KT-583-857

90571

90571

UCA
university for the creative arts

Farnham, Falkner Road, Farnham, Surrey, GU9 7DS 01252 892709
Return on or before the last date stamped below. Fines will be charged on overdue books.

2 5 SEP 2009

2 5 NOV 2009

1 2 NOV 2009

1 4 DEC 2009

2 5 OCT 2010

- 8 DEC 2010

7 DAY
BOOK

WITHDRAWN
FROM STOCK

The Players' Realm

Studies on the Culture
of Video Games and Gaming

Edited by J. Patrick Williams
and Jonas Heide Smith

McFarland & Company, Inc., Publishers
Jefferson, North Carolina, and London

90571

A companion title: *Gaming as Culture: Essays on Reality, Identity and Experience in Fantasy Games,* edited by J. Patrick Williams, Sean Q. Hendricks and W. Keith Winkler (McFarland, 2006)

Library & Learning Centre
University for the Creative Arts
Farnham

794.
8
PLA

LIBRARY OF CONGRESS CATALOGUING-IN-PUBLICATION DATA

The players' realm : studies on the culture of video games and
gaming / edited by J. Patrick Williams and Jonas Heide Smith.
    p.   cm.
    Includes bibliographical references and index.

    ISBN-13: 978-0-7864-2832-8
    (softcover : 50# alkaline paper) ∞

    1. Video games — Social aspects.   2. Computer games —
Social aspects.   I. Williams, J. Patrick, 1970–   II. Smith,
Jonas Heide.
GV1469.34.S52P53   2007
794.8 — dc22   2007002390

British Library cataloguing data are available

©2007 J. Patrick Williams and Jonas Heide Smith. All rights reserved

*No part of this book may be reproduced or transmitted in any form
or by any means, electronic or mechanical, including photocopying
or recording, or by any information storage and retrieval system,
without permission in writing from the publisher.*

Cover image ©2007 Brand X Pictures

Manufactured in the United States of America

McFarland & Company, Inc., Publishers
  Box 611, Jefferson, North Carolina 28640
  www.mcfarlandpub.com

Table of Contents

Introduction:
From Moral Panics to Mature Games Research in Action

J. PATRICK WILLIAMS AND
JONAS HEIDE SMITH

Digital games and digital gaming cultures have become increasingly visible, salient aspects of everyday life in the 21st century. The cultures that encapsulate digital games are complex and vary across historical, linguistic, and national boundaries, yet there are also trans-cultural patterns that connect players worldwide. In this chapter, and more broadly in this book, we explore the space(s) within which an emerging field of social scientists, computer scientists, and humanists engage in the cultural study of digital games and digital gaming.[1]

Digital games themselves have inundated our everyday lives. We either play or personally know people who play at almost any time of the day and night. We or they play at home, at school, at work, and increasingly at the bus stop, on the train, and on the way to the next meeting. We or they play on powerful multi-media desktop and laptop computers, on gaming consoles in bedrooms and family rooms, on handhelds, PDAs, cellphones and other mobile devices. Some games seem almost mindless distractions that take only moments to play; others are persistent online worlds with no end, where players' investments rival or outweigh family, school and work. Increasingly, new communication technologies allow communities to form *among players* as we or they share in the gaming experience. As these new media become less expensive and spread around the world — and as the depth and complexity of networked games increases — scholars are becoming increasingly savvy in how we approach digital games.

The study of digital games and digital gaming is neither new nor easily summarized, yet it is obvious that the field has seen immense growth since the late 1990s. While aesthetic and psychological approaches to the study of games have tended to garner the most attention in the past, in an important sense scholars have only recently begun to study the social and cultural aspects of games. Below, we sketch some of the various trajectories of digital games in modern Western societies, first by looking at the growth and persistence of public interest in digital games — especially in terms of moral panic. We then contrast this outsider perspective with two different insider perspectives: one that has tended toward studying *gaming* and one which primarily attends to *games* themselves. We conclude by discussing some exemplars of what we call mature games research in action by providing an overview of the substantive chapters in this book.

Digital Games and the Persistence of Moral Panics

Digital games are a culturally embattled phenomenon. In the wake of many high-profile cases of violence, games are now regularly cited as a *cause* of deviant behavior through a variety of public channels, including parent-led campaigns to expunge games from schools; congressional hearings about the culpability of, and lawsuits against, game developers for their programming and products; news reportages and psychological research that focus on game effects; and cultural myths fueled by anecdotal evidence and gossip. A few examples illuminate our point. For instance, legal action was taken in 2003 against game developers Take Two after a car thief in Alabama shot several policemen. Similarly, after the 1999 Columbine High School shootings, the family of a victim charged a large number of game developers with complicity and the United States Senate convened hearings in which they demanded that scholars and other experts testify as to the relationship between video games and violence (Jenkins 1999). At other times, news media have singled out games as a probable cause of violence. In May 2002, a Danish Broadcast Corporation news byte (DR 2002) claimed that a recent high school shooting in Erfurt, Germany, could be explained by the perpetrator's fascination with *Counter-Strike*, while a 2006 American Broadcasting Company report claimed that the new Nintendo DS system could be used by pedophiles to interact with children (ABC 2006). Meanwhile, private citizens, including church leaders, parents, and lawyers, continue to argue that first-person shooter games are nothing less than simulators for would-be teenage murderers. In short, contemporary media regularly construct discourses of fear and panic. From the threat posed by the spread of the telephone in the 20th century (Betteridge 1997; Umble 1992), to mass-mediated consumption of terrorism (Altheide 2004) and sex and violence (Biltereyst 2004) via television, panics surrounding the politics of leisure and everyday life remain especially prevalent when it comes to mediated communication and entertainment.

Professionals and scholars that work with and within the computer industry are also partly responsible for the spread of negatively-biased information about games and gaming. Kelly begins his book on massively multiplayer online games (MMOGs) with a self-portrait of the "addicted" gamer:

> Rubbing my inflamed eyes, I realize that I've been staring at the computer screen for 20 straight hours. My back hurts. My head is spinning. My tongue is coated with a gummy rind. I can hardly keep my chin off the keyboard. But I can't go to bed yet. It's only 2:00 AM and I have many important things to do [Kelly 2005: 1].

He goes on in the first chapter to highlight a number of instances of "shocking" behavior online: players of MMOGs sell virtual goods for real money; some players sit for so long, they develop deep vein thrombosis; a Korean youth dies after playing Lineage for 86 hours straight; an American youth allegedly kills himself after being spurned by a female player online ... and the list goes on (ibid.: 13–17). His goal is not to overemphasize these events, but to argue that there is a culture surrounding digital games that explains these out-of-the-ordinary events and processes. While Kelly's intentions are laudable, the result serves to reinforce a set of media-driven stereotypes about gaming cultures.

The rhetoric Kelly employs is not new. In fact, some social scientists have for years searched for causal relationships between games and social psychological conditions such as aggressive behavior (Anderson 2004; Anderson and Bushman 2001; Arriaga, Esteves, Carneiro, and Monteiro 2006; Uhlmann and Swanson 2004) and addiction (Bellamy and Hanewicz 2001; see also Griffiths and Davies 2005).

Sociologist Stanley Cohen first described moral panics based on his analysis of youth subcultures in Britain in the 1960s. In his characterization, moral panics progress through stages:

1. a condition, episode, person or group of persons emerges to become defined as a threat to societal value and interests;
2. its nature is presented in a stylized and stereotypical fashion by the mass media;
3. the moral barricades are manned by editors, bishops, politicians and other right-thinking people;

4. socially accredited experts pronounce their diagnoses and solutions;
5. ways of coping are evolved or (more often) resorted to;
6. the condition then disappears, submerges or deteriorates and becomes less visible [Cohen 2002: 1].

Cohen's model is linear. Although the stages may overlap, the situations which characterize the panic are worked through and eventually recede from the limelight. Digital games and digital gaming, however, continue to go through cycles of panic and never seem to reach the final stages of resolution. Perhaps this is because the digital game is not a homogeneous category but instead refers to a plethora of computer-mediated environments with and within which human beings interact. Perhaps also (or instead) this is because digital games are simply one part of a still-emerging, highly-mediated social structure in which mass mediated images, rather than new communication media, have thus far dominated our understandings of reality. Regardless of why digital games and gaming remain objects of moral panic, we can trace this panic through at least two trajectories: fantasy gaming and the diffusion of personal computers.

Fantasy gaming, epitomized by the classic role-playing game *Dungeons and Dragons* (*D&D*), passed through a cycle of moral panics primarily during the late 1970s and 1980s. In their review of fantasy gaming cultures, Williams, Hendricks and Winkler characterize the early stages of the panic:

> *D&D* was defined as a threat to societal values and interests soon after it emerged on the American mainstream cultural radar in the late 1970s. The threat was manifested primarily in fears of occult worship (Martin and Fine 1991) and negative psychological conditions including suicide, all of which the mass media presented in a stylized and stereotypical fashion (Adler and Doherty 1985; Brooke 1985; Dear 1984; Elshop 1981; Weathers and Foote 1979). In these and many other popular culture sources, staff writers, apparently unfamiliar with fantasy games, reported the concerns of adults — parents, politicians, police, and religious leaders — over fantasy games as a source of child corruption [Williams, Hendricks, and Winkler 2006: 8].

Pop cultural moralists did not argue alone. Soon, "socially accredited experts" (Cohen 2002: 1) initiated research to diagnose the problems associated with fantasy gaming. This work shared a number of features as most of the "experts" involved were non-gamers working within a deductive, positivist paradigm. Researchers applied a traditional arsenal of psychological tests to gamers and displayed little consideration for the cultural differences among types of fantasy games. Generally speaking, the results were anything but clear, although they were often biased towards negative findings. As an example, Douse and McManus (1993: 508) found that role-playing gamers "show clear personality differences from controls"— they were "significantly more introverted, [...]

showed less empathic concern," and were more likely to treat people as objects than members of a control group. Another study (DeRenard and Kline 1990) concluded that *D&D* play correlated positively with high levels of cultural estrangement but negatively with feelings of meaninglessness. Over time, researchers failed to "prove" that fantasy games were responsible for deviant behaviors. Consequently, games with bases in high fantasy passed through the final stages of moral panic by the late 1980s and have not garnered significant or sustained media criticism since then.

At the same time that fantasy gaming was experiencing considerable growth (as well as media and social scientific attention), methods of computer-mediated interaction were also burgeoning. The internet, usenet and telnet, email, and other forms of digital communication forms were just emerging as cultural processes that would come to affect people's everyday lives. Like fantasy gaming, computer-mediated culture was also quickly perceived by many as another new cause for panic. Unlike fantasy gaming, however, moral panics about computer-mediated culture have continued to develop alongside successive improvements in technology. The establishment of the internet as a social space, for example, sparked controversy among many politically- and morally-minded writers through the 1990s. These writers, acting as moral entrepreneurs, tended to take one of two sides in the debate on digital technology. From a "technotopianist" perspective, writers such as Sherry Turkle (Turkle 1984; 1995) and Howard Rheingold (Rheingold 1991; 2000) enthused about the potential for human development through interaction with and through computers by focusing explicitly (and almost exclusively) on what they saw as the positive outcomes of computer usage. "Welcome to the wild side of cyberspace culture," Rheingold wrote, "where magic is real and identity is a fluid. [...] You can be a man or a woman or something else entirely.... Identity is the first thing you create" (Rheingold 2000: 149, 152). Similarly, Robins (1995: 139) described how cyberspace promised to deliver its user "from the constraints and defeats of physical reality and the physical body."

In turn, "dystopian" moralists such as Neil Postman (Postman 1992) bemoaned the alleged loss of face-to-face community and the estranging effects of new technology, tending instead toward pessimistic characterizations of information and communication technologies. "Reduced to its essentials, we stand on the threshold of turning life itself into computer code, of transforming the experience of living in the physical world — every sensation, every detail — into a product for our consumption. [...] The implications of these new technologies are social; the question they pose, broadly ethical; the risks they entail, unprecedented" (Slouka 1999: 98, 102). Other writers, such as Kenneth Gergen (1991) similarly hyperdramatized the relation between computers and society through concepts such as "multiphrenia." Rhetoric about the dan-

gers of computer-use continues today, despite the fact that few empirical studies support it.[2]

Digital games and digital gaming cultures today are inextricably linked
to these earlier developments in fantasy games and computer technologies.
Given the ubiquity of digital games in contemporary Western societies, it
seems that they should have long since passed through all the stages of panic
and emerged, like role-playing and other fantasy games, to become normal-
ized commodities for leisure consumption. It seems, however, that digital games
have not completely escaped a conservative cultural bias that both assumes
and signals that games should be viewed as something strange, as we have
shown. In sum, after forty years of video gaming history, games are still sometimes treated as a phenomenon which is different, dangerous and in need of
special attention and/or legislation.

Analyzing the various social forces that support biases against digital
games and digital gaming warrants a book in its own right. However, we can
still quickly point to several possible reasons. First, the digital games genre is
undergoing rapid, constant change. Today's games, while certainly building
on a host of predecessors, are much more complex comparatively and display
a dramatically higher degree of audiovisual realism. For non-playing adults,
the realism can be quite shocking compared to the games from only a few
years ago.[3] Second, while dedicated game systems (including PCs and consoles) are increasingly common among households throughout the industri-
alized world, they differ from older "mass" media systems such as television
in an important way. Specifically, televisions attracted a much larger audience
initially than games have done. TVs provided not only a source for entertainment — adult entertainment has always been more prevalent on TV than
youth entertainment — but for news and information as well. Thus, the television was a more attractive piece of technology to more people. Not so with
games, as many adults simply are not interested. Third, games have served as
a convenient scapegoat for larger social problems. Much like fast food is
blamed for America's obesity, games may serve to some as a whipping boy
and an opportune target for moral outrage which allows a comfortable shifting of responsibility. Last, many game developers are not entirely opposed to
having a somewhat risqué, counter-cultural image. When, for instance, programmers at Rockstar Games inserted hidden sexual material into *Grand
Theft Auto: San Andreas* they were obviously not too concerned with trying
to dispel all notions of dubious morals in their product. The mixed motives
behind game production create a complex interplay among developers, consumers, moral entrepreneurs, and those trying to clear the games industry of
its subcultural connotations.

Studying Games, Studying Gaming

Against this background of worries about game effects, an intentional emphasis toward both more value-neutral and more positively-biased studies of digital games and digital gaming has occurred. To oversimplify things, this perspective — known widely as "game studies"— sees that games may be fruitfully treated like any other topic within media studies, sociology, cultural studies, and so on; that is, as an activity which, if you care to look, is varied both in its structure, substance and function.[4] Within game studies, two somewhat overlapping research foci are apparent. Some researchers are primarily interested in games as artifacts or texts, while others tend to emphasize the activity of gaming.[5] Both approaches to games preceded the invention of video games. For example, folklorists have studied the transmission of particular games through history and anthropologists have studied the function and meaning of games in particular cultures (e.g., Avedon and Sutton-Smith 1971).

Within contemporary game studies, humanist scholars have tended to study the structure and meaning of particular games, game types or of video games generally. Such approaches have shed light on the narrative aspects of games, the structure of time, spatiality and experience, and the relationship between game aesthetics and other forms of expression. Methodologically, this approach often builds on careful study of particular games (which constitute the empirical data) and may draw specifically on the researcher's own experience of playing. Social scientists, on the other hand, have more often studied either gamers or the activity of gaming (or both). In these approaches, games are likely to constitute a backdrop to the research, rather than being the focus of attention. There has been some antagonism between scholars of the two traditions. In particular, scholars analyzing concrete games (without explicitly considering empirical player experience) have faced concerns about considering the structure or content of games to be all-important (which echoes debates in media studies over assigning too much importance to the text itself). Gaming researcher Carsten Jessen is explicit that the first question to be asked is "not what the computer and the games do to children, but the opposite: what do the children do with the computer and the games?" (Jessen 1999). Similarly, Ermi and Mäyrä voice the opinion that "...the essence of a game is rooted in its interactive nature, and there is no game without a player [....] If we want to understand what a game is, we need to understand what happens in the act of playing, and we need to understand the player and the experience of gameplay" (2005: 1).

Although some game scholars seem to privilege one approach over others, we have organized this book with the intention of looking past such territoriality. The editors and authors recognize that games have concrete features, differ structurally, and display different approaches to design challenges. Because of this, games may be categorized, discussed and dissected with only indirect reference to players — the study of games themselves needs no further justification. Similarly, gamers are influenced by games as well as by wider cultural and social forces. Their behavior is not determined by what occurs during gameplay, nor is their behavior entirely divorced from their experience with and within games. In short, the study of gamers and the activity of gaming is clearly also justified. Differences between these two approaches should also not obscure the fact that they share many ideals. Within "mainstream" game studies, the days are over when researchers would approach their topic of interest without an understanding of games and gaming culture. Today, game researchers can generally be presumed to have a deep understanding of their research topic (something which is clearly true for the contributors to this volume). Of course, this requirement of understanding is not, and should not be, demand a love of or devotion to games and gaming. Students of games should be free to approach the study of anything entertaining with a critical eye, if not outright skepticism.

The editors and authors in this volume both *know* and *care* about games as a matter of course. We find games to be important and we draw on our experience with games. By doing so, without any fanfare and probably without giving it special thought, our collective efforts represent a new phase in the history of game research. As long as we take the time and effort to become familiar with our subject matter and approach it in a methodologically sound manner,[6] game studies will continue to grow as an important academic discipline.

The Maturation of Games Research

The new phase of games research exemplified by this book is one of increasing maturity displayed by the authors' commitment to research questions of a type which might also be applied to other social and cultural phenomena. The authors represented here "simply" wish to systematically examine specific aspects of digital games and digital gaming using a variety of methods and strategies inspired by a variety of academic fields. There is no need to defend games as a worthwhile topic or to make all-encompassing statements about the universal applicability (or lack thereof) of some particular theory or approach. And while the authors do not ignore methodological considerations, neither do they lose themselves in them.

The chapters are divided into four sections. Section 1 consists of four chapters that collectively speak to the issue of control versus authorship. In Chapter 1, Jonas Heide Smith examines issues of political legitimacy in persistent game worlds. Beginning with an historical analysis of game world design and then moving into two case studies — *Star Wars Galaxies* and *Dark Age of Camelot* — Smith describes power structures in contemporary MMOGs by comparing games to traditional nation-states in terms of rulers' need for political legitimacy. His analysis exposes the deep historical roots of controversies surrounding the relationships between citizens-players and rulers-designers. Smith discusses the function and form of end-user-license-agreements and argues that they are central to a "battle over meaning [...] that will shape the near and distant future of game worlds." Like Smith, Sara M. Grimes focuses on end-user-license-agreements in Chapter 2. As Grimes notes, young people are increasingly adopting participatory roles in the creation of online content. Showing how children are increasingly required to enter legal agreements on gaming websites and thus surrender parts of their immaterial rights, Grimes argues that "...not only are children engaged in much more than simple play when they visit these spaces. They are also being enlisted in intrusive market research strategies that make full use of the creativity, community and agency contained in their online contributions." Both of these chapters generally question the extent to which players and designers create and control players' experiences.

The other two chapters in this section deal specifically with the negotiation of power in text-based game worlds. In Chapter 3, Nadezhda Kaneva studies the virtual city of Cybertown, a text-based role-playing community accessible through the internet. Participation in the Cybertown community is relatively unstructured and the depth of engagement varies from user to user. Using ethnographic methods, she explores three basic questions: how a sense of community is constructed within the mediated virtual environment; who holds authorial power (and how) within the playing space; and how players negotiate between interactive authoring and the development of a sense of belonging to the virtual community. In Chapter 4, Mel White shows how a number of different styles of justice in virtual game worlds have emerged in recent years, each of which is shaped by how a game is structured, how many players are involved, and who controls the hardware and software. White discusses these various systems of justice by drawing upon her many years of personal experience as a system administrator. She illustrates the dilemmas facing MUD admins and emphasizes how the various solutions to deviance and disagreement which have sprung up over the years are based on an amateur, trial-and-error form of community control: "rules that govern social behavior in text based gaming environments form autopoietically from case-lore and knowledge acquired from other MUDs."

Section 2, titled "Discourse and Ideology," begins with Aaron Delwiche's position (in Chapter 5) that the very traits that make digital games an exciting vehicle for educators also make them attractive to those engaged in commercial and political persuasion. Synthesizing recent findings on the educational potential of video games with insights from propaganda research, Delwiche shows how games seem particularly well-suited to propaganda purposes. Delwiche's approach makes plain the critical insight that games are not developed in a cultural vacuum, but rather are packed with ideological substance. In Chapter 6, Lars Konzack discusses some of this substance through an analysis of several ideological rhetorics that games studies scholars have identified — either implicitly or explicitly — in recent years. Through a semiotic examination of "product oriented," "socially and culturally oriented," and "aesthetically oriented" rhetorics, Konzack reminds us of the degree to which basic assumptions shape the direction of research within the field. His work also provides insight into how rhetorical frames influence one another and impact players' orientations toward digital games more generally.

In line with Konzack's notion of rhetorical frames, Jon Dovey and Helen W. Kennedy (Chapter 7) identify "a particular hegemonic version of game culture complete with its own origin myths, founding fathers and idealized or preferred producers and consumers." This emergence is not accidental, but has happened because producers inhabit key structural roles within the system of symbolic production. Drawing on a case study of game developers Pivotal Games, the authors argue that digital games culture has witnessed the construction of a privileged subjectivity that is grounded in the production of dominant truths about particular people, practices and tastes. Whereas Dovey and Kennedy focus on the hegemony of gaming culture, in Chapter 8 Rafael Miguel Montes offers a critical cultural analysis of the hegemony that exists within games themselves. Through his analysis of the game *Tom Clancy's Ghost Recon: Island Thunder,* Montes reflects on what happens when he — a Cuban American — is asked to take on the role of a U.S. soldier engaged in military action in Cuba. Montes questions Janet Murray's (1997: 99) assertion that "the experience of being transported to an elaborately simulated place is pleasurable in itself, regardless of the fantasy content" by acknowledging a first-person, ethnic standpoint epistemology. What happens when the Cuban exile community's longed for commencement of a post–Castro Cuba is instantaneously rendered for immediate consumption? What happens when the player identifies more with the enemy than with her/his avatar? These issues, like the issues in the other chapters in this section, highlight the cultural webs within which games are produced and consumed, designed and played.

Section 3 focuses on the concepts of experience and identity. Mirjam Eladhari's chapter (Chapter 9) examines game design features that relate to players' self-characterization within digital game worlds. Focusing on how game designers create the possibilities for players to create meaningful personas through narrative, she uses the concept of a "character arc"—which she calls the player's journey—to contextualize her discussion of how player characters undergo development through problematic situations and decision-making processes. In her research she finds "not only that virtual game world creation is an art, but also that playing is an art in itself, providing performances both for the individual player and for the virtual society of the specific game world." Eladhari suggests techniques for supporting characterization which might in turn enhance player immersion. In Chapter 10, Torill Elvira Mortensen also writes about play as an embodied and pleasurable experience. Players move back and forth between modes of playing and different types of media consumption, rather than staying locked to their monitors. Personal development, mastery, social development, friendships, explorations of identity and social roles are vital to players, and their delight in playing is embedded in the social rewards of multi-user games. Mortensen argues that much current game research has too narrow a conceptualization of the pleasure of playing. Drawing on results from her study of life in a MUD, she argues that "games are so attractive because they release us from the boundaries of our achievements in other arenas and set us free to measure ourselves by different standards, not just because they reduce the world to factors that can be learned, controlled and mastered." She sees play not as a postmodern activity, but as an expression of a new sincerity attached to the use of media, as players are not just "active audiences" but participants in their own mediated experiences.

While Mortensen's research provides important insight into how players experience games, Mia Consalvo (Chapter 11) offers a very different, but equally useful, perspective on players' experiences. She presents a comparative analysis of *The Sims* and *The Sims Online*, asking as a starting question why the success of the former did not carry over to the latter. Her study, based on over 350 game "days" in *The Sims*, more than one year of play in *The Sims Online*, analysis of popular and business accounts of the two games, and industry interviews and documents, highlights key design differences between the games, such as the games' interfaces, the conventions and limitations of playing each game, and the role of game objects vis-à-vis the players as potential reasons for their varying levels of success. In the final chapter of the section, Laurie N. Taylor (Chapter 12) argues that game studies have tended to ignore crucial differences between the cultures that surround different gaming platforms. Focusing too readily on PC games and gamers, and on multiplayer games rather than communities surrounding single-player games, game studies has often failed to address substantial portions of game culture. Taylor's work calls on games scholars to increase our collective focus on these marginalized aspects of gaming culture and to take the relationship of the game platform to gaming cultures more seriously. Her call is particularly relevant at this moment in time, as PDAs, cell phones, and other mobile devices are just beginning to experience accelerated growth within the digital gaming industry.

Section 4, "Consumption and Community," explores a final set of links between the producers and consumers of games and the gaming cultures within which these actors are embedded. Jason Wilson reminds us in Chapter 13 that game design takes many forms. Supporting and extending Dovey and Kennedy's (Chapter 7) analysis of hegemonic games culture, Wilson begins from the position that games scholars often focus on the increasingly concentrated industrial nexus of what he calls "big gaming": the linked complex of big developers, big publishers and big retailers supplying users of the major platforms with bleeding-edge digital play. Wilson shifts the focus to a necessarily selective survey of the sprawling diversity of indie game development and explores a small but diverse group of sites and practitioners that use the freedom that independence from the games industry gives to struggle against the limitations of their marginal positions for a range of purposes. His study is a call to take seriously the cultures of indie game development, both for game studies and for the future of the games industry.

In Chapter 14, Mike Molesworth and Janice Denegri-Knott explore the connection between virtual goods and consumer culture. The authors are particularly interested in how digital games stimulate desire for both virtual and "real world" commodities that are represented in digital games. Drawing from literature on consumer desire and hedonic consumption, they offer a richly-woven analysis of how "desire for consumer goods easily finds its way into digital games, [how] some experiences in games may ask players to re-examine their consumer lifestyles, and [how] some games open up the potential for consumption experiences based on fantasies beyond what is available in the material world."

Finally, Daniel Keller (Chapter 15) explores the culture surrounding text-based adventure games (or "interactive fiction"). Interactive fiction (IF) as a computer game genre became virtually extinct in the 1980s as text-based games were replaced by games with impressive audiovisuals. Keller believes that the main reason IF is still around twenty years later is because of the communities that formed in internet and usenet groups to create and play these games, even after commercial outlets collapsed. Intrigued by the apparent resurgence of interest in the genre, Keller conducted a survey seeking to hear the voices of the players themselves. The results of his research offer insight into the culture that surrounds IF communities. His multi-faceted analysis shows us that, while nostalgia plays a role in the renewed popularity of the genre, the players are also "drawn to a combination of factors that are only made available through IF: the potential to feel in control of a narrative; the ability to play and read at the same time; the opportunity to become the story's protagonist; and the chance to use one's imagination to make the reading experience more personal." The opportunities Keller lists function as cultural mana that sustains players, just as the cultural desires for "real" and virtual goods sustains the players in Molesworth and Denegri-Knott's work. And like Wilson's emphasis on the power of alternate modes of game production, Keller highlights the communal aspects of building new culture together.

As the chapters in this book make abundantly clear, the cultural study of digital games and digital gaming is growing stronger all the time. After reading the following chapters, we hope you will return to your games and your own research with renewed inspiration.

Notes

1. The social sciences, computer sciences, and the humanities are distinct academic disciplines in universities around the globe, yet game scholars often bring skills from multiple disciplines to bear in their research. In this way, game studies is an interdisciplinary project that (ideally) eschews academic insularity.

2. And when empirical evidence does suggest causal relationships between games and human behavior, the findings are often difficult to replicate.

3. A March 2006 blog post on Pixelante Nation (http://www.pixelantenation.com/) exemplifies our point. Discussing *Metal Gear Solid 3*, the blogger writes: "From a distance, or in the middle of a firefight, its easy to count lethal force as matter of survival or detachment. However, in any properly stealthy playthrough of the game, you WILL get the drop on a few lone opponents. It is entirely to your advantage to intimidate and shake down a live guard for supplies and ammunition. However, in the game, a cornered enemy will express fear. Train a weapon on them and they will freeze immediately. Tilt it towards their head and they will panic, even plead. The more I play it, the more unnerving that actually gets. Finishing off a frightened, now-unarmed opponent feels just a little surreal. The animation is grisly, the blood is a little exaggerated, and the vocal bit, a shout of surprise, is a little bit disturbing. Through this, the game actually encourages me not to use lethal force. In these instances it has actually made me feel uncomfortable with the simulated killing of a disarmed enemy soldier. They are well-animated, well-voiced and they emote well. No other game has had this sort of effect. Some have given inklings of it; the first few FPSs I played that had actual voiceovers for enemies would occasionally unnerve me just a little." As opponent AI and their details become more and more complex, they will continue to seem more and more human to us. For people like me, it could make games more and more difficult.

4. This variation is perhaps most obvious in the growing (and sometimes contradictory) range of research literature focused on digital games. In addition to a host of new research monographs and anthologies, websites and blogs, two journals are establishing themselves as legitimate, scholarly outlets of game research: *Game Studies* (since 2001) and *Games and Culture* (since 2006).

5. A third focus is on the broader cultural aspects of games and gaming.

6. Of course, enthusiasm generally speeds up this process which is why those who actually study games are often fond of the medium.

References

ABC. 2006. "The Nintendo DS System." WPVI-TV Philadelphia. Retrieved March 28, 2006 (http://abclocal.go.com/wpvi/story?section=special_coverage&id=3905371#)

Adler, Jerry, and Shawn Doherty. 1985. "Kids: The Deadliest Game?" *Newsweek*, September 9, 1985, p. 93.

Altheide, David L. 2004. "Consuming Terrorism." *Symbolic Interaction* 27: 289–308.

Anderson, Craig A. 2004. "An Update on the Effects of Playing Violent Video Games." *Journal of Adolescence* 27: 113–122.

Anderson, Craig A., and Brad J. Bushman. 2001. "Effects of Violent Video Games on Aggressive Behavior, Aggressive Cognition, Aggressive Affect, Physiological Arousal, and Prosocial Behavior: A Meta-Analytic Review of the Scientific Literature." *Psychological Science* 12: 353.

Arriaga, Patrícia, Francisco Esteves, Paula Carneiro, and Maria Benedicta Monteiro. 2006. "Violent Computer Games and Their Effects on State Hostility and Physiological Arousal." *Aggressive Behavior* 32: 146–158.

Avedon, Elliott M., and Brian Sutton-Smith. 1971. *The Study of Games*. New York: John Wiley & Sons Inc.

Bellamy, Al, and Cheryl Hanewicz. 2001. "An Exploratory Analyses of the Social Nature of Internet Addiction." *Electronic Journal of Sociology* 5 (Mar).

Betteridge, Jenie. 1997. "Answering Back: the Telephone, Modernity and Everyday Life." *Media, Culture and Society* 19: 585–603.

Biltereyst, Daniel. 2004. "Media Audiences and the Game of Controversy." *Journal of Media Practice* 5: 7–24.

Brooke, James. 1985. "A Suicide Spurs Town to Debate Nature of a Game." *New York Times*, August 22, 1985, p. B1

Cohen, Stanley. 2002. *Folk Devils and Moral Panics*. London: Routledge.

Dear, William. 1984. *The Dungeon Master: The Disappearance of James Dallas Egbert III*. Boston: Houghton Mifflin.

DR. 2002. "Søndagsmagasinet 5 May." Denmark: DR.

Elshop, Phyllis Ten. 1981. "D&D: A Fantasy Fad or Dabbling in the Demonic?" *Christianity Today*, September 4, 1981, p. 56.

Ermi, Laura, and Frans Mäyrä. 2005. "Fundamental Components of the Gameplay Experience: Analysing Immersion." In *DIGRA 2005: Changing Views: Worlds in Play*, edited by J. Castells. Vancouver, Canada: Simon Fraser University Press.

Griffiths, M.D., and M.N.O. Davies. 2005. "Videogame Addiction: Does it Exist?" Pp. 359–368 in *Handbook of Computer Game Studies*, edited by J. Goldstein and J. Raessens. Boston: MIT Press.

Jenkins, Henry. 1999. "Congressional Testimony on Media Violence." Testimony presented before the U.S. Senate Commerce Committee, Washington, D.C. May 4, 1999. Retrieved March 29, 2006 (http://web.mit.edu/m-i-t/articles/index_dc.html)

Jessen, Carsten. 1999, "Computer Games and Play Culture: An Outline of an Interpretative Framework." Retrieved March 7, 2006 (http://www.carsten-jessen.dk/compgames.html).

Martin, Daniel, and Gary Alan Fine. 1991. "Satanic Cults, Satanic Play: Is 'Dungeons & Dragons' a Breeding Ground for the Devil?" In *The Satanism Scare*, edited by James T. Richardson, Joel Best, and David G. Bromley. New York: de Gruyter.

Murray, Janet. 1997. *Hamlet on the Holodeck: The Future of Narrative on Cyberspace.* Cambridge: The MIT Press.

Postman, Neil. 1992. *Technopoly: The Surrender of Culture to Technology.* New York: Knopf.

Rheingold, Howard. 1991. *Virtual Reality.* New York: Summit Books.

_____. 2000. *The Virtual Community: Homesteading on the Electronic Frontier.* Cambridge, Mass.: MIT Press.

Robins, Kevin. 1995. "Cyberspace and the World We Live In." *Body and Society* 1(3–4): 135–155.

Turkle, Sherry. 1984. *The Second Self: Computers and the Human Spirit.* New York: Simon and Schuster.

_____. 1995. *Life on the Screen: Identity in the Age of the Internet.* New York: Simon and Schuster.

Uhlmann, Eric, and Jane Swanson. 2004. "Exposure to Violent Video Games Increases Automatic Aggressiveness." *Journal of Adolescence* 27: 41–52.

Umble, Diane Zimmerman. 1992. "The Amish and the Telephone: Resistance and Reconstruction." in *Consuming Technologies: Media and Information in Domestic Spaces,* edited by R. Silverstone, and Eric Hirsch (eds.): Routledge.

Weathers, Diane, and Donna M. Foote. 1979. "Beware the Harpies!" *Newsweek,* September 24, 1979, p. 109.

Williams, J. Patrick, Sean Q. Hendricks, and W. Keith Winkler. 2006. "Fantasy Games, Gaming Cultures, and Social Life." Pp. 1–18 in *Gaming as Culture: Essays in Reality, Identity, and Experience in Fantasy Games,* edited by J. P. Williams, Sean Q. Hendricks, and W. Keith Winkler. Jefferson, NC: McFarland and Company.

Section 1: Control versus Authorship

1. *Who Governs the Gamers?*

Jonas Heide Smith

*You set out to make a game, and quickly discover that you're suddenly a
politician running a game the size of a city. You're suddenly a social
architect worrying about issues you never had a clue about.*
— Raph Koster, quoted in Pika (2004)

When Martigano stepped off the space shuttle and onto the sandy surface of Tatooine he was instantly overwhelmed by the exotic sounds and the
proximity of large numbers of locals chatting in a language which he did not
understand (although his player recognized it as French). Slowly making his
way through the darkened streets, his mind was fully occupied by the novelty of the situation and by the opportunities hinted at by what would soon
appear to be a huge danger-filled world. He had little energy at this point to
worry about the contract he had just signed; being intent on mundane matters of movement and survival he did not ponder his new-found status as citizen of a virtual world.

But a citizen was just what he had become. He, or rather his player, had
just consented to a contract in a process which bears more than a passing
resemblance to the semi-mythical instance of entering into a "social contract"
imagined by certain political philosophers. A constitution normally specifies
the rights and obligations of a state and its citizens and the *Star Wars Galaxies* End-User License Agreement (EULA) is no exception.

Of course, whether the EULA should really be seen in this light depends
on our conceptualization of the game world that it governs. If we consider
the *Star Wars Galaxies* gamespace to be a toy, or perhaps a playground, then

little seems to be riding on the phrasing of a semi-obscure document that few users are likely to read fully. If, on the other hand, we consider the gamespace to be a world (albeit a virtual one) in which people play, interact, and sometimes work in ways that are highly comparable with physical-world activities, then we should take an interest in the ways in which such a world is governed. Ancient concerns over the legitimacy and distribution of power suddenly become relevant.

The EULA of another gameworld, *Dark Age of Camelot*, explicitly favors the former perspective.[1] If you (the player) want to enter the game you must "specifically acknowledge that the time you spend playing Dark Age of Camelot™ is for entertainment purposes only." But a number of recent developments seem to challenge this view. Massively multiplayer online role-playing games (MMORPGs) are having tangible physical-world consequences as players trade in-game objects and characters for physical-world money (Castronova 2001; Dibbell 2003). Also, players are increasingly showing concern over their in-game rights. For instance, professor of philosophy and player of *The Sims Online* (Maxis Software Inc. 2001) Peter Ludlow was evicted from the gameworld in what turned into a controversy over freedom of speech in the game (Feldman 2003; Harmon 2004). Fully realizing the extent of these tensions, creative director at Sony Online Entertainment (who run *Star Wars Galaxies*) Raph Koster has sparked discussion with a (somewhat experimental) declaration on the rights of players (Koster 2000). Koster sets forth nineteen articles following from logical deliberation on the status of game worlds, suggesting for instance that avatars should be free and have equal rights as well as property rights and the right to protest against perceived oppression.

Accepting that EULAs may be conceived of as constitutions and game characters as citizens who might be entitled to certain rights requires adopting a non-obvious perspective. Game developers themselves strongly argue that they are producing entertainment rather than societies in any non-metaphorical sense and many players agree. Nevertheless, it has recently been argued that the player-as-citizens perspective may well make legal sense and will become increasingly relevant as the pervasiveness and scope of game worlds grow. More specifically, Lastowka and Hunter (2003) offer three reasons to seriously consider the legal implications of online interaction in social or game worlds. First, studying contemporary game worlds will enable us to prepare for the legal issues sure to face online worlds in the future. Second, there is no clear distinction between real-world and virtual-world economies as one constantly bleeds into the other through sales of in-game objects for real-world currency, and so on. Third, these worlds represent useful experiments in law-making and provide a challenge for real life legal systems (see also Castronova 2001; 2003b).

From a slightly different angle Jack. M. Balkin of Yale Law School makes a supporting claim:

> Even at this early stage of technological development, people have simply invested too much time, energy, and money in virtual worlds to imagine that the law will leave these worlds alone, and allow them to develop their own norms and resolve their own disputes unhindered [Balkin 2004].

In the light of this challenge to the traditional perspective, this chapter analyzes the power relation between game designers and players in two large MMORPGs in order to answer the question: How is power distributed and exercised within these game worlds? From a brief introduction to the games in question, I move on to a discussion of the nature of power in game worlds before analyzing the two EULAs in depth. Finally, I discuss the relationship between game worlds and physical-world societies by looking at the role of social (and political) theory in the analysis of game world sociality.

Star Wars Galaxies and *Dark Age of Camelot*

Star Wars Galaxies and *Dark Age of Camelot* (henceforth *SWG* and *DAoC* respectively) are commercially produced and managed massively multiplayer role-playing games. Players buy the boxed game and must then pay a monthly fee to access the game worlds running on servers managed by the game owners. Players can create one or more characters (often referred to as "avatars") through which they can experience the three dimensional game worlds, interact with other players and computer-controlled characters.[2]

SWG and *DAoC* are often classified as second generation graphical game worlds. Game architecture inspiration is drawn from pen-and-paper role-playing games (most clearly TSR's *Advanced Dungeons & Dragons*), from text-based computer ancestors known as Multi User Dungeons and from first generation commercial graphical game worlds such as *Meridian 59* (Archetype Interactive 1996) and *Ultima Online* (ORIGIN Systems Inc. 1997). In terms of audiovisuals and content, *SWG* draws upon the Star Wars universe while *DAoC* players enter one of three medieval "realms" based on Arthurian legends, Celtic mythology, or Norse mythology. Once logged on, players can choose a wide range of activities and the games have no hard-set winning conditions as such. Most players attempt to advance their characters through the level or skill progression system, often teaming up with others to complete advanced missions and engage powerful enemies. Inter-player combat is strictly regulated and a player can choose whether to engage in this activity (either by choosing a non-player-vs-player server or by actively switching the option on/off).

In order to truly progress in the game a player must spend a considerable number of hours within the world, where weekly play time of 20 hours (or more) is not uncommon (Castronova 2001). Presently, each game has approximately 250,000 paying subscribers (*SWG* has slightly more).[3]

I chose to analyze these games because of their status as second generation game worlds, believing them to be more indicative of the direction of the genre than older titles. Also, at the time of this research they were among the most popular of the mainstream Western game worlds, although their success was later dwarfed by that of Blizzard's (2004) *World of Warcraft*. For later work it would be worthwhile to compare mainstream games with more experimental approaches that tend to take more progressive stands regarding player rights.

The Problem of Power

If politics is a struggle to get power, much political theory can be seen as a struggle to define power. The concept of power has proven elusive as well as controversial. In *Leviathan*, Thomas Hobbes (1997: 72) claimed that "[t]he power of a man, to take it universally, is his present means, to obtain some future apparent good...." In a more modern context, Max Weber's (1978: 926) famous view that power is "the chance of a man or a number of men to realize their own will in a social action even against the resistance of others who are participating in the action" stresses the social nature of power. It also corresponds with Hobbes' notion that power is a substance which someone can be said to possess.

These substantial notions of power contrast relational views, particularly the poststructuralist perspective of Michel Foucault, who believed that power was a far more fundamental aspect of human life than often assumed and one which should be seen as existing in and supporting concrete interactions between people, rather than a substance residing with or within people. While the meta-question of how to conceptualize power is important, political philosophers have often glossed over disagreements by focusing on the formal distribution of power in a society (i.e., the law and the system of government) and the ways in which agents and coalitions manage to further their interests. To some extent this is the approach taken in the following analysis, but in addition to considering the formal conditions of power I will discuss the ways in which players can and do resist or alter the structures of power laid down by both the game code and the EULAs.

Power in Game Worlds

While most aspects of game world power are well-known from more traditional contexts, some are new. Karl Popper (1995: 121–122) writes:

> No political power has ever been unchecked, and as long as men remain human (as long as the "Brave New World" has not materialized), there can be no absolute and unrestrained political power. So long as one man cannot accumulate enough physical power in his hands to dominate all others, just so long must he depend upon his helpers.

Popper here indirectly reflects on an important premise of political philosophy: political philosophers usually take much for granted. They do not, as a rule, propose to radically change the laws of nature but rather concentrate on constructing systems which ensure their desired balance between individual freedom, justice and the collective interest. Thinkers from Plato to Rawls assume that air is generally transparent, that things do not fall upwards, that no-one is immortal, that citizens pose a potential physical threat to each other and that objects age and generally deteriorate over time. Indeed, Thomas Hobbes builds a good part of his famous analysis on the same premise which Popper highlighted:

> Nature hath made men so equal, in the faculties of the body, and mind; as that though there be found one man sometimes manifestly stronger in body, or of quicker mind than another; yet when all is reckoned together the difference between man, and man, is not so considerable as that one man can thereupon claim to himself any benefit, to which another may not pretend, as well as he [Hobbes 1997: 98].

No such conditions can be assumed in game worlds. As Lawrence Lessig (1999: 6) notes, in cyberspace "there is no choice that does not include some kind of building. Code is never found; it is only ever made...."[4] But in a sense these games constitute the brave new world(s) that Popper mentions. Here, at least in principle, political power can be unchecked and the power of the game designer is certainly far beyond that imagined by even the most ambitious of political philosophers.

While, interestingly, game world designers do usually respect well-known rules (or should we now say conventions?) of physics as they manifest themselves on Earth, we can easily spot exceptions. Hobbes' premise of equal physical power, for instance, is blatantly disrespected as leveling within these games creates an extreme dichotomy between experienced characters and new ones.[5] Other breaks with physical-world assumptions include the fact that some players cannot be attacked by others, the convention that death is never final, that players often cannot steal from one another and, of course, the use of magic.

Game designers (including day-to-day managers, helpers, and so on) seem tremendously powerful. One might be excused for thinking that the unquestionable power to completely restrict undesired action types and the control over all in-game communication modalities would give designers a degree of control far beyond anything experienced by real-world leaders. But on the level of administrator experience this (surprisingly perhaps) seems not to be the case. Statements of relative impotence are frequent. In their seminal article on the early graphical world *Habitat* (Lucasfilm Games 1985), designers Chip Morningstar and F. Randall Farmer (2003: 671) note that:

> Again and again we found that activities based on often unconscious assumptions about player behavior had completely unexpected outcomes (when they were not simply outright failures). It was clear that we were not in control. The more people we involved in something, the less in control we were. We could influence things, we could set up interesting situations, we could provide opportunities for things to happen, but we could not dictate the outcome. Social engineering is, at best, an inexact science (or, as some wag once said, "In the most carefully constructed experiment under the most carefully controlled conditions, the organism will do whatever it damn well pleases").

Even if the authors are in part reflecting on the limits of their own disciplinary backgrounds they are also asserting that, despite all their apparent control, social dynamics within *Habitat* felt mostly unpredictable. Similarly, a recent design manual states that, when designing online games,

> you're more than a game designer; you must also be a social architect.... An online game isn't an experience that you lead a player through; it's a Petri dish for growing social situations, and it's nearly impossible to predict in advance what will happen there [Rollings and Adams 2003: 500–501].

Now, there may be reasons for downplaying one's power. First, the dynamics of privileges are surely often hidden to the privileged; no matter how much influence we may have we will always be restrained by various factors. Game designers, of course, are heavily constrained by time, (lack of) funds, and the current state technology and thus cannot do *exactly* what they want. We should also acknowledge that any game which grants its players a large degree of autonomy (and MMORPGs usually advertise the joy of freely exploring their vast worlds) leaves the players able to do unexpected things (see for instance Castronova 2003a: 45). This point was driven home in *Ultima Online* where "the detailed ecological model employed broke down when players rapidly killed everything that moved" (Bartle 2003: 22) and where at one time a horde of angry and naked protesters stormed the king's castle displaying their anger over the problematic game service (King and Borland 2003: 160).

Additionally, MMORPGs are populated by players who do not all follow the clear path of level progression but instead choose to use the game to play their own sub-games, for various artistic endeavors, or to make a (physical-world) living by brokering in-game objects (e.g., Terdiman 2004). The power of the game designers does not determine the players' preferences although much is done to shape them (e.g., streamlining game mechanics to encourage players to travel in groups). While creative players can clearly subvert some of the intentions manifested in the game code there is one power technique over which — although less direct than the game code — they have little say: The game's EULA.

Reading the EULA

The existence of the state, argued the original contractarians of political philosophy, is justified by its necessity in making individuals act according to the common good. To various extents Thomas Hobbes, John Locke, and Jean-Jacques Rousseau argued that individuals could realize this necessity and that they would therefore join together in a relationship characterized by a "social contract." They speculated that in a natural pre-state condition people (rational, autonomous individuals) would have agreed to enter into a condition of mutual limitation to achieve an advantage, both individually and collectively.

Such problems of legitimacy do not apply to EULAs. The act of consent in the case of our two games is concrete and entirely non-hypothetical:

> By clicking on the "I Accept" button, you accept the terms and conditions below. By clicking the "Decline" button, you decline our offer, in which case you must not install or use the software....
>
> 1. Accounts are available only to adults or, in their discretion, their minor child of at least thirteen years of age.... If you are a minor child, your parent or guardian must complete the registration process, in which case he or she takes full responsibility for all obligations under this Agreement. By clicking the "I Accept" button, you represent that you are an adult and are accepting this Agreement either on behalf of yourself or your minor child.... You are liable for all activities conducted through the Account, and parents or guardians are liable for the activities of their minor child ... [*Star Wars Galaxies*].

Two main documents regulate rights within *SWG*. The EULA itself, consisting of fifteen numbered paragraphs, defines terms related to the player accounts, while the Community Standards Document specifies the rules of social interaction within the game space. *DAoC* players submit to rules specified in the EULA itself and a Rules of Conduct document. The EULAs are detailed statements of ownership and rights in addition to a number of disclaimers freeing Sony and Mythic from liability in various unfortunate circumstances. Technically the player buys and enters the game based on the then-current EULA. If the EULA is suddenly changed in a way which the player cannot accept, he or she would suddenly be unable to (rightfully) play the game. The problems associated with changing basic rules constitute one of the reasons why physical-world constitutions impose various conservative guarantees on legislators such as demanding that the change be approved by two separate legislative assemblies. The *SWG* EULA clearly states that Sony "may amend this Agreement at any time on our sole discretion," at which point the player is given the choice to either accept or decline the new EULA (the latter, of course, means being unable to play).

Physical-world laws specify sanctions which are ultimately a consequence of the constitution and which, for recognized citizens, take the form of various unpleasant measures like fines or imprisonment. In contrast, the *SWG* EULA concentrates on one rather more drastic sanction: Banishment. At least in principle, the grounds for banishment are rather expansive:

> 6. We may terminate this Agreement and/or suspend your Account immediately and without notice: (i) if you violate any provision of this Agreement; (ii) if you infringe any third party intellectual property rights; (iii) if we are unable to verify or authenticate any information you provide to us; (iv) if you violate any of the player rules of conduct located at the Game Site or The Station ... rules of conduct located at www.station.sony.com/en/termsofservice.jsp (either of which we may amend or supplement from time to time, in our discretion), or (v) if you engage in game play, chat or any player activity whatsoever which we, in our discretion, determine is inappropriate and/or in violation of the spirit of the Game.

Clause (v) is the most problematic here. Sony here forces anyone who wants to play the game to agree that he or she may be banished for any action which Sony deems inappropriate, a license further strengthened by the addendum that the player will lose "*the balance of any prepaid period, without any refund.*" Considered in a constitutional light this clearly undermines essential ideas of legal rights manifest in physical-world democracies.

Another paragraph (Paragraph 8) arguably defines most in-game player actions as "content" uploaded to the game server (for a discussion of game EULAs in relation to intellectual property see Taylor [2001]). This content can either be derivative, in which case it belongs fully to Sony, or non-derivative, in which case the player must

> exclusively grant and irrevocably assign to our licensors and us all rights of any kind or nature throughout the universe to such Content ... in any languages and media now known or not currently known.

This transfer of rights creates a tension between the desire of the game developers to encourage web-based fan activity (often making liberal use of screenshots and chat logs) and the desire to ultimately "own" everything which takes place in the game world.

The *Dark Age of Camelot* EULA wrestles with the same issue. Here, all elements originating from the game are considered the sole property of Mythic:

> ... your Account(s), and all attributes of your Accounts, including all guilds, groups, titles, and characters, and objects, currency and items acquired, developed or delivered by or to characters as a result of Game play through your Accounts are part of the System and the Game Content, and are the sole and exclusive property of Mythic, including any and all copyrights and intellectual property rights in or to any and all of the same, all of which are hereby expressly reserved.

This is different from "user content" which covers specifically user-generated elements like chat messages.

> As to all User Content, you hereby grant to us an exclusive, perpetual, worldwide, irrevocable, assignable, royalty-free license, fully sublicensable through multiple tiers, to exercise all intellectual property rights, in and to all or any part of your User Content, in any medium now known or hereafter developed....

Whereas the EULAs themselves describe in general terms the legal status of in-game activities and the distribution of rights, players also consent to obey various, more concrete, rules of conduct. These are listed in documents providing details on how players are allowed to interact within the gamespace. Judging by its prominent position in these documents one rule is all-important: Players must not harass each other:

> *SWG*: You may not harass or threaten other players.
> *DAoC*: [A player may not use the game to] Harass, threaten or embarrass another Player of the Services or to cause distress, unwanted attention or discomfort of such Player, or any other person or entity.

Considering the design of both games, the prominence (and explicitness) of the anti-harassment rule is striking. Both games are usually considered low on inter-player violence since players are physically unable to attack each other personally[6] (which explains why the anti-violence rule does not feature in the documents). This constraint is hard-coded and very easy to uphold since one's stand toward another character (or non-player character) is a binary one of fighting/not-fighting. In-game communication is quite different as no algorithm can effectively disallow offensive statements.[7] This also means, however, that harassment cannot be entirely specified in the rules of conduct, which explains the curious definition offered *SWG* players: "Harassment is defined as specifically targeting another player or group of players to harm or inconvenience them. Harassment can take many forms, as it goes to the state-of-mind of the person or Squad on the receiving end of the action." This definition basically claims that harassment must be intentional but that it also depends on the interpretation in the receiving end, which seems somewhat contradictory. *DAoC* takes a slightly different approach to the definition issue by emphasizing that no playing style directly supported by "game mechanics" is considered harassment. Harassment, then, "consists of flagrant misuse and abuse of game mechanics with the intention of distressing and offending other players." The question then becomes one of defining game mechanics. Mythic offers the following definition: "Game mechanics allow players to interact with the world and each other." With such a general definition of game mechanics the player must again consider harassment a question of intention.[8]

Another prominent rule seeks to ensure the general non-aggressive atmosphere of the gamespace. With identical formulations, both games disallow player groupings based on or espousing any "racist, sexist, anti-religious, anti-ethnic, anti-gay or other hatemongering philosophy." This rule clearly serves to uphold the playful status of the game-space by trying to keep it clear of real-world politics or antagonisms (as well as ensuring that no player group feels unwelcome). Apart from the marketing concerns reflected in such attempts, the desire to preserve the "world apart" atmosphere — the desire to uphold the "magic circle" (Salen and Zimmerman 2004: 93–99) — most likely is also motivated by the wish to stay in control of the game. If the game space and physical life gets too intertwined, real-world legislators, tax authorities and so on are likely to take a more active interest in the games, creating tensions over player rights and obligations. This concern is particularly apparent in the *DAoC* EULA which, as mentioned above, stresses that the player must only use the game space for entertainment purposes and by accepting the EULA claims no interest in the value of the game beyond the time spent playing. Finally, the EULA strenuously forbids the sale of game objects, characters and so on through any system other than the official account transfer system offered by Mythic themselves.

Another rule that attempts to ensure a positive atmosphere between players in *SWG* forbids fraud, defined as "falsely representing one's intentions to make a gain at another's expense." For instance, someone playing an artisan is not allowed to promise to improve someone else's weapon only to disappear with that same weapon. As with other rules discussed here, the anti-fraud rule is one you would expect to be in place in a physical-world society. If we look at the worlds portrayed in our MMORPGs' pen-and-paper ancestors such a rule might also have existed, but it would have been a fictitious law and not a game rule. In other words, the in-game powers in such worlds might try to punish those guilty of fraud but fraud would not be against the spirit of the games. If fact, it might even be rewarded since pen-and-paper role-playing encourages players to assume the role of citizens of dubious professions like thieves and assassins and to above all play the role to the best of their ability. But MMORPGs evidently are not meant to work like this. Instead, one must be honest and generally act in a socially responsible fashion. Both EULAs stress that "role-playing" can never be an excuse to violate any of the rules of conduct. Thus, even if one specifically wishes to play an evil character, arguably fully consistent with the medieval and space frontier settings, one must not annoy or defraud others. The choice to emphasize social responsibility over the drama and danger inherent in role-playing clearly supports a very specific playing experience.

The EULAs, to sum up, may be seen as documents which perform two functions. First, they attempt to specify that which cannot be regulated algorithmically. Importantly, they do not list actions that are illegal within the game spaces, but mention only those activities that are illegal and indefinable through code. Some such activities can be described quite clearly (even if they cannot be prevented by code). For instance the EULAs can unambiguously disallow certain types of player use of game content, yet some behavior (e.g., harassment and dishonorable combat) are situationally defined and thus always ambiguous. In these latter cases both EULAs are adamant that the game managers have the final say in any dispute. The second function, most prevalent in the *DAoC* EULA, is the separation of the game from the physical world. The game managers go to great lengths to ensure that outside concerns and most obviously outside law will not apply within the game world. Many have argued that this is a difficult position to defend and one likely to be further challenged in the very near future (Balkin 2004; Castronova 2003b; Lastowka and Hunter 2003).

The Distribution of Power

A player, unlike a citizen of a democracy, has no direct say regarding the contents of the EULAs. In fact, the developers act as the legislative, executive, and judicial powers within the two worlds. Of course, the developers have clear incentives to take player complaints and suggestions seriously (as is often done), but there are no formal channels of player influence over these governing texts. Should a player feel unable to conscientiously comply with the EULAs as described above, he or she can opt to leave the game. Game worlds aplenty beckon any homeless player towards their shores. Thus, a common response to unsatisfied players is "If you don't like the game, you're free not to play it," often followed by the qualification that the game developers have incurred the costs of creating the game world and thus have the right to control the game world as they see fit.

In an important sense, this is an echo of another classical debate. In David Hume's view, expressed in the mid eighteenth century, we cannot seriously say "that a poor peasant or artisan has a free choice to leave his country, when he knows no foreign language or manners, and lives, from day to day, by the small wages which he acquires" (Hume 1748). In contrast, Jean-Jacques Rousseau argued that for citizens of free states, leaving one's home was quite possible (Rousseau 1762). It's very likely, however, that Rousseau had a different and more local idea of "state" than did Hume. And of course, the specific type of community in question is important. Lessig (1999) notes that the exit solution may at first glance seem highly plausible for online community members (see also Galston 1999). After all, the next community is just a mouse click away. But since, in an online community, all investments are tied to one's non-transferable character, leaving would mean losing everything one has earned within the system (both in terms of items, wealth, and social capital). As Lessig (1999: 83) puts it,

> it becomes increasingly hard for members of a successful [game world] to move elsewhere. They have the right to exit, but in the sense that Soviet citizens had the right to exit — namely, with none of the assets they had built in their particular world.

Raph Koster, in the above-mentioned document on player rights, makes a similar point when he considers it self-evident

> That the ease of moving between virtual spaces and the potential transience of the community do not limit or reduce the level of emotional and social involvement that avatars may have with the community, and that therefore the ease of moving between virtual spaces and the potential transience of the community do not in any way limit, curtail, or remove these rights from avatars on the alleged grounds that avatars can always simply leave [Koster 2000].

Arguably, then, when a player is in a position to start caring about her rights she will no longer be able to easily (or cheaply) just leave the system without looking back. While it is technically easy to move between game worlds, other forces tie the player to her present world. Such forces are being partly remedied by the widespread clan system common to online games. If one cannot transfer her position from a community then perhaps one should redefine that community. Clans often function in multiple games and when members move between games (although loosing the character and items associated with their former account) they can transfer their in-clan social capital from one game world to the other.

Present-day game worlds, with some exceptions,[9] are autocratic structures in which basic rights known from the outside world are blatantly disrespected (even if players consent to these conditions). How problematic this is depends entirely on how we conceive of these worlds. Regardless, we can expect the position that game worlds are purely means of entertainment that should be kept separate from physical-world concerns to be increasingly challenged. Additionally, regardless of the power balance between the two competing perspectives we can see that the very existence of these special social spaces reframes issues as old as the social sciences themselves.

It is increasingly evident that, no matter how often or how explicitly players consent to consider online gaming as mere entertainment, they attach value to their activities and genuinely care about the worlds that they populate and help shape. This attachment manifests itself in multiple ways. Players protest loudly against game changes that diminish the value of their investment (such as when the relative power of a character class is reduced, a process known as a "nerf"[10]). Other players see it as their mission to cause distress in others,[11] and these others often react in highly emotional ways (for a discussion of grief play see Foo and Koivisto [2004]). Furthermore, players construct elaborate social structures and relationships often including in-game weddings.[12] This suggests that no matter if, or to what extent, it will prove possible to uphold the barriers separating in-game sociality from the outside world in legal terms, there is no denying that what goes on in the game is socially very real.

We also see that, although the medium matters and particular games inspire particular patterns of behavior, what is striking about multiplayer sociality is not its strangeness but its similarities with social dynamics well-known and well-studied in the physical world. Yet, it is tempting to be lured by apparent novelty into abandoning what amounts to centuries of knowledge. Consequently some scholarly approaches to games do seem to lack a sense of history in a way which mirrors the state of internet studies (and debate on internet sociality) in parts of the 1990s (Wellman and Gulia 1999). To some extent the blank slate approach to games (although never framed in such terms) has been recommended to the extent that it was seen as a necessary counter-measure to the theoretical imperialism of disciplines that seemed eager to subsume games under their own theoretical headings (Smith 2004). But while the study of game ontology and the formal relationship between game aspects like rules, game-play, and aesthetics may warrant such a fresh approach social theory is not medium specific. Social science (in most distillations at least) looks for general patterns and does not generally start over when new frameworks for social interaction appear; particularly when those patterns seem quite compatible with tried-and-tested paradigms. This does not mean that cutting-edge persistent game worlds represent nothing new but the challenge is one of adaptation not one of starting from scratch.

Conclusions

In *Star Wars Galaxies* and *Dark Age of Camelot*, two popular contemporary game words, all formal power resides with the game developers. The power over algorithmically definable actions is exercised through the game code while the power to define the spirit of the game and the way players should interact (on punishment of being banished) is exercised through the game EULA and related documents. These EULAs also serve another function, namely to uphold or strengthen the separation of the game world from the world outside in order to maintain maximum control, limit player recourse to outside law and to accommodate those many players who would not be attracted to a game which resembled the outside world too much.

Whether the substantial power imbalance characterizing the player-developer relationship is problematic cannot be answered in the abstract but depends to a large extent on the status that we assign to the worlds. This is a two-way relationship as the conceptual framework that one applies is also in itself a means to support the player-developer relationship that one prefers. Thus, this battle over meaning (which increasingly is a losing one for the "purely entertainment" side) is one that will shape the near and distant future of game worlds.

Although almost all formal power rests with developers, players are hardly powerless puppets. They are fully free not to enter a specific game and fully free in principle to leave whenever they chose (although certain conditions may compel them to stay). Game worlds often attract players by emphasizing the freedom of movement and exploration that they offer and this freedom can of course be used by players in ways practically unforeseeable by developers. Players can organize in-game protests and generally challenge the spirit of the game by exploiting it for their own purposes; whether artistic, commercial or personal. Many such practices will of course be welcomed by the developers as they add flavor and variation to the game space.

Finally, what I have framed here as a conflict is also a mutually beneficial relationship. Players enjoy the vast, and often beautiful, expanses of game worlds and feel that the service provided is worth the monthly fee. For their part, game developers are not just power mongers but also artists working to challenge the boundaries of a rapidly evolving medium. But the relationship, we would be foolish not to accept, will not remain unaffected by outside forces. Games will not be left alone; they are simply too important.

Notes

1. The EULA versions referred to in this article were in effect on October 20th 2004 and were located at *http://starwarsgalaxies.station.sony.com/tos.jsp* (*SWG*) and *http://support.*

darkageofcamelot.com/kb/article.php?id=072 (*DAoC*). At times, I will use the term EULA to also refer to documents other than the license agreements themselves (e.g. rules of conduct etc.).

2. For a general introduction to the history and design of world-based online games see Richard Bartle's (2003) *Designing Virtual Worlds.*

3. Numbers are based on Bruce Sterling Woodcock's (2004) *An Analysis of MMOG Subscription Growth.*

4. While Lessig is right in principle we should also remember that the statement is almost never true in practice as new games build vastly on the structure (and often the code) of older specimens (see for instance the history of MUD code-bases in Bartle [2003]).

5. Even if clearly inspired by pen-and-paper role-playing this situation in fact (almost) never occurred in games like *Advanced Dungeons & Dragons* where player characters of remarkably different skill levels would rarely interact.

6. Both games restrict this option to higher level characters although *DAoC* players can choose to log on to special player-vs-player servers.

7. Unless one simply disallows or severely restrains real-time communication. This approach is taken by Disney's child-friendly *Toontown Online* (Disney 2003).

8. A recent fan column on the *Star Wars Galaxies* Warcry website (*http://swg.warcry.com*) exemplifies the ambiguities of harassment (Waylander 2004). A crafter is continuously badgered by an impatient customer. Although the crafter tries to reason with the other player he is plagued by more or less rude messages throughout the crafting process. There's nothing to indicate that the customer is being intentionally abusive, but arguably his impatience and thoughtlessness is a nuisance to the crafter.

9. *A Tale in the Desert* (eGenesis 2003) and *Second Life* (Linden Lab 2003) for instance both take more experimental approaches.

10. The term refers to the foam-plastic material used in certain types of toy weapons, indicating that the object or character class has been rendered harmless.

11. See for instance the "Player Killer Headquarters" at *http://www.pk-hq.com/*.

12. For an example of an *SWG* wedding see *http://www.rebscum.com/viewtopic.php?t=833*.

References

Archetype Interactive. 1996. *Meridian 59.* Version: PC. Published by: The 3DO Company.

Balkin, Jack M. 2004. "Virtual Liberty: Freedom to Design and Freedom to Play in Virtual Worlds (Yale Law School, Public Law Working Paper No. 74)."

Bartle, Richard. 2003. *Designing Virtual Worlds.* Indianapolis: New Riders.

Castronova, Edward. 2001. "Virtual Worlds: A First-Hand Account of Market and Society on the Cyberian Frontier." in *CESifo Working Paper Series No. 618.*

_____. 2003a. "On Virtual Economies." *Game Studies* 3.

_____. 2003b. "The Right to Play." in *State of Play.* New York: New York Law School.

Dibbell, Julian 2003. "The Unreal Estate Boom." *Wired,* December 2003.

Disney. 2003. *Toontown Online.* Version: PC. Published by: Disney.

eGenesis. 2003. *A Tale in the Desert.* Version: PC. Published by: eGenesis.

Feldman, Curt 2003. "Q&A: Banned Sims blogger bites back." *Gamespot.com.*

Foo, Chek Yang, and Elina M.I. Koivisto. 2004. "Defining Grief Play in MMORPGs: Player and Developer Perceptions." in *International Conference on Advances in Computer Entertainment Technology (ACE 2004).* Singapore.

Galston, William. 1999, "Does the Internet Strengthen Community?" Retrieved 1st of November, 2004 (http://www.puaf.umd.edu/IPPP/fall1999/internet_community.htm).

Harmon, Amy. 2004. "A Real-Life Debate on Free Expression in a Cyberspace City." in *The New York Times*. New York.

Hobbes, Thomas. 1997. *Leviathan — Or the Matter, Forme and Power of a Commonwealth Ecclesiasticall and Civil*. New York: Touchstone.

Hume, David. 1748. *Of the Original Contract (online version by Jon Roland)*.

King, Brad, and John Borland. 2003. *Dungeons and Dreamers: The Rise of Computer Game Culture from Geek to Chic*. New York: McGraw-Hill.

Koster, Raph. 2000, "Declaring the Rights of Players," Retrieved 20th of October, 2004 (http://www.legendmud.org/raph/gaming/playerrights.html).

Lastowka, F. Gregory, and Dan Hunter. 2003. "The Laws of the Virtual Worlds." SSRN Working Papers.

Lessig, Lawrence. 1999. *Code and Other Laws of Cyberspace*. New York: Basic Books.

Linden Lab. 2003. *Second Life*. Version: PC. Published by: Linden Lab.

Lucasfilm Games. 1985. *Habitat*. Version: Commodore 64. Published by: Lucasfilm Games.

Maxis Software Inc. 2001. *The Sims Online*. Version: Published by: Electronic Arts Inc.

Morningstar, Chip, and F. Randall Farmer. 2003. "The Lessons of Lucasfilm's Habitat." in *The New Media Reader*, edited by N. Wardrip-Fruin and N. Montfort. Cambridge: The MIT Press.

ORIGIN Systems Inc. 1997. *Ultima Online*. Version: PC. Published by: Electronic Arts Inc.

Pika. 2004, "Interview with Raph Koster, Chief Creative Officer for SOE," Retrieved 13th of May, 2004 (http://www.warcry.com/scripts/columns/view_sectionalt.phtml?site= 15&id=102&colid=1712).

Popper, Karl. 1995. *The Open Society and its Enemies*. London: Routledge.

Rollings, Andrew, and Ernest Adams. 2003. *Andrew Rollings and Ernest Adams on Game Design*. Boston: New Riders Publishing.

Rousseau, Jean-Jacques. 1762/1998. *The Social Contract — Or Principles of Political Right*. Ware: Wordsworth Editions.

Salen, Katie, and Eric Zimmerman. 2004. *Rules of Play — Game Design Fundamentals*. London: MIT Press.

Smith, Jonas Heide. 2004, "Does gameplay have politics?" Retrieved 1st of November, 2004 (http://www.game-research.com/art_gameplay_politics.asp).

Taylor, T.L. 2001. ""Whose Game is this Anyway?": Negotiating Corporate Ownership in a Virtual World." in *Computer Games and Digital Cultures*, edited by F. Mäyra. Tampere: Tampere University Press.

Terdiman, Daniel 2004. "Virtual Trader Barely Misses Goal." *Wired News*, 16th of April.

Waylander. 2004, "Good Grief," Retrieved 27th of October, 2004 (http://swg.warcry.com/ scripts/columns/view_section.phtml?site=13&id=298).

Weber, Max. 1978. "The Distribution of Power Within the Political Community: Class, Status, Party." Pp. 926–940 in *Economy and Society*, vol. 2, edited by G. R. a. C. Wittich. Berkeley: University of California Press.

Wellman, Barry, and Milena Gulia. 1999. "Virtual communities as communities — Net surfers don't ride alone." in *Communities in Cyberspace*, edited by P. Kollock and M. A. Smith. London: Routledge.

Woodcock, Bruce Sterling. 2004, "An Analysis of MMOG Subscription Growth — Version 10.0," Retrieved 20th of October 2004, (http://pw1.netcom.com/~sirbruce/ Subscriptions.html).

2. Terms of Service and Terms of Play in Children's Online Gaming

SARA M. GRIMES

As children and youth continue to expand their access to, and presence on, the internet they increasingly adopt participatory roles in the creation of online content — contributing in meaningful ways to online environments, games and communities. The fact remains, however, that the most popular among these sites are often commercially owned and operated, and respond primarily to corporate interests. This has resulted in what Montgomery (2000) terms a "children's digital media culture," which creates new levels of intimacy between marketers and children by dissolving the traditional barriers between content and commerce. Nowhere is this relationship more clearly illustrated than within popular branded children's websites and online games. Online game communities provide young users with virtual tools and playspaces, enabling them to interact, adopt virtual pets, play sponsored "advergames," and serve as a stable data-mining resource for marketers and toy companies. This phenomenon, and the corporate mechanisms that drive it, is reflective of a larger trend in online gaming conventions — one that increasingly incorporates marketing research strategies into game content and design.

Concurrently, digital multiplayer games are becoming the site of mounting legal conflict and academic inquiry. Whereas public discourse and political debate during the late twentieth century centered on music sharing and other forms of digital piracy, attention has now shifted to issues of intellectual property and the nature of participatory design and authorship. Through these debates, online gamers and creators are contributing to a transformation in contemporary notions about the nature and limits of copyright, as well as the legality and fairness of the terms of service (TOS) agreements (also called end-user license agreements (EULAs) and terms of use (TOU) contracts) that aim to control and define the activities and experiences of users. The scope and nature of these online contracts becomes all the more questionable in cases where the user group consists predominantly of minors — children who remain largely ignorant of the labor relations and legal implications of the activities in which they are engaged, the true value of the intellectual property they are voluntarily revoking, and the loss of privacy and cultural meaning in which these interactions may result. Furthermore, policies aimed at protecting children's interests online, such as the Children's Online Privacy Protection Act (COPPA)[1] in the US, do not currently address the more indirect forms of privacy invasion and intellectual property appropriation that occur within commercial game spaces.

This study provides an overview of the TOS contracts contained within some of the most frequented children's online games, in order to compare the nature and scope of these online (but allegedly legally binding) contracts to existing laws and policies relating to children online. I provide a review of the content and activities that take place within popular online children's games in order to assess the nature and intensity of users' participation in the construction of commercially-driven digital playspaces. I also emphasize the exchange of information and culture that occurs between children and corporate entities in order to identify the nature of these interactions, and the legal and economic implications of children's participation in this exchange. This project thus explores the hypothesis that children's cultural participation in online gaming is highly structured by commercial interests through the incorporation of advertising and marketing research into children's digital culture, the appropriation of children's contributions and creativity, and the commodification of children's online practices. I will couch my analysis within a consideration of how children's online games are seen to operate vis-à-vis the greater trends and business practices found within children's cultural industries, as well as the issue of children's rights in the information age.

The Rise of "Cyber"-Childhood

Over the last two decades, children's media usage has increased substantially. In the average North American home, children have access to a variety of media options — from TVs and DVD players, to personal computers and videogame consoles. In the US, 73% of children have a computer at home and nearly half (49%) have a videogame console (Rideout, Vandewater, and Wartella 2003). Among children aged 6 years and under, "nearly twice as many ... live in a home with internet access (63%) as with a newspaper subscription (34%)" (p. 4). Internet usage studies conducted over the past five years continue to show that families with children remain among the fastest growing demographics of internet users (Edwards 1999; Montgomery 2000; Statistics Canada 2004). In Canada, single-family households with children under the age of 18 have the highest rate of home internet use, comprising nearly 4.9 million households or 73% of this demographic in 2003 (Statistics Canada 2004). Recent studies by Nielsen/Netratings (2003a; 2003b) report that children account for one out of every five internet users in the US (totaling more than 27 million), while 13.1 million children across Europe are now online. Children are also using media at an increasingly younger age. "Nearly half (48%) of all children six and under have used a computer, and more than one in four (30%) have played video games" (Rideout et al. 2003: 4).

Research also indicates that the most popular children's sites are often commercially owned and operated, responding primarily to industry interests and an advertising-based economic model (Montgomery 2000; Seiter 2004; Shade, Porter, and Santiago 2004). This has resulted in a children's digital media culture (Montgomery 2000: 636) shaped by "powerful commercial forces" that attempt to create new levels of intimacy between marketers and children by dissolving the traditional barriers between content and advertising. Seiter (2004: 93) notes that, as internet use became more and more prevalent among Western children, their "interests, habits, and abilities in the online environment became the subject of intense interest by marketers." The resulting relationship that has formed between marketing, information and communication media, and children's culture has made childhood "inseparable from media use and media surveillance" (Cook 2001: 82). This is due in part to the increasingly central role market research has taken in both the creation and manipulation of children's digital content. As Montgomery (2000: 638) describes, the "intense focus on research within the new media industries has produced a wealth of information, much of it proprietary, which is guiding the development of digital content and services for children." The internet also allows market researchers to construct richly detailed consumer profiles from the aggregate data gathered from thousands of subjects belonging to a demographic group that is otherwise extremely difficult to gain access to.

This practice is part of a growing trend in consumer research that Russakoff (1999) has labeled "cool hunting," a practice in which marketers, "get kids talking about their taste-worlds" (Quart 2003: 42). Cool hunting is manifested in various formats, including sponsored or "branded chats" hosted by popular, youth-oriented chatrooms (Selling to Kids 2001) as well as the invisible data-mining technologies online games use to gather information about their users. While children's personally identifying information is protected in the US and on many US-based websites through COPPA, little protection exists for children and websites located outside the US.[2] Furthermore, no protection currently exists for information that is collected and stored in aggregate form (e.g., through detailed studies of whole demographics) and interest groups are often what marketers and advertisers value most (Lindström 2003; Smith and Clurman 1997; Sutherland and Thompson 2001).

The modest academic attention given to these processes, as well as what impact they might have on children's newfound roles as online cultural producers, is particularly significant when we consider the types of online activities children reportedly prefer. As Livingstone (2003: 13–14) argues, "while to adults the internet primarily means the world wide web, for children it means email, chat, games — and here they are already content producers." Children also contribute to the creation of online content by building personal websites (Grunwald Associates 2003) or maintaining "weblogs" (Grimes 2003). Furthermore, numerous media education programs stress the importance of content creation to children's acquisition of media literacy skills (Buckingham 2003). However, whereas issues such as children's online privacy and copyright infringement through unsanctioned file-sharing are exhaustively researched and highlighted in the mainstream press, the legal aspects of children's direct participation in cultural production — including children's potential intellectual property rights and other authorship rights over the ideas and cultural content they produce and distribute online — are often overlooked.

Conversely, questions of authorship and cultural production are at the center of escalating public and legal debate concerning adult internet users, particularly within the realm of online gaming. Unlike the ongoing conflicts surrounding music file-sharing software (including Napster and KaZaA!), cases involving online multiplayer games (most often involving Massively Multiplayer Online Games [MMOGs] such as *EverQuest* [Sony Online Entertainment 1999–2004], *The Sims Online* [Electronic Arts, Inc. 2002–2004], and *Lineage* [NCSoft. 1998–2003]) illustrate how the interactive nature of many internet applications problematizes traditional notions of authorship. Online multiplayer games consist of ongoing cultural productions, the result of the combined efforts and participation of both corporate employees (designers, programmers, customer support agents, and so on) and the games' players. The collaborative and often symbiotic aspects of these shared production processes are presenting new challenges to legal concepts like intellectual property and ownership (see e.g., Stephens 2002). The emerging debates have the potential to both significantly alter the structure of the internet and redefine future articulations and treatments of intellectual property worldwide. Thus, while file-sharing cases may effectively demonstrate conflicts between corporate interests and the notion of a cultural commons, online games present a unique venue for a critical investigation of how virtual environments and communities are redefining social conceptualizations of cultural work, copyright and intellectual property.

In many of the cases to date, tensions arise as players and the game industry both seek to exert control over the characters and in-game items created as a result of the hours, weeks and months of gameplay players dedicate to MMOGs and game communities.[3] From players' perspectives, the time, money and creative energy dedicated to the construction of game characters, as well as the ongoing maintenance of consistent and entertaining game communities is justification for a claim to partial authorship and co-ownership over characters and player-generated creations. On the other hand, the industry argues that its ownership of the game code (not to mention the original narrative, visual and audio elements of the game, and the rules of play) legitimately extends to the players' actions within the game environment. At the center of the industry's claim is the controversial institutionalization of TOS or EULA contracts. TOS agreements consist of online contracts that players must agree to upon entering a game by clicking in confirmation that they have read and accepted the terms and conditions outlined by the game owners/operators. By clicking "Yes" or "I Agree," the user consents to waive a number of significant rights, such as the "rights to own the fruits of labor, rights to assemble, rights to free speech" (Castronova 2003: 8).

Player resistance to the intellectual property clauses of a number of TOS contracts found within online games has spurred widespread debate and speculation among legal experts and digital game scholars, a number of whom argue that it remains unclear whether TOS agreements, in their current form, will prove strong enough to survive the growing challenge posed by players and other opposing parties (Castronova 2003; Lastowka and Hunter 2004). Castronova (2003) argues that game owners cannot prevent fair and equal treatment of individuals and virtual property just because they have a TOS that says so. He writes, "[s]ynthetic worlds are being treated as special cases, but no law has defined when and how this special treatment should apply" (p. 9). Lastowka and Hunter (2003: 71) note that courts are likely to reject TOS contracts on the basis that they are "overly restrictive upon the economic interests of the participants."

The fact remains, however, that only a small proportion of adult players and internet users pay attention to the contents of TOS contracts and privacy policies, let alone fully understand their legal implications. According to Turow (2003: 3), the majority of adult internet users in the US "misunderstand the very purpose of privacy policies," believing incorrectly that the mere presence of a privacy policy indicates that a website "will not share their personal information with other websites or companies." While little research has been conducted on children's understanding of website policies and contracts, emergent studies do suggest a similar set of trends among child internet users. In a sixteen-week study of children's internet use within a public library setting, Sandvig (2000) found only nine requests for privacy policies of any kind among the 203,647 page requests submitted by children during that time period. More recently, Shade, Porter, and Santiago (2004) report that young children have difficulty understanding questions about privacy, know very little about common internet business practices such as sending "cookies" to track users, and oftentimes did not fully comprehend why personal information should not be divulged online. Furthermore, Turow (2001) reports that children are more likely than adults to give out sensitive information, particularly in exchange for a free gift or reward. These findings support a growing body of academic research demonstrating the limitations of children's understanding of internet (especially corporate) processes (Seiter 2004; Shade et al. 2004), as well as children's overall lack of critical literacy when it comes to new media (Kline 2001; Livingstone 2003).

The Terms and Conditions of Children's Online Play

Whereas the issues of children's privacy and media literacy are the focus of growing scholarly interest, to date little mention has been made in the literature of children's relationship and potential claims to intellectual property online. Not only do online games — through their incorporation of interactivity, entertainment, community, and cultural participation — represent a unique site for the study of online digital culture. They also constitute an important dimension of children's online experience. In 2003, 87% of children aged 7–12 years reported "playing online games" as their favorite online activity (Greenspan 2003), and all five of the "top five" online destinations most visited by children aged 2–11 featured online games of some sort (either MMOG environments, such as Disney's *Toontown Online* [Walt Disney Company 2003], or an assortment of interactive mini-games, as found on Polly-Pocket.com [Mattel, Inc. 2003c]). Since one of the key areas in which the conflict between adult players and game owners/operators has manifested itself has been the contestation (in the case of the players) and defense (in the case of the industry) of TOS contracts, I will focus on TOS contracts within children's online gamesites.

My methods consisted of a multiple-case embedded case study design incorporating nine unique cases. Yin (1984: 23) described the case study approach as an "empirical investigation of a contemporary phenomenon within a real-life context," in which the "boundaries between context and phenomenon are not immediately evident," and multiple sources of evidence are examined. This approach appears consistent with the nature of children's online gamesites, wherein the commercial content of the site and the autonomous activities that occur within it interact as both hegemonic and oppositional forces. Furthermore, because these virtual playspaces represent a new, emergent form of children's culture, the boundaries between context and phenomena remain elusive and difficult to determine. I chose a comparative, multiple-case design to allow a preliminary mapping of the norms or conventions that are being established within TOS contracts present within children's online games.

I selected cases based on popularity rankings measuring the top online destinations most frequented by "children" (aged 2–12 years) and the more general category of "youth" (users under 18 years), as reported by internet audience research firms Nielsen/Netratings and Hitwise (Greenspan 2003; Nielsen/Netratings 2002). While this approach initially yielded seventeen cases (including the *Disney Online* and *EverythingGirl.com* [Mattel, Inc. 2003b] portals), the fact that a number of the sites listed were actually subsets of a larger, umbrella brand or web environment (and therefore shared the same TOS contract and privacy policy), meant that only nine distinct TOS documents were retrieved for analysis. I constructed a coding protocol drawing upon Turow's (2001) inventory of the contents of privacy policies found on children's websites. I also used Russo's (2001) checklist of "fifteen significant points" to look for when analyzing EULAs in order to identify and categorize key clauses contained within the agreements. I performed a comprehensive overview of the contents of each site to allow for comparison between the findings from the EULA or TOS content analysis with activities featured on the sites, as well as the type of information users either could or were required to provide in order to participate. Table 2.1 provides a full listing of the cases selected for analysis.

Overview of Site Contents and Activities

In addition to a primary focus on interactive games (either multiplayer, downloadable, or simple, one-player Flash games), the majority of the sites

Game	Rank	Source	Date
Yahoo!Games	1	Nielsen/Netratings	August 2003
Yahoo! Fantasy Sports — Baseball	3	Hitwise	July 2003
Yahoo! Fantasy Sports	7	Hitwise	July 2003
Yahoo! Fantasy Sports — Football	8	Hitwise	July 2003
EA Online	2	Hitwise	July 2003
Pogo	2	Nielsen/Netratings	August 2003
MSN Game Zone	6	Hitwise	July 2003
	3	Nielsen/Netratings	August 2003
Kraft Entertainment	6	Nielsen/Netratings	August 2003
NeoPets	4	Hitwise	July 2003
EverythingGirl (included in the analysis)			
Diva Starz	1	Nielsen/Netratings	September 2003
Polly Pocket	3	Nielsen/Netratings	September 2003
Barbie	4	Nielsen/Netratings	September 2003
Disney Online (included in the analysis)			
Toon Town Online	2	Nielsen/Netratings	September 2003
DisneyChannel.com	5	Nielsen/Netratings	September 2003
gURL.com	4	Nielsen/Netratings	July 2002

Table 2.1: Online gamesites selected for analysis; rankings based on frequency of visits

I reviewed also featured "advergames" — games containing themes, activities or images that directly related to a specific (set of) product(s) or brand(s). The brands and products featured varied from sugar cereals, to movies, to toys and clothing lines. In some cases, particularly within branded sites like Barbie/Mattel's EverythingGirl.com (Mattel, Inc. 2003b) and Kraft Foods' Candystand.com (KF Holdings 2004a), nearly all of the games and activities related directly or indirectly to products and related merchandise. The vast majority of the sites collected some form of personally identifiable information from the player — email addresses, date of birth and gender being the most common, though some also asked for the user's name and at least some components of their home address (such as state/province, country, or zip code/postal code). The vast majority also included some form of social software or community-building tools, such as multiplayer components, game-related forums or chat rooms, and in some cases an email or e-card service. While little more than half of the sites allowed participants to contribute creative submissions (such as game reviews, poetry contest submissions, or fan art), very few allocated space within the site for players to create webpages, user polls, or other features of the website design. Two-thirds of the sites solicited players to complete polls or surveys (such as gURL.com's [iVillage, Inc. 1995–2004] "Are you going away for spring break?" poll, or the General Mills consumer awareness survey featured on Neopets.com [Neopets, Inc. 2004]), or to customize some aspect of the site or gameplay (as in the EverythingGirl.com site, for example, where the player could decorate Polly Pocket's bedroom or customize a new outfit for Barbie). Often, these surveys, polls and customizable features directly related to (and solicited customer opinion about) particular products or brands.

In all of the cases reviewed, membership to the site was required in order to access the entirety of the sites' contents. A small majority of these sites allowed non-members access to a limited portion of the game or a small selection of mini-games. The remainder required that players sign-up or register for membership before gameplay could commence. While membership to the majority of the sites was free — only two sites featured games or areas that required a paid subscription, while one became fee-based after an initial 10-day free trial period — in all cases, players were required to divulge personal information in order to join.

Placement and Visibility of TOS

All the sites displayed a hyperlink to a privacy policy on the homepage, and a vast majority also displayed a hyperlink to the TOS agreement. In almost all cases, both hyperlinks were placed at the bottom of the page. Most often, hyperlinks to the TOS and privacy policy were placed at the bottom of most or all the pages of the site (excluding pop-up windows). In two-thirds of the cases, no special markers (measured as "color," "font size," "font type or effects," and "other distinguishing feature") were used to enhance the visibility of the TOS hyperlink, though hyperlinks to privacy policies most often included at least one marker aimed at enhancing visibility. As a rule, if the player was asked to read the privacy policy he/she was also asked to read the TOS agreement (conversely, the player was unlikely to be asked to read just one). The same goes for the presence of mechanisms designed to encourage player to read the TOS contract (such as re-directing the player's browser to the TOS upon registration, or forcing the player to scroll through the TOS in order to accept). If such a mechanism was in place, it was likely to include both the privacy policy and the TOS.

Content Analysis of TOS Contracts

The length of the TOS contracts varied significantly both in terms of the total printed pages they produced, as well as in terms of the time required to read through the contents in their entirety. In printed pages, TOS contracts produced anywhere from 3–5 pages to 9–12 pages, with a slight majority in the later category. There was even more dispersion in terms of the time required to read the contracts, thus no significant patterns or tendencies could be identified. The TOS contracts took anywhere from 4–5 minutes to read, to a surprising 17–18 minutes, depending on length, complexity of language, font size, and so on. The longest TOS contract was found on the EA Games Online website, while the shortest was one provided by Kraft Entertainment sites. A small majority of the TOS contracts were characterized by a moderate language style (in terms of complexity of sentence structure, vocabulary used, and formality of writing style), while the rest were predominated by an "advanced" style of language. Most of the TOS agreements also contained a significant amount of legal terminology and convoluted sentence structure, with nearly half comprised almost entirely of a "legalese" style of writing. A number of sites did attempt to clarify their use of legal terminology by providing examples, definitions or other forms of clarification for less common legal terms and concepts. Whereas the majority of the case studies either directly targeted or allowed participation by children under the age of 13, (only three, MSN Game Zone [Microsoft Corp. 2003], gURL.com and Neopets.com restricted access to some areas to users aged 13 years and older), none of the TOS contracts contained much, if any, "child-friendly" or easy-to-understand language. Furthermore, only two gamesites, Postopia.com (KF Holdings 2004b) and Neopets.com, provided a separate child-friendly version of the TOS, wherein effort was made to explain elements of the TOS to younger players, using a child-accessible vocabulary. For example, the child-friendly version of the Postopia.com TOS agreement stipulates, "Just by visiting Postopia, you are saying you will always follow the rules here" (KF Holdings 2001–2004).

In eight of the TOS contracts, the specific parties entering into the agreement were not explicitly identified (the only exception being MSN Game-Zone). Instead, most merely stated that the user, often vaguely referred to as "you," was agreeing to terms and conditions put forth by the company (defined as including any number of subsidiaries and sometimes affiliates). Two cases referred to the user and/or the user's parent somewhat interchangeably and failed to clearly outline where the responsibilities of each the child and the parent were assumed to begin and end, or how the actions of one might be distinct from the actions of the other. Little more than half of the contracts specified the negotiability (or lack thereof) of the terms contained within the agreement.

While all of the TOS contracts reviewed warned users that the terms and conditions could change at any time, less than half made a clear designation of responsibility for notification of these changes. In these cases, responsibility was either assumed by the site operator (as in the case of the Disney games and sites) or bestowed upon the user, who was given the express responsibility of periodically reading the TOS and monitoring any changes thereof. The rest of the gamesites simply suggested that the user should review the TOS periodically, without specifying that it was their legal responsibility to do so. More than half explicitly alerted the user that external websites, games and tools linked through the site could contain a different set of terms and conditions, and advised the user to become familiar with the various TOS contracts they might enter into upon navigating the site's hyperlinks.

A large majority of the TOS contracts contained the stipulation that any and all user submissions to the site became the unlimited and irrevocable property of the site owners/operators. In most cases, both the types of user submissions included in this claim and the nature and breadth of the copyright assumed by the gamesite were somewhat ambiguous. In no case was the user explicitly identified as the owner of his/her submissions. For instance, the TOS contract for EverythingGirl.com stated:

> You grant Mattel a non-exclusive, royalty-free, perpetual, irrevocable, and sublicensable right and license to reproduce, distribute, publish, transmit, modify, adapt, translate, display, distribute, sell, license, publicly perform, prepare derivative works based upon, and otherwise use or exploit Your Submissions throughout the world in any and all media [Mattel, Inc. 2003a].

Other TOS contracts included exhaustive lists of items that would be considered proprietary content, as well as the various ways in which the gamesite might use this content. The *gURL.com* site (a subsidiary of popular women's online community iVillage), for instance, listed nine types of user contributions that the site considered to be "submissions" (including poetry, artwork, creative works, message board/forum submissions, and responses to games and quizzes), as well as twenty different ways the site might subsequently use these submissions. Furthermore, users were required to agree to grant *gURL.com* (and iVillage) "a royalty-free, perpetual, irrevocable, non–exclusive right (including any moral rights)" (iVillage, Inc. 2004) to own and use their submissions. Limitations to the gamesites' ownership claims were rarely addressed, and in only one case did a gamesite (*Yahoo! Games*) claim less than sweeping proprietary rights over player-submitted contents (Yahoo!, Inc. 2003a).

In addition to the sites' claims of intellectual property ownership over players' submissions and communications, TOS contracts invariably included highly detailed and specified limitations on the users' usage and appropriation of site contents and applications. These clauses provided the gamesites with the intellectual property and copyright protections that the TOS contracts were concurrently denying the players. Items disclaiming the site's reliability and liability were also ubiquitous, as were statements outlining the gamesite's right to terminate user accounts without notice and at the owners/operators' discretion. All the agreements reviewed included a stipulation concerning the jurisdiction or legal venue for any legal claims made by or against the site, and a majority of the agreements also required that players consent to the exclusivity of this venue.

A number of gamesites also included a description of the site's "rules of conduct" within their TOS documents. These rules described the types of activities or actions that could result in the termination of a player's account, as well as the player's responsibilities in terms of representation (for instance, that any personal information provided must always be accurate), interactions with other players, and so on. In addition, the rules of conduct section of the TOS agreements of both Neopets.com and EA Online (Electronic Arts, Inc. 2004b) contained statements pertaining to off-site trade and for-profit player auctions. For instance, EA Online warned players that it "does not recognize or condone any outside service that may be used for the exchange of points, assets or attributes that you may accumulate as a result of participating in the Service of playing your EA game" (Electronic Arts, Inc. 2004a), including eBay and Yahoo! Auctions. Neopets.com stated that it reserved the right to permanently freeze the accounts of players engaged in this type of activity.

Comparison of TOS Contracts by Target Audience

Among the six TOS contracts associated with gamesites identified as targeting a primarily child audience segment, only two (Neopets.com and Postopia.com) provided a child-friendly version of the TOS. Four of these TOS contracts contained only a small proportion of child-friendly language within the text of the TOS, and tended instead to include a predominantly "moderate" language style (in terms of complexity of sentence structure, vocabulary used, and formality of the writing). In terms of length, four of the TOS contracts on sites directed toward children were under eight printed pages, and took over 10 minutes to read from start to finish. However, cases within the kids' sites category also included the two shortest documents, indicating a significant amount of variation in terms of the length and complexity of TOS contracts. Nonetheless, despite minor deviations between sites aimed at children and those aimed at a general audience (including adults and children) in terms of language use and length, every contract reviewed contained all fifteen of Russo's (2001) "15 significant points" commonly found in the TOS/EULAs of adult-oriented internet applications. This clearly suggests that children and their unique legal status as minors are granted very little (if any) special consideration in terms of how TOS contracts are formulated and applied. The failure of these sites to address children's special legal status within contract law is particularly problematic, as oftentimes minors' contracts (especially for goods or services not deemed a necessity) are considered void or at the very least void-able by Canadian and US courts.

Only two cases included a separate, child-friendly version of the TOS contract: Kraft Entertainment's kid-oriented Postopia.com and Neopets.com (a child targeted, "virtual pet" game community). In both cases, the agreement began by advising young players to read through the terms and conditions with a parent. The reader was then provided with an easy-to-read, easy-to-understand summary of "the rules you need to know to use our Web site" (KF Holdings 2001–2004). Yet, while every TOS contract analyzed included Russo's (2001) fifteen key items, as well as a number of additional clauses, child-friendly versions were significantly shortened and simplified. Postopia.com's child version consisted of only four items, namely that the child agree to the terms as they appeared (non–negotiability of terms); agree to respect the "Postopia rules" (rules of conduct and privacy policy); agree to respect and abide by the site's intellectual property rights; and agree to grant intellectual property ownership of their submissions to the site owners/operators. The child-friendly Neopets.com TOS displayed a similar pattern. Users were advised that by using the site they were automatically agreeing to the terms and conditions (non–negotiability of terms), and then warned about the site's own copyrights:

> The accounts, activities, items, faeries, games and pets are for you to play while on the site. Except as permitted by the functionality of this site, you can't sell them (for money or Neopoints), give them to anyone, trade them for anything (including Neopoints), or pretend you made them [Neopets, Inc. 1999–2004].

The *Neopets.com* TOS contract also provided an overview of the rules of conduct, warned that non-compliant accounts could be terminated permanently, and told readers that by posting or sending any content or comments to the site, "you (and your parents) are agreeing that [...] we can use it in any way we want, anywhere, until the end of time" (Neopets, Inc. 1999–2004).

The majority of sites in some way limited membership or access to certain portions of the gamesite based on the reported age of the player. Membership was fully restricted by age in only two cases: MSN Gamezone, which required that players be at least 18 years old to participate, and gURL.com, which restricted access to its site to players 13 years and older. However, not all sites asked for or verified the player's age. Among those that did, in almost every case the reported age or date of birth could be immediately adjusted to the required age by clicking on the browser's "Back" button and changing the year of birth. The one exception to this was the gURL.com site, which automatically sent a cookie to the user's computer once an age of less than 13 years was reported, indicating that the user was barred from participating. Upon each subsequent visit to the gURL.com site, unless the cookie was removed, the user was automatically re-directed to a page reminding them of their illegibility to participate, and asking them to return once they turned 13. While the majority of sites stated that parental permission was required for children 12 years and under, only three of the sites took any steps to ensure that parental consent was granted. Furthermore, very few asked or required that parents read the TOS before registering (or confirming registration for) their child.

Of further significance was the discovery that among the cases reviewed, the majority contained a high proportion of advergames or other branded components. Sites like Postopia.com, Candystand.com, and EverythingGirl.com contained little content other than games featuring interactive advertisements and/or product preference surveys. Neopets.com incorporated a blend of game genres and activities with a number of embedded product placements (for McDonald's restaurants, Disney movies and General Mills cereals, for instance) in a strategy the company has termed "immersive advertising" (Neopets, Inc. 1999–2004). For example, during the period of study, users could visit a McDonald's kiosk in the Neopian marketplace to purchase a Happy Meal for their pet and play games with a McDonald's theme. These sites often mixed advergames and other forms of advertising with market research initiatives, soliciting players to fill out surveys, participate in polls, or perform online product comparisons in exchange for game-related rewards (such as "Neopoints" in Neopets.com, or "Pippa Points" in Everything Girl.com). In some cases, advancement in the game required the real world purchase of certain products. For example, in Postopia.com most of the site's mini-games required "Postokens" to play — coins "purchased" with codes only available inside specially marked boxes of Post kids' cereals. Within the context of the increasingly invasive approach taken by child marketers, it is apparent that these types of features consist not only of an interactive form of advertising, but also of a new form of online market research — collecting data from child users as they play and interact with the games' embedded advertisements.

Terms of Service, Terms of Play?

While the TOS contracts reviewed varied significantly in some respects (such as length, structure, and so on), a number of shared patterns or conventions were apparent. One of the most striking was the way in which TOS contracts on sites known to be highly frequented by children dealt with issues involving intellectual property. In almost all cases, intellectual property ownership was claimed not only in relation to game items (the focus of the debates between adult online game players and game owners), but also encompassed players' online communications, postings to forums and chatrooms, and even email contents. Only a minimum effort was made to make the contents of these contracts accessible to children. In some cases, sites did not even direct players to read the TOS agreement, assuming instead a prior knowledge and experience of copyright and contracts that many children do not have. It remains questionable whether it is reasonable to expect children to have the skills and knowledge required to understand the implications of many of the clauses included in TOS contracts — assuming, of course, that they are inclined and able to read through these lengthy and difficult texts in the first place. It is also unclear whether current contract laws, in Canada, the US or elsewhere, even allow for corporations to enter children (either directly or via parental consent) into legal contracts of this nature.

In terms of parental consent, there appears to be no standard format for establishing the parent's roles and responsibilities in terms of their children's interactions and activities within these sites. In cases where parental consent was sought, the sites did not display any consistent strategy for ensuring that an actual parent was granting consent. Furthermore, while the inclusion of clauses naming the parent as an agreeing party (or requiring that parental consent be granted for children to participate in the sites) may offer some degree of protection to the sites in terms of liability, they did not adequately account for the rights of the child player who would be engaging with the sites on a regular (often unsupervised) basis. Sites also failed to establish that the consent being granted by child users and/or their parents truly consisted of informed consent. Very few details were provided about how children's non-personally identifiable data was collected and used, and practically no mention was made of the nature and function of data-mining and market research practices within these sites. The ethical implications of conducting research without first establishing informed consent from the participants are immense, particularly when the respondents are under the age of legal majority.

In comparing these sites with the MMOGs at the center of the adult player debates (see e.g., Smith in this volume), it also becomes clear that popular children's gamesites do not contain the same opportunities for social interaction and cultural participation as games directed more specifically at teens and adults. Most of the games reviewed were much smaller and less sophisticated than adult-oriented MMOGs, both in terms of design and levels of interactivity and interaction allowed. This was true even in the case of Disney's *Toontown Online*, the one game reviewed that truly qualified as a MMOG comparable to *EverQuest* or *Ultima Online* (Origin Systems 1997–2003). Here, players were limited to a pre-defined selection of "Speedchat" text options that the player must choose from in order to communicate with others,[4] as opposed to the open chat format found in adult games. Nonetheless, the content analysis findings did show that a significant amount of cultural participation does occur within children's online games, through forums, creative submissions, and even gameplay — despite the fact that these environments are perhaps more confined and commercially defined than adult-oriented MMOGs. That space for participation in these sites is more limited, and oftentimes specifically directed to yield valuable market research and information about consumer preferences, only strengthens the argument that children's online culture is undermined by sweeping TOS contracts. If children's cultural participation can legitimately be transformed into intellectual property for commercial purposes, then it is only logical that corporate entities will attempt to evoke and extract the most commercially valuable forms of content from them.

The assimilation of children's culture and play activities into corporate branding initiatives recalls Kinder's (1991) description of the media "supersystem"— the type of cross-media intertextuality that occurs when a brand or cultural icon becomes extended and diversified to the point of cultural saturation. Within children's culture, the supersystem

> works to position consumers as powerful players while disavowing commercial manipulation. It levels all ideological conflict within the single narrative of an all-encompassing game. And it valorizes superprotean flexibility as a substitute for the imaginary uniqueness of the unified subject [Kinder 1991: 119–120].

The contradictory positioning of consumers as the active agents of their own commercial manipulation and ultimate commodification is particularly evident in the cases reviewed herein. Through their enframement of advertising and market research as a new form of play, commercialized gamesites create an illusion of power and agency that works to obscure the true functioning and motivations of these spaces. The fact that children flock to these sites over non-commercial, or even self-generated, websites is indicative of how successful this obfuscation truly is. The endless barrage of fun and entertainment offered on commercial gamesites, oftentimes paired with opportunities for participation and decision-making, privileges the child user (their preferences, thoughts and autonomy) in a way that most contemporary children's spaces do not. At the same time, however, commercial sites value the child player primarily in terms of their function as an audience (for advertisements), as a commercially valuable source of research data, or even as a commodity product to be packaged and sold in the form of research and trend reports. Thus, while commercial gamesites do provide children with a somewhat interactive and participatory playspace, they do so within the context of economic and legal processes which reconstruct "childhood as a cultural space constituted by consumerism" (Langer 2004: 260).

As in the case of the adult MMOG players and owners engaged in intellectual property conflicts over in-game assets, the TOS contracts contained within children's gamesites create a highly industry-focused copyright system. Yet, as Taylor (2002) argues, online games are not merely pre-packaged cultural products, they are also spaces in which groups of players invest significant amounts of time communicating, developing characters and storylines, and participating in shared leisure activities. As a result, online games foster the development of compelling cultures and communities that require the collective participation of their players in order to produce shared and cohesive social meanings. Players occupy a central role in the creation and maintenance of online games — a role which is not recognized in current TOS contracts. The key difference between the adult cases and the children's cases examined herein is the amount of resistance that corporate game owners have encountered in their attempt to enforce stringent intellectual property regimes onto the adult player community. The unsanctioned secondary economy that has arisen out of online player auctions continues to infiltrate new MMOGs as they are introduced, encompassing an ever-greater assortment of items and activities. Game owners are now scrambling to reconsider the industry's initial, somewhat united stance on intellectual property. The owners of the popular online game *Second Life* (Linden Lab 2003–2004), for instance, recently transferred all intellectual property ownership of player-created items, storylines and characters back to the players themselves. As children's online games have yet to receive the same level of attention as adult-oriented MMOGs, an equivalent level of discourse around the TOS contracts contained therein has yet to arise. The risk in this case, however, is that children lack sufficient knowledge and familiarity with the processes and concepts involved — including intellectual property, privacy and authorship — to produce a comparably effective form of player resistance.

A further concern in the case of child players is the negative impact excessively stringent copyright systems could have on children's emerging rights as cultural producers. Whereas children are encouraged through the press and media education programs to participate in online culture and form online communities, TOS contracts undermine many of the potential benefits and value that children might otherwise derive from their newfound roles as cultural producers. Gamesites seemingly empower children by providing them with the tools and venues required to create and sustain an authentic, online children's culture. Yet this culture is simultaneously appropriated and commodified as potential fodder for marketing initiatives and new product development. By claiming ownership over children's autonomous online culture, the TOS contracts delimit and define children's online play as merely a new source of market research. This process is only minimally hindered by newly implemented internet laws and policies, such as COPPA in the US (which focuses almost exclusively on "protecting" children's privacy instead of promoting children's rights and participatory roles in relation to ICTs), and PIPEDA in Canada (which was explicitly designed "to encourage the ongoing accumulation and trade of digitized personal and other information" [Barney 2000: 229]), as the threat to privacy is but one of the more obvious consequences of data-mining and other forms of commercial surveillance. Of equal significance is an interrelated process at work within these practices, namely the commodification of the users themselves. Market research strategies and data-mining technologies are used "to refine the process of delivering audiences of ... computer users, to advertisers. Companies can package and repackage customers in forms that specifically reflect both their actual purchases and their demographic characteristics" (Mosco 2004: 158). In this way, internet users are reduced to mere audience commodities (Smythe 1981), as the "use value" of users' online experiences and relationships are made subordinate to the "exchange value" of packaged user trend reports and data-mined demographic profiles. The users thus become alienated from the digital products of their online interactions and activities, which are aggregated and reconstituted in commodity form as the intellectual property of marketers and website operators.

Conclusion

The example of intellectual property disputes among adult MMOG players and game owners presents an important starting point for further analysis of children's online games, as it forces a consideration of the meaning of culture and community — in addition to economic themes such as authorship and ownership. Whereas research to-date on children's usage of the internet has predominantly ignored children's experience as cultural producers, the case of online games offers an important point of departure from this tendency, through its repositioning of users as active players, and highlighting of the central function of the user in the construction and maintenance of online culture. By positioning children as active producers instead of passive audience members, the current analysis reveals that children's interests are not adequately represented in many of their favorite online destinations. Even though the legality of these contracts remains dubious at present, the as yet unchallenged authority of these agreements could nonetheless potentially allow them to determine how authorship and intellectual property in children's online games and communities come to be defined in the future. As Coombe (1998: 9) argues, "People's anticipations of law (however reasonable, ill informed, mythical, or even paranoid) may actually shape law and the property rights it protects."

While the findings drawn from the present analysis are preliminary, and a survey of a broader, more representative sample still needs to be conducted, the patterns found in the TOS contracts of the most popular children's sites certainly present justification for further research in this area. Above all, it is clear that the legal terms and conditions of children's online play are not accessible to young readers. Current measures aimed at ensuring that informed consent is granted by either children or their parents are inadequate and inconsistent. In addition, the intellectual property issues raised herein warrant a deeper analysis, especially in terms of how children's online content is shaped and used for commercial interests. Similarly, better insight into children's production of online content and culture is required, in order to determine how children interpret and potentially resist the imposition of commercial copyright systems.

In contrasting the findings of the content analysis with the activities featured in popular children's gamesites, it becomes clear that not only are children engaged in much more than simple play when they visit these spaces. They are also being enlisted in intrusive market research strategies that make full use of the creativity, community and agency contained in their online contributions. The underlying legal and economic implications suggested by the stringent intellectual property claims found in TOS contracts are confirmed in the greater branding strategies of the companies involved, as well as offline initiatives such as Neopets.com's successful business practice of creating and selling youth trend reports and behavioral studies. As international conventions and national laws have previously established that minors warrant special status and consideration in such commercial (as well as legal) matters, the limited attention that has thus far been granted to this exchange must be remedied if children's rights are to be effectively upheld and protected online. If children's online contributions and activities are to continue to be used and defined as fodder for market research, then internet and media policies, as well as accepted ethical standards for online market research conducted on children, need to be updated and revised. On the other hand, if children's cultural participation is something we truly wish to foster and promote, then the appropriateness and potential consequences of these exchanges need to be evaluated and redefined through rigorous public and legal debate. In the meantime, however, contrary to the widespread rhetoric of the savvy "cyberchild," or perhaps because of the false expectations and assumptions this discourse produces about children's knowledge of internet processes, children's interests are not yet truly represented within some of the most important arenas of their emerging digital culture.

Notes

1. The Children's Online Privacy Protection Act (COPPA), passed by the US Federal Trade Commission in 1998, established a set of new laws aimed at regulating children's online privacy by requiring that children's websites (both those directly aimed at children and those knowingly gathering information from users under the age of 13) give parents notice about their data-collection activities; obtain verifiable parental consent; and provide parents with access to any information collected from their children, as well as the opportunity to discontinue any further uses of the data collected.

2. Notable exceptions are The European Union Directive on Privacy and Electronic Communications (2002) and Canada's Personal Information Protection and Electronic Documents Act (PIPEDA) (2004), each of which includes certain prohibitions against using personal data for purposes other than that for which they were originally collected.

3. In 2000, for instance, Sony Entertainment secured the cooperation of popular online auction sites, including eBay and Yahoo!, to prevent *EverQuest* players from selling game characters and other in-game items for real-world profit.

4. *Toontown Online* players have the option, however, of placing other players on their "Friends" list and providing them with a "Secret" password outside of the game, which would then allow them to communicate through open chat.

References

Barney, Darin. 2000. *Prometheus Wired: The Hope for Democracy in the Age of Network Technology.* Vancouver, BC: UBC Press.

Buckingham, David. 2003. *Media Education: Literacy, Learning and Contemporary Culture.* Cambridge, UK: Polity Press.

Castronova, Edward. 2003. "The Right to Play." Paper presented at the *State of Play Conference*, November 13–15. New York: New York Law School.

Cook, Daniel T. 2001 "Exchange Value as Pedagogy in Children's Leisure: Moral Panics in Children's Culture at Century's End." *Leisure Sciences* 23: 81–98.

Coombe, Rosemary J. 1998. *The Cultural Life of Intellectual Properties: Authorship, Appropriation and the Law.* Durham, NC: Duke University Press.

Edwards, Ellen. 1999. "Kids, Alone and Unsupervised, Use All Media More." *The Washington Post*, November 18: A1.

Electronic Arts, Inc. 2002–2004. *The Sims Online (TSO).* Platform: PC. Electronic Arts, Inc.

_____. 2004a. "EA Online Terms of Service." Retrieved October 18, 2004 (http://www.ea.com/global/legal/tos.jsp).

_____. 2004b. *EA Online.* Platform: PC/online.

Greenspan, Robyn. 2003. "Kids Are Media Users Too." *ClickZ*, October 9. Retrieved October 18, 2004 (www.clickz.com/stats/big_picture/demographics/article.php/5901_3089701).

Grimes, Sara M. 2003. "All About the Blog: Young People's Adoption of Internet Technologies and the Marketers Who Love Them." *Computers and Society* 32(5).

Grunwald Associates. 2003. "2 Million American Children Have Their Own Websites, Broad New Internet Survey Shows." *News Release*, December 4. Retrieved October 18, 2004 (http://www.grunwald.com/surveys/cfi/newsrelease.html).

iVillage, Inc. 1995–2004. *gURL.com*. Platform: PC/online. iVillage, Inc.
_____. 2004. "Terms of Service." Retrieved October 27, 2004 (http://www.gurl.com/about/privacypolicy/pages/0,,621916,00.html).
KF Holdings. 2001–2004. "Kids Read Here." Retrieved October 26, 2004 (http://www.postopia.com/miscContent/terms_conditions.aspx).
_____. 2004a. *Candystand.com*. Platform: PC/online. Kraft Entertainment.
_____. 2004b. *Postopia.com*. Platform: PC/online. Kraft Entertainment.
Kinder, Marsha. 1991. *Playing with Power in Movies, Television, and Video Games: From Muppet Babies to Teenage Mutant Ninja Turtles*. Berkeley, CA: University of California Press.
Kline, Stephen. 2001. *Media Use Audit for B.C. Teens*. SFU Media Lab: Burnaby, BC, Canada. Retrieved August 18, 2004 (http://www.sfu.ca/media-lab/research/report.html).
Langer, Beryl. 2004. "The Business of Branded Enchantment: Ambivalence and Disjuncture in the Global Children's Culture Industry." *Journal of Consumer Culture* 4(2): 251–77.
Lastowka, F. Gregory, and Dan Hunter. 2004. "The Laws of the Virtual Worlds." *California Law Review* 92(1): 3–73.
Linden Lab. 2003–2004. *Second Life*. Platform: PC. Linden Lab.
Lindström, Martin. 2003. *BRANDchild: Remarkable Insights into the Minds of Today's Global Kids and Their Relationships with Brands*. Sterling, VA: Kogan Page.
Livingstone, Sonia. 2003. "The Changing Nature and Uses of Media Literacy." In *Media@LSE Electronic Working Papers* (4), edited by Rosalind Gill, Andy Pratt, Terhi Rantanen and Nick Couldry. London School of Economics and Political Science: London, UK.
Mattel, Inc. 2003a. "Terms and Conditions of Website Use." Retrieved October 26, 2004 (http://www.everythinggirl.com/common/legals.aspx).
_____. 2003b. *Everythinggirl.com*. Platform: PC/online. Mattel, Inc.
_____. 2003c. *PollyPocket.com*. Platform: PC/online. Mattel, Inc.
Microsoft Corp. 2003. *MSN Game Zone*. Platform: PC/online. Microsoft Service Network.
Montgomery, Katherine C. 2000. "Digital Kids: The New On-line Children's Consumer Culture." Pp. 635–648 in *Handbook of Children and the Media*, edited by Dorothy G. Singer and Jerome L. Singer. Thousand Oaks, CA: Sage Publications.
Mosco, Vincent. 2004. *The Digital Sublime: Myth, Power, and Cyberspace*. Cambridge, MA: MIT Press.
NCSoft. 1998–2003. *Lineage*. Platform: PC. NCSoft.
Neopets, Inc. 1999–2004. "Terms/Conditions." Retrieved October 26, 2004 (http://www.neopets.com/terms.phtml).
_____. 2004. *Neopets.com*. Platform: PC/online.
Nielsen/Netratings. 2002. "Nearly 20 Percent of the Active Online Population Are Kids and Teens, Creating Opportunities for Marketers." *News Release*, August 13, New York. Retrieved October 18, 2004 (http://phx.corporate-ir.net/phoenix.zhtml?c=82037&p=irol-newsArticle&ID=538963&highlight=).
_____. 2003a. "Kids Account for One Out of Every Five Internet Surfers In the U.S.; More Than 27 Million American Kids Connect Online." *News Release*, October 21. New York. Retrieved August 10, 2004 (http://www.nielsen-netratings.com).
_____. 2003b. "13 Million Kids Using the Internet Across Europe." *News Release*, September 30. New York. Retrieved August 10, 2004 (http://www.nielsen-netratings.com).
Origin Systems. 1997–2003. *Ultima Online*. Platform: PC. Electronic Arts, Inc.
Quart, Alissa. 2003. *Branded: The Buying and Selling of Teenagers* Cambridge, MA: Perseus Group.
Rideout, Victoria J., Elizabeth A. Vandewater and Ellen A. Wartella. 2003. "Zero to Six:

Electronic Media in the Lives of Infants, Toddlers and Preschoolers." A *Kaiser Family Foundation Report*, Fall. Washington, DC: Program for the Study of Entertainment Media and Health/Henry J. Kaiser Family Foundation. Retrieved September 5, 2004 (http://www.kff.org/entmedia/loader.cfm?url=/commonspot/security/getfile.cfm&Page ID=22754).

Russakoff, Douglas. 1999. "Marketers following youth trends to the bank." *The Washington Post*, April 19: A1.

Russo, Jack. 2001. "How to Read "Terms of Use" Agreements." Presented at the *Computer Systems Laboratory Colloquium*, April 11, Stanford University. Palo Alto, CA: Stanford University.

Sandvig, Christian. 2000. "The Internet Disconnect in Children's Policy: A User Study of Outcomes for Internet Access Subsidies and Content Regulation." Presented at the *28th Conference on Communication, Information, and Internet Policy*, September 23–25, Alexandria, VA. Ann Arbor, MI: Telecommunications Policy Research Conference/ School of Information, University of Michigan.

Seiter, Ellen. 2004. "The Internet Playground." Pp. 93–108 in *Toys, Games and Media*, edited by Jeffrey Goldstein, David Buckingham, and Gilles Brougere. Mahwah, NJ: Lawrence Erlbaum Associates.

Selling to Kids. 2001. "Marketers Find an Audience in Chatty Kids." March 21. Retrieved September 5, 2004 (http://www.findarticles.com/p/articles/mi_m0FVE/is_5_6/ai_ 72614513).

Shade, Leslie, Nikki Porter and Wendy Karina Sanchez Santiago. 2004. "Everyday Domestic Internet Experiences of Canadian Children and Youth." Presented at *Digital Generations — Children, Young People and New Media*, July 26–29, University of London. London, UK: Center for the Study of Children, Youth and Media, Institute of Education.

Smith, Jonas Heide. 2006. "Who Governs the Gamers?" Pp. 17–32 in *Among Players: Cultural Studies on Digital Games and Digital Gaming*, edited by J. Patrick Williams and Jonas Heide Smith. Jefferson, NC: McFarland.

Smith, J. Walker, and Ann S. Clurman. 1997. *Rocking the Ages: The Yankelovich Report on Generational Marketing*. New York: HarperBusiness/HarperCollins Publishers, Inc.

Smythe, Dallas W. 1981. *Dependency Road: Communications, Capitalism, Consciousness and Canada*. Norwood, NJ: Ablex.

Sony Online Entertainment. 1999–2004. *EverQuest*. Platform: PC. Sony Online Entertainment.

Statistics Canada. 2004. "Household Internet Use Survey." *The Daily*, July 8. Retrieved September, 5 2004 (http://www.statcan.ca/Daily/English/040708/d040708a.htm).

Stephens, Molly. 2002. "Sales of In-Game Assets: An Illustration of the Continuing Failure of Intellectual Property Law to Protect Digital-Content Creators." *Texas Law Review*, 80: 1513–1515.

Sutherland, Anne, and Beth Thompson. 2001. *Kidfluence: Why Kids Today Mean Business*. Toronto, ON: McGraw-Hill Ryerson Ltd.

Taylor, T.L. 2002. "Whose Game Is This Anyway?: Negotiating Corporate Ownership in a Virtual World." In *Proceedings of Computer Games and Digital Cultures Conference*, edited by Franz Mäyrä. Tampere, Finland: Tampere University Press. Retrieved August 28, 2003 (http://social.chass.ncsu.edu/~ttaylor/papers/Taylor-CGDC.pdf).

Turow, Joseph. 2001. "Privacy Policies on Children's Websites: Do They Play by the Rules?" *Report Series*, March. Philadelphia, PA: Annenberg Public Policy Centre of the University of Pennsylvania.

_____. 2003. "Americans and Online Privacy: The System is Broken." *Report Series*, June. Philadelphia, PA: Annenberg Public Policy Centre of the University of Pennsylvania.

Walt Disney Company. 2003. *Toontown Online*. Platform: PC. Walt Disney Internet Group.

Yahoo!, Inc. 2003a. *Yahoo!Games*. Platform: PC/online. Yahoo!, Inc.
_____. 2003b. *Yahoo!Fantasy Sports — Baseball*. Platform: PC/online. Yahoo!, Inc.
_____. 2003c. *Yahoo!Fantasy Sports*. Platform: PC/online. Yahoo!, Inc.
_____. 2003d. *Yahoo!Fantasy Sports — Football*. Platform: PC/online. Yahoo!, Inc.
Yin, Robert K. 1984. *Case Study Research: Design and Methods*. Newbury Park, CA: Sage
   Publications.

3. Narrative Power in Online Game Worlds: The Story of Cybertown

Nadezhda Kaneva

Virtual Promises

The homepage of the virtual colony of Cybertown displays the image of a female figure dressed in a science fiction inspired costume in silver and blue colors with the word GUIDE printed on her chest. She smiles invitingly as she points to the image of a futuristic looking city in the distance. The text on the homepage encourages you to enter a "virtual civilization for the future" and states that the year is 2090.[1] A flashing sign promises "3D chat, virtual homes, pets, roles and more!" To become a member of this virtual colony, one does not "register" or "join." One "immigrates" to Cybertown, symbolically crossing a border between "real life" (RL) and "virtual reality" (VR). Entering Cybertown as a new virtual immigrant and an ethnographer, I was bound to discover a rich and complex world of interaction and play.

Simply put, Cybertown is a complex online graphical simulation, which falls within the genre of massively multiplayer online role-playing games (MMORPGs). As Kolo and Baur (2004) have pointed out, MMORPGs can be purely text-based or they can provide graphic environments that resemble the real world. Either way, their central characteristic is that "players control their online personae, which we will call characters, via a variety of modes of the human–computer-interface, confined by technical restrictions and more, or less, formalized and sanctioned rules. This thereby creates a parallel space of social interactions among the characters in the gameworld" (Kolo and Baur 2004).

I began my study of Cybertown as an exploration into the nature of online game worlds and the intersections of game play and communal interaction that emerges in them. I was particularly interested in two sets of questions. First, how is a sense of shared reality constructed and maintained within an online game world? Is there a relationship between the process of interactive authoring within the game world and the development of a sense of belonging to an online community within the game? And second, who are the authors of players' mediated experiences? Does the digital medium of the Internet allow for a different balance of power in the relationship between producer and receiver, compared to more traditional media? If so, how is this relationship different?

I chose not to focus on the technological aspects of virtual environments. Instead, I was interested in the social dynamics that emerge in virtual environments and through which the shared reality of an online game world is constructed. My goal was two-fold: to be able to produce, in Geertz's (1973) terms, a "thick description" of this virtual world; and to develop the kind of interpretive understanding that could explain what made this game feel like a community to its players.

Crossing Borders

To understand the new and enchanting worlds of online games and gaming communities the field of Game Studies draws on various theoretical traditions among psychology, sociology, anthropology, communication, and literary theory. Early research of computer-mediated communication claimed that communication through a computer network that is limited to the exchange of textual messages could not sustain complex and nuanced levels of interpersonal communication because the medium eliminates non-verbal cues, such as gender, race, body language, and intonation (Kiesler, Siegel and McGuire 1984; Sproull and Kiesler 1986; 1991). This view was gradually supplemented by increasingly context-based research from a range of methodological traditions (Bruckman 1992; Jones 1995; 1998; Smith and Kollock 1999). Rheingold's exploration of an online group called the WELL (World's 'Lectronic Link) and of text-based multi-user domains (MUDs) was particularly influential in the development of a new understanding of online social formations as communities (Rheingold 1993). Rheingold argued that text-based communication is capable of sustaining highly elaborate symbolic environments in which participants evolve various forms of relationships that may cross over the virtual border and translate into close relationships in the offline world. Text-based MUDs, among the earliest iterations of virtual game worlds, were the object of many studies (e.g., Kendall 1996; Mortensen 2002; Nakamura 1995; Reid 1996; Schaap 2002; Turkle 1995).

The emerging genre of MMORPGs marks an important shift in online game research (Taylor 2004) inasmuch as many game researchers (including those represented in this volume) focus on commercially released titles with significant market penetration, such as *Ultima Online* (Electronic Arts 1997; Kolo and Baur 2004), *Everquest* (Sony Online Entertainment 1999; Jacobson and Taylor 2003; Yee 2001), and *World of Warcraft* (Blizzard 2004). My ethnography of Cybertown offers a look into a different type of virtual world — one that emerged as a free, non-commercial space created by a set of volunteers as their own virtual playground, which only later transitioned to a subscription-based model.

Two of the strongest influences on my thinking about online gaming communities derive from literary and communication theory, which have been invoked by other game and community scholars as well. First, in my examination of the relationship between author and reader and its transformation within the digital medium of the Internet, I have drawn from Janet Murray's *Hamlet on the Holodeck: The Future of Narrative in Cyberspace* (1997), which discusses the applicability of fiction-writing narrative techniques to the Internet and provides insights into the way users relate to narratives presented in this new medium. Murray's approach combines literary theory with an analysis of the Internet as a digital culture complete with its own aesthetic and symbolic rules. I find this approach particularly useful as it allows analyses of online experiences to move beyond questions of authenticity and focus on the narrative and performative aspects of these experiences.

Second, my analysis of the nature of shared realities in game worlds leans on the theoretical work of James Carey (1988), and particularly on his ritual model of communication and its relevance to understanding reality as constructed through communication. In Carey's definition, communication is "a process through which a shared culture is created, modified and transformed" (1988: 43). The ritual view of communication emphasizes the process of "creation, representation, and celebration of shared *even if illusory* beliefs" and centers on "the sacred ceremony that draws persons together in fellowship and commonality" (1988: 43, emphasis added). In sum, following Carey, I adopt a constructivist theoretical perspective that understands communication and communicative rituals as the vital material from which shared identities and realities are brought forth into life and sustained over time.

Living in Cybertown

My approach to conducting fieldwork online relies on the methodological insights offered by a number of "virtual ethnographers" (e.g., Cherny 1999; Hine 2000; Kendall 2002; Schaap 2002). Each of these authors conducted a long-term ethnographic study of an online game or community in order to develop an understanding of its cultural codes and practices through a sustained presence and participation as a member of the group.

Most of the data for this chapter were collected through participant observation and informal interviews conducted online. I visited the Cybertown community approximately 80 times over the course of 6 months, from September 2002 through February 2003, the average duration of each visit being approximately one hour. Overall, my presence in Cybertown was not the presence of a detached observer but of an involved participant as I tried to gain full membership. In this sense, my interpretations are necessarily the result of my self-reflective engagement with the field. I kept detailed field notes and captured visual and textual information from chat rooms and bulletin boards in Cybertown. To supplement my experiences, observations, and conversations, I examined a number of documents created by the players, i.e., legal texts, ethical guides, news bulletins, and public notices. I also selected for examination several narratives about Cybertown posted on sites external to Cybertown. These include personal websites, electronic journals and commentaries on life in Cybertown by members, as well as marketing documents created by Blaxxun Interactive (2001a; 2001b), the original corporate owner of Cybertown.[2]

Players entering Cybertown may choose between a two-dimensional (2D) and a three-dimensional (3D) interface mode. Graphics are fewer and mostly static in 2D and users communicate by typing into a chat window as they would in most web-based chatrooms. In 2D players and objects are represented by text descriptions. To enter the 3D mode users must download custom software and select a 3D avatar. In this mode players can visit a number of richly designed, futuristic looking 3D spaces and interact with virtual objects and other players represented by avatars. Navigation is accomplished through keystroke combinations and mouse clicks and players can choose between text and voice-chat.

My exploratory journey in the virtual game world of Cybertown was quite literally that of a foreigner, unfamiliar with the culture, eager to learn and adapt, anxious to be accepted by those I met. As I spent more time in the game, my range of activities and responsibilities increased. I purchased a virtual home in a virtual neighborhood, accepted a virtual job and attempted to perform the duties of the job to the best of my abilities. I was compensated for my work in the local virtual currency of "citycash" (or "cc's" as Cytonians would call it) and was offered a promotion on a number of occasions. My first job was on the lowest step of the hierarchical ladder. My job title, as well as my low number of experience points and accumulated cc's established me as a "newbie." This particular role served my research purposes well as it allowed me to ask multiple questions on all sorts of subjects and not look suspicious. At the same time, I had to make my identity as a researcher known to other players for the purpose of ethical disclosure. At various points in the fieldwork I was also engaged on a rather basic human level as a friend and confidant who attempted to provide emotional support to people I had met in Cybertown.

I interacted with people in various social settings. I attempted to get to know my neighbors. I followed the virtual news and aimed to learn as much as possible about the laws and rules of this world. Moreover, I accepted these laws as binding for my behavior in Cybertown and acted in accordance with them even when I disagreed with some of them. I engaged in discussions with other Cybertown citizens on current issues, such as elections, security policies, financial or technical threats to the continued existence of Cybertown, employment practices and ways of being involved in communal life. Through these interactions and through the routine practices that came with the performance of my appointed duties, I tried to make sense of my life and the lives of others within the game world. My study was discovery oriented and exploratory in nature. In keeping with the principles of ethnographic research, I attempted to develop a presence in the scene and an *emic* identification with the goals and meaning systems of the community of players, as well as to gain an understanding of their symbols and practices, cultural rules, and linguistic codes (Thompsen et al. 1998).

Cybertown and the Aesthetics of the Digital Medium

Cybertown is a *fictional* space populated by *characters*.[3] While the authors of the space, as well as of the characters populating it, are real people and in some cases have face-to-face interactions offline, it would be misleading to assume a one-to-one correlation between player and character identities. In the same way, we would not assume that a writer only writes about herself, or that an actor only acts out his actual personality. The virtual space of Cybertown is an imaginary space and the creation of community within it is an act of the imagination more than anything else — participating in the communal aspects of the simulation is an integral part of the act of playing the game. In this sense, to borrow a phrase from Benedict Anderson (1991), the community of Cybertown is an "imagined community."

Once this is understood, a new player can begin to understand events and behaviors within Cybertown that may seem meaningless outside of the game world. For example, upon getting my first job as a Block Deputy (BD) I had to undergo training before I could begin performing the duties of the job. The training consisted of visiting a designated chat area, named BD's Training House, and interacting for approximately two minutes with a trainer bot, a program that informed me of my duties and how to perform them. The bot was only programmed to respond to three basic commands and in the face-to-face world I would not have viewed this experience as a form of job training. However, this experience made sense within the conventions of the fictional narrative of Cybertown. Once immersed in the narrative of the simulation, I did not question the bot's competence as my trainer and proceeded with the training without which I would have not been able to play the role of a Block Deputy.

Murray (1997) examines the aesthetics of the digital medium and identifies three underlying elements: (i) it is immersive; (ii) it requires agency, and (iii) it involves transformation. Murray explains the concept of *immersion* and one's engagement with the immersive nature of a fictional narrative in the following way:

> *Immersion* is a metaphorical term derived from the physical experience of being submerged in water. We seek the same feeling from a psychologically immersive experience that we do from a plunge in the ocean or swimming pool: the sensation of being surrounded by a completely other reality, as different as water is from air, that takes over all of our attention, our whole perceptual apparatus. We enjoy the movement out of our familiar world, the feeling of alertness that comes from being in this new place, and the delight that comes from learning to move within it [1997: 98–99].

From the moment one "immigrates" to Cybertown, one is immersed in a new environment. The mere act of moving your newly acquired avatar in a 3D world requires practice and skill. In this sense, the experience is quite analogous to Murray's metaphor of swimming. Many new immigrants ask endless questions about 3D and try to learn various tricks of moving and positioning their avatars. Otherwise simple acts, such as waving or blinking, are not instantly and easily accomplished through an avatar. At the same time, the newness and otherness of the experience reinforces the sense of being in a completely different world and enables the "willing suspension of disbelief"[4] necessary for a convincing narrative immersion. The act of logging on to Cybertown serves as a crossing of the metaphorical boundary known in theatrical terms as "the fourth wall" between the "representational world" and the "actual world" (Murray 1997: 103). It signals the beginning of the immersive experience of playing and takes the user into the "enchanted space" in a manner similar to Alice's entrance into Wonderland through the looking glass.

Another important element of the immersive experience is the ability to discover and successfully engage with "functional virtual objects" (Murray 1997: 111). This process creates a feedback loop that urges one to get even more involved with the game narrative. One manifestation of the importance of virtual objects is evidenced by the proliferation of virtual items that can be exchanged in Cybertown. The availability of a wide range of items, most of which are completely non-functional for practical use, provides the players with an opportunity to actively sustain the belief of engagement with the imaginary world through successful interactions with its virtual objects.

For example, one of the characters I met in Cybertown, who had been a member for more than 3 years, had an impressive collection of more than 200 virtual items. His virtual house featured 53 items, among which several swords, multiple bathrooms, multiple tables, and many items of unidentified function. Interestingly, this player spent most of his time in Cybertown in the two-dimensional (2D) mode of interaction, which allows players to see virtual items only in the form of a textual list of names and descriptions. This suggests that the 3D visual appearance of the items is not necessarily of primary importance to this player's character but their possession is. My conversations with him revealed that in RL this person was of modest means, which could probably explain the importance he ascribed to the ownership of items and the accumulation of cc's in Cybertown. However, beyond specific, individually situated explanations such as this one, the virtual items can be interpreted as valuable tools for the "active creation of belief" (Murray 1997: 110).

In confirmation of this more general interpretation, another member of the community confided the following:

> *Cytonian1*[5]*:* I am a victim of item lust too ... and I agree it's weird. I started out collecting round objects ... and started liking other things too.

Cytonian1 explained her fascination with items with the fact that she was interested in learning how to make them.

> *Cytonian1:* I wanted to learn how to make objects, so I would buy them and then look at them in a VRML[6] program like Spazz3d.

However, she agreed that this was not the case for everyone. She told me of many schemes invented by CT members to obtain more items, one of which includes registering under a new name and then showing up at the Flea Market area of Cybertown "begging for newbie gifts of free items."

It would be too simplistic to explain users' eagerness to accumulate items as merely a manifestation of human greed, thus naturalizing greed as an uncontrollable impulse. It would also be insufficient to attribute "item lust" to a speculation that people, socialized in a RL capitalist society where commodity-exchange is central, respond naturally to the existence of an economic structure of exchange within Cybertown. After all, few of the virtual items can be used for any real purpose. One possible explanation, regardless of the personal motivations of individual players, is that in interacting with the items — being able to obtain them, sell them, collect them, arrange them, or even lose them — players further the shared illusion of inhabiting their characters in the game and sustain their sense of immersion and involvement with the game narrative.

Murray's second characteristic of the digital medium is *agency.* Agency is also commonly referred to in discussions of online games as "interactivity." In Murray's work agency refers specifically to the shared responsibility over the content of the interactive story between producer and user. Murray is careful to avoid using the term "authorship" instead of agency. She insists that the user's participation, however active and imaginative, is still restricted by the intentions of the original author, or "main author." The producers of Cybertown, through narrative and technological means, set the limitations for "authoring" by players.

Given the structures that simultaneously enable and limit authoring, it becomes clear that agency is a useful way of thinking about players' involvement with the production of their own game experiences. Cytonians can decorate their houses in a number of ways, create a personal profile, write instant messages, post on bulletin boards, and produce a range of short-lived narratives in instantaneous chat. Those who are more skillful with 3D modeling software can create their own avatars, virtual pets, and virtual items for sale or for sharing. On several occasions, I witnessed the instantaneous creation of battle narratives by a group of characters who met at the Cybertown Café. These imaginary battles among warriors were executed by typing the actions of the different fighters in the chat window. Winning or losing depended on being a fast typist and not making typing mistakes. A typo would result in the action not being executed and could lead to losing the battle. These examples show the importance of agency for the quality of the immersive experience and the last one, in particular, is an illustration of unexpected forms of adapting the capabilities of the medium to the narrative needs of particular players. At the same time, these examples demonstrate that agency is exercised within the limits of a "master narrative" provided by the producers of the game world.

The third aesthetic principle recognized by Murray is *transformation.* She calls the digital storytelling medium a "shape-shifting" environment and refers to the capabilities of morphing programs, as well as to the opportunity of users to be present in more than one environment at the same time. Transformation also relates to issues of identity and our ability to identify with the various characters in a fictional narrative. Because of the interactive nature of the medium, players do not simply narrate events but enact them, thereby undergoing a transformation of self. In this way it could be said that the players become their characters.

The importance of transformation is illustrated by the fact that many Cybertown players have multiple characters that they use in different situations. Cytonian1 admitted to having eight different login names (or "nics" for various characters). She used different nics depending on what she was doing at any given moment. For example, one of her nics was reserved for use when she was working on a particular website:

> *Cytonian1:* [This nic] is for my craft website. [That other one] is my very old and favorite nic, you could say it's the "real cyber me." LOL
>
> *Researcher:* So, it's like wearing different uniforms, or aprons?
>
> *Cytonian1:* Yes ... like a job I guess ... my friends know my other nics. Just not public about it. Most people aren't. I have had friendships with people and found out later that two friends were actually just one. LOL

This comment fits Murray's analysis of the use of characters as masks in a theatrical performance. When Cytonian1 changed among nics, she did so to send particular signals to those who knew her. It was not an arbitrary switch but a communicative act, a strategic choice in the course of playing the game of living in Cybertown.

Sherry Turkle points to a similar phenomenon —a multiplicity of characters, which she interprets as multiple aspects of a decentered self. Her widely quoted example is of a Midwestern college student she names Doug, who talks about four different characters he plays in various MUDs. In Doug's case, he often has several windows open on the screen that allow him to be present in a different MUD in each window, and be a different character in each of them. He concludes that in this kind of arrangement, "RL is just one more window and it's not usually my best one" (Turkle 1995: 13).

This sweeping conclusion was not supported by my observations since most of the Cytonians I met appeared to draw a clear line between life in Cybertown and RL. Many admitted to using multiple nics but none said that they ever appeared in the same space as more than one character. In sum, the act of switching between characters is not a random act for players, nor is it intended to confuse others around them. Rather, it is a form of expression and self-transformation consistent with the aesthetics of the digital medium.

Narrative and Power

I now turn to the question of power over the shared game reality of Cybertown and the specific ways in which it is exercised and negotiated through narrative means. Game scholars have previously examined the question of the balance of power between game structures and players' actions in several commercially released games. For example, Taylor and Kolko (2003) discuss Electronic Arts' *Majestic*, while Atkins (2003) pays particular attention to the problem of power in his discussion of *SimCity*. What makes the case of Cybertown different from commercially released games, such as *Majestic* and *SimCity*, is that it emerged as the love child of a group of volunteer programmers, some of whom have remained active players in the game over its evolution from a free online world to a subscription-based one. Thus, there is a less obvious and strict separation between producers and players compared to ready-made commercial game worlds. Indeed, Cybertown began with the assumption that anyone with the right set of skills can build parts of the game world. From there the game gradually developed into a simulation where one can simply play by interacting with what is available.

From a narrative perspective, Cybertown's central metaphor — a growing virtual colony — encourages players to take active part and pride in the shared building of their game world. The game is predicated on the idea of constant construction and players are encouraged to develop new areas and objects within the game world. From their first day in the game, players are urged to buy houses, take up jobs, organize neighborhood activities and contribute items for sale and exchange. Despite this narrative of creativity, however, power and control over the shared game world is far from equal.

Cybertown's homepage claims that this is a "global community" and has links to chat-windows in eight languages — English, German, Spanish, Italian, French, Japanese, Hebrew, and Russian. However, based on my observations, most of the citizens spend their time in the English-speaking chat rooms and in RL reside in North America or Western Europe. Even though the site allows one to switch to a different language chat window, the materials surrounding the chat window, such as system notices, banner ads, welcome messages, menus, options, and directories, are presented in English in all of the eight language versions. Hence, it is reasonable to assume that the larger cultural backdrop against which Cybertown emerges is one of Western, and specifically English-language, contemporary culture as it is known in the United States.

The U.S. cultural environment has a political focus on democracy and participation in elections, an economic focus on market exchange, and a popular climate of informal interaction and entertainment consumption through which sociality is created and affirmed. From this vantage point, the logic behind the structure of Cybertown as a community becomes clear — it is a structure that emulates current Western social practices, rather than attempting to imagine new modes of sociality. Further, it is a structure produced by a community of designers, programmers and engineers that work within the social, historical and economic circumstances of Western society. Because of its embeddedness in the cultural codes of Western political economy, the Cybertown simulation has elected officials, a process of self-governance, an economic structure of commodity exchange, recognition of private property, and a civic structure of citizen interaction and debate. The community simulation built around this structure has to face some of the same questions that are at the core of contemporary Western social thought. Some such questions that came up during my life in Cybertown related to freedom of speech, discipline and punishment, distribution of power, safety and privacy, labor practices and compensation, as well as social volunteering and organizing. Thus, the shared sense of community evolving out of the fictional game narrative of Cybertown found constant cultural referents in the offline realities of Western capitalist society. As Atkins (2003) finds in his analysis of *SimCity*, the game narrative is inevitably ideologically inscribed.

Within a fictional narrative context, conflicts and tensions emerge through narrative means and must be resolved within the limitations of the narrative structure of the game. As a result, the ideological conflicts are superimposed on the relationships among game producers and game players, despite the fact that the game's narrative tries to obscure distinctions between them. For example, Cybertown has a simulated system of self-governance evidenced by an election process for Mayor and an administrative body called the City Council. Yet the society is highly dependent on the role of a god-like character called the Founder — a figure referred to in many of the historical and legal documents of the game world, such as its Constitution, its City Council Guidelines, and various other texts. A document entitled *Cybertown City Council Guidelines and Ordinances* provided Figure 3.1 (see page 67) of the organizational structure of Cybertown and called it "Founders Hierarchy."

It is evident from this chart that there is a clear hierarchy of power in which the character of the Founder retains the highest level of authority. The Founder exercises this power through narrative tools, such as providing the texts of the Constitution, issuing open letters to the populace and acting very much as the authority that holds the future of the community in his hands. In fact, the character of the Founder is almost mythical among Cytonians, though not necessarily liked or accepted. There are Cytonians who have suggested that the Founder is not a real person and that even if there ever was such a person, s/he never appears in Cybertown to interact with the ordinary citizens.

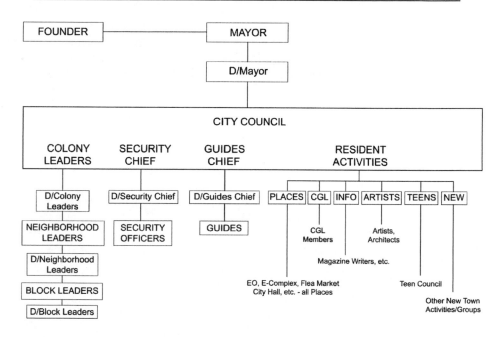

Figure 3.1 Founders Hierarchy of Cybertown

One of the Cytonians I met, whom I will call Cytonian2,[7] maintained an online journal on a site separate from Cybertown, and referred to the Founder in his writings as "the absentee landlord." By using this phrase, Cytonian2 comments on the asymmetrical amount of power held by the Founder who was seen as disinterested in the life of the community within the game world. However, this structural imbalance of power can be understood as reflective of the relationship between "producer" and "player" in respect to the game narrative. By having control over the master narrative of the game, the Founder acts as the "main author," in Murray's terms, and retains the highest level of power even when s/he chooses not to exercise it.

The *Cybertown City Council Guidelines* state that the Mayor of Cybertown (an important character in the simulation), while being the highest-ranking elected official, is not able to make major changes to the structure of the simulation without the consent or cooperation of the Founder. This arrangement is perceived as unfair by Cytonian2 who wrote the following in response to a question about his understanding of the distribution of power in Cybertown:

> *Cytonian2:* Faking Place[8] is purported to be a family site and a society of the future, at least that is the ideal. What is forgotten in all of that, however, is that it is still a money making attempt. The landlord still has control over every

single decision that is ultimately made in the place. Thus, there is really no distribution of power at all. This, in effect, amounts to a dictatorship, and all the elections in the place ain't gonna change that until the landlord relinquishes the stranglehold he currently has. Another factor in this is the fact that the place is still run on the blaxxun servers, and they don't seem willing to release their hold on the place either anywhere in the near future.

Here Cytonian2 pointed to elements external to the fictional game narrative of Cybertown, yet he interpreted these externalities from the point of view of his character: a Cybertown citizen. His comments were also quite consistent with the structure of Cybertown's simulated self-governing society. Yet his frustration came from the unjustified impossibility of reconciling the tension between "external" authorial control and the "internal" communal practice within the game. Cytonian2 was, in short, reacting to the imbalance in the structural nature of a fictional game narrative that maintains the separation between "producer" and "player." However, drawing on Murray's insights, if the "main author" of a text were to permanently give up control over the text to its "readers" this would render the experience of immersion impossible.

The relationship between narrative and power was evidenced in a number of other cases in Cybertown. One poignant example was found in an announcement made by the Founder on November 17, 2002, stating that as of January 1, 2003, Cybertown would cease to be a free site and would become a subscription-based service. The rights to this kind of major alteration of the master narrative are reserved only for the primary author (or producer) of the game, and its authority is not questioned by the members of Cybertown. The choice that each individual player had to make at this point was whether to continue his or her engagement with the game. This was not a choice of narrative. Rather, it was a choice of access and participation. To continue playing the game, one must agree to its rules. To use a metaphor of reading a book, the reader may choose to close the book but cannot rewrite the story in it.

Before the shift to a subscription-based service was announced to players, a banner ad appeared in every public space in Cybertown, stating that a major announcement from the Founder was forthcoming and listing the time and date when it would be made. For those who were not able to "attend" the announcement event, a transcript of the Founder's speech was later available through a link in the *CT News*. By contrast, if an ordinary player, acting in character as a Cybertown citizen, wanted to get any message out he or she would have had to rely on posting it on multiple bulletin boards, submitting a story to the *CT News* staff with no guarantee of getting it published, and engaging in interpersonal communication with other game characters.

This was the path that I had to take, for instance, in order to inform as many Cytonians as possible that I was conducting research on the site.

It is important to note that the character of the Founder is only a symbolic representation of the main author behind the existence of Cybertown, just as the director of a film is only symbolically its creator. In reality, the master narrative of Cybertown is not created by a single person or player but by a team of individuals, some of whom are also active players in the simulation. However, the Founder and those closest to her or him in the organizational structure (see Figure 3.1, page 67) are the visible symbols of ultimate narrative authority.

A point of view external to the game may underplay the significance of the main author. Consider the way in which Blaxxun Interactive summarizes the producer's (or operator's) role in a marketing brochure about Cybertown:

> Cybertown is the ultimate self-sufficient Virtual World. Without regulation or interference from the operator, the citizens govern their world themselves — from adoption of social roles to looking after new members to even mayoral elections. This results in an identification with one's own world, which couldn't be stronger [Blaxxun Interactive 2001b].

From this vantage point, "the operator" (i.e. the Founder) has no particular interest in controlling the internal dealings of the game community and, in fact, minimal intervention is seen as proof of a successful communal structure among the characters within the simulation. At the same time, such minimal intervention is only possible after the main rules of the game's master narrative have been established and they have been internalized by the players through the processes of immersion, agency, and transformation. Interestingly, even Cytonian2, who is an admitted critic of the power distribution in Cybertown, abides by the rules of the master narrative, as this is the only way of continuing participation:

> *Cytonian2:* I have never been much in favor of many of the rules in Faking Place. The vast majority of them are just plain silly, make no sense, and are enforced arbitrarily at best. That doesn't mean that I don't abide by them. I do. Well, okay, not always, but certainly within the guidelines for posting messages and in chat.

Having power in Cybertown means having control over various aspects of the narrative of the simulation. When I obtained a job as a Block Deputy, one of the lowest ranking jobs in the game structure, I was given access rights to delete messages from the bulletin board on my block. In other words, my narrative power had increased as I was able to alter the textual history of the block. Members with job titles higher in the hierarchy have access rights to delete virtual houses that have not been visited for more than two weeks, while members with programming skills have the ability to alter the narrative through creating objects and uploading them for sale in the Mall. Some are even able to create new neighborhoods, provided of course that they can solicit the support and approval of the Founder. In this sense, as agents able to author many parts of their experiences, all Cytonians are invested with some degree of power. In fact, it is through such narrative power that they sustain their sense of belonging to the game community. Yet the power to create is counterbalanced by the power to delete, which is selectively conferred on players by the game's master narrators.

Why Do We Do It?

As many ethnographic researchers have noted, an ethnographic research project should ultimately help the researcher answer the question, "Why do people do what they do?" While it is often easy to observe *what* people do or *how* they do it, many times it is not a simple task to explain *why* they do it. Why do people log on to a website on a daily basis, create virtual homes, work in virtual jobs, buy virtual items, and carry out virtual elections? Many explanations can be given but the most common one that Cytonians shared with me sounded very much like this:

> *Cytonian1:* It's fun. There could be better ways of running this place, but I love it here. Even the stuff that pisses me off is still fun. LOL

In these concluding remarks I wish to offer a twofold interpretation of why living in Cybertown — or any virtual game world — is "fun." According to Murray (1997), the interaction with/in the mediated environment is entertaining because it provides the sense of immersive trance. The experience of participating in Cybertown can easily be compared to watching a movie, reading a book, or following a soap opera on TV. The only difference is that in this particular soap opera you play one of the characters and get to talk to many of the other characters. Thus, participation in Cybertown is a form of active play with an incredibly rich set of characters and props that offer numerous combinations. As Murray (1997: 98) succinctly puts it, "The experience of being transported to an elaborately simulated place is pleasurable in itself, regardless of the fantasy content."

Second, the shared assumptions, interests, practices, codes, and rituals of the participants in online interactions that are maintained over time elevate these interactions to the level of community (Hine 2000). My ethnographic immersion into the world of Cybertown confirms Hine's conclusions and is also in agreement with Schaap's research on text-based MUDs:

> "Playing" a character in a MUD is more than just a game. Players indicate that they enjoy playing in the MUD because it usually is fun ... but the whole "game" revolves not around winning, but around the social relations and social interactions between the characters [Schaap 2002: 2].

In this sense, Cybertown is an elaborate example of how community is constructed within the game through the process of communication. Communication scholar James Carey has noted that,

> For the ordinary person communication consists merely of a set of daily activities: having conversations, conveying instructions, being entertained, sustaining debate and discussion, acquiring information. The felt quality of our lives is bound up with these activities and how they are carried out within communities [Carey 1988: 33].

Having observed and participated in the daily activities of Cybertown, there is no doubt in my mind that the game community of Cybertown characters, produced and maintained through communication, is dramatically alive for its players. At the same time, as any media product, Cybertown stands for more than the communal utopia of people seeking entertainment made possible by technological innovation. Indeed, it is the result of a process of narrative production and consumption similar to that of other cultural products. As such, it is also a site of struggle over the power to control the narrative and define the shared reality. My observations show that, as in all forms of media, here again the producer has dominance over the user. However, embedded in the structure of the new, interactive medium of virtual game worlds is a greater challenge to the producers' "author-ity." A game narrative cannot move forward without some degree of player agency. Thus, there is a greater opportunity for members of Cybertown to move closer to the producer's side of the line than they may find in other forms of media narratives. Yet the kinds of narratives that players can construct remain limited by the structural and technological arrangements of Cybertown.

The intricate ways in which power can be exercised through narrative means are evident in the story of Cybertown. The shared reality of Cybertown is constructed and struggled over through communication practices. The outcome of any struggle for control over a fictional narrative must be won by a "main author" if the narrative is to retain its nature as a fantasy and the online world is to remain a game world. Similarly, any ethnographic study is predicated on the belief that "the journey is not just about getting to know a strange land and understanding the Other and his culture, it is also, and maybe more importantly, a way to better understand the Self, one's own country and culture" (Schaap 2002: 1). It is my hope that through understanding the tensions present in virtual narrative struggles we may gain insights into the struggles over the master narratives of our real lives.

Notes

1. This date reflects the time when fieldwork was conducted — autumn 2002.

2. Cybertown was launched in 1995 by the German-based company Blaxxun Interactive, which continued to host it until October 2002. Currently, the site is hosted by the US-based Integrated Virtual Networks.

3. It is difficult to estimate the actual number of players in Cybertown. The stated number of members is over one million. However, many users admit to having multiple login names which are included in this estimate. During my observations during the six months of fieldwork, the number of characters present online at any given time was between 350 and 500.

4. Murray borrows this phrase from Coleridge (1817).

5. To protect the privacy of CT players their real nicknames have been replaced by the generic name "Cytonian" followed by a numeral to differentiate between the different respondents.

6. VRML is the name of a programming language used for the creation of 3D objects and spaces.

7. In online correspondence with Cytonian2 he explicitly requested that I use his real name in this study and give him credit for his comments. Regrettably, the ethical and procedural requirements for research involving human subjects prohibit me from doing this. However, I wish to acknowledge the help and insights that Cytonian2 provided me and I am happy, with his permission, to disclose his name to interested readers of this chapter.

8. Faking Place is the name that Cytonian2 has adopted for Cybertown in his online journal and he used the same phrase to refer to the site in our correspondence as well. In addition, he posted as entries to his online journal all of his answers to my questions.

References

Anderson, Benedict. 1991. *Imagined Communities: Reflections on the Origins and Spread of Nationalism.* New York, NY: Verso.

Atkins, Barry. 2003. *More Than A Game: The Computer Game as Fictional Form.* Manchester, UK: Manchester University Press.

Blaxxun Interactive. 2001a. "Virtual worlds for entertainment: Interest worlds. Product Management." (http://www.blaxxun.com/pdfs/blaxxunplatform_interest_wp_e.pdf)

_____. 2001b. "Cybertown. Virtual worlds for entertainment: Science fiction community on the Internet." (http://www.blaxxun.com/pdfs/blaxxun_reference_cybertown_e.pdf)

Blizzard Entertainment. 2004. World of Warcraft. Platform: PC.

Bruckman, Amy. 1992. "Identity Workshop: Emergent Social and Psychological Phenomena in Text-based Virtual Reality." (http://ftp.cc.gatech.edu/pub/people/asb/papers/identity-workshop.ps)

Carey, James W. 1988. *Communication as Culture: Essays on Media and Society.* Boston, MA: Unwin Hyman.

Cherny, Lynn. 1999. *Conversation and Community: Chat in a Virtual World.* Stanford, CA: CSLI Publications.

Coleridge, S. T. 1817. *Biographia Literaria, Or, Biographical Sketches of My Literary Life and Opinions.* New York, NY: Kirk and Mercein.

Electronic Arts. 1997. Ultima Online. Platform: PC. Origin Systems.

Geertz, Clifford. 1973. "Thick Description: Toward an Interpretive Theory of Culture." Pp. 3–30 in *The Interpretation of Cultures.* New York, NY: Basic Books.

Hine, Christine. 2000. *Virtual Ethnography.* Thousand Oaks, CA: SAGE.

Jacobson, Mikael, and T. L. Taylor. 2003. "The Sopranos Meet EverQuest. Social Net-working in Massively Multiplayer Online Games." In *Melbourne DAC — the 5th International Digital Arts and Culture Conference*. School of Applied Communication, Melbourne, Australia. (http://hypertext.rmit.edu.au/dac/papers/index.htm)

Jones, Steven G. 1995. Editor. *Cybersociety: Computer-mediated communication and community*. Thousand Oaks, CA: SAGE.

_____. 1998. Editor. *Cybersociety 2.0: Revisiting Computer-mediated Communication and Community*. Thousand Oaks, CA: SAGE.

Kendall, Lori. 1996. "MUDder? I Hardly Know 'Er! Adventures of a Feminist MUDder." Pp. 207–223 in *Wired Women: Gender and New Realities in Cyberspace*, edited by L. Cherney & E. R. Weise. Seattle, WA: Seal Press.

_____. 2002. *Hanging out in the virtual pub: Masculinities and Relationships Online*. Berkeley and Los Angeles, CA: University of California Press.

Kiesler, S. L., Siegel, J. and McGuire, T. W. 1984. "Social Psychological Aspects of Computer-Mediated Communication." *American Psychologist* 39(10): 1123–1134.

Kolo, Castulus, and Timo Baur. 2004. "Living a Virtual Life: Social Dynamics of Online Gaming." *Game Studies* 4(1). (http://www.gamestudies.org/0401/kolo)

Mortensen, Torill E. 2002. "Playing With Players: Potential Methodologies for MUDs." *Game Studies* 2(1). (http://www.gamestudies.org/0102/mortensen)

Murray, Janet H. 1997. *Hamlet on the Holodeck: The Future of Narrative in Cyberspace*. Cambridge, MA: MIT Press.

Nakamura, Lisa. 1995. "Race In/For Cyberspace: Identity Tourism and Racial Passing on the Internet." *Works and Days* 25/26, 13(1–2): 181–193.

Reid, Elizabeth M. 1996. "Communication and Community on Internet Relay Chat: Constructing Communities." Pp. 397–412 in *High Noon on the Electronic Frontier*, edited by Peter Ludlow. Cambridge, MA: MIT Press.

Rheingold, Howard. 1993. *The Virtual Community: Homesteading on the Electronic Frontier*. Menlo Park, CA: Addison-Wesley.

Schaap, Frank. 2002. *The Words That Took Us There: Ethnography in a Virtual Reality*. Piscataway, NJ: Transaction Publishers.

Smith, Marc A., and Peter Kollock. 1999. Editors. *Communities in Cyberspace*. New York, NY: Routledge.

Sony Online Entertainment. 1999. Everquest. Platform: PC. Sony Online Entertainment.

Sproull, Lee and Sara Kiesler. 1986. "Reducing social context cues: electronic mail in organizational communication." *Management Science* 32(11): 1492–1512.

_____, and _____. 1991. *Connections: New Ways of Working in the Networked Organization*. Cambridge, MA: MIT Press.

Taylor, T. L. 2004. "The Social Design of Virtual Worlds: Constructing the user and community through code." Pp. 260–268 in *Internet Research Annual Volume 1: Selected Papers from the Association of Internet Researchers Conferences 2000–2002*, edited by Mia Consalvo, Nancy Baym, Jeremy Hunsinger, Klaus Bruhn Jensen, John Logie, Monica Murero, and Leslie Regan Shade. New York, NY: Peter Lang.

Taylor, T. L., and Beth E. Kolko. 2003. "*Majestic* and the uncertain status of knowledge, community and self in a digital age." *Information, Communication & Society* 6(4): 497–522.

Turkle, Sherry. 1995. *Life on the Screen: Identity in the Age of the Internet*. New York, NY: Touchstone.

Yee, Nick. 2001. "The Norrathian Scrolls: A Study of Everquest (version 2.5)." (http://www.nickyee.com/eqt/demographics.html)

4. *Law and Disorder in Cyberspace: How Systems of Justice Developed in Online Text-Based Gaming Communities*

Mel White

For you will not be Superman
For you will not be Superwoman
For you will not be Solomon
but you will be asked the question nevertheless
— John Stone, "Gaudeamus Igitur," 1982.

The Internet has long been seen as one of the few places where freedom "truly" exists. In places such as forums, chat rooms, web pages, and game arenas there is an expectation of individual liberty and individual privacy where anyone can, in theory, express any view s/he likes and espouse any idea s/he finds reasonable. In practice, this simply is not true. Governments do try to control and censor some web pages and websites and cyber-communities, rather than being completely rule-less, usually have a set of regulations that their members are expected to obey. In order to maintain community, site administrators take advantage of common regulations that develop within the meta-group to establish and maintain systems of justice.

Communities in Cyberspace

It is tempting for those unfamiliar with online gaming to think that its culture is homogenous, with only small differences in communities, programs and interfaces. In reality, online gaming culture is a complex phenomenon and the types of societies and social rules that form within it depend on the general type of game that the culture centers around. The games familiar to most people on the Internet include corporate sponsored entertainment games such as Bejeweled (Astatix N.d.), gambling sites, graphic-heavy Massively Multiplayer Online Games (MMOGs) such as Guild Wars (NCSoft 2005), Real-Time Strategy games (RTSs) such as Age of Empires III (Microsoft Game Studios 2005), and First Person Shooter games (FPSs) such as *Half-Life II* (Valve Corp. 2004). Most of these online spaces control the behavior of their visitors through code within the game and by rules laid down by corporate lawyers (see also Grimes in this volume; Smith in this volume). In many cases they are ruled in a sort of "laissez faire" style, with the community itself being left to deal with social problems and deviant behaviors. The communities themselves use behavior control structures that have evolved from the early days of online gaming and more specifically from older text-based MUD systems including MOOs, MUCKs, and MUSHes.[1]

Social and Administrative Roles on Muds

The role perhaps most-often overlooked when examining social interactions on a MUD is the group of administrators that have the final say in what happens to the virtual space. The owner, who may be either the person who set the game up, the person who owns the server space, or the one who inherited both of those functions from the person who originally set up the MUD is usually referred to as the "archwizard." In addition to being responsible for the technical details of where the MUD resides, archwizards also control access to the game, set the overall game policies, create initial characters, and designate members of the community to become the MUD "wizards," who administer the game on behalf of the archwizard.

Players who are given wizard characters are expected to keep the game running by addressing software and hardware problems and by resolving interplayer conflicts. Wizards are literally "all knowing and all seeing" characters; residents of the Panopticon, who have programming-level access to the game space as well as access to the logs of all actions and conversations on the game space. In most cases, wizards are the only group who can create other characters or remove other characters from the game. Other roles include "programmers" and "builders," specialized types of characters who have the ability to create programs and environments within the game space. Builders usually have access to some of the programming functions on the MUD. Good builders are sometimes recruited from other MUDs to create adventure areas within the newly-set up game and to program specialized commands for the new MUD. Player characters (PCs) have a more limited range of options. On some MUDs they are allowed to build a small number of rooms, but are not allowed to do any programming. On systems that allow guilds, players can rise to positions of influence within their community subgroup. The last type of character is the guest account for visitors to the MUD. This account can be used by anyone with access to the MUD itself. Guest characters usually only have the ability to move and speak and may be subject to time limits for their visit.

Beyond the status-related roles that determine one's position in the game, community is developed by the type of interactions of the specific category of the MUD. MUD and MUSH code offers a set of enhancements that make it easy for players to build adventure rooms and monsters. The focus of these games tends to be on game skills (e.g., monster-killing skills), particularly in the early stages when a player is attempting to build up points for their character. Social hierarchy in these communities is usually based on skill level acquired through monster-killing, area-creating, and programming (Muramatsun and Ackerman 1998); interaction generally takes place while "in character" and with a small number of other players. Promotion within the social ranks is also based on point systems. Players with high levels of programming skills or with high levels of game kill points usually become leaders of individual guilds. Wizards are almost always selected from the top players on MUDs and MUSHes.

In contrast, MUCKs (and MOOs to some extent) tend to emphasize player interactions rather than solo or limited team play. The original MUCKs were designed for freeform role-playing similar to tabletop role-playing games, where a group of players would interact in the context of their characters and create a story or a game together rather than wandering around and killing pre-programmed monsters. One or more players acts as a "game master," directing play and changing the environment as needed. There is no limit to the number in a party, and many areas are available for social chat.

Because good gaming skills do not result in status change in these environments, there are not many guild-type hierarchies set up on MOOs and MUDs. Instead, the focus is on the individual and players with good social skills tend to form sub-communities around them and to act as a stabilizing point for the community. Often these players will set up special events on a game space that helps bring the community together, such as the "Truth or

Dare" games of Tapestries or the live "Short-Short Storytelling Night" activities on FurryMuck. These events, because they usually don't require specialized coding of the environment, are easily portable to other MUCKs and MOOs. Because of the low emphasis on programming to achieve specific ends, the flow of cultural practices seems to move more quickly between various MUCKs and MOOs than between heavily game-oriented environments such as MUDs and MUSHes.

Setting Down the Rules

The first online game spaces were chat rooms on large services such as CompuServe and Genie, where the player paid by the hour for access to these realms. The games were controlled by corporate entities, and the rules were carefully set out by teams of legal experts. Moderators had fairly limited powers of enforcement, and generally were not able to give any help beyond offering advice in resolving player to player disputes or helping someone with a technical problem related to the game program itself. Major infractions of the rules were sometimes settled by the ISP, but in general the wheels of justice were exceedingly slow. In the worst cases, the ISP itself could — and sometimes did — ban troublemakers. Within game areas such as Genie's Gemstone adventure, very little was done to resolve common interplayer issues and gripes within the community about the unfairness of the actions of some players. Left to their own, players attempted to deal with social problems by interpersonal controls such as shaming and shunning, which, while effective in everyday life, are too easily ignored or circumvented in virtual communities.

Many saw MUDs as a rebellion against the strict regulations of the commercial, fee-based games. MUD players did not have to pay to have access to the game, since the majority of MUDs were hosted on university student computer accounts rather than on more expensive commercial sites. The students who owned accounts and provided the space controlled the community resources and people were let in or booted out according to the owners' wishes. The stability and longevity of game spaces were always in question, for MUDs tended to hog expensive computer resources. Universities struck back with frequent system audits and would sometimes suspend students caught running illegal MUDs.

In addition to external sources, there were also internal threats to stability. Disgruntled players could, and would, report the MUD to the university's computer administrators in revenge for perceived injustices. Angry coders could also cause problems by tweaking the MUD code until the system crashed or causing it to slow down the university's servers to the point where an

administrator would investigate. By 1995, as computing resources became
cheaper, more archwizards were beginning to host MUDs on their own personal servers.

Initially, there was no consistent set of rules beyond "have fun" and "don't
break the system;" a paradigm that worked only as long as the population was
small. Once the number of players increased to where more than about 25 at
a time were online together, interpersonal conflicts were certain to arise. Sometimes issues were settled by community negotiation and discussion, but in
many cases they were resolved when the archwizard would step in and pronounce a fiat. There was no inherent right of appeal and the archwizard was
judge, jury, and executioner. It was a feudalistic way of doing things, but the
Golden Rule became the community standard: "he who owns the gold makes
the rules." If players disagreed with the way the laws were set or the way justice was served, they were free to find another community to join.

Early legal issues usually revolved around some sort of coding problem.
It was possible for a skilled coder to "bend" the rules of the environment so
that their characters could gain points (and rise in status) quickly. Tips on
how to make such programs were spread quickly in MUD communities.
When abuse was discovered, coder wizards would fix the issue by simply
tweaking the MUD program to make the "cheat" impossible and sometimes
by removing the coder's ability to program on the MUD. With fairly sparse
populations, social conflicts were relatively infrequent and matters such as
where/when a player should be "In Character" (IC) and where/when players
could have their characters socialize in an "Out Of Character" (OOC) fashion were simply resolved by archwizard fiats.

After a MUD reached a certain size, coding issues and player quarrels
became frequent enough that they were difficult for a single person to handle. Although there is no hard and fast rule about the preferred ratio of wizards to active players, experience has shown that a ratio of about 1 wizard to
every 75 players connecting simultaneously is enough to ensure that requests
for help are answered in a timely manner. Archwizards usually selected friends
to be wizards and staff for the MUD. While this benign sort of nepotism
worked reasonably well in the early stages of a MUD, it proved unworkable
as a strategy with communities of a thousand or more players. Accusations
of favoritism were frequent and small conflicts in viewpoint could turn a small
issue on a MUD into an outright war. Friendships could be, and were,
destroyed by fairly trivial differences in opinion and hot-tempered wizards
could turn a player quarrel into a donnybrook that could destroy a small
cyber-community. In more than one case, a rogue wizard has exacted revenge
by destroying ("toading") players and large areas of a MUD.

Archwizards who survived early struggles and saw their MUDs enter a strong period of growth were forced to become more particular about who they selected as administrators and law-givers. Because the tide had turned to a point where player issues became more common than coding problems, wizards became more valued for their ability to maintain an atmosphere of calm cooperation in difficult situations than for their ability to be friendly with the MUD's archwizard. This frequently resulted in the older, more experienced players being promoted to wizard levels, where their knowledge of other types of organizations helped form the basis of rules that "made sense" for the MUD. In addition to selecting experienced players to be administrators, archwizards would also recruit wizards from other MUDs to serve on their staff in either a temporary or permanent position. The experiences of these players often enabled them to make suggestions when unusual problems arose and to construct morally-based solutions in a cooperative fashion (Cooper 1996).

Toward a System of Justice

Prussian general Karl von Clausewitz said that no battle plan survives the first encounter with the enemy. In a sense this is also true of systems of justice. The first MUDs had no real sets of rules for players because programmers and wizards naively assumed that everyone who joined would understand the simple "sign on and have fun" concept. This utopian vision worked only on a limited scale and in situations where the number of players online at any given time was fairly small. As population grew and player interactions in various areas increased, complaints became more frequent and archwizards and wizards found themselves spending most of their time online settling arguments rather than enjoying the game environment.

Many archwizards and wizards resorted to a parental-like policy in dealing with infractions by simply insisting that their judgment was final and no argument would be tolerated. It wasn't always a fair and balanced type of justice, but what it lacked in equity, it made up for in speed. Abuses were common on some MUDs, particularly when one of the parties involved was a personal friend of a wizard or of the archwizard. Not everyone was happy with this parental form of justice. In 1990–1991, a number of archwizards and wizards announced to their communities that they were tired of threatening others into conforming to the system's rules and were going to try other methods of governing the games. Several MUDs set up anarchies where wizards were to simply function as code maintainers and server administrators; player conflicts would be resolved by the players themselves.

One of the first challenges to the law of anarchy came on a MUD called

Islandia. Because one of the ways of gaining points was to "kill" another player's character, a group of players decided to emulate the outlaws of the American West in the late 18th century and form a band of cyber-criminals. Calling themselves "the Black Rose," members stalked the rest of the community and "killed" players that they came across. While this "killing" did not actually destroy a character, it had the annoying effect of removing some of the "dead" character's accumulated points and sending them back to a distant area with no equipment or personal belongings. Complaints mounted, and eventually the wizard Lynx (Conrad Wong) decided to step in and held meetings with the Black Rose players and the players who complained about them.

The Black Rose gang pointed out that while their actions might be annoying, there was nothing in the rules that said their actions were illegal. The community itself wasn't united in its feelings about the Black Rose gang and accusations, frequently tinged with heavy sarcasm, were leveled against those who complained about the cyber-killings. Others who supported this form of entertainment pointed out that the job of the wizards was to tweak the code; not to make social policy. Lynx attempted to talk the Black Rose gang into limiting their killing to a "combat arena" where only the willing would be killed. The Black Rose players countered that this unfairly hindered their rights of access and free play. A temporary solution was tried with Lynx posting a "do not kill" list of players who didn't want to be bothered by the Black Rose gang. This worked to some degree, but the final solution enacted on *Islandia* was really one of the pat responses to MUD issues: if the issue appears to be unresolvable, change the MUD program itself. Revar, the head coder, added an option that made every player — including the Black Rose gang — un-killable. After that the only way to kill another player's character was to convince that person to type out a set of commands that would change their status to "killable;" something that most players refused to do. The "no kill" flag became standard setting in the newly revised MUD code that Revar was writing; a type of MUD which came to be called a "Fuzzball MUCK."

As a social justice policy, the "no kill flag" was a notable success. Deprived of their entertainment, the Black Rose gang's notoriety and importance faded and the concept of player-killing on MUCKs ended quietly — though on MOOs, MUDs, and MUSHes where the code change was not implemented, player-killing was and is still common (Conrad Wong, personal communication). Code changes couldn't address other social issues that began emerging, however. As people spent more time immersed in online communities, the question of whether harm to the virtual self was actually a crime arose to challenge the idea of how laws in cyberspace ought to be constructed and enforced (Williams 2000).

The most notorious of these incidents involved the *LambdaMOO* virtual rape. This event, which occurred in the early 1990's (Dibbell 1993), involved a character named Mr. Bungle who went on a "power-game" trip through *LambdaMOO*, showing up in rooms and sending as a series of text messages that described violent sexual acts being performed by characters within the rooms he visited. Messages describing anal rape by sharp knives were part of his repertoire, along with the gleeful commentary that seemed to mock the players' powerlessness against him: "You hear Mr. Bungle laughing evilly [sic] in the distance" (Dibbell 1993: 3).

Players were outraged and horrified, but the reaction of the administration was neither swift nor immediate. Four months before the incident, the wizards of *LambdaMOO* declared that they were tired of dealing with the complex issues of social justice. In a document prepared by the archwizard Haakon (Pavel Curtis, *LambdaMOO*'s principal architect), the wizard staff declared that their only function was technical support and that the community itself should police any problems that came up (Curtis N.d.). The community, unable to form any coherent policies about any issue, simply let things slide into anarchy. The resulting anarchy made it difficult for Bungle's victims to seek any form of redress. The community itself was the only body capable of action since it was not clear that a crime in the legal sense of the word had been committed and since there was no way to identify and bring legal proceedings against the person playing Mr. Bungle (Williams 2000). The violated players reacted in the only way they thought sensible, by promptly publicizing the event on the main *LambdaMOO* mailing list.

As the news spread, there were calls for the removal of Mr. Bungle, but to the surprise of the abused players, this sentiment was not unanimous. A number of players felt that the virtual act was not relevant since the offended players could have disconnected at any time during the attack. Bungle himself showed up on *LambdaMOO* a few days later and when questioned, reiterated the logic that this was simply game play in cyberspace. No real harm had been done to anyone, though the players whose characters had been violated argued that the virtual rape was nearly as traumatic as a real rape. A few dissenters tried to blame the players whose characters were attacked, saying that the victims should have simply ignored Bungle by using the @gag command in the code, which would have prevented them from seeing the offensive messages. A backlash followed this, spearheaded by women on *LambdaMOO* already weary of what Dibbell calls the "gag-and-get-over-it school of virtual-rape counseling" (Dibbell 1993). Eventually a town meeting was called and after the discussion had raged and cooled, one wizard who had been listening in on the process very quietly took justice into his own hands and removed Bungle's character by toading it.

Unfortunately, this solution was ineffective. Mr. Bungle's player simply created a new character named "Dr. Jest" and rejoined *LambdaMOO*. After a month or so of inaction, Dr. Jest went on another long series of virtual rape attacks. Once again, the character was removed by community consent and *LambdaMOO* struggled to find a system for enforcing community standards that would allow freedom while controlling those whose actions were harmful to other players. LambdaMOO then tried a form of democracy with a system of petitions and ballots. The purpose of this was that the community would govern and police itself. Issues that passed were binding on both the wizcorps and on the individual players and wizards could remove players by toading if the community felt it necessary. This continued for a number of years until in May of 1996 a weary and disgusted Haakon announced:

> The wizards will no longer refrain from taking actions that may have social implications. In three and a half years, no adequate mechanism has been found that prevents disruptive players from creating an intolerably hostile working environment for the wizards. The [original proposal's] ideal that we might somehow limit ourselves solely to technical decisions has proven to be untenable [Haakon 1996].

The social experiment failed, and in doing so it may have laid the seeds of the decline of *LambdaMOO*. I visited *LambdaMOO* a number of times in 2000–2004, and never found more than 30 people online. Many times when I logged in, nobody was there.

At the other extreme were experiments in anarchy that tried to address issues of justice by giving nearly everyone wizard-level powers. One of the larger MUCKs, *Sociopolitical Ramifications* (*SPR*), tried this experiment on a more modest scale shortly after the *LambdaMOO* fiasco. Initially set up for a group of friends, *SPR* had the largest proportion of wizard level players to regular players of all the active MUCKs. Young and idealistic, the owners of the MUCK felt that it should be easy to promote players to wizard status, and that with a large number of wizards, the twin goals of freedom and order in the community could be maintained. They quickly discovered that giving someone power doesn't ensure that they have any concept of control or fairness. Stripped of a system of checks and balances, abuses of power quickly became rampant. Cliques formed, spying on player interactions became common, and wizard vendettas against single players or groups of players were common. With no one to control the actions of the watchmen of the society, the it disintegrated as players left, carrying word with them that an anarchy of the powerful was a poor way to run an online gaming environment.

Social Changes and Internet Societies

In the late 1980s and early 1990s online gaming populations were still relatively homogenous. Internet access was expensive and available only to those who had the ability to deal with shell programs, modem strings, and basic Unix programs such as telnet. As a result, most of the people in the online population were male, lived in North America, and a large percentage of the population was in college. This picture changed radically when commercial servers entered the marketplace. The greatest impact came when AOL began offering inexpensive accounts that connected to the Internet, which changed the makeup of the online population dramatically within the space of a few years. Internet was no longer an exclusive circle of computer literati, but was an environment where anyone could play — regardless of age or gender — and early players' expectations that things would always stay the same came to a rather abrupt end as women entered the games and began to influence policy. One of the most prominent "hot button" issues in the early 1990s was "virtual sex."

In the early days, casual virtual sexplay among player characters was fairly common. Pundits suggest that female-presenting characters were often males who were playing out fantasies as nymphomaniacs who were sexually attracted to "all" male characters. The pseudo-female character would be courted and given a lot of social attention in exchange for "hot chatting" — virtual sexplay sessions. This led to the commonly held perception that any female character on a MUD was either there simply for sex, or was a male in disguise. This community paradigm was rather shocking to the first women who signed onto MUDs as female characters.

Women found that in many areas they couldn't enjoy playing a character similar to their own concept of themselves since female-presenting personas found themselves constantly pressured for virtual sex and were forced to deal with textual displays of sexual acts committed on their character either in one-to-one interactions (whispers) or displayed for all the users in the room to read (posed). Many women dealt with the situation by killing off their female characters and re-presenting themselves in virtual worlds as male. A few who decided that interpersonal communication practices, rather than their own gender, needed to be challenged held the position that their characters should be given the same kind of rights and protections that they would be granted in ordinary society and insisted that MUD wizards implement laws about sexual harassment. However, there was no clear community consensus on what sorts of rights could and should be granted to virtual persons (Cooper 1996). Many wizards were young males who enjoyed these kinds of interactions and who conceived women's protests as some kind of extremist feminist reaction. While the few female wizards sympathized and prodded for action, many of their male colleagues preferred to let the matter be handled by social controls, overlooking the larger issue that online gaming as a whole was mainly composed of college-aged males.

In 1992, *Brazilian Dreams* MUCK helped change that paradigm. It was a fairly large MUCK and, unusually, had a female archwizard. Most of the wizards on *Brazilian Dreams* were either female or presenting as female and a number of the help staff was also female. Because the archwizard had experienced enough unwanted attentions to push the sexual harassment issue, she laid down a strong anti-harassment policy very clearly in an electronic text. Players had the right to complain about unwanted attentions, and those players who didn't seem to understand the concept of "no thank you, I don't want to hot chat with you" were removed from the MUCK. Word spread quickly in online communities and players began urging archwizards of other MUDs to make a similar policy to protect female players. Within two years of the *Brazilian Dreams* anti-harassment policy statement, most MUCKs and MUDs with existing legal systems adopted these rules or a similar set of to protect players from stalking and harassment.

Cyberculture resigned itself to the truth that MUDs with more than about 100 players online at a time needed active administration and policy enforcement rather than benign anarchies and wizards began taking a more active role in enforcing the rules and in writing legal policies for the MUDs. Coder wizards helped develop some specialized tools to help investigate and track player complaints and concerns. A policy of having the MUD record all player actions to a master MUD "log file" made the resolution of player arguments much simpler, moving it from a "he said-she said" arena into an exact record of who wrote and did what to whom. Situations like the *LambdaMOO* rape became increasingly rare as wizards became able to quickly determine the truth from the system logs. The MUDs also watched the watchmen as well as the citizens and ensured that wizards were not immune to the rules they were expected to enforce. The occasional rogue wizard was identified quickly and legitimate complaints of abuse by a wizard were quickly dealt with by the entire wizcorps.

Real Life Meets Unreal Life

"Real" life has a way of intruding on cyberlife, of bending the rules in unexpected ways and forcing archwizards and wizards to make difficult moral and social decisions in a very short time-frame. One common issue of real and unreal worlds meeting revolves around protection of intellectual property. Although an infinite number of characters can be created, some players prefer to make characters that resemble known heroes or cartoon characters such as Rambo or Bugs Bunny. The player may see it as a tribute to a favorite character, but the icon's creators are often unwilling to allow unlicensed use of their intellectual property. Artists have written administrators to demand that players stop pretending to be a character that they do not have the rights to. Unauthorized Pern MUSHes were threatened by legal action by author Anne McCaffrey, who was irate to find her worlds translated to the cyber-realm. Negotiations with the author came to an amiable conclusion when she sanctioned a set of strict rules and legitimized some of the Pern MUSHes (McCaffrey 1993). On the heels of this and several other high-level complaints, most MUDs began including copyright ownership concepts into their standard terms of service.

More emotionally complex issues of intellectual property ownership occur on those rare occasions when a player dies. The wizcorps, as justices and janitors of the gaming space are the ones who decide what should be done about the intellectual property of the player. Such difficult decisions stem from trying to determine what to do when the player who died was someone who wrote specialized programs for the MUD that are heavily used by the other players. As with situations involving estates in the real world, these are not easy to resolve and often require compromise to come to a solution that makes almost everyone happy. Moral issues are not merely legal in nature. Threats of suicide are one of the most common and difficult issues that wizards deal with. Few MUDs have policies or help systems that tell the wizard how to react when a concerned player reports that another player is trying to kill him/herself. "Munchausen by Internet" (Feldman 2000) cases are not uncommon, particularly when a player feels that s/he needs to extricate a character from a potentially uncomfortable social situation or when the player makes a bid for sympathy or attention (Ducheneaut and Moore 2004). On rare occasions, the threat is carried out and the wizard in charge of the case must try to decide where the victim is and which authorities to alert and how to convince those who could help that this is a report of a real crisis. In several instances, wizard intervention has been successful in saving a life (K'has, personal communication).

In addition to dealing with internal legal and moral dilemmas, MUD archwizards and wizards may be affected by legislation in the countries where their host machines are located. Following close on the heels of the sexual revolution in cyberspace came the 1996 legislation from the United States Senate called the "Communications Decency Act:" a law that attempted to define and regulate "obscene behavior" in cyberspace. Its passage into law created a number of problems for MUD communities. With internally-derived no-harassment policies in place, cyber-community leaders often felt that they had resolved such matters to the satisfaction of all. In the months between the time that the bill was passed in February 1996 until it was struck down by the United States Supreme Court in June 1997, cyberspace gaming and chat areas struggled to find out how they should respond to the new law. *Furry-Muck* was the first MUD to respond by setting up a cyberlaw that segregated the MUCK's areas into "adult" and "non-adult" areas. In order to gain access to the "adult" areas, a player had to register with the MUCK and divulge their real name and real age and real email account. This raised a furor in the community and a small number of players left to join other MUDs that didn't require adult registration, but the wizcorps stood firm on this unpopular policy.

Then the other shoe dropped. The ACLU contacted *FurryMuck* to ask it to join in as a test case in the lawsuit against the Communications Decency Act. The wizcorps was caught off-guard and asked for clarification. They were told that a *FurryMuck* player contacted the ACLU to complain that *Furry-Muck* and other game environments were being hampered by this policy and to ask that the ACLU fight the law on behalf of all MUCKs (ACLU Online Archives 1996). After investigation and some discussion, the wizards determined that the ACLU was unaware that the 17-year-old male who appealed to the ACLU for help was making a number of misleading statements in his affidavit. The special areas he built on *FurryMuck* and other MUCKs were in fact areas designed for sex slave fantasies, and he had been "selling" himself and others for online sexual pleasure in these auctions since he was 14 years old. If the wizards continued with their "adults-only" area lockdown, he would not be able to participate in his preferred online sexual activities for another six months. K'has, on behalf of the *FurryMuck* wizards, replied to the ACLU's email and quietly explained to the ACLU lawyer what the youngster's motive was and why they felt an adult registration policy was for the good of the community. The characters that the young man had created were toaded and his areas were removed from the MUCK, though date and time stamped archives were kept for evidence if the case was ever reopened. To the wizcorp's collective relief, the ACLU dropped *FurryMuck* from the lawsuit. But that didn't mean that the issue was fully resolved, for *FurryMuck* community reaction was fast and furious. There was talk of a player rebellion and talk of leaving the MUCK for other gaming areas that did not enforce such restrictive rules. The wizard corps still stood their ground on the policy and the threatened exodus never really materialized. Within three years, community awareness of minors gaining access to sex areas was at a high, and after dealing with a number of angry parents, many other MUDs began copying *FurryMuck*'s registration policy to keep these issues from threatening the stability of their community.

A Collision of Paradigms

It is difficult enough to deal with the laws of a single country, but the ever-growing interconnectedness of cyberspace sometimes test MUD legal systems in ways never imagined. A number of years ago when I was a newly-hatched wizard, a player approached me and asked me for help with issues involving harassment by another player. I asked her for more information and she told me that she had just been through a very messy divorce and her ex-husband had been stalking her. The police had been called in and an injunction was issued against him, but she was so frightened that she moved to New Zealand. Since both she and her ex-husband were players on the MUCK, she feared that his harassment might continue in cyberspace.

I pressed for more details and learned that the divorce court and the abusive ex-spouse were in Australia and at this point I was at a loss to decide whose laws held sway here. The MUCK's server was in Michigan, but the "owner" lived in New York. I lived in Texas, while the other MUCK administrator-wizards lived on the East Coast and West Coast of the United States. Were we empowered to enforce a judicial ruling that was set down in Australia — and if so, how could we figure out just what constituted "inappropriate contact" in cyberspace? It was a dilemma of Solomonic proportions. After talking to a number of law enforcement officials including a lawyer and a police officer, the wizcorps came to the conclusion that the only sane thing we could do was to enforce the anti-harassment policies of the MUCK itself and its host ISP. Anything else simply was outside our jurisdiction. The player was concerned and stated that she thought this was not a good enough guarantee. Our response, that the laws of the local community are the only ones that are truly enforceable by the wizards, was no comfort to her.

Where international expectations of behavior are concerned, it can become difficult to decide whose rules should be enforced. For example, some games allow "age play." In these sexual fantasies, adults pretend to be children for the purpose of attracting other adults to engage in sex with the minor character. Although the players who are indulging in this sex play are both adults, it is difficult to decide what the legal status of this form of play should be. In some jurisdictions, this is considered obscene and is legally punishable. In other jurisdictions it is an action that is protected by the concept of free speech. In some areas of the world, the age of consent is far lower than that of the United States and the issue of obscenity would never arise. In short, there are still many social and legal issues yet to be addressed in multicultural and multinational cyberspaces.

Who Are You?

One issue that has become increasingly salient over time regards privacy and how much of a player's real life information should be available to administrators and other players. The right to anonymity was one of the earliest freedoms embraced in online game spaces, but situations involving threats of stalking and personal injury among community members and questions of age-based entry into adult areas led to a policy of MUDs requesting verification of the player's information. Many players protested these policies and some have offered intriguing and unbelievable excuses (such as "I'm in a Federal Witness Protection Plan" or "I'm an undercover FBI agent") to explain why they should be given membership without having to reveal any further details about themselves. Although privacy concerns are justified in rare instances where the player is being stalked or harassed by a wizard, MUDs in general have stood firm on a "no exceptions" policy in regard to age registrations.

A number of MUDs found themselves in situations where they needed to divulge the identity of a character. Shortly after the Communications Decency Act was passed, a parent contacted the wizards of FurryMuck and several other MUCKs to complain that a player had been sending his under-age daughter pornographic pictures and suggested that the girl meet him at a motel so that she could become his lover. The parent turned the messages over to the police, a case was set up, and the parent then contacted the MUCKs to ask that they cooperate with the investigation. Deciding the proper course of action was difficult. After deliberation and some cross–MUD chatter in various wizcorps, a cyber-investigation was launched. The parent's complaint was verified, and one of the FurryMuck wizards (K'has) then verified that there was a real criminal investigation taking place. K'has relayed the details of the court case and the officer contact information to the administrators of the other MUDs that the parent had emailed. After talking to legal counsel, K'has was appointed to be the liaison between the police and FurryMuck. The parent/player then contacted the police department, confirmed that the case was both real and active, and then gave the officer in charge the information that the lawyer agreed was legal to divulge. The abuser was convicted in a court of law and sentenced to a jail term. This turned out to be the "opening shot" in a number of similar cases. By the time the second incident occurred, the paradigm of "investigate on the MUCK, confirm all claims in the real world, and if it's confirmed then cooperate after seeking legal counsel" had spread to other game spaces. Although this type of multi-state and multi-site legal action is still relatively uncommon, on the rare occasions when it happens, walking the fine line between privacy and right to know is a source of stress for administrators and wizards.

In my own career as a MUD wizard I know of only one case involving multiple national jurisdictions. A player contacted me once saying that his character had been hacked and that he was being spammed by hate messages that came from his system. An extensive check of the logs showed that someone had broken into his computer and his account and that, in fact, the entire classroom network of his particular school (a small college in Taiwan) had been compromised by a hacker who was using an automated program to spew racist hate literature on the system. We launched an investigation and tracked the hacker via his ISP to an address in Florida, then filed a complaint with his ISP. Documents and supporting evidence were forwarded to his ISP and also turned over to the Taiwanese system administrators so that they could file formal complaints. We learned later that the hacker's account had been disconnected and that security at the college had been upgraded; no other actions had been taken.

Conclusion

In cyberspace, issues of justice and authority are often laced with unusual social parameters seldom encountered in the outside world. Although some solutions can be modeled on real life systems, justice often proves to be an unwieldy concept in liminal, virtual environments. Because of this, rules that govern social behavior in text based gaming environments form autopoietically from case-lore and knowledge acquired from other MUDs. Although currently active MUDs usually developed fairly sophisticated "Terms of Service" (TOS) to guide player behavior, archwizards and wizards are constantly amused and bemused by how players still find loopholes in community standards that have evolved over the lifetime of gaming in cyberspace.

I gratefully acknowledge the following FurryMuck wizards, who provided details about many of the anecdotes mentioned in this chapter: K'has, Lynx, Chip Unicorn, Nightwind, Tugrik, Shaterri, and Drew as well as former wizards Riss and Centaur.

Note

1. These four terms are often used interchangeably for text-based networked virtual reality game spaces that can be modified by players to allow for gaming or chatting. There are a significant number of differences among them, but those differences are only perceptible at the code level; not at the player level. Originally there was just one variety of code; the "MUD" code, but as MUDs became popular and demand grew for different kinds of options, programmers modified the code into what became three other types of virtual realities: MOOs, MUSHes, and MUCKs. Except in instances where a specific virtual world is mentioned, I will refer to all games of this type as "MUDs."

References

ACLU Online Archives. 1996. "Affidavit of Christopher O'Connell Ransohoff." Retrieved September 29, 2004 (http://archive.aclu.org/court/kit.html).

Astatix. N.d. *Bejewled*. Platform: Online.

Cooper, Wes. 1996. "Wizards, Toads, and Ethics. Reflections of a Moo Administrator" *CMCMagazine*, January 1996. Retrieved September 28, 2004 (http://222.december. com/cmc/mag/1996/jan/cooper.html).

Curtis, Pavel. 1996. "Lambdamoo Takes a New Direction" Retrieved October 25, 2004 (http://www.cc.gatech.edu/classes/ay2001/cs6470_fall/ltand.html).

Dibbell, Julian. 1993. "A Rape in Cyberspace or How an Evil Clown, a Haitian Trickster Spirit, Two Wizards, and a Cast of Dozens Turned a Database into a Society." *The Village Voice*, December 21, 1993: 36–42.

Ducheneaut, N., and Moore, R.J. 2004. *The Social Side of Gaming: A Study of Interaction Patterns in a Massively Multiplayer Online Game*. In: Proceedings of the ACM conference on Computer-Supported Cooperative Work (CSCW2004), ACM, New York, 2004. Retrieved October 29, 2004 (http://pdf.textfiles.com/academics/cscw2004-swg.pdf).

Feldman, M.D. 2000. "Munchausen by Internet: Detecting Factitious Illness and Crisis on the Internet." *Southern Medical Journal* 93: 669–672.

Haakon, 1996. LambdaMOO Policy Statement. Retrieved February 20, 2005 (http://www.sscnet.ucla.edu/soc/faculty/kollock/classes/cyberspace/resources/LambdaMOO%20 Takes%20a%20New%20Direction.htm)

McCaffrey, Anne, 1993. "Public Text of Subject: A Post-Atwop Pern MUSH." Retrieved August 4, 2004 (http://www.idyllmtn.com/mush/dawnsisters/anne.html).

Microsoft Game Studios. 2005. *Age of Empires III*. Platform: PC. Ensemble Studios.

Muramatsu, J., and Ackerman, M. 1998. "Computing, Social Activity, and Entertainment: A Field Study of a Game Mud." *Computer Supported Cooperative Work* 7: 87–122.

NCSoft. 2005. *Guild Wars*. Platform: PC. ArenaNet.

Stone, John. 1982. "Gaudeamus Igitur" Retrieved September 4, 2004 (http://www.npr.org/programs/atc/features/2003/jul/bellevue/johnstone.html).

Valve Corp. 2004. *Half-Life II*. Platform: PC. Valve Corp.

Williams, Matthew. 2000. "Virtually Criminal: Discourse, Deviance, And Anxiety Within Virtual Communities." *International Review Of Law Computers & Technology* 14(1): 95–104.

Section 2: Discourse and Ideology

5. *From* The Green Berets *to* America's Army: *Video Games as a Vehicle for Political Propaganda*

AARON DELWICHE

In February 2003, the video-game *Special Force* began circulating on the Internet. Structurally similar to *Counter-Strike* and *Call of Duty*, it is a classic example of the first-person shooter genre. Such games offer "three-dimensional navigation in virtual environments, in which the player interacts in single or multi-player combat sequences by using a range of weaponry in order to complete a mission or objective" (Nieborg 2004: 1). While *Special Force* embodies many characteristics typically associated with the genre, its storyline is unique: players assume the role of Islamic militants repelling an Israeli invasion of Lebanon. Designed by Hezbollah, a militant Shia group widely viewed as a terrorist organization (Westcott 2002), *Special Force* is intended to attract new recruits while bolstering support for the fight against occupation. Within a few months of its release, more than 10,000 copies had been distributed in Lebanon, Syria, Iran, and the United Arab Emirates.

Another first-person shooter, *America's Army* is also available via the Internet. Developed for the U.S. Army by the Modeling, Simulation and Virtual Environments Institute (MOVES) at the Naval Postgraduate School, *America's Army* deliberately taps into the immersive game context in the hopes of recruiting young Americans into the Army. "If you don't get in there and engage them early in life about what they're going to do with their lives," explains one of the game developers, "when it comes time for them to choose, you're in a fallback position" (Ryan 2004: B1). With more than 1.5 million copies downloaded over a six-month period, the release of *America's Army* has been called "the most successful game launch in history" (O'Hagan 2004). As of June 2005, the game hosted more than 5 million players — most of them men.

Special Force and *America's Army* are consciously designed to foster support for the military objectives of their creators, while recruiting youth to pick up arms in pursuit of those goals. By many measures, both titles could be considered political propaganda. However, the development teams responsible for these games classify their handiwork as educational entertainment. Mahmoud Rayya, a spokesperson for Hezbollah, explains that "*Special Force* offers a mental and personal training for those who play it, allowing them to feel that they are in the shoes of the resistance fighters" (Soussi 2003). Colonel Casey Wardynski, the director of *America's Army*, sounds a similar note when he suggests that the game allows children to "try the army on for size and get more information about the many job opportunities." According to one internal report, the game has been a wild success, engendering "positive awareness of Soldiering among twenty-nine percent of young Americans age 16 to 24" (Wardynski 2004).

It is time for game researchers to acknowledge that video-games have enormous persuasive potential. "Whatever the power of images," Penny (2004: 80) tells us, "interactive media is more. 'Not just a picture,' it is an interactive picture that responds to my actions." Pioneer game designer Chris Crawford agrees, noting that the compelling worlds created by game designers have the potential to shape attitudes in dangerous ways. "Goebbels was so frightening," he writes, "because he had a pretty good grip on how to use modern media for propaganda purposes. Right now, we're all too dumb to figure it out. Someday, we'll have our interactive Goebbels" (Crawford, cited in Peabody 1997).

In the following pages, I argue that video-games have the potential to shape attitudes and behavior in ways that Goebbels could never have dreamed. After addressing common misconceptions about the term propaganda, I identify four traits of video games that might function as mechanisms for influencing attitudes. These characteristics — the four I's — are immersion, intense engagement, identification, and interactivity. This essay does not prove that video games can shape beliefs, but it points to research on each of these characteristics which suggests that they play a role in changing attitude and behavior. Applying this framework to recent games that are explicitly political, I speculate that the most successful propaganda games will exploit all four of these dimensions. Finally, I call on game designers and scholars to acknowledge the ethical responsibilities that accompany this powerful medium.

What Is Propaganda?

Neil Postman (1979: 46) warns that "of all the words we use to talk about talk, propaganda is perhaps the most mischievous." One could devote an entire dissertation to the nuances of this term, and interested readers are encouraged to consult Stanley Cunningham's (2002) *The Idea of Propaganda: A Reconstruction.* The discussion that follows is based on an operational definition adapted from Garth Jowett and Victoria O' Donnell (1986), in which they suggest that propaganda refers to the deliberate and systematic attempt to shape perceptions, manipulate cognitions, and direct behavior to achieve a response that furthers the desired intent of the propagandist. This tool of ideological, physical, or economic conflict is typically aimed at more than one person and wielded by an organized group. Propaganda encompasses advertisements, public relations campaigns, political commercials, political leaflets, and persuasive messages embedded in most forms of entertainment, including video games.

Propaganda is closely related to ideology, but the terms have distinct meanings. Ideology refers to shared values and beliefs — often experienced as natural — that shape individuals' understandings of institutions and social relationships (Sturken and Cartwright 2001). Churches, schools, family, and the media are some of the institutions responsible for the transmission of ideology (Althusser 1996), but the process is largely unconscious and nondirected. In contrast, propaganda is developed by an organized group and systematically disseminated with the intent of prompting certain attitudes and behaviors. Savvy propagandists tap into the affective power of dominant ideologies, but they do so with the conscious desire to shape attitudes and behavior.

Propaganda can be as blatant as a swastika or as subtle as a joke. Though widely viewed as sinister and dishonest, it is also used to disseminate prosocial messages such as "don't drink and drive" or "practice safe sex." For better or for worse, it thrives in democratic systems as an alternative to the physical force that underpins totalitarian regimes, and some theorists suggest that it is inevitable in a technologically advanced society (Ellul 1973). Propagandists love short-cuts — particularly those which short-circuit rational thought. They encourage this by agitating emotions, by exploiting insecurities, by capitalizing on the ambiguity of language, and by bending the rules of logic. As history shows, they can be quite successful.

Though propaganda has existed throughout human history, it achieved unprecedented power during World War I, fueling public support for "the war to end all wars." In America, when citizens discovered that many atrocity stories had been fabricated, widespread disillusionment provided fertile ground for the propaganda analysis movement. An interdisciplinary group of journalists, scholars, and activists distributed critical rubrics and instructional materials widely throughout the country (Sproule 1996), and key figures within the movement later went on to become prominent scholars in the field of communication.

Communication research is heavily indebted to propaganda critics of the early twentieth century, but the term almost disappeared from the vocabulary of social scientists in the postwar era. In 1966, the psychologist Leonard Doob (1966: *vi*) noted that

> The word propaganda is no longer popular either in general usage or among social scientists and philosophers. The polite terms have come to be communication and information, since they imply no value judgment and since the latter more gracefully embraces widely scattered phenomena ranging from physical systems (telephones, computers) to many of the intricate perplexities inherent in developing societies and international diplomacy.

Forty years later, polite language dominates research on the persuasive impact of video games. This can be seen in the "serious games" movement that brings together game developers, scholars, policymakers, and military planners. In October 2004, the developers of *America's Army* co-hosted a Serious Games Summit in Washington, DC. The conference was intended to build "links between the traditional video-game industry and program managers for homeland security, state and local governments, military agencies and educational institutions." Of thirty-seven sessions listed in the conference program, thirty-two were identified as military in nature. In all of the sessions at the Serious Games Summit, the word "propaganda" never appeared once in a title or abstract. Speakers instead framed their research in instructional terms, stressing "behavior modification," "training," "learning," "simulation," and "altered perception." This vocabulary may be slightly more precise, but it also soft-pedals the fundamental desire to shape gamers' opinions, attitudes and behaviors.

Are games such as *Special Force* and *America's Army* educational or propagandistic? Some would argue that they are both. Ever since Plato penned *Republic*, political theorists have recognized that education is a process that systematically influences perceptions, cognition, and behavior. Lambert (1938) argues that "education is a form of communal propaganda, approved by the State and guided by tradition," noting that both practices "depend for their dissemination on much the same media — the spoken word, the Press, the book, the film, and so forth" (p. 158). Teachers and political propagandists both seek to transform audience attitudes and behavior, and the underlying persuasive processes are closely related.

Mechanisms of Effectiveness

During the past few years, game studies researchers have gradually established a shared vocabulary for interpreting digital games. One only needs to scan the chapter heads of contemporary anthologies to identify recurring themes. From *The Videogame Theory Reader* (Wolf and Perron 2003) to *First Person: New Media as Story, Performance and Game* (Wardrip-Fruin and Harrigan 2004), researchers highlight four key characteristics of this new medium. Games are *immersive*, which means that they are capable of transporting users into compelling virtual environments (McMahan 2003; Murray 1997). They are *intensely engaging*, provoking states of intense concentration that can last for hours on end (Oblinger 2004). They foster intense *identification* between players and game characters (Filiciak 2003), and they are *interactive* media that dynamically modify content in response to user actions (Smith 1999). All four of these characteristics are central to the gaming experience. In studies scattered across disciplines, each dimension has been independently linked to attitude change. The combined persuasive strength of these characteristics is potentially multiplied as players compulsively revisit their favorite video games.

Immersion

One can watch television or listen to the radio in a distracted state, but most video games demand and receive rapt audience attention. Murray (1997) calls this domination of player senses "immersion," comparing participation in virtual environments to swimming. She explains that we experience "the sensation of being surrounded by a completely other reality, as different as water is from air, that takes over all of our attention, our whole perceptual apparatus" (98). The sensory domination experienced from video games is particularly profound. While film and television content enter via two perceptual channels, video games make it possible for communicators to influence sight, sound, touch, and even proprioception (the perception of bodily movement). As Lahti (2003) notes, gamers often perceive representations on the screen as extensions of their bodies.

Of course, immersive states have also been observed in audience relationships to other media. Many of us have experienced the feeling of being lost in a good book. Movie theaters dim lights and encourage patron silence in an attempt to intensify immersion. More than seventy years ago, Herbert Blumer (1933: 74) recognized that cinema is capable of inducing "emotional possession." In this state, "the individual suffers some loss of ordinary control over his feelings, his thoughts, and his actions. Such a condition results usually from an intense preoccupation with a theme, in this case that of a picture. The individual identifies himself so thoroughly with the plot or loses himself so much in the picture that he is carried away from the usual trend of conduct. His mind becomes fixed on certain imagery, and impulses usually latent or kept under restraint gain expression or seriously threaten to gain such expression." Ellul (1973) would later note that this is precisely how propaganda operates. It "tends to make the individual live in a separate world; he must not have outside points of reference. He must not be allowed a moment of meditation or reflection in which to see himself vis-à-vis the propagandist, as happens when the propaganda is not continuous. At that moment, the individual emerges from the grip of propaganda" (p. 17).

Recently, Green, Brock and Kaufman (2004) have drawn our attention to an audience phenomenon called *transportation*: a "convergent mental process, a focusing of attention that may occur in response to either fiction or nonfiction. The components of transportation include emotional reactions, mental imagery, and a loss of access to real-world information" (p. 703). Noting that transported individuals are less likely to break the spell by challenging a story's embedded assumptions, Green and Brock (2000) argue that transportation has the potential to amplify a narrative's persuasive effects. They observe that the feeling of "being there" approaches the feeling of real experience, which is also known to affect attitude formation. In four separate experiments, Green and Brock (2002) have correlated the mechanism of transportation with changed beliefs, even when "belief change dimensions were not explicitly articulated in the story" (p. 718).

Intense Engagement

Video-game immersion is often accompanied by intense player engagement. Focused gamers display many characteristics of what Csikszentmihalyi terms a "flow state" (Douglas and Hargadon 2000). This state is characterized by focused concentration, time distortion, a sense of control over one's actions, and satisfaction derived from factors intrinsic to the activity being practiced (Nakamura and Csikszentmihalyi 2002: 90). Sherry (2004) argues that video games are uniquely well suited to induce the flow state because they offer clear objectives, precise feedback, immersive audiovisual material, and content that is dynamically adapted to reflect user choices.

This has important implications for persuasion, because the "motivation for an extended engagement" is crucial to mastering complex bodies of knowledge (Gee 2004: 4). Peng (2004: 10–11) suggests that "students learn in a flow state where they are not just passive recipients of knowledge, but active learners who are in control of the learning activity and are challenged to reach a certain goal." Garris, Ahlers, and Driskell (2002: 454) agree, pointing out that "motivated learners more readily choose to engage in target activities, they pursue those activities more vigorously, and they persist longer at those activities than do less motivated learners." Such claims apply equally well to political persuasion: when audiences are motivated and engaged, they are more likely to interact with a game's ideational content.

Identification

In many of the most popular video games, we identify ourselves *bodily* with our character in the game-world, and *psychologically* with the broader narrative arc defined by our character's choices. While early video games such as *Pong* and *Asteroids* relied on distancing third-person perspectives, interfaces have steadily evolved to invite greater bodily identification with on-screen characters (Rehak 2003). This type of corporeal identification is closely linked to the notion of presence. As Rob Fullup puts it, "in a game, Mario isn't a hero. I don't want to be him: he's me. Mario is a cursor" (cited in Frasca 2001: 167). Video-game identification is potentially more powerful than that fostered by cinema. "It is easier to identify ourselves with something that is partly created by us," argues Filiciak (2003: 91) "than with pictures imposed on us by somebody else."

Filmmakers have long recognized the psychological power of such identification processes. In the opening sequence of Fritz Lang's *Man Hunt* (1941), the spectator views Hitler through the scope of a sniper's rifle (Figure 5.1). Arguing that this "compulsively allies the spectator with the whole motivation of the picture and its main character," Furhammer and Isaakson (1971: 187) explain that "the audience has been placed in a situation which forcibly produces exactly the moral perspective that the film itself will eventually arrive at." In this example, the identification is also corporeal in nature — extending the viewer's eyesight to the scope of the rifle and even the bullet itself. Other propaganda films, such as *Casablanca* (1941), encourage viewers to identify with the protagonists' psychological struggles and moral choices (Nachbar 2000).

From the standpoint of those who seek to influence cognition and behavior, player identification with a game character is particularly intriguing. Gee (2003: 55) observes that three types of identity are at work when gaming: virtual identity, real-world identity, and a projective identity that synthesizes both. Unlike the identification experienced with film and literature, video-game identification is active (making choices that develop the character) and reactive (responding to conditions that stem from these choices). Players learn, "through their projective identities, new identities, new values and new ways

Figure 5.1. In Fritz Lang's *Man Hunt* (1941), spectators are encouraged to identify with the would-be assassin.

of being in the world based on the powerful juxtaposition of their real-world identities ... and the virtual identity at stake in the learning..." (p. 66). Ultimately, "the power of video games for good or ill, resides in the ways in which they meld learning and identity" (p. 199). This is as true of games that seek to impart political messages as of those that are explicitly educational.

Interactivity

Unlike movies and television programs, video games are *interactive*: the user chooses and the computer responds. In the context of video games, Smith (1999) argues that interactivity most usefully refers to interaction with virtual objects (what players can do to those objects, the ways those objects can respond, and the ability of those objects to act upon avatars without prompting) and with the game's underlying narrative. In all of these contexts, there is a cybernetic feedback loop between the user and the machine. According to Penny (2004: 83), "it is the ongoing interaction between these representations and the embodied behavior of the user that makes such images more than images."

Similar feedback systems are used in video games. Garris, Ahlers and Driskell (2002), theorists with extensive experience designing military simulations, argue that judgment-behavior-feedback loops are crucial to recognizing any instructional benefits from games. In their view, "the game cycle focuses attention to a critical chain of dependencies: (a) To elicit desirable behaviors from learners, (b) they first need to experience desirable emotional or cognitive reactions, (c) which result from interaction with and feedback generated from game play" (p. 452). This loop underpins all video games, from *Pac Man* to *Counter-Strike*. Players are rewarded for engaging in certain behaviors (e.g. eating dots, shooting their opponents), and they experience positive feelings when such rewards are given. When players make choices discouraged by the game designers (e.g. walking off a cliff or shooting civilians), they are punished. For example, *America's Army* "rewards Soldierly behavior and penalizes rotten eggs" (Davis, Shilling, Mayberry, Bossant, McCree, Dossett, Buhl, Chang, Champlin, Wiglesworth, and Zyda 2004: 11). Friedman (1999) argues that the cognitive outcomes of such interactive loops are particularly pronounced. After all, "the way computer games teach structures of thought — the way they reorganize perception — is by getting you to internalize the logic of the program." This means "thinking *along with* the computer, becoming an extension of the computer's processes" (p. 4).

Case Studies

These four dimensions provide a useful rubric for designing and critiquing persuasive video games. The following case studies demonstrate how this framework might be applied. These are not the only issues worth considering, but they are a valuable starting point. While some games appear on the surface to be breathtaking propaganda accomplishments, they fall short when examined through the framework described above.

Kuma\War

Kuma\War, a first-person and third-person shooter developed by Kuma Reality Games, invites gamers to participate in such missions as "Uday and

Qusay's last stand," "Fallujah Police Station Raid," and "Najaf: al Mahdi Ceme-
tery Battle." The names and locations are ripped from the headlines. Each
mission is accompanied by links to articles from third-party media outlets,
satellite images of the battlefield, and explanatory video clips presented in the
form of faux news broadcasts. Created with the help of a former ABC news
producer and a retired marine commander, the clips use "exclusive" video
footage obtained from the Associated Press and the Department of Defense.

The game's creators rapidly adjust their content to reflect real-world
events. For example, in July 2005, within hours of terrorist bombings in London, the company posted a game module pitting British troops against Iraqi
tanks. In an accompanying blurb, the editors remarked that "today's terror
attacks in London remind us of Britain's many acts of courage during these
years of crisis. In this weeks' episode, British forces confront Saddam's elite
tank corps in the opening days of Operation Iraqi Freedom. We offer this tale
in honor of our friends and defenders overseas." It should be noted that, at
the time that the module and blurb were uploaded to the *Kuma\War* site, real-
world authorities had not yet established any link between the terror attacks
and events in Iraq.

At first glance, *Kuma\War* seems to be a textbook example of how video
games might function as propaganda. The close relationship between game
developers and the Department of Defense suggests that the designers' agenda
does not deviate radically from that of the US military. The developers are
obsessed with authenticity, but they base their notion about the "real facts"
upon military briefings. Game modules are uncritically aligned with the military objectives of U.S. foreign policy. Much like soldiers who have been
deployed in Iraq, the game's players fight on battlefields that have been pre-
selected by political leaders and military planners.

Evaluated in terms of the mechanisms identified above, *Kuma\War* has
not been an overwhelming success. The game has been widely panned by
reviewers for dated visuals, weak audio and unconvincing artificial intelligence,
all flaws that undermine immersion. Judging by sparsely populated forums
and the dearth of third-party sites, *Kuma\War* has also failed to promote
player engagement. It has earned 53% on *Metacritic* (based on 13 reviews)
and a 0% on *Rotten Tomatoes* (based on 5 reviews)—failing grades by any
measure. Furthermore, *Kuma\War* does little to foster identification between
players and their game characters.

Serious Games

Some of the most well-known attempts to influence attitudes and behavior via video games have been implemented by game designers who are also

scholars. Gonzalo Frasca and Ian Bogost's web log *Water Cooler Games* is a clearing house for discussion of these issues. Frasca (2001) has long advocated the use of video games as tools for social change. As the lead designer and producer of *Newsgaming.com*, he spearheaded the creation of two recent political games: *September 12th* and *Madrid*. The first game, designed shortly after the second anniversary of attacks on the World Trade Center, asks players to contemplate the consequences of the War on Terror. "This is not a game," announces the opening screen. "You can't win and you can't lose. This is a simulation. It has no ending. It has already begun. The rules are simple. You can shoot. Or not." After this introduction, players are presented with a topographic view of a populated city somewhere in the Middle East. Civilians and gun-toting terrorists wander the streets. In a visual display reminiscent of Fritz Lang's *Man Hunt*, the user is invited to move cross-hairs around the screen (Figure 5.2). When the mouse is clicked, a cruise missile is fired into the crowded streets. The message of the game quickly becomes clear. It is impossible to kill terrorists without also leveling buildings and killing civil-

Figure 5.2. *September 12th* demonstrates that it is impossible to bomb suspected terrorists without leveling buildings and killing civilians (by permission of Gonzalo Frasca).

ians. With the death of each civilian, new converts to the militant cause are born. The press release accompanying *September 12th* explains that its intent is "to encourage players to think critically about the efficacy of the United States' current strategy against terrorism."

Viewed within a web browser, this *Shockwave*-based game is neither immersive nor engaging. The graphics are simple and cartoon-like. There is little capacity for identification, for the user is distanced from the action through the targeting cross-hairs. A forced time-delay between shots decreases the likelihood that the missiles will be experienced as an extension of the user's body. The persuasive power of this simulation rests on the interactive loop between the player and the game itself. Violence is rewarded with further violence. Nonviolence prevents further escalation of terrorism. The applet is a clever parable about the futility of violence, but it is unlikely to alter the views of Americans who endorse the War on Terror.

Frasca created *Madrid* in March 2004, three days after Al Qaeda militants bombed a train station in Madrid. The opening screen depicts a diverse crowd of people who have gathered for a candle-light vigil. Each wears a T-shirt emblazoned with the names of world cities that have been the target of terrorist attacks. The player is instructed to "click on the candles and make them shine as bright as you can." As a timer counts down, the player must continually click on the candle flames to make them glow brighter. With each click, time is extended. When the player stops clicking, time runs out and they are chastised for not trying hard enough. The message of this game is exactly opposite that of the first. In *September 12th*, it is at least possible for players to end the game with a sense of accomplishment. *Madrid* always ends in failure because, at some point, the user must stop clicking.

Ian Bogost creates political games that are more closely linked to electoral politics. Working with Frasca, he created a game aimed at volunteers working for the presidential candidate Howard Dean during the 2004 primaries (See Figure 5.3). In this *Flash*-based game, players guide a virtual member of the Dean campaign through the process of delivering literature, waving signs, and knocking on doors. The game does not elaborate the candidate's policy positions and could be used for any candidate with very little modification (Trimble 2004).

Bogost's second project makes more explicit connections to substantive issues. Designed for the state GOP in Illinois, *Take Back Illinois* contains components focused on medical malpractice reform, education, public participation, and economic reform (Figure 5.4). In each of these mini-games, play unfolds under the watchful eye of a gigantic representation of House GOP Leader Tom Cross. In the component focused on educational reform, a map of Illinois displays eight school districts. Players must balance educational

Figure 5.3. Aimed at volunteers working for Howard Dean, this game could be adapted to any political candidate with only cosmetic changes (by permission of Ian Bogost).

standards with teacher allocation to improve overall educational performance. A fixed number of teachers can be added to the game, and teachers can be relocated between districts. Players must allocate instructors while periodically "teaching" by quickly clicking a series of colored buttons according to a predetermined sequence.

Bogost predicts that games can have a greater impact on audiences than traditional forms of political communication because "you've got a player learning to understand principles by performing them himself rather than hearing someone talk about them idly in casual conversation" (cited in Foster 2004: A32). Yet, both games could do much more to link game mechanics with political principles. The process of rapidly clicking colored icons does not convince users of the importance of educational standards, and controlling a virtual campaign worker is unlikely to foster understanding of policy positions of the Dean campaign. Furthermore, neither of these games is immersive, user engagement is limited at best, and there are few opportunities to identify with game characters.

Frasca and Bogost are visionary designers, but the works described here

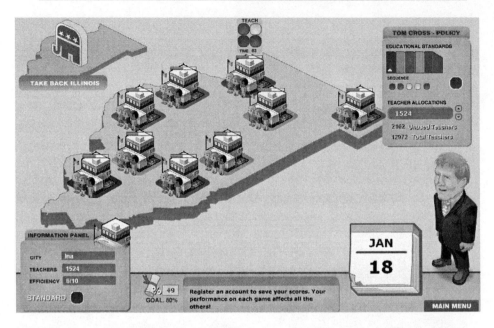

Figure 5.4. In the education reform component of *Take Back Illinois*, players "teach" by rapidly clicking colored buttons (by permission of Ian Bogost).

only hint at the true persuasive potential of video games. Of all four games, only *September 12th* succeeds in tightly coupling game mechanics and visual feedback with its political message.

Conclusion

From *America's Army* to *Kuma\War* and *September 12th*, persuasive games challenge video-game researchers who care about the potential of this fledgling medium. Game scholars celebrate research demonstrating the educational benefits of video games, but they have hesitated to acknowledge that games might have other effects. Perhaps to avoid providing ammunition to would-be censors, researchers have remained strategically silent about the ways in which games transform those who play them. However, it is possible to acknowledge the potential effects of video games without blaming the medium for all social ills.

Game researchers should take moral and political responsibility for the medium that we love. In celebrating the accomplishments of video games, we should also scrutinize their more questionable uses. For example, many are troubled by the use of *America's Army* to entice new military recruits. As of March 2007, more than 3,100 U.S. soldiers have been killed and close to 13,000 have been wounded in the Iraq War (Iraq Coalition Casualty Count 2007). The number of Iraqi civilian casualties is estimated at 60,000 (Iraq Body Count 2007). Whether one supports or opposes American involvement in the region, the use of video games for recruiting purposes warrants serious attention.

As demonstrated in the preceding pages, there are many reasons to believe that games such as *America's Army* have an effect on audiences. The four I's commonly referenced in the games literature have been independently linked to attitude change, and their combined persuasive power may be reinforced through repetition. Yet, accepting that games might have some effects does not mean that they affect all players in the same way. Players can approach games such as *America's Army* and *September 12th* from a variety of subject positions, engaging in negotiated readings that mitigate or reject the intended messages of game developers.

Sharing critical insights with the general public is one way that game scholars can take moral and political responsibility for the medium that we love. The four I's could be one starting point for evaluating the persuasive effectiveness of video games. The simplicity of this approach makes it a valuable tool for media literacy educators who seek to understand the new media landscape. These concepts can be explained in ways that are accessible to K-12 students, encouraging them to think more critically about their relationship to video-game content. Furthermore, the analytical power of this framework will strengthen with time, because game scholars are collectively building a more sophisticated understanding of each one of these dimensions.

This essay is only intended to *initiate* a conversation about propagandistic applications of video games — much more work needs to be done in this area. One obvious direction of inquiry would be to distinguish characteristics common to video-game genres (e.g. role-playing, first-person shooters, massively multiplayer environments, real-time strategy) from characteristics linked to video-game content. It would also be interesting to know more about the relative importance of each dimension in shaping attitudes. Are immersion and intense engagement more important than identification? What about a game that excels on three dimensions while lacking any sort of interactive message modulation? Audience studies could also be conducted to understand the extent to which gamers are sensitized to these dimensions of play.

As research continues, we should keep our eyes on the horizon for the first video-game propaganda masterpiece. It is possible to imagine a game that transcends theoretical disputes in our community to synthesize immersion, engagement, identification, and interactivity with compelling, politically charged narrative. Although one has not yet emerged, it is helpful to remember that 34 years lapsed between the invention of the Kinetescope and Serge Eisenstein's *Battleship Potemkin* (1925). When such a game is created, we can only hope that it looks more like *Casablanca* (1941) than *Triumph of the Will* (1934). If we continue to share our findings with the broader gaming community, audiences will be more prepared to greet such a title with the scrutiny it deserves.

References

Althusser, Louis. 1996. *For Marx (Verso Classics 1)*. London: Verso Press.

Anderson, Craig A., and Brad J. Bushman. 2001. "Effects of Violent Video Games on Aggressive Behavior, Aggressive Cognition, Aggressive Affect, Psychological Arousal, and Prosocial Behavior: A Meta-Analytic Review of the Scientific Literature." *Psychological Science* 12(5): 353–359.

Atari. 1972. *Pong*. Platform: Arcade. Atari.

_____. 1979. *Asteroids*. Platform: Arcade. Atari.

Bavelier, Daphne, and C. S. Green. 2003. "Action Video Game Modifies Visual Selective Attention." *Nature* 43: 534–537.

Benedict, James O. 1990. "A Course in the Psychology of Video and Educational Games." *Teaching of Psychology* 17(3): 206–208.

Blumer, Herbert. 1933. "Emotional Possession: Sorrow and Pathos." Pp. 95–102 in *Movies and Conduct (A Payne Fund Study)*. New York: Macmillan and Company.

Chaffee, Steven, and Miriam Metzger. 2001. "The End of Mass Communication?" *Mass Communication and Society* 4(4): 365–379.

Crawford, Chris. 1982. "Why Do People Play Games?" Pp. 16–24 in *Art of Computer Game Design* (pp. 16–24). Berkeley: McGraw-Hill.

Csikszentmihalyi, Mihaly. 1990. *Flow: The Psychology of Optimal Experience* New York: Harper and Row.

Cunningham, Stanley B. 2002. *The Idea of Propaganda: A Reconstruction* Westport, CT: Praeger Publishers.

Davis, Margaret, Russell Shilling, Alex Mayberry, Phillip Bossant, Jesse McCree, Scott Dossett, Christian Buhl, Christopher Chang, Evan Champlin, Travis Wiglesworth and Michael Zyda. "Making *America's Army*: The Wizardry Behind the U.S. Army's Hit PC Game." Pp. 9–15 in *America's Army PC Game: Vision and Realization*. Monterey, CA: The Wecker Group.

Delwiche, Aaron. 2003. "MMORPG's in the College Classroom." Invited presentation at *The State of Play: Law, Games, and Virtual Worlds*. New York Law School. November 13–15.

Doob, Leonard. 1954. "Goebbels' Principles of Propaganda." Pp. 508–521 in *Public Opinion and Propaganda* edited by Daniel Katz, Dorwin Cartwright, Samuel Eldersveld, and Alfred McClung Lee. New York: Holt, Rinehart and Winston.

_____. 1966. *Public Opinion and Propaganda* Hamden: Archon Books.

Douglas, Yellowlees, and Andrew Hargadon. "The Pleasure Principle: Immersion, Engagement, Flow." Pp. 153–160 in *Hypertext 2000*. San Antonio, Texas: ACM.

Ellul, Jacques. 1973. *Propaganda*. New York: Alfred A. Knopf.

Filiciak, Miroslaw. 2003. "Hyperidentities: Postmodern Identity Patterns in Massively Multiplayer Online Role-Playing Games." Pp. 87–102 in *Video Game Theory Reader*, edited by Mark J. P. Wolf and Bernard Perron. London: Routledge.

Frasca, Gonzalo. 2001. "Rethinking Agency and Immersion: Video Games as a Means of Consciousness-Raising." *Digital Creativity* 12(3): 167–174.
Friedman, Ted. 1999. "*Civilization* and Its Discontents: Simulation, Subjectivity, and Space." Pp. 132–150 in *On a Silver Platter: CD-ROMs and the Promises of a New Technology,* edited by Greg M. Smith. New York: New York University Press.
Furhammer, Leif, and Folke Isaksson. 1971. *Politics and Film.* London: Studio Vista.
Garris, Rosemary, Robert Ahlers, and James E. Driskell. 2002. "Games, Motivation, and Learning: A Research And Practice Model." *Simulation and Gaming* 33(4): 441–467.
Gee, James P. 2003. What Video Games Have to Teach Us About Learning and Literacy. New York: Palgrave Macmillan.
_____. 2004. "Learning about Learning from a Video Game: Rise of Nations." Retrieved October 22, 2004, from http://distlearn.man.ac.uk/download/RiseOfNations.pdf.
Goebbels, Joseph. 1938. "The Radio as the Eighth Great Power." *German Propaganda Archive.* Grand Rapids, MI: Calvin College. (http://www.calvin.edu/academic/cas/gpa/ww2era.htm)
Green, Melanie C., and Timothy C. Brock. 2000. "The Role of Transportation in the Persuasiveness of Public Narratives." *Journal of Personality and Social Psychology* 79(5): 701–721.
Green, Melanie C., Timothy C. Brock, and Geoff F. Kaufman. 2004. "Understanding Media Enjoyment: The Role of Transportation into Narrative Worlds." *Communication Theory* 14(4): 311–327.
Hezbollah. 2003. *Special Force.* Platform: PC.
Infinity Ward. 2003. *Call of Duty.* Platform: PC. Activision.
Iraq Body Count. 2007. Retrieved March 7, 2007 (http://www.iraqbodycount.net/database/).
Iraq Coalition Casualty Count. 2007. Retrieved March 7, 2007 (http://icasualties.org/oif/).
Jowett, Garth, and Victoria O' Donnell. 1986. *Propaganda and Persuasion.* Newbury Park: Sage.
Kuma Reality Games. 2004. *Kuma\War.* Platform: PC. Kuma Reality Games.
Lahti, Martti. 2003. "As We Become Machines: Corporealized Pleasures in Video Games." Pp. 157–170 in *Video Game Theory Reader,* edited by Mark J. P. Wolf and Bernard Perron. London: Routledge.
Lambert, Richard. 1938. *Propaganda.* London: Thomas Nelson and Sons.
Lynch, Jim. 2004. *The Detroit News,* December 1. Retrieved February 10, 2005 (*http://www.detnews.com/2004/technology/0412/01/A01-20800.htm*).
McMahan, Alison. 2003. "Immersion, Engagement and Presence: A Method for Analyzing 3-D Video Games." Pp. 67–86 in *Video Game Theory Reader,* edited by Mark J. P. Wolf and Bernard Perron. London: Routledge.
Murray, Janet. 1997. *Hamlet on the Holodeck: The Future of Narrative in Cyberspace* New York: Free Press Books.
Mussi, Silvano. 2003. "Providing Websites with Capabilities of One-to-One Marketing." *Expert Systems* 20(1): 8–19.
Nachbar, Jack. 2000. "Doing All of Our Thinking for Us: *Casablanca* and the Home Front." *Journal of Popular Film and Television* Retrieved February 10, 2005 (http://www.findarticles.com/p/articles/mi_m0412/is_4_27/ai_59599087).
Nakamura, Jeanne, and Mihaly Csikszentmihalyi. 2002. "The Concept of Flow." Pp. 89–105 in *Handbook of Positive Psychology* edited by C.R. Snyder and S.J. Lopez. New York: Oxford University Press
Namco. 1980. *Pac-man.* Platform: Arcade. Midway.
NewsGaming.Com. 2003. *September 12th.* Platform: Web.
_____. 2004. *Madrid.* Platform: Web.

Nieborg, David B. 2004. "*America's Army*: More Than a Game?" In *Bridging the Gap: Transforming Knowledge into Action through Gaming and Simulation*. München: Ludwig Maximilians University. CD-ROM.

Oblinger, Diana G. 2004. "The Next Generation of Educational Engagement." *Journal of Interactive Media in Education*. Retrieved February 10, 2005 (http://www-jime.open. ac.uk/2004/8/oblinger-2004-8-disc-paper.html).

O'Hagan, Steve. 2004. "Recruitment Hard Drive: The U.S. Army is the World's Biggest Games Developer, Pumping Billions into New Software." *The Guardian (London)*, June 19. Available: LEXIS-NEXIS Academic Universe.

Peabody, Sue. June 17, 1997. "Interview with Chris Crawford: Fifteen years after *Excalibur* and *The Art of Computer Game Design*." Retrieved July 1, 2004 (http://www.vancouver.wsu.edu/fac/peabody/game-book/Chris-talk.html).

Peng, Wei. 2004. "Is Playing Games All Bad? Positive Effects of Computer and Video Games in Learning." Paper presented at 54th Annual meeting of the International Communication Association. New Orleans. May 27–31.

Penny, Simon. 2004. "Representation, Enaction and the Ethics of Simulation." Pp. 73–94 in *First Person: New Media as Story, Performance and Game*, edited by Noah Wardrip-Fruin and Pat Harrigan. Cambridge, MA: MIT Press.

Persuasive Games. 2004. *The Howard Dean for Iowa Game*. Platform: Web.

_____. 2004. *Take Back Illinois*. Platform: Web.

Picard, André. April 9, 2004. "Videogames May Help Surgeons." *Toronto Globe and Mail*. p. A13.

Postman, Neil. 1979. "Propaganda." *Etc.* 36(2): 128.

Rehak, Bob. 2003. "Playing at Being: Psychoanalysis and the Avatar." Pp. 103–128 in *Video Game Theory Reader*, edited by Mark J. P. Wolf and Bernard Perron. London: Routledge.

Ryan, Joan. 2004. "Army's War Game Recruits Kids." *San Francisco Chronicle*, September 23. Retrieved October 25, 2004. Available: LexisNexis Academic Universe.

Sherry, John L. 2004. "Flow and Media Enjoyment." *Communication Theory* 14(4): 328–347.

Singhal, Arvind, Michael J. Cody, Everett M. Rogers, and Miguel Sadibo. 2004. *Entertainment-education and Social Change*. Mahwah, NJ: Erlbaum.

Smith, Greg M. 1999. "Introduction: A Few Words about Interactivity." Pp. 1–34 in *On a Silver Platter: CD-ROMs and the Promises of a New Technology*, edited by Greg M. Smith. New York: New York University Press.

Soussi, Alasdair. 2003. "War Games Becoming All Too Real." *Sunday Herald (Scotland)*. Retrieved February 10, 2005 (http://www.sundayherald.com/print31960).

Sproule, J. Michael. 1996. *Propaganda and Democracy: The American Experience of Media and Mass Persuasion*. Cambridge: Cambridge University Press.

_____. 1998. "Progressive Propaganda Critics and the Magic Bullet Myth." *Critical Studies in Mass Communication* 6: 226.

Sturken, Marita, and Lisa Cartwright. 2001. *Practices of Looking: An Introduction to Visual Culture*. Oxford: Oxford University Press.

Turkle, Sheri. 1995. *Life on the Screen: Identity in the Age of the Internet*. New York: Simon and Schuster.

U.S. Army. 2002. *America's Army*. Platform: PC. Activision.

Valve Software. 2000. *Counter-Strike*. Platform: PC. Vivendi Universal.

Wardynski, Casey E. 2004. "Informing Popular Culture: The *America's Army* Game Concept." Pp. 6–7 in *America's Army PC Game: Vision and Realization*. Monterey, CA: The Wecker Group.

Westcott, Katherine. 2002. "Who Are Hezbollah?" *BBC News*. Retrieved February 10, 2005 (http://news.bbc.co.uk/1/hi/world/middle_east/1908671.stm).

Wolf, Mark J. P., and Bernard Perron. 2003. *The Video Game Theory Reader.* London: Rout-
　ledge.
Worldnet Daily. March 3, 2003. "Hezbollah's New Computer Game." Retrieved Novem-
　ber 3, 2004 (*http://www.worldnetdaily.com/news/article.asp?ARTICLE_ID=31323*)
Yee, Nick. 2003. "Ariadne: Understanding MMORPG Addiction." Retrieved October 1,
　2003 (http://www.nickyee.com/hub/addiction/home.html).

6. Rhetorics of Computer and Video Game Research

Lars Konzack

In recent years video game[1] research has been growing — especially in areas like game-design (Fullerton, Swain and Hoffman 2004; Rollings and Adams 2003; Salen and Zimmerman 2003), psychology (Gee 2004; Gunter 1998; Prensky 2001) and aesthetics (Atkins 2003; Newman 2004; Poole 2000). Researchers are no longer just approaching video games as technology and through market research, but as a new kind of culture with significant meanings in contemporary society. Each approach to the study of video games is constituted by a specific rhetorical frame that shapes how video games are understood and each of these rhetorical frames shape what is (and can be) said about video games. In this sense video game rhetorics limit video game research. However, if we consider the relation between video games and rhetoric from a more optimistic angle, we might instead argue that, indeed, each rhetoric helps create a new school of video game research.

This chapter on rhetorics of video game research is inspired by Brian Sutton-Smith's (1997) analysis of play rhetoric. Eight kinds of influential rhetorics will be identified: 1) technology, 2) economy, 3) anxiety, 4) learning, 5) gender, 6) ideology, 7) narratology, and 8) ludology. These eight influential rhetorics should not be seen as the only possible rhetorics that surround video game research. Rather they show how researchers tend to work within sets of controversial statements. The above mentioned rhetorics were chosen because they are perceived by many in the field as influential and controversial, giving rise to what may sometimes seem as endless discussions

(Newman 2004, McAllister 2004). By recognizing and drawing attention to these rhetorics, researchers may on the one hand become aware of how to deal with them, knowing what to expect from each of these different points of view. On the other hand, researchers may also become encouraged to talk outside these rhetorics in order to present other ways of thinking about video games, thereby providing new insights into the practice of video game research.

It is not my purpose here to take every angle of each rhetoric into account, but rather to sketch out the most salient ways in which each of these kinds of rhetorics function. Consequently, my representation will focus on bringing about a generalized overview. The danger of using this approach of course may be a resulting caricatured presentation, but I hope to suggest many nuanced positions as well. Nevertheless, it may seem as if some of my discussion is indeed a caricature although this is not meant to be. Each rhetoric is complex and space prohibits more than an exploratory survey at this point.

Technology

The technology rhetoric of video game research seems obvious, since video games are dependent upon video game technology such as television and computers. This rhetoric is primarily concerned with technological development of video games in terms of sound, graphics, number of calculations, memory size and overall performance. From the perspective of technology, video games are valued primarily in terms of whether they match the technological development of computer science, i.e., whether they are cutting edge (or even "bleeding edge"). To understand this rhetoric, one has to recognize the explosive development of the computer industry during the last 50 years. Accordingly, there is nothing enigmatic about the technological euphoria we frequently witness among users.

Computer development is mirrored in video games from the black and white *Pong* (Atari 1972) to the colorful *Pac-Man* (Midway Games 1980); from fairly simple 3D-graphics in *Wolfenstein 3D* (id Software 1992) to *Max Payne* (Remedy Entertainment 2001) with full 3D graphics, bullet time effects, and recognizable facial features; and likewise from the 2D strategy game *SimCity* (Maxis Software 1989) by Will Wright to his upcoming 3D creation *Spore* (Maxis Software forthcoming), which provides an opportunity to raise your own evolutionary race. These are just a few games; it does not end there. It looks as if each new video game sets a new standard for what is technologically feasible. Computer technology is constantly increasing its capacity, giving rise to even more technologically advanced video games — especially action games, strategy games, and simulator games. In this sense, computers and video games are supporting one another, pushing technology forward.

The technology rhetoric becomes more apparent when Charles Bernstein (2003: 155) writes in his game analysis, "[m]ore and faster: better graphics and faster action, so fast you transcend the barriers of gravity, so vivid it's realer than real." Ralph Baer — the inventor of video games — primarily focuses on technological development (along with patent rights) in his account of video game history (Baer 2003). Within this rhetoric, it becomes evident that we ought to invent faster and more advanced video games in order to invent even faster and much more advanced video games. If one suggests another approach to video games, s/he is perceived as a Luddite who wants to put technological development at a standstill.

Outside video game research there have been attempts to address how technological rhetoric frames modern or contemporary society. Michel Foucault is especially famous for his effort at showing how technology is in itself a sign system of semiologically constructed power structures (Foucault 1975; Poster 1990). In this sense our culture is a socio-technological construction. Following this line of thought Sherry Turkle (1995: 67) argues that

> Current video games are still recognizably rule-based, although they are far more sophisticated, with more random elements and branching points. Indeed they have become so complicated that an industry of fan magazines, computer bulletin boards, and such institutions as a Nintendo Information Hotline has grown up around them.

What is being said is in fact that the sophistication of video games as such through the use of more advanced technology creates more cultural impact. One often finds within the rhetoric of technology a vision of how video games will be even more advanced in the future due to even more advanced technology. Mark Pesce (2002: 131) puts it this way: "Of all the revolutions kindled by the personal computer, electronic gaming faces the brightest future." These visions of what is to come are frequently based on science fiction like William Gibson's *Neuromancer* (Benedikt 1991, Suzuki 2003). Whether or not these dreams in fact come true remains to be seen.

Economy

The economy rhetoric is concerned with video game sales. The economic importance of video games is the key factor. The games that sell well on the free market are of course labeled as "bestsellers" and, if we choose to view video games from this angle, they are inevitably the best video games. This leaves us with a clear-cut success criterion: either the game sells and is a hit or it is not. Two vignettes exemplify this rhetoric:

> When 1987 began videogame consoles were once again selling at a phenomenal pace. In the six months since the 7800 became available Atari sold 10,000 of them. Atari managed to sell 125,000 Master Systems in only four months [Herman 1999: 123].

> Released well behind schedule, too close to Christmas to have even a chance at the lofty sales goals that EA held, *The Sims Online* proved initially to be a deep disappointment. [...] Electronic Arts' president John Riccitiello said that only 40,000 people had started paying the monthly fee by February 2003. Those numbers didn't appear to get much better. By the end of April 2003 the company had sold just south of 100,000 games. That was frustrating, acknowledged EA executives, who had originally projected that 200,000 paying subscribers would be signed by the end of March 2003 [King and Borland 2003: 242].

This is necessarily a narrow view of video games, and no doubt video games still sell, which means they are an economic success. As long as there are gamers who wants to buy games, there will be made and sold games — accordingly, there will be a focus on the bestselling games.

In the rhetoric of economy the goal is to produce video games and earn a profit by doing so. If one wants to say differently, s/he appears as just another spendthrift or idealistic philanthropist. Advertising in games, like product placement in movies, appears to be part of the natural growth of profit margins; another is advergaming.

> All forms of marketing, including both "advergaming" and product placements represent areas of opportunity since one of the most sought after advertising demographic groups are now the primary gamers. Other services, such as product exchange, will also grow as the online/MMOG market, in particular, grows [Haigh 2005: 3].

Another notable approach within the rhetoric of economy, is Ted Castranova's famous analysis of the world of Norrath in *Everquest* (Verant Interactive 1999) as an economic system. Castronova found that Norrath's gross national product per-capita was $2,266 and provocatively argued that, if Norrath were a country, it would be the seventy-seventh wealthiest in the world, just behind Russia (Castronova 2005). In short, what we encounter in such (economic) rhetorics is a tendency to understand every aspect of gaming from the perspective of worth, value, and profit. This does not necessarily mean that these researchers do not accept or respect creative and aesthetic views of games; rather these views are seen as of minor importance.

Anxiety

The rhetoric of anxiety refers to concern about video game effects on players. Anxiety manifests itself in terms of psychological and social problems.

In the first case, psychologists and moralists are afraid that playing video games too often or too much might harm video game players. This anxiety stems from the fear of video game addiction (Griffith and Davies 2005; Gunter 2005; Loftus and Loftus 1983). Fears about the psychological damage to (especially young) players are not new. Not only do gamers themselves revel in running the knife's edge between fun and "addiction" (e.g., Kelly 2005), but researchers have for some time considered electronically-mediated worlds psychologically dangerous space. The following example shows how anxiety is present in recent on neurological health:

> Not only can excessive video game playing cause behavioral and social changes in a person, but it can also result in neurological changes as well. A recent study utilized positron emission tomography in order to show that levels of the neurotransmitter dopamine increased while playing video games. [...] If future studies demonstrate these patterns, and if they are considered in unison with the psychological and social ramifications of excessive video game playing, it can be concluded that the video game addiction can and does exist. In that case, the answer to the initial question of "Do we need a Video Gamers Anonymous?" is most certainly yes [Sclimme 2002].

The greatest worry, however, appears to be more interpersonal or social, that video games might influence players by producing callous aggressive criminals and vicious, sadistic citizens through violent game content. In particular, "ultra-violent" games like *Carmageddon* (Stainless Software Ltd. 1997), *Doom* (id Software 1993), *Grand Theft Auto* (DMA Design Ltd. 1997), Manhunt (DMA Design Ltd. 2003), *Mortal Kombat* (Midway Games 1993), *Postal* (Running with Scissors 1997), and their sequels have brought about this fear of video games by serving as exemplars of depravity, latched onto by moral entrepreneurs who seek to advance the agendas of conservative organizations.

Historically, we find anxiety toward a range of new media — e.g., movies, comics, radio and television — due to people in modern history perceiving these new media with suspicion (Kirsch 2006). Such anxiety has caused numerous controversial debates and "solutions" to the problem range from censorship to interventions to banning the media from home, work and other private and public spheres. Researchers, oftentimes psychologists, emphasize the negative effects of gaming through their research designs. It is therefore not surprising when they write that their

> results clearly support the hypothesis that exposure to violent video games poses a public-health threat to children and youths, including college-age individuals. Exposure is positively associated with heightened levels of aggression in young adults and children, in experimental and nonexperimental designs, and in males and females [Anderson and Bushman 2001: 358].

Perhaps more controversial is Helga Zepp-LaRouche, founder of the Schiller Institute, and her right-wing politically inclined speech to an audience at the São Paulo State Appellate Criminal Court:

> It is a great honor for me to be able to speak to you on the subject of the New Violence today. Actually, this is a phenomenon, which threatens human civilization in the same way as a new global epidemic, and I have launched an international campaign for the banning and outlawing of this media violence and of media products which glorify violence [Zep-LaRouche 2002].

Some researchers have responded negatively to this kind of critique, suggesting there is no proof of any danger in playing video games (Williams, Hendricks, and Winkler 2006). Barrie Gunter concludes that, "[e]ven with experimental studies, there are problems of validity that derive from the fact that they do not measure 'real aggression' but rather simulated or pretend aggression" (Gunter 1998: 109). Other researchers have taken a more political approach to counter the standard rhetoric of anxiety by highlighting it. Henry Jenkins has tried to support video game as free speech:

> We are afraid of our children. We are afraid of their reactions to digital media. And we suddenly can't avoid either. These factors may shape the policies that emerge from this committee but if they do, they will lead us down the wrong path. Banning black trench coats or abolishing violent video games doesn't get us anywhere. These are the symbols of youth alienation and rage — not the causes [Jenkins 1999].

Jenkins' statement, while sincere, is nonetheless not very convincing, partly because it continues the anxiety rhetoric. Consequently, he implies that there is something to it. Arguing that video games are not dangerous or mostly harmless is very difficult, simply because it is the non-controversial statement. If we want people to listen to us then we need to show them that we are worth listening to — relying on a rhetoric of anxiety helps achieve that goal.

Learning

The learning rhetoric focuses not on the danger of video games but on the possibility that the players may gain a worthwhile learning experience through their use. Playing and learning are said to go hand in hand. The idea is that if children and adolescents spend a lot of time using video games, this activity should at the same time enhance (at least) their physical, mental and social skills and capabilities, which ought to prove useful in an information society in which computers play a central role. Physical skills may be learned and/or improved through the use of action games; mental skills primarily through strategy games; and social skills through role-playing games. Mainly edutainment and edugames like simulators, construction and strategy games, and to some degree adventure games are emphasized as applications encouraging advanced learning potential. Likewise the fact that young people play games via the internet is seen as an opportunity to learn social skills in cyberspace (Gee 2004; Loftus and Loftus 1983; Prensky 2001).

It is often teachers and psychologists who argue in favor of this notion. Seymour Papert has, since the early 1980s, been claiming that children gain a special kind of learning opportunity through use of computers, i.e., constructivist learning (Papert 1980; 1994). Others, as a way of thinking video games and learning as closely related, have extended this idea.

> Seymour Papert is an expert on "hard fun." [...] Papert proposes that we think about computers in education, literally and metaphorically, as if creating a country called, say, Mathland. While Mathland is an odd geopolitical concept, it makes perfect computational sense. In fact, modern computer simulation techniques allow the creation of microworlds in which children can playfully explore very sophisticated principles [Negroponte 1997: 197].

Following this trend, Marc Prensky has stated that, because young adults have grown up with video games, they learn better through the use of digital game-based learning. This way of thinking refers to Seymour Papert as well as media critics like Marshal McLuhan and Neil Postman.

> So, in the end, it is *all these cognitive differences*, resulting from years of "new media socialization" and profoundly affecting and changing the generations' learning styles and abilities, that cry out for new approaches to learning for the Games Generation with a better "fit" [Prensky 2001: 65].

In any case, the aspiration turns out to be the creation of video games in which learning is the most important issue. When the learning rhetoric is introduced it becomes difficult to argue against; after all, nobody in her/his right mind would argue against learning through the use of video games. As such the rhetoric of learning assumes a central role in explaining why video games are good for children, as Gee (2004: 48) notes: "I am convinced that playing video games actively and critically is not 'a waste of time.' And people playing video games are indeed, learning 'content,' albeit usually not the passive content of school-based facts." This rhetoric seems to emphasize the creation of games with a large amount of learning potential. The more children (or players in general) can learn from a game, the better. Accordingly, there is a quest for the perfect digital game-based learning (Prensky 2001).

Gender

The rhetoric of gender might just as well go by the name of the feminist rhetoric, because it is almost entirely within a feminist rhetoric that gender and video games has been discussed. Although there are exceptions (e.g., Schut 2006), "boy" games are largely absent from the rhetoric or scorned in some way.

An early concern among feminist researchers was that more boys than girls play video games (Kinder 1991). The consequence, it seems, is that boys are getting better at using computers because they play with computers more than girls. Hence, it becomes significant for the researchers to get girls into playing video games.

> The problem in the differential attractions to computer games stems from the fact that here, as is often the case, the cultural constructions of gender are not separate from those of power. It is not just that girls seem to like today's computer games less than boys do, but that these differential preferences are associated with different access to technological fields as the children grow older, and this differential access threatens to worsen as technological literacy increasingly becomes a general precondition for employment" [Cassell and Jenkins 1998: 11].

In this way, the gender rhetoric consists almost entirely of the argument that we ought to invent and produce more girl games. This is known as the pink games approach to girl gaming in which games are designed to please or reflect female play drives.

> A final concern is whether we need games designed specifically for girls versus games for gamers, that is, androgynous games. Perhaps in an ideal world girls would be included in the digital revolution through the development of games that appeal equally to boys and girls. In reality, however, most games have attracted at least three boys for every girl. Therefore games targeted specifically towards girls may be necessary to reach a mass audience for girls [Subrahmanyam and Greenfield 1998: 66].

This approach to girl gaming is not a question on how to make girls have fun while playing video games, but to raise and educate these girls for them to become an integral part of the computerized information society, e.g., grow up to become a fashion designer due to having played *Barbie Fashion Designer* (Digital Domain 1996; Subrahmanyam and Greenfield 1998). In this sense it is very closely related to the rhetoric of learning, as we shall see later.

Another way to approach this gender rhetoric is to examine the female role model and possibilities for female identification in video games. Implicit in much gender research are the ideas that girls have trouble identifying with male characters in video games and that female characters in video games are

presented in narrow, highly gendered ways (suggesting girls have trouble identifying with these kinds of characters too).

> Content analysis has highlighted a general lack of female game characters, and
> the sexualized and stereotypical representation of those included female charac-
> ters. [...] This contributes to the perception that computer games embody mas-
> culine interest and activities, making computer games at best unappealing, or at
> worst offensive, to females [Bryce and Rutter 2002: 246].

One might argue that male characters are stereotypically portrayed as well,
but that is not normally (if ever) part of the gender rhetorics on video games.
Hence, Lara Croft as female role model has been scrutinized in numerous
analyses of *Tomb Raider* (Core Design Ltd. 1996) via discussions of whether
or not girls ought to identify with this gun-slinging, fitness character (Kennedy 2002; Mikula 2004; Richard and Zaremba 2005). Consequently, this
criticism debates whether or not girls ought to play action games. The gender rhetoric suggests that most games are designed for boys, yet girls too may
be able to squeeze them into their own gendered culture. Hence, as a reaction to the *pink games* movement, the so-called *game grrlz* entered the scene
with an attitude.

> Aliza Sherman: Looking at the games on today's market for girl, I get a little
> concerned. Where are the games that teach competitiveness? Assertiveness? And
> that take advantage of a female's natural hand-eye coordination? I think that as a
> society, we have big taboos against strong women and a greater fear of women as
> warriors [Jenkins 1998: 335].

The rhetoric of gender has mostly come from a feminist point of view in
which girl gaming appears victimized. Yet, it looks like this accustomed way
of thinking gendered gaming has at least been challenged by the game grrlz.

Ideology

The latest controversial video game rhetoric is the rhetoric of ideology.
It is based on the belief that video games might be used as propaganda and
dissemination of political ideology. On one hand it shows anxiety regarding
the use of propaganda and as such it appears to be closely related to the rhetoric of anxiety, but on the other hand the rhetoric sometimes shows great
expectations towards political awareness and the possibilities of enlightenment
through the use of video games.

Gonzalo Frasca (2001) reflects this ambiguity: "While the only objec-
tion that I would make to the game is its blatant consumerism, this is not
The Sims' most important ideological claim. The Sims' most powerful statement is that human life, both on its personal and social levels, can be simu-

lated." Aaron Delwiche (in this volume) demonstrates how Frasca has tried to come up with political counterstrategies in short games toward propaganda games like *America's Army* (U.S. Army 2001) and Kuma\War (Kuma Reality Games 2004). In addition, Helene Madsen and Troels Degn Johansson (2002) have shown how satire may be constructed through short computer games.

Anna Everett (2005) centers her attention to how video games present racist ideologies implicitly in most games, yet explicitly in a game such as *Ethnic Cleansing* (Resistance Records 2002), thereby highlighting the neo-colonialist, Eurocentrist tendencies underlying game production (Everett 2005; see also Montes in this volume). On a different level Alexander R. Galloway (2004) makes an effort to explain the potential for social realism in video games, saying that "[t]o find social realism in gaming one must follow the tell-tail traits of social critique and through them uncover the beginnings of a realist gaming aesthetic."

What is at stake here is a difference between on the one hand problematic and to some extent illegitimate propaganda games, and on the other hand what is presented as important and legitimate counterstrategies in the ideological struggles that are played out in political video games. The dilemma with this strategy, however, is that what from one point of view is seen as a legitimate political game stressing the problems of today's world may, from another point of view, be seen as some kind of illegitimate propaganda tool.

Narratology

In the rhetoric of narratology — or the storytelling rhetoric — we find an aesthetic understanding of video games in which researchers study how games might live up to the demands and requirements of narratives in literature and movies. Usually literary and film theorists are involved as representatives for this kind of rhetoric. Looking for narratives, the focal point of attention has explicitly been narrative-based games like adventure and role-playing games (Aarseth 1997).

There seems to be an expectation that, when the media has matured, exciting interactive narratives will become the norm. This implies that, if video games are narrative, they are art as well. Janet Murray (1997: 145) articulates this notion by writing that "the violence and simplistic story structure of computer skill games are therefore a good place to examine the possibilities for building upon the intrinsic symbolic content of gaming to make more expressive forms." Likewise, Barry Atkins (2003: 24) states: "One day, perhaps, the computer game will even produce its *À la Recherche du Temps Perdu* or *Ulysses*, its *Casablanca* or its *Citizen Kane*."

At one extreme, this rhetoric all games to be narrative games. Even the game *Tetris* (Pajitnov and Pavlovsky 1985) is a narrative; there exist only games that in varying degrees live up to the ideal of a narrative format. Murray (1997: 143–144) expresses this point of view when declaring that "even a game with no verbal content, like Tetris, the wildly popular and powerfully absorbing computer game of the early 1990s, has clear dramatic content."

The rhetoric of narratology stems from the hypertext rhetoric in the early 1990s in which writers conceived that, when computers were common place and fast enough, the users of computers would like to read non-linear hypertext narratives (Aarseth 1997; Bolter 1991; Landow 1992). The most important inspiration to this rhetoric may in fact be Brenda Laurel, who tried to redefine the computer as a narrative medium back in the 1980s when computers were foremost conceived as a field belonging to the natural sciences, certainly not the humanities. By suggesting a narratological approach to computers based on Aristotle, she succeeded in changing this condition (Laurel 1986; 1991). To summarize, this rhetoric states that videogames ought to be analyzed from a narratological point of view in which every single game is seen as a would-be-narrative. The more these game narratives resemble film or book narratives, the better game it is.

Ludology

The rhetoric of ludology or the game rhetoric arose as a response to the rhetoric of narratology, and in this sense it was a reaction to the one-dimensional notion that video-games-as-narrative was the final goal of video game development. As Markku Eslinen (2001) concludes:

> ... both the number of game elements and the relations between them can be different in specific ways that are typical of (computer) games and only of them, and don't have to respect any conventions and traditional boundaries inherited from oral or written narratives, drama, theatre or films.

In this rhetoric the center of attention is the gameplay and game mechanics of video games. As a result, the ambition is to conceive a better understanding of game and play, i.e., to conceive a ludology (Frasca 2003a; Eskelinen 2004). Ludologists have several time pointed to *Tetris* (1985) as the prime example of a video game without any narrative, thereby suggesting games do not need to have any narratives at all (Aarseth 2004; Eskelinen 2001; Juul 2005). Here, the notion is that ludology is seen as an alternative to narratology, stating that game fictions may have a game structure rather than a narrative structure, or if there is a narrative structure, it must be perceived as subordinate to the game structure. As Espen Aarseth (2004: 51) puts it: "Adventure games seldom, if at all, contain good stories." Apart from all this ludological rhetoric against a narratological one, the ludic perspective has actually generated a new way of understanding video games (e.g., Costikyan 2002; Juul 2005; Salen and Zimmerman 2003).

Eight Kinds of Rhetoric

Based on the above (necessarily brief) descriptions, we are able to generate a table that gives us an overview of these influential and controversial rhetorics (see Table 7.1, page 122). The table is divided into General Rhetoric, Representative, Main Question, Game Type, and Common Conclusion.

General Rhetoric refers simply to the name I have given to each of these eight rhetorics. The "representatives" are those professions that often become attracted to the rhetoric in question (although this is certainly a rule of thumb rather than a precise indication). The Main Question is the question which each rhetoric asks and consequently focuses its attention on answering. The Game Type refers to those genres on which each rhetoric tends to focus, including any positive or negative bias expressed in the rhetoric. Finally, Common Conclusion contains the most frequent answer to the Main Question.

Grouping Game Rhetorics

In order to form a general view of the above mentioned eight different rhetorics, we may divide them further into three categories: 1) the product-oriented rhetorics, 2) the socio-culturally oriented rhetorics, and 3) the aesthetically oriented rhetorics. Technology and Economy are both product-oriented rhetorics, since they are both oriented toward the video game as a product. Anxiety, Learning, Gender and Ideology are all socio-cultural rhetorics that focus on players and how they are affected socially and culturally by the video games. Finally, Narratology and Ludology are both aesthetically-oriented rhetorics, given that they both focus on the form and expression of the video game. These categories are not mutually exclusive and, in fact, it is possible to see how all of the rhetorics may in fact blend, creating friends and enemies in the process. The different rhetorics are never static, because the representatives of each are trying to figure out new ways of comprehending video games and video game culture. Therefore the interesting matter becomes how all of these different rhetorics relate to one another at the present moment in the academic study of video games.

General Rhetoric	Representatives	Main Question	Game Type Positive (+) or negative (-)	Common Conclusion
Technology	Engineers Programmers	How may we improve video games technologically?	State of the art (+)	We must develop technologically improved video games
Economy	Sales people Economists	How may we benefit financially from video games?	Bestsellers (+) Advergames (+)	We must sell more video games and advertise more in video games
Anxiety	Psychologists* Moralists	Are video games dangerous?	Violent action games (-) War games (-)	We must censor or ban video games
Learning	Psychologists* Teachers	Is it possible to learn from playing video games?	Edugames (+) Edutainment (+)	We must develop video games with learning opportunities
Gender	Feminists Gender researchers	Is there a difference between boys and girls using video games?	Boy games (-) Girl games (+)	We must develop games for girls
Ideology	Sociologists Media theorists	How do video games work as propaganda?	Propaganda games (-) Political games (+)	We must be aware of the political implications of video games
Narratology	Literature and media theorists	How do video games work as narratives?	Adventure games (+) RPG (+)	We must analyze video games as narratives
Ludology	Game and interactive media researchers	How do video games work as play and games?	Action games (+) Simulators (+) Strategy games (+)	We must analyze video games as gameplay

*The psychologists arguing within the rhetorics of anxiety and the psychologists arguing within the rhetorics of learning are rarely the same psychologists — on the contrary they are usually seen in opposition to one another.

Table 7.1

Rhetorical Interplay

The two product-oriented rhetorics play well together. Continuously, technology is improved, creating faster games with better graphics to be sold on what seems to be a growing global market. Games that turn into bestsellers become guides on how new video games should be developed. In this perspective video games are an advanced, active enterprise. Product-oriented rhetorics may accordingly be inscribed with the notion of competing, capitalist and technological progressive development of video game history (Finn 2002; Herman 1997; Malliet and de Meyer 2005).

The four socio-culturally oriented rhetorics, on the other hand, do not engage in a productive interplay of collaboration. Far from it. The rhetorics of anxiety and learning have commonly been seen as opposites, contrasting one another as if they were dichotomous. The argument implicit in the rhetoric of learning goes like this: video games are not dangerous to children because children may learn while playing.

> The meaning of playing *Counter-Strike* is not merely embodied in the graphics or even the violent game play, but in the social mediations that go on between players through their talk with each other and by their performance within the game. Participants, then, actively create the meaning of the game through their virtual talk and behavior borrowing heavily from popular and youth culture representations. Players learn rules of social comportment that reproduce codes of behavior and established standards of conduct, while also safely experimenting with the violation of these codes [Boria, Breidenbach and Wright 2002].

This is to some extent established on the false assumption that learning negates any dangerous effects of video games. In response the rhetoric of anxiety implicates violent games as media through which children learn about, and learn to accept, violence as a part of everyday life. As David Grossman (2001: 6) puts it: "Every time a child plays an interactive video game, he is learning the exact same conditioned reflex skills as a soldier or police officer in training."

The rhetoric of gender connects the rhetorics of anxiety and learning, stressing the difference between girl games and boy games. The gender rhetoric implies that boy games are violent while girl games contain learning potential. One could argue that the gender rhetoric further claims that boy games are subversive, while girl games are just right. Subrahmanyam and Greenfield (1998) assert as much when they write that:

> Research on children's play suggests that boy's liking for violent games is paralleled by the aggressive nature of their play. [...] However given that girls' avowed dislike for aggression and their preference for cooperation over competition, we speculate that in order to appeal to girls, the mystery/action component in girls' games must be nonviolent and must allow players to solve problems or mysteries and arrive at solutions by relating to and cooperating with others [pp. 51, 55].

In this way, the rhetoric of gender emphasizes educational girl games that counter boy games often known to have violent content. Thus, the rhetoric of gender apparently encapsulates both the rhetorics of anxiety and learning. Even so, this enforced alliance may of course be challenged since neither the rhetoric of anxiety nor the rhetoric of learning is fully satisfied within such an arrangement.

There is yet a fourth rhetoric meddling among the socio-cultural approaches, the rhetoric of ideology. Here one finds rhetorical video game ideology regarding learning, anxiety, and gender. Simon Penny (2004: 82), discussing serious play and interactive media politics, ends up referring to all of these rhetorics:

> There is a possibility that [serious play] might be expressed in situations which resemble the visual context of emotional tenor of the gameplay. Which is to say, games and interactive media in general can be powerful inculcators of behaviors, and these learned behaviors can be expressed outside the realm of the game. And if this is true, then it is hard to escape the conclusion that an interactive work might encourage misogynistic violence or that first person shooters actively contribute to an increase in gun violence among kids.

Finally, the two aesthetic oriented rhetorics — narratology and ludology — are divided against one another. Naturally, researchers within each rhetorical field maintain that video game aesthetics must be grasped through the principles they espouse. Narratologists have not been pleased with the content of existing video games and suggest that more effort ought to be spent on creating nicely structured narratives (Crawford 2003). Meanwhile, ludologists find that the narrative gets in the way of the game — cut scenes, for example, have been especially admonished (Eskelinen 2001). That is why Rune Klevjer (2002) felt the urge to defend cut scenes in video games; suggesting cut scenes potentially contain an exceptional aesthetic mode of expression.

It seems as if a stalemate has taken place between the two aesthetically oriented rhetorics, though there have been attempts at mediating between these two rhetorics, calling for some kind of compromise that will, with a bit of luck, satisfy both ludologists and narratologists (Frasca 2003b; Jenkins 2004). Unfortunately, each attempt usually ends up stating that one part in the conflict is just a bit more correct than the other, thereby ensuring continued upheaval in this debate.

Other Rhetorical Interplay

There are also controversies cutting across the three discursive orientations, giving rise to plenty of opportunities to construct alliances and enemies within the community of game researchers. It would, however, be impossible to examine all such possible interplays. Still, here are a few examples of how these rhetorical exploitations take place.

Marsha Kinder (1991) operated within the rhetorics of anxiety and economy in order to establish a feminist critique of boy gaming based on a Freudian analysis. Her work conceived of the joystick as a symbolic phallus which, when taken away from a boy, symbolized Freud's Oedipal castration. She remarks: "[t]he marketing of video games seems to be geared primarily to those with, potentially, the most fear of castration" (p. 101). Not only does she belittle boy gaming, she makes the economy of video games into an enemy of feminism as well.

Another way to deal with the rhetoric of economy and the rhetoric of gender comes from Sheri Graner Ray (2004). In order to promote girl gaming, she implied there was a new overlooked market, suggesting an opportunity for investment, by stating:

> ... the more economic reason is that the game industry must expand to other markets if it wishes to sustain growth. There are only so many males age 13–25 in the world at any given time. If no other audiences are farmed, then the game industry will outgrow its market, resulting in loss of revenue and ultimately a contraction of the industry [p. 183].

In this prospect, the rhetorics of gender and economy instead become a coalition, expectantly saving the video game industry from a collapse that would occur if only boys played games.

Perhaps the most speculative exercise of rhetoric interplay is Gonzalo Frasca's (2003a) way of exploiting the conflict between narratologists and ludologists as a stepping-stone to inaugurate his own political rhetoric of ideological critique. At first it just seems as if Frasca wants to point to the fact that indeed games need to be analyzed as game simulations, but later it becomes evident that there is much more at stake:

> I previously described stories as being heavily associated with the concept of fate. This idea is the backbone behind the Marxist drama school, developed by Bertolt Brecht and more recently by Augusto Boal. Marxists argue that Aristotelian drama and storytelling neutralize social change because they represent reality as an inexorable progression of incidents without room for alteration. Boal's answer to this problem can be found in his corpus of drama techniques, The Theatre of the Opressed, which combines theatre in order to encourage critical debate over social, political, and personal issues" [p. 228].

Here, ludology is suddenly translated into a Marxist ideology, and as a result ludologists ought to be seen as a sub-group of Marxist ideologists. By suggesting this, Frasca rhetorically takes the ludologist hostage to his own political views. All of these examples show that one needs to read video game research very carefully. Otherwise one risks being unintentionally caught up in rhetorical interplays that may serve or establish unknown agendas, regardless of the researcher's own wishes.

End Game?

Do only eight rhetorics exist, one might ask? The answer is most definitely, "No!" In this chapter I have identified eight influential and controversial video game rhetorics, but there are certainly many other rhetorical strategies at play in game studies. New rhetorics may come and go, but only few will have the potential to become controversial rhetorics, gaining plenty of supporters and critics. Another question might be whether or not all of these rhetorics are equally valuable. This is a very relevant question. To answer this correctly one must try to uncover the truth-value of each of these rhetorics for her/himself. Each rhetoric needs to be judged according to not just how fellow representatives perceive them, but whether they live up to our notion of reality.

Notes

1. For the purpose of this chapter I shall not distinguish between video games and computer games. I have used the term "video game" throughout the article for consistency-except of course in quotations, but this term "video game" might as well be replaced with the term "computer game."

References

Aarseth, Espen. 1997. *Cybertext: Perspectives on Ergodic Literature.* Baltimore, MD: The John Hopkins University Press.

_____. 2004. "Genre Trouble: Narrativism and the Art of Simulation." Pp. 45–55 in *First Person: New Media as Story, Performance, and Game*, edited by N. Wardrip-Fruin and P. Harrigan. Massachusetts, MA: MIT Press.

Adams, Ernest, and Andrew Rollings. 2003. *Andrew Rollings and Ernest Adams on Game Design.* Indianapolis, IN: New Riders Publishing.

Anderson, Craig A., and Brad J. Bushman. 2001. "Effects of Violent Video Games on Aggressive behavior, Aggressive Cognition, Aggressive Affect, Physiological Arousing, and Prosocial Behavior: A Meta-Analytic Review of the Scientific Literature." *Psychological Science* 12(5): 353–359.

Atari. 1972. *Pong.* Platform: Arcade.

Atkins, Barry. 2003. *More than a game: the computer game as fictional form.* Manchester, UK: Manchester University Press.

Baer, Ralph. 2003. "Foreword" in *The Medium of the Video Game*, edited by M. J. P. Wolf Austin: TX: University of Texas Press.

Benedikt, Michael. 1991. *Cyberspace: First Steps.* Massachusetts, MA: MIT Press.

Bernstein, Charles. 2003. "Play it again Pac-Man" in *The Medium of the Video Game*, edited by M. J. P. Wolf Austin: TX: University of Texas Press.

Bolter, Jay D. 1991. *Writing Space: The Computer, Hypertext, and the History of Writing.* Hillsdale, NJ: Lawrence Erlbaum Associates.

Boria, Eric, Paul Breidenbach and Talmadge Wright. 2002. "Creative Player Actions in FPS Online Video Games: Playing Counter-Strike." *Game Studies* 2(2). Retrieved January 18, 2006. (http://www.gamestudies.org/0202/wright/)

Borland, John, and Brad King. 2003. *Dungeons and Dreamers: The Rise of Computer Game Culture from Geek to Chic.* Emeryville: CA, McGraw-Hill.
Bryce, Jo, and Jason Rutter. 2002. "Killing Like a Girl: Gendered Gaming and Girl Gamers' Visibility." Pp. 243–256 in *Computer Games and Digital Cultures: Conference Proceedings,* edited by F. Mäyrä. Tampere, Finland: Tampere University Press.
Crawford, Chris. 2003. "Interactive Storytelling." Pp. 259–274 in *The Video Game Theory Reader,* edited by M. J. P. Wolf. London, UK: Routledge.
Cassell, Justine, and Henry Jenkins. 1998. "Chess for Girls? Feminism and Computer Games." Pp. 2–45 in *From Barbie to Mortal Kombat: Gender and Computer Games,* edited by Cassell and Jenkins. Massachusetts, MA: MIT Press.
Castronova, Edward. 2005. *Synthetic Worlds: The Business and Culture of Online Games.* Chicago, CA: University of Chicago Press.
Core Design Ltd. 1996. *Tomb Raider.* Platform: PC. Eidos Inc.
Costikyan, Greg. 2002. "I Have No Words and I Must Design." Pp. 9–34 in *Computer Games and Digital Cultures: Conference Proceedings,* edited by F. Mäyrä. Tampere, Finland: Tampere University Press.
Digital Domain. 1996. *Barbie Fashion Designer.* Platform: PC. Mattel Media.
DMA Design Ltd. 1997. *Grand Theft Auto.* Platform: PC. BMG Interactive.
_____. 2003. *Manhunt* (2003). Platform: PC. Rockstar Games Inc.
Eskelinen, Markku. 2001. "The Gaming Situation." *Game Studies* 1(1). Retrieved January 18, 2006. (http://www.gamestudies.org/0101/eskelinen/)
Everett, Anna. 2005. "Serious Play: Playing with Race in Contemporary Gaming Culture." Pp. 311–326 in *Handbook of Computer Game Studies,* edited by J. Raessens and J. Goldstein. Massachusetts, MA: MIT Press.
Finn, Mark. 2002. "Console Games in the Age of Convergence." Pp. 45–58 in *Computer Games and Digital Cultures: Conference Proceedings,* edited by F. Mäyrä. Tampere, Finland: Tampere University Press.
Foucault, Michel. 1975. *Surveiller et punir,* Paris, France: Gallimard.
Frasca, Gonzalo. 2001. "The Sims: Grandmothers are cooler than trolls by Gonzalo Frasca" in *Gamestudies* 1(1). Retrieved January 19, 2006. (http://www.gamestudies.org/0101/frasca/)
_____. 2003a. "Simulation versus Narrative: Introduction to Ludology." Pp. 221–236 in *The Video Game Theory Reader,* edited by M. J. P. Wolf. London, UK: Routledge
_____. 2003b. "Ludologists Love Stories, Too: Notes from a Debate That Never Took Place." Pp. 92–99 in *Level Up, Digital Games Research Association (DiGRA) Conference Proceedings,* edited by M. Copier and J. Raessens. Utrecht, Holland: Utrecht University.
Fullerton, Tracy, Christopher Swain and Steven Hoffman. 2004. *Game Design Workshop: Designing, Prototyping, and Playtesting.* San Francisco, CA: CMP Books.
Galloway, Alexander R. 2004. "Social Realism in Gaming." *Game Studies* 4(1). Retrieved January 19, 2006. (http://www.gamestudies.org/0401/galloway/)
Gee, James P. 2004. *What Video Games Have to Teach Us About Learning and Literacy.* New York, NY: Palgrave Macmillan.
Griffith, Mark, and Mark N. O. Davies. 2005. "Does Video Game Addiction Exist?" Pp. 359–372 in *Handbook of Computer Game Studies,* edited by J. Raessens and J. Goldstein. Massachusetts, MA: MIT Press.
Grossman, Dave. 2001. "Trained to Kill." *Professoren-forum-Journal* 2(2). Retrieved January 19, 2006. (http://www.professorenforum.de/volumes/v02n02/artikel1/gross.pdf)
Gunter, Barrie. 1998. *The Effects of Video Games on Children: The Myth Unmasked.* Sheffield, UK: Sheffield Academy Press.
_____. 2005. "Psychological Effects of Video Games." Pp. 145–160 in *Handbook of Computer Game Studies,* edited by J. Raessens and J. Goldstein. Massachusetts, MA: MIT Press.

Haigh, Charles. 2005. *The Video Game Industry: An Industry Analysis from a VC Perspective*. Retrieved January 19, 2006. (http://mba.tuck.dartmouth.edu/digital/Programs/MBAFellowsProgramArchive/05_shah.pdf)

Herman, Leonard. 1997. *Phoenix: The Fall and Rise of Videogames, 2nd ed.* Kearney, NE: Rolenta Press

id Software. 1992. *Wolfenstein 3D*. Platform: PC. Apogee Software Ltd.

_____. 1993. *Doom*. Platform: PC. Id software Inc.

Jenkins, Henry. 1998. "Voices from the Combat Zone: Game Grrlz Talk Back." Pp. 328–341 in From *Barbie to Mortal Kombat: Gender and Computer Games*, edited by J. Cassell and H. Jenkins. Massachusetts, MA: MIT Press.

_____. 1999. *Professor Jenkins Goes to Washington*. Retrieved January 20, 2006. (http://web.mit.edu/cms/People/henry3/profjenkins.html)

_____. 2004. "Game Design as Narrative Architecture." Pp. 117–130 in *First Person: New Media as Story, Performance, and Game*, edited by N. Wardrip-Fruin and P. Harrigan. Massachusetts, MA: MIT Press.

Johansson, Troels Degn, and Helene Madsen. 2002. "Gameplay Rhetoric: A Study of the Construction of Satirical and Associational Meanings in Short Computer Games for the WWW." Pp. 73–88 in *Computer Games and Digital Cultures: Conference Proceedings*, edited by F. Mäyrä. Tampere, Finland: Tampere University Press.

Juul, Jesper. 2005. *Half-Real: Video Games between Real Rules and Fictional Worlds*. Massachusetts, MA: MIT Press.

Kelly, R. V. 2005. *Massively Multiplayer Online Role-Playing Games: The People, the Addiction and the Playing Experience*. Jefferson, NC: McFarland.

Kennedy, Helen W. 2002. "Lara Croft: Feminist Icon or Cyberbimbo? On the Limits of Textual Analysis." *Gamestudies* 2(2). Retrieved January 23, 2006. (http://www.gamestudies.org/0202/kennedy/)

Kinder, Marsha. 1991. *Playing with Power in Movies, Television and Video Games*. Los Angeles, CA: University of California Press.

Kirsch, Steven J. 2006. *Children, Adolescents, and Media Violence: A Critical Look at the Research*. London, UK: Sage Publishing.

Klevjer, Rune. 2002. "In Defence of Cutscenes." Pp. 191–203 in *Computer Games and Digital Cultures: Conference Proceedings*, edited by F. Mäyrä. Tampere, Finland: Tampere University Press.

Kuma Reality Games. 2004. *Kuma\War*. Platform: PC. Kuma Reality Games.

Landow, George P. 1992 *Hypertext: The Convergence of Contemporary Critical Theory and Technology*. Baltimore, MD: The John Hopkins University Press.

Laurel, Brenda Kay. 1986. "Interface as Mimesis." Pp. 67–85 in *User Centered System Design: New Perspectives on Human-Computer Interaction*, edited by D. A. Norman and S. W. Draper. Hillsdale, NJ: Lawrence Erlbaum Associates.

_____. 1991. *Computer as Theatre*. New York, NY: Addison-Wesley Publishing

Loftus, Geoffrey, and Elizabeth Loftus. 1983. *Mind at Play: The Psychology of Video Games*. New York, NY: Basic Books.

Malliet, Steven, and Gust de Meyer. 2005. "The History of the Video Game." Pp. 23–46 in *Handbook of Computer Game Studies*, edited by J. Raessens and J. Goldstein. Massachusetts, MA: MIT Press.

Maxis Software. 1989. *SimCity*. Platform: PC. Brøderbund Software.

_____. Forthcoming. *Spore*. Electronic Arts Inc.

McAllister, Ken S. 2004. *Game Work: Language, Power, and Computer Game Culture*. Tuscaloosa, AL: The University of Alabama Press.

Midway Games. 1980. *Pac-Man*. Platform: Arcade.

_____. 1993. *Mortal Kombat*. Platform: Amiga. Acclaim Entertainment Inc.

Mikula, Maja. 2004. "Lara Croft, Between a Feminist Icon and a Male Fantasy." Pp.

57–69 in *Femme Fatalities: Representation of Strong Women in Media*, edited by R. Schubart and A. Gelsvik. Gothenburg, Sweden: Nordicom.

Murray, Janet H. 1997. *Hamlet on the Holodeck: The Future of Narrative in Cyberspace.* Massachusetts, MA: MIT Press.

Negroponte, Nicholas. 1995. *Being Digital.* New York, NY: Vintage Books

Newman, James. 2004. *Videogames.* London, UK: Routledge.

Pajitnov, Alexander, and Dmitriy Pavlovsky.1985. *Tetris.* Platform: Arcade

Papert, Seymour. 1980. *Mindstorms: Children, Computers and Powerful Ideas.* New York, NY: Harvester Wheatsheaf.

_____. 1994. *The Children's Machine: Rethinking School in the Age of the Computer.* New York, NY: Harvester Wheatsheaf.

Penny, Simon. 2004. "Representation, Enaction, and the Ethics of Simulation." Pp. 71–84 in *First Person: New Media as Story, Performance, and Game*, edited by N. Wardrip-Fruin and P. Harrigan. Massachusetts, MA: MIT Press.

Pesce, Mark. 2002. "Head Games: The Future of Play." Pp. 130–137 in *Game On: The History and Culture of Videogames*, edited by L. King. London, UK: Laurence King.

Poole, Steven. 2000. *Trigger Happy: Videogames and the Entertainment Revolution.* London, UK: Fourth Estate Limited.

Poster, Mark. 1990. *The Mode of Information: Poststructuralism and Social Context.* Cambridge, UK: Polity Press.

Prensky, Marc. 2001. *Digital Game-Based Learning.* New York, NY: McGraw-Hill

Ray, Sheri G. 2004. *Gender Inclusive Game Design: Expanding the Market.* Hingham, MA: Charles River Media.

Remedy Entertainment. 2001. *Max Payne.* Platform: PC. Rockstar Games Inc.

Resistance Records. 2002. *Ethnic Cleansing.* Platform: PC. Genesis3D.

Richard, Birgit, and Jutta Zaremba. 2005. "Gaming with Grrls: Looking for Sheroes in Computer Games." Pp. 283–300 in *Handbook of Computer Game Studies*, edited by J. Raessens and J. Goldstein. Massachusetts, MA: MIT Press.

Running with Scissors. 1997. *Postal.* Platform: PC. Ripcord Games.

Salen, Katie, and Eric Zimmerman. 2003. *Rules of Play: Game Design Fundamentals.* Massachusetts, MA: MIT Press.

Schlimme, Mary. 2002. *Video Game Addiction: Do we need a Video Gamers Anonymous? Neurology and Behaviour 2.* Retrieved January 23, 2006. (http://serendip.brynmawr.edu/bb/neuro/neuro02/web2/mschlimme.html)

Schut, Kevin. 2006. "Desktop Conquistadors: Negotiating American Manhood in the Digital Fantasy Role-Playing Game." Pp. 100–119 in J. Patrick Williams, Sean Q. Hendricks, and W. Keith Winkler (eds.). *Gaming as Culture: Essays in Reality, Identity and Experience in Fantasy Games.* Jefferson, NC: McFarland.

Sony Online Entertainment. 1999. *Everquest.* Platform: PC. 989 Studios.

Stainless Software Ltd. 1997. *Carmageddon.* Platform: PC. Interplay Entertainment Corp./ SCi Games Ltd.

Sutton-Smith, Brian. 1997. *Ambiguity of Play.* Cambridge, MA: Harvard University Press.

Subrahmanyam, Kaveri, and Patricia Greenfield, 1998. "Computer Games for Girls: What Makes Them Play?" Pp. 46–71 in From *Barbie to Mortal Kombat: Gender and Computer Games*, edited by J. Cassell and H. Jenkins. Massachusetts, MA: MIT Press.

Suzuki, Shigeru. 2003. "Cyborg Agency in the Digital Age: On William Gibson's Neuromancer." *Lore: Rhetoric, Writing, Culture* 3(1). Retrieved January 24, 2006. (http://www-rohan.sdsu.edu/dept/drwswebb/lore/lore.html)

Turkle, Sherry. 1984. *The Second Self: Computers and the Human Spirit.* New York, NY: Simon and Schuster.

_____. 1995. *Life on the Screen: Identity in the Age of the Internet.* New York, NY: Simon and Schuster.

U.S. Army. 2001. *America's Army*. Platform: PC. Online.

Williams, J. Patrick, Sean Q. Hendricks, and W. Keith Winkler. 2006. "Fantasy Games, Gaming Cultures and Social Life." Pp. 1–18 in J. Patrick Williams, Sean Q. Hendricks, and W. Keith Winkler (eds.) *Gaming as Culture: Essays in Reality, Identity and Experience in Fantasy Games*. Jefferson, NC: McFarland.

Zepp-LaRouche, Helga. 2002. *Stop the New Violence: Create a New Renaissance*. Retrieved January 24, 2006. (http://www.schillerinstitute.org/lar_related/2002/brazil/hzl_new_viol.html)

7. From Margin to Center: Biographies of Technicity and the Construction of Hegemonic Games Culture

Jonathan Dovey and Helen W. Kennedy

> *In our reviews over the years we've always talked about how gamers are the early adopters of technology in the home and we've discussed ways to better serve them.*
> Bill Gates, cited in Asakura (2000: 20).

Computer games culture is diverse, differentiated and subject to processes of flux, change and development; yet for all this diversity we have seen the emergence of a particular hegemonic version of game culture complete with its own origin myths, founding fathers and idealized or preferred producers and consumers. Games culture is also a critical site where discourses around technology, technological innovation and technological competence converge with dominant conceptions of gender and race. In this chapter we will trace the development of contemporary games culture through a number of different case studies. These case studies draw together material taken from both the center and the margin of a hegemonic version of the history of the development of game culture and of game culture production.

The chapter is informed and underpinned by interview material drawn from a case study of Pivotal Games made in December 2003. Pivotal Games

131

is a mid-sized development studio based between Bristol and Bath in the West of England. It employs seventy people and produces the *Conflict Desert Storm* tactical squad based military shooter games. We interviewed a cross section of ten development staff, from quality assurance game testers, through artists and programmers, to the managing director, in order to build a picture of the culture and process of game production. In addition, we interviewed female participants in game culture in order to explore potentially counter-hegemonic discourses of game design. Lastly, we examine some apparent absences and blindspots that exist in popular texts surrounding game culture — texts which regularly offer up forceful and compelling histories of key figures in the industry.

Our primary conceptual development in this chapter for the study of games is that of "technicity." We deploy the concept in order to interrogate the ways in which technological competence becomes raced and gendered as part of a particular idealized game producer subjectivity. As part of this interrogation, we discuss two dominant tropes — the hacker and the cyborg — which have emerged as preferred subjectivities in the narratives of technoculture in general and how each is re-invoked in popular narratives of game culture development. We also make use of the work of cultural theorist Pierre Bourdieu and his notions of "taste cultures," "symbolic production" and "cultural capital" in order to explore the hegemonic forces at work in the shift in subjectivities from gamer enthusiast (a largely marginal identity within mainstream culture) to "founding fathers" (key figures who have become the accepted and mythologized originators of a dominant version of game culture). Bourdieu's work enables us to explore to dialectic processes simultaneously. First, how it is that these ideal and idealized subjects — those with the greatest technicity, i.e., the "early adopters" and the "early adept" — are also those most able to exploit the system — to use and deploy their technicity for the accumulation of personal wealth and cultural status and power. And second, how the prowess, playful creativity and skill of those most exploited by the system are redeployed in the service of further capital accumulation on the part of those that set the terms of the industry. These processes, which is to say technicities, condition the entrance into the games business for many of the key producers today.

Identity, Culture and Technology

The contemporary subject is invited to accept their connections with machines and to seek to be an early adopter of each technological advance which brings them into greater connection with the multitude of global communities among which they will find their new "kin." Profits in global economies depend increasingly on consumers' willingness to participate in a permanent upgrade culture by buying the next generation of digital media — PC, DVD, iPod, digital camera, and so on. The desirability of these products is generated through a regime of symbolic production for which digital representation is a key signifier. The computer game both creates symbolic worlds and generates consumer technology demand. The identities and sensibilities that have driven the development of game cultures can therefore be seen as being actively produced through the interaction of counter cultures, consumer markets and symbolic production.

The idea of technicity emerges as a key concept for understanding games culture. By technicity we refer to the interconnectedness of identity and technological competence. Particular tastes, aptitudes and propensities towards technology become part of a particular "identity" through which affiliation is generated and networks and connections formed. To be subjects within the privileged West is to be increasingly caught up in technically and mechanically mediated networks of people who share the same tastes and attitudes, pleasures and preferences. This idea has been developed within theories of cyberculture, which seek to understand how technologies (particularly, but not exclusively, computer technologies and biotechnology) contribute to social relationships, cultural practices and subjectivity (Escobar 2000; Featherstone and Burrows 1995; Haraway 1989; Poster 1995; Stone 1995). Technologically-mediated life in the West is subsequently perceived and experienced by Westerners as naturally superior.

In order to argue that certain kinds of identity, behavior or taste are somehow "dominant," we must acknowledge that there is a range of marginal, subaltern or oppositional identities that are defined in reference to the dominant group. Technicity can thus be understood as a site of cultural hegemony in the 21st century. Here we take our lead from interpreters of Gramsci who use his work to understand the processes of struggle over cultural meaning (e.g., Storey 2002). Cultural Studies approaches to understanding culture have insisted on foregrounding and interrogating the ways in which some meanings come to be circulated, accepted and eventually taken for granted or naturalized. This process is dependent upon a network of power through which those who have the power to produce and circulate their meanings and interpretations ultimately generate a set of "'hegemonic truths' which [...] assume an authority over the ways in which we think and act; that is they invite us to take up 'subject positions' from which meaning can be made and actions carried out" (Storey 2002: xi).

However, just as we assert the power of dominant technicities within contemporary Western culture, we equally assert that this power is a dynamic process through which other, alternate and subversive identities are also constantly generated. The field commanded by the dominant is neither fixed nor finalized, but exists in constant contestation and redevelopment through the dynamics of popular culture. While we wish to point out the dominance of very particular kinds of technicity, we also want to redefine the culture of games by drawing attention to the many other forms of subjectivity that get written out of dominant accounts. For every group of hardcore online first-person shooter (FPS) gamers that takes its play very seriously, there is another group playing ironically, creating new characters that challenge hardcore orthodoxies and generally building a culture that defines itself in opposition to the norm. Female *Quake* clans like PMS — "Psycho Men Slayers" — are a good example because they contest the orthodox dominant identities associated with online FPS play.

Framing Technicity — Hackers and Cyborgs

Each new technological epoch brings about a period of instability which is greeted by both enthusiasm and suspicion. This was as true of the advent of the printing press, the telegraph, the telephone and electricity (Marvin 1988) as it is with computers and computer gaming. Each period therefore requires adjustments in our lived relations with machines and technological processes, which then produce cultures that function through the meanings of these lived relations. The instability that surrounds each new set of inventions produces questions. "What do these technological changes mean?" "How will they affect the way we live our lives or communicate with one another?" "How will we be defined as subjects or governed as citizens?" These questions are never finally answered, just as the instability which prompts them is never finally resolved, but remains potentially open to contestation through localized situated practices. These same processes have been in play since the advent of digital technologies. The two decades preceding the new millennium were seen as just such a period of instability, during which critical and enthusiastic responses to the innovations brought about through digital technology emerged. The way in which we all respond to such questions of instability is informed by what Lister (2003: 60, after de Lauretis et al. [1980]) call "the technological imaginary," the desires and fears which we project onto technologies.

If the idealized modern subject has always been marked by an enthusiastic acceptance of its connection with machines, then the contemporary version of this ideal subject is the digitally competent producer/consumer whose "technicity" plays a key role in formations of taste and lifestyle. This is the subjectivity so enthusiastically embraced by the authors of publications like *Wired* and *Mondo 2000*. Sobchack (2000: 140) describes the latter as being characterized by a "utopian plunge into the user friendly future of better living, not only through a chemistry left over from the 1960's, but also through personal computing, bio- and nano-technologies, virtual realities and an unabashed commitment to consumerism." The formation of these tastes and lifestyles do important work in the creation and maintenance of consumer markets for hi-tech consumption. *Mondo 2000*, in its editorial for their second edition in 1990, offers this subjectivity as both a source of pleasure and also a *requirement* for full participation and citizenship in the new digital age:

> Call it a hyper-hip wet dream, but the information and communications technology industry require a new *active* consumer or it's going to stall ... This is one reason why we are amplifying the mythos of the sophisticated, high complexity, fast lane/real time, intelligent, active and creative reality hackers... A nation of TV couch potatoes (not to mention embittered self-righteous radicals) is not going to demand access to the next generation of the extensions of man [Sobchack 2000: 140–141].

Contrasting this populist perspective, two dominant figures of technicity have emerged in critical writing on technology and culture over the last twenty years: the hacker and the cyborg. Each was produced simultaneously in the mid–1980s as a key figure representing positive models of technicity, models which potentially offered subversive, critical and progressive ways in which the new technologies of digital communications could be repurposed for progressive or even utopian ends. The hacker and the cyborg may be twenty-year-old paradigms of technicity, yet they continue to reverberate through the study of contemporary gaming cultures.

The Hacker Ethos and Mythos

A key feature of the hacker identity inherited by game designers and manufacturers is an attachment to what cyber theorists — after cyberpunk author William Gibson — termed "edge." "Technological edge can be defined as the product of a successful conjunction of advanced technological hardware and contextually sophisticated techniques" (Tomas 2000: 179). "Contextually sophisticated techniques," in turn, refers to the innovative uses of technology in unexpected or unprescribed ways, stretching or adapting technologies to perform functions for which they weren't designed. This might be anything from learning how to make free phone calls by whistling the right combinations of dial tones (phone phreaking) to using level editors to spray anti-war graffiti in online game worlds (e.g., www.opensorcery.net/velvet-strike/). The archetypal edge identity is that of the hacker. Gibson's fictional "console cowboys," who featured as the wily and resourceful heroes of the bad new future, contributed to how "real life" hackers were able to represent themselves "to the rest of us (particularly those of us intrigued by, but generally ignorant of, electronics) as sexy, hip and heroic, as New Age Mutant Ninja Hackers" (Sobchack 2000: 141). Inheriting some of the libertarian ideologies of late 1960s, California hackers promised to lead us to a non hierarchical networked environment of democratic data.

The dominant representations of this hacker identity have been problematized, however. Sobchack is particularly critical of how this identity is founded on access to computers, a social process mitigated by the lived realities of race, class and gender. Scratch the surface and the hacker is revealed as an idealized white, male subject. This is nowhere more tellingly portrayed than in Steven Levy's (1984) *Hackers: Heroes of the Computer Underground*, which contributed to the mythologizing of hacker identity and culture. Karen Coyle (1996: 44) notes the consequences of this mythology:

> With little review of the facts, Levy also concludes that women are genetically unable to hack. He never considers relevant that this hacking took place in a campus building between midnight and dawn in a world where women who are mugged at 2 am returning from a friend's house are told: "What did you expect, being out at that hour?" Nor does he consider that this hacking began at a time when MIT had few women students. And though he describes his male hackers as socially inept, he doesn't inquire into their attitudes toward women and how those attitudes would shape the composition of the hacking "club."

Finally, Levy fails to acknowledge the fact that hacking clubs and cultures typically emerge in spaces that are almost exclusively white as well as exclusively male. "Other" hackers have existed and continue to exist, but their stories are not included in the dominant mythos.

The Cyborg: Manifesto and Manifestations

The figure of the cyborg, as developed by Donna Haraway in an article which was first published in 1985 in *Socialist Review*, offered up the idea that our new intimate connection with machines could create a fluid zone of identity affiliation and agency which would destabilize conventional relationships between body, machine and nature, challenging the "command, control and conquer" logic of state and corporate digital domination. Critical in these ideas was the introduction of what appeared to be a move away from other political critiques of technology which had been motivated by either a "revisionist" or "revolutionary" impulses (See Wacjman [1991] for a review of the various feminist positions taken in relation to technology since the 1970s). The dawning of the cyber age was met with a sense of new opportunities as Haraway (1991a; 1991b; 1997) and others offered the figure of the cyborg as a way to move beyond the potentially essentializing association of women with nature. The cyborg became a metaphor for an alternative subjectivity and thus as a "site of possible resignifications ... to expand the possibilities [of subjectivity] to enable an enhanced sense of agency" (Butler 1992: 16). These resignifications were a rallying call for those deemed to be marginal by technoculture to embrace their affinity with technology and to offer new symbols, new uses and practices through which to "code" their subjectivities. The newly emergent post-digital technicities would, it was argued, produce hybridized identities, a "technologically creolized cultural laminate with a different set of ethnic type rules of social bonding" (Tomas 2000: 185).

In truth, both hacker and cyborg were always also caught up in their own cycles of opposition and dominance. For every hacker hero created by Gibson or even by Disney, such as *Tron* (Lisberger 1982: 96), there was also a Kevin Mitnick, public enemy number one, alleged to have cost billions of corporate dollars in the late 1980s (see Levy 1986). For every decentered cyborg self experimenting with online identity masquerade (Turkle 1995) there was another fantasy of militarized masculinity in *Terminator* form, confirming Claudia Springer's (1991) reading of the cyborg as a fascist fantasy rather than a radical subjectivity.

Since the formulation of these progressive discursive models of technicity, their context has shifted radically. The early, technophilic aspirations for digital technology envisaged between 1985 and 1995 have been succeeded in the last ten years by a firming up of the parameters of what is possible (a closing of the borders) as digital media have come to occupy key sites of symbolic and economic power within contemporary "networked society" (Castells 2000). The outsider identity of the hacker now finds itself in command of substantial corporate budgets, while the progressive aspirations of the cyborg often seems to have been overcome by the very worst forms of the militarized command, control and conquer war machine that Haraway's (1991a) concept sought to resist.

From Margin to Center: Dominant Technicities

We were all in it from a sense of wonder. [...] All of us either had no lives before or had thrown them over because of these stupid machines. We hung out together because we were all the same sort of jerks [Doug Carlston, co-founder of Broderbund software, cited in King and Borland 2003: 47].

The recent tendency within the game industry has been toward anything but the production of creolized hybridized subjects. Instead there has
been a tendency toward a narrowing of possibility and potential driven by
highly controlled, though decentralized, forms of production economy. Producers themselves articulate a post-fall narrative from innocent days of hacking pleasure to life in the digital sweatshop. In the following biographies,
which articulate a specific dominant technicity, there is in fact a remarkable
homogeneity rather than creolization. The stories constitute the dominant discourse which structures the history of computer games, the histories of its
founding "fathers" and key players. Other histories and other subjects are
either marginalized or absent altogether. However, rather than view these
accounts as primary historical evidence, we must understand that they are part
of the hacker mythos, the lone individual genius, breaking into hi-tech equipment and repurposing it for pleasure and fun. Similarly, cyborg discourse
informs these accounts in the notions of early designers with machine-like
minds and inhuman propensities.

We found it common for "star" biographies to point to a childhood passion for games of all kinds and an early engagement with computer games
specifically. Sean Blackley, one of the driving forces behind XBox, was
described as designing and programming games from the age of ten (Takahashi 2002: 40). Richard Bartle, the co-author (with Roy Trubshaw) of the
first MUD environment in 1980 was described as having a father who was
"an avid board game player" and who "quickly instilled the love of dice and
competition in his two sons" (King and Borland 2003: 52). John Romero and
John Carmack, who established their own company id Software and went on
to create the successful games *Doom* and *Quake*, have been described as having grown up "with a love of programming in general and games in particular" (King and Borland 2003: 90). In a pure cyborgian hyperbole, "Romero
was so good at Pac-Man that he could maneuver the round yellow character
through a maze of fruit and dots with his eyes shut" (Kushner 2003: 5).

An associated feature of game designers' backgrounds was an interest in
engineering — the construction of complex systems. As a teenager Blackley
allegedly amused himself by building go-carts and bombs (Takahashi 2002:
39). Will Wright, lead designer of *SimCity* and *The Sims*, was encouraged by
a chemical engineer father with projects that included building radio controlled models: "mostly I built a lot of models, ... then I blew them up and
built more" (King and Borland 2003: 82). This interest then extended in his
teenage years to robotics: "writing the software that would control robot brains
was like model making taken to an extreme..." (King and Borland 2003: 82).
Richard Garriot, "Lord British" and early designer and developer of the highly
successful and influential *Ultima* virtual game world, was brought up by a

NASA astronaut father who "routinely brought home expensive government toys from NASA headquarters, tinkering with them for days on end and taking them apart to see what made them work" (King and Borland 2003: 15). Ken Kutaragi, the inspirational leader of Sony's Playstation project is an electronic engineer by training. "I'm confident in matters of technology. That's my hobby, and I consider myself second to none in these matters" (Asakura 2000: 221) Kutaragi built himself a computer at home as soon as the components became available (Asakura 2000), while Romero's step-father was an engineer and Carmack was described by those working with him as 'the engineer' (King and Borland 2003).

In this male- and engineering-structured version of a dominant technicity, there is also a hint that such predispositions go hand-in-hand with a certain level of obsessive, asocial or even anti-social behavior. This we might also see as both cyborgian in its post-human aspect, as well as typical of the hacker in "his" loner identity. Asakura (2000: 6) reported that Ken Kutaragi was an "'A' student in elementary school in every subject but two, physical education ... and social studies." Much is made by Kushner (2003) of Carmack and Romero's misfit status. A psychologist examining Carmack following his attempt to steal an Apple computer made the following observation, replete with a description of chillingly cyborgian tendencies: "Boy behaves like a walking brain with legs ... no empathy for other human beings" (Kushner 2003: 24). Carmack was described as having some strange mannerisms, for example, "he developed a unique speech impediment, adding a short robotic humming sound to the end of his sentences, like a computer processing data: 12 times 12 equals 144 ... mmm" (Kushner 2003: 19). Carmack was also alleged to have been heavily influenced by both Neal Stephenson's metaverse in Snow Crash and the Holodeck in Star Trek. As the narrative goes, it was this passion which drove him to continually push the boundaries of possibility in his programming of these alternative worlds. Kushner portrayed Carmack's obsession as the means through which he gained a sense of power and control and which consoled his subsequent aversion to external authority, allowing his subjectivity to dissolve into the machinic. Kushner's devotional description of Carmack's abilities blend the lone hero of the hacker world with the language of the cyborg: "He had never worked on a computer before but took to the device as if it were an extension of his own body. It spoke the language of mathematics; it responded to his commands and, he realized after seeing some games on the monitor, it contained worlds" (Kushner 2003: 20).

King and Borland (2003: 90) alleged that the *Doom* duo Carmack and Romero "found programming to be a refuge from unhappiness elsewhere in their lives." They further argue that Bartle found a social space in the Computer Society at Essex University in 1978 because programmers were regarded as "social misfits" by the predominantly radical left student body. Alongside these implications of social dis-ease we found frequent references to the obsessive and driven qualities possessed by the "star" programmers. One of Carmack's co-workers described him as a classic cyberpunk console cowboy figure: "When he was programming there was nothing but programming, I'm sure there were days when he didn't eat" (King and Borland 2003: 95). Finally, there was a marked sense of counter cultural rebelliousness typical of the hacker in the constructions of these biographies. Romero and Carmack were both described as having an intolerance of authority, Carmack in particularly is alleged to hate the authority of parents, school and religion (Kushner 2003). Both Asakura and Takahashi portrayed their subjects (Ken Kutaragi at Sony and Sean Blackley at Microsoft, respectively) as spanners in the corporate works rather than as "company men," yet also as rebels on a mission to establish games within the heart of the corporate body. Kushner made explicit the connection with the hacker subjectivity when he described Carmack's encounter with Steven Levy's book as a kind of personal epiphany — it was this book that reassured Carmack that he was not alone.

In this narrative, playing and programming computer games figure as key means through which these individuals were able to articulate their defiance of the corporate system; yet also the means through which they developed the specific technical skills which were recognized as commercially highly valued and valuable. Kushner claimed that Romero was able to sneak onto university campuses to play on the computers there; the gatekeepers to this technology, the young male students, recognized his skills and were "charmed by his gumption" (Kushner 2003: 7).

> Since the seventies, the electronic gaming industry had been dominated by arcade machines like Asteroids and home consoles like the Atari 2600. Writing software for these platforms required expensive development systems and corporate backing. But computer games were different. They were accessible. They came with their own tools, their own portals — a way inside. And the people who had the keys were not authoritarian monsters, they were *dudes*. Romero was young, but he was a dude in the making, he figured. The Wizard of this Oz could be him [Kushner, 2003: 7].

We see here the idea of "cool" to which Sobchack referred earlier in this use of the term dude." The hyper-hip hacker and cyborg subjectivities invoked in these accounts bear out their roots in *Mondo 2000*, *Wired*, cyberpunk rhetoric.

These accounts are formed through the discursive frameworks of the technological imaginary, conjuring up both the popular and the theoretical tropes and mythos of hacker and cyborg in their articulation of what is now *the* dominant technicity of game cultures. Critical here is the story of a particular journey from a marginal or rebellious position in relation to corporate power or the mainstream towards an occupation of a central, or hegemonic, position in the construction of a dominant version of game culture and of a designer technicity. In the process, these narratives reinforce and adapt existing tropes around masculinity, technology and creativity.

Magical Things of Wonderment

Our analysis of the popular discourses that shape our knowledge of game production's history was prompted by our own findings in our Pivotal Games case study. There we encountered evidential accounts in interviews, rather than narratives in popular cultural histories, yet we found many of the same discursive frameworks in operation, suggesting that the mythos of a dominant technicity is well and truly internalized. We asked each of our ten respondents a series of common questions concerning their first contact with computers and computer games, as well as questions about their cultural appetites when these first contacts occurred.

The results were startlingly homogenous. Nine out of ten claimed computer game playing histories that stretched back into childhood, beginning between the ages of 7 and 13, depending on the age of the respondent. Older employees were less likely to have started playing at a very early age simply because the technology was less available. Pivotal Games is a hobbyist, fan led group of individuals who found their way into an industry for which they showed an early passion. The similarities in responses suggest the evolution of a creative programmers' sensibility of early encounters with computers and games. This sensibility is characterized by a fascination with how things work "under the bonnet," combined with a fascination with the creative possibilities of the computer as a manipulation machine. Each characteristic is linked to an interest and facility with mathematics. For several of our respondents the computer-as-gameplay entertainment quickly became the computer-as-creative tool as young boys began to explore beyond the boundaries of the software provided. An account by the company's Technical Director was typical; he described himself as "essentially a mid to late 80s bedroom programmer." He went on to explain,

> I am the type of person, have the type of mind that does get excited and interested by new technology or gadgets, so even though I was only a teenager then, when home computers became fairly common place the first time I saw them, they just held an interest for me like any other gadget or VCR or anything that was new. But I got into it and discovered that there was more depth in

computers than there was in any other device by orders of magnitude and I was interested in the complexity of them. So it was just the technical challenge, it happened to be something that I was good at and enjoyed hugely and that is true today, I mean programming today remains as much of a hobby as it does a vocation or a commercial interest.

Similarly, a member of the "core tech" game engine programming team recalled how he became a programmer through his fascination with how things work:

> I was just fascinated by how it all worked you know because when I first played games they were these magical things of wonderment really. I had no idea about computers or what computer programs were. I kind of had a driving desire to find out how things worked. I have always liked to know how things worked and I have always liked to build things. As a kid I used to play with Lego rather than with action man toys and that sort of thing and I would be quite happy to take apart things in the house. I would get into quite a lot of trouble because I couldn't put them back together, radios and that kind of thing. Just to have a look at them and poke about and see how they worked.... So I was spending my time of an evening playing with computers and playing with games and then finding how the games worked and trying to cheat at them I guess initially was what got me really into the technical side of them to be honest.

Common experiences of early games as "magical things of wonderment" opened up a field of technical and creative expression that has become a key part of the professional identity of these game developers. Part of this shared nostalgia for early games was based not just on experiences of being a consumer of a new product, but also in the real possibilities that such consumption opened up for becoming a producer. These key figures were able to intervene in the processes of technological innovation and development by altering, extending and manipulating the technology in unexpected, playful and often illegitimate ways.

A second dominant narrative in the Pivotal developers' accounts of the evolution of their tastes was a common experience (particularly among senior members of the team) of playing table-top fantasy role-playing games such as Dungeons and Dragons (see Williams, Hendricks, and Winkler [2006] for recent research). Mathematically calculated game mechanics based in sprawling rule books were perfectly adaptable to the algorithms of computer programs. Pivotal's Managing Director, who already had a long history in table-top game design before his involvement in the computer game industry explained the link between role-playing and programming:

> The fundamental mechanic is all down to numbers and probabilities, percentage chances of hitting and missing; all our vehicles are just a bunch of numbers. There is a 3D model there and there are 3D surfaces set, as a number value, hit point value and then something that says what happens when you penetrate and

destroy that. Is it catastrophic damage? That is stuff I played with for years, just on table tops or role-playing and ditto with characters, movement speeds, hit points, actions you can do and it is all number based.

A second outcome of a common taste for fantasy role-play is the continuing appeal of "sword and sorcery" imaginary worlds in computer game content. Computer games have continued to draw from and develop the archaic fantasies of the Dungeons and Dragons (D&D) world (for example *Fable* 2004). Four of the ten respondents — significantly all senior figures within the company both in age and authority — expressed strong childhood and adolescent attachment to paper gaming, to the mathematically systematized pastime of role-play gaming, fantasy and D&D. As a lead designer described it,

> I was about nine when I started playing Dungeons and Dragons. I mean I had been into fantasy stuff for quite a while which I think stemmed from the fact that both my parents were quite into Lord of the Rings and I used to get read The Hobbit as a bedtime story by my mum,.... so I'd always been really interested in that whole fantasy thing, and had you know, fantasy toys and soldiers and that.... I was really quite hooked on that sort of thing and absolutely loved it. Then I discovered the War Hammer stuff a bit later, probably when I was about twelve or thirteen and again got really into that, which some of my earliest ever attempts to write serious rule systems was for War Hammer 40,000, which I sent into Games Workshop and they liked enough to send back release forms to say, "Well we might use this, so sign the copyright over to us...." I read a lot of the Dungeons and Dragons sort of novels, a lot of the fantasy stuff.

These marked features of technicity are consistent with our analysis of popular game industry histories. However the issues around dominant and marginal tastes are made more complex by the fact that the particular taste preferences articulated here are generally deemed quite marginal or subcultural in relation to a hierarchy of "quality" versus "trash" tastes. The movement of games themselves from bedroom subculture to mainstream big media business has had the effect of repositioning the hacker/programmer from margin to center.

All the evidence above suggests a consistency of taste, sensibility, aptitudes and propensities which we have defined as a dominant technicity. Accounts and stories further serve to root this version of technicity implicitly and naturally in a masculine identity. Those who do not fit the hegemonic mold become differentiated and excluded as "the other." If one particular group is dominant, however, then we can be sure that there are other stories, identities and creative processes that get written out of the dominant discourse. We will now explore some of these in detail in order to show how technicities are never fixed, never completely determined, but rather are

contested and negotiated, becoming most visible when they are susceptible
to market commodification.

Edge as Cultural Capital

Table-top role-playing game development, pleasures in engineering or
math, a fascination with systems ... these are all aspects of a particular taste
culture and have specific functions in the formation of a particular technicity. In order to address how these processes have shifted from margin to center, we rely on some of the theoretical structures developed by Pierre Bourdieu
for thinking about taste cultures. Bourdieu (1986) undertook large-scale sociological empirical research to show how class functioned in consumer- and
information-society, which succeeded the industrial age. He was able to show
that "taste" and "lifestyle" were part and parcel of the generation of "symbolic capital," which did important work for (what was in the 1980s called)
the New Economy.[1] The dominant technicities we have begun to uncover can
be identified as part of a class culture identifiable by specific "tastes" in technoculture.

Bourdieu emphasized the importance of symbolic production in the generation of the desires that drive consumer economies, and in the accumulation of capital. In relation to technicity and its place in the order of symbolic
production and taste generation, we would add new media designers and programmers who, since Bourdieu's (1986) thesis, have come to play a lead role
in the creation of symbolic capital. In recent cultural history, to be a web
designer or games programmer is to have maximum cool. Thus, the development of a dominant technicity within game production has not happened
by accident — it has happened because new media designers do important
work in the system of production of symbolic goods. The vibrant virtual
worlds which they create are in some ways the domain of the technological
imaginary, the place where our desires are played out (and played at). The
technological imaginary is a driver of consumption in a never-ending upgrade
culture; the next gadget or software upgrade always brings us ever-closer to
a sense of completion and wholeness which day-to-day reality so painfully
lacks but which we are certain to find in the friction-free world of the imaginary future.

Bourdieu also offers us a framework for understanding the discomfort
experienced by game designers who have found their youthful pleasures
eclipsed by business realities. The fan-based culture of 1980s bedroom programmers was founded on a hacker ethos. It was an "outsider" identity, a
mutant strain of techno-masculinity that took root in the cultural crevices

offered by first generation PCs, Amigas and Commodores. The sense of group belonging generated within this subculture offered status based on the technical virtuosity deployed in turning the new computer tools of the workplace into objects for pure pleasure. However this same generation, now nearing middle-age and finding themselves in the driving seat of the cultures of new media, have to reconcile a subcultural history and dominant present.

> [T]he new cultural intermediaries are inclined to sympathize with discourses aimed at challenging the cultural order and the hierarchies which the cultural "hierarchy" aims to maintain. [...] But in fact these occupations condemn their occupants to the essential ambiguity resulting from the discrepancy between the (symbolically) subversive dispositions linked to their position in the division of labor and the manipulative or conservative functions attached to the position, between the subjective image of the occupational project and the objective function of the occupation [Bourdieu 1986: 366].

This precisely describes the tensions between designers' sense of themselves as "outsiders" and rebels ("the subjective image of the occupational project") on the one hand and their position within a very tight production machine ("the objective function of the occupation") on the other.

The supreme "edge" adapters and disseminators of game culture play a key role in creating the entertainment technologies of tomorrow and their multiply-desired imaginaries. There is therefore something at stake in embracing this form of technicity. In the culturally central process of mediation and entertainment, the future is geek. The economic importance of this group of early adopters, whether designers or players or both, is not underestimated by corporate new media industries, as the Bill Gates quote at the head of this chapter underlines.

Gendering and Racializing Technology

While Bourdieu may be able to help us to understand the broader framework within which dominant technicity operates he does not obviously give us much purchase on why this particular "taste culture" is so highly gendered and racialized. For some commentators the very masculine nature of game cultures is simply the way things are. Gary Gygax for example has argued that,

> [m]ales dominate RPG design because 90% or more of the players are males. Males dominate all games, for that matter, as they are more oriented towards game play. Do I think that male-designed games prevent more females from playing games? No way! If there was a significant portion of the market female, female game designers would have tapped it long ago [Gel214th N.d.].

In fact, Gygax's observation is an all-too-common example of dominance in action. It represents the triumph of an ideological perception over the facts —

the ESA claims that nearly forty percent of gamers are women, and we know from the cultural history of games that a significant proportion of players on early MUDs as well as existing MMORPGs and other fantasy-based games are female. It seems equally clear that anyone who looks at the history of literature can see that women have played a significant role in both the consumption and production of fantasy fiction (e.g., Margaret Atwood, Octavia Butler, Ursula K. LeGuin, Marge Piercy, Joanna Russ, Margaret Weiss, and so on), many of whom are drawn to fantasy by the possibilities it offers to imagine power and subjectivity differently. If we are to begin to understand gender and dominance in this respect, we need to turn to theorizations of gender and technology.

There is a matrix of determination at play in the gendering of the computer itself, which is central to the histories of games cultures. Karen Coyle (1996: 43) argues that "to question the masculinity of computers is tantamount to questioning our image of masculinity itself: computers are power, and power, in our world, must be the realm of men." Thus, while not all men are adept with computers (or other highly valued forms of technology), "what is experienced as failure by individual men may not affect the general image of hegemonic masculinity. Those who are masters demonstrate not only that they are 'real men' themselves, but they demonstrate a phenomenon recognized as masculinity and confirm the meaning of the concept" (Lie 1995: 391). This is a critical point — not all men love computers (much less computer games) and not all women are technophobic. In fact, any empirical investigation reveals a rich and diverse range of technicities in play at any point in cultural history. However, the power of hegemony is such that first, technicities that do not fit the dominant model are made invisible by those that do and second, those of us who do not belong to the dominant group also internalize their power and make ourselves invisible.

Established feminist scholarship has explored the massive range of engagements that women with digital technologies (see e.g., Danet 1998; Hayles 1999; Stone 1995). McRae (1996) examined the ways in which MUDs offered a version of virtual reality through which identity play could also include experimenting with other kinds of sexuality and sexual pleasure. Players can role-play sex from a range of identity positions, choosing mates from either gender or "non-gendered" or even non-humans. Through these experiences different kinds of power and agency emerge.

This work of cultural reclamation in the digital realm has also extended to race. Wakeford (2000), for instance, signals the work of River Ginchild — director of Digital Sojourn — who was motivated to produce her site because "I wanted to see myself— women of African descent — on the web. I think I had seen one or two but in June 1995 it was — overwhelmingly — white male, it still is, but there are a lot more of us online with pages" (Wakeford 2000: 353). The Afrofuturism movement draws on a long history of understanding the relationships between race, technology and culture and seeks to undermine the notion that African Americans are somewhat "naturally" outside of technoculture. The movement also seeks to examine how whiteness is implicitly and explicitly inscribed in technoculture. Similarly, Nakamura's (2002) Cybertypes offers some insightful analyses of how Asian-American identity is (de)constructed through identity tourism in MUDs and MOOs. In doing so, she contributes to the ongoing endeavor to attend to issues of race in cyberculture studies.

Part of this process requires excavating those "others" who have played a significant role in the development of technoculture and interrogating how they have contributed to popular cultural meanings around technology as producers and consumers. Furthermore, it requires highlighting how race is constructed in contemporary cyberculture, such as how blackness bestows coolness on characters in cyberpunk fiction (e.g., Hiro Protagonist's hybrid identity in Snow Crash). There is also of course a largely unwritten history of African American and Caribbean engagements with technologies in the music industry where 1970s artists like George Clinton, Lee Scratch Perry and Sun Ra were experimenting with new technologies and sci-fi imagery — succeeded by the entire reinvention of popular music led by the sampling artistry of hip hop artists like Afrika Bambaata (Guins 2005). In sum, cyberculture, as a material reality and lived practice, provides both the opportunities for the articulation of outsider identities and is also the means through which existing normative meanings around gender and race are circulated.

"Other" Histories of Computer Gaming Cultures

We have to attend critically to the exclusions and blind spots which occur within these popular histories and biographies of computer games and computer games culture. Roberta Williams is perhaps best known for helping create and define the genre of online adventure games (Pemberton 1999) as well as co-founding the massively successfully company Sierra Online. She thus serves as a key example of females who are significantly engaged in the production of computer game culture. Kushner (2003: 12) indicates that Williams and her husband "pioneered the Ziploc distribution method, turning their homemade graphical role-playing games into a $10 million-a-year company, Sierra On-Line — a haven of hippie digerati with hot tub parties to boot." Yet accounts of the rise of computer game culture and its roots in hacker culture have often played down Roberta's significance in this pioneering innovation. Coyle (1996) figures things differently. She argues that Roberta Williams was the one more involved in the technical side of the endeavor while husband Ken "ran the computer shop." She counterposes this against Levy's (1984) account, wherein "Roberta is portrayed as a housewife and mother whose authorship of the popular games was the least important part of the process" (Coyle 1996: 44). Roberta Williams is also credited with introducing the first ever female game protagonist in *Kings Quest IV*[2].

Other female designers or developers often have had their work on particular games similarly overlooked or ignored. *Centipede* (Atari 1981) one of the most popular early computer games among both male and female audiences was celebrated as being designed by a woman, Dona Bailey. Frequently however, her contribution is belittled and Ed Logg features as the most important contributor to the game. *River Raid*, published in 1982 by Activision (a firm formed in 1979 by disgruntled ex–Atari programmers), was developed by one of the first female game designers, Carol Shaw. Having designed *Video Checkers* and *3D Tic Tac Toe* for Atari, Shaw moved to Activision and has gone down in history as one of the pioneers in the mostly male dominated world of game programming. Unfortunately, these women are rarely mentioned in popular texts that mythologize computer game culture and are recognized today mainly because of the intervention of female gamers and website producers who are chipping away at the dominant version of computer game history and culture through the creation and circulation of marginal images and alternative histories.

Our own research and correspondence with female designers and producers confirms this understanding of their position as marginal to the accepted or authoritative version of game culture. Raina Lee is the producer and editor of a self-published metazine entitled *1-Up*, which contains cartoons, stories and essays based on a heterogeneous range of computer games and computer games pleasures. It also contains review essays of and critical commentary on current and classic game titles (although it seems to display some nostalgia for classic games and "simpler" pleasures). As a second generation Chinese-American with feminist sensibilities, Lee is positioned outside the normative construction of the computer games player. As Lee (2002) describes her motivation for producing the metazine, "I publish *1-Up* to make sense of our relationship to technology as well as to chronicle the culture surrounding video games." The metazine is also clearly an intervention into dominant gaming culture and the discourse that surrounds it: "some brush off video games as mindless entertainment, there is little written about them as a cultural experience. Most of the material comes from game publications that are written in the voice of a 14-year old boy, which is OK if you are a 14-year old boy. Many of us are not, and have never been, which is why we have this publication" (Lee 2002).

The articles included in *1-Up* offer feminist readings of games and also tackle the issue of race in game representation (an enduringly overlooked aspect of game culture). In one article, Lee critiques a first-person-shooter game distributed by Aryan record label Resistance Record — a company owned by the largest active Neo-Nazi organization in North America.

> Like mainstream mediums [sic] such as film, television, and the Internet, gaming is an influential cultural outlet where values of hate and intolerance can be perpetuated. Like those mediums [sic], gaming is also a form of communication where liberating, anti-racist, and feminist values can be spread, and better yet, experienced. For those who want to make a difference in the war against hate, I suggest they embrace the do-it-yourself ethic and hack *Ethnic Cleansing* back into a decent game [Lee 2003: 85].

1-Up represents a range of responses to computer games, from passionate engagement and enthusiastic articulation of playing pleasures to systematic critique. Lee's production activities along the margins of gaming culture are unlikely to find their way into the dominant stories of hardcore gamers and producers, even though her self-narratives parallel the tastes and aptitudes as those recounted in the popular biographies of these "founding fathers:"

> Video games introduced me to computers and other gadgets (walkmans, audio equipment etc) and even today I am kind of a gadget nerd. I don't mind figuring out VCR's or digital cameras or any other kinds of personal technology, and perhaps I got used to it because I spend so much time with games. My father was also into techie/ audio equipment, and he always encouraged me to take those interests [personal correspondence 2004].

Another interviewee, Mari Soderburg (designer of the *Spite and Malice* computer card game), offers a compelling example of the degree to which these dominant tastes and technicities are gendered. We begin with a familiar story of early encounters with computer technology. As Soderburg told us, "It was late at night alone at the computer center when I came upon "Adventure" (Colossal Cave), a text adventure game. This was before CRTs so it was on a teletype machine. I was hooked. I can still recall the "rush" I used to get as I solved different parts of the adventure." Yet despite this very typical set of both tastes and aptitudes (Soderberg worked in IT in a variety of different roles for many years), she was frequently confronted by very particular assumptions based solely on the fact that she was female. She recounted a few of those experiences for us as well.

> [M]y experiences with technical support in the 1980–90s were disheartening. I received responses like, "I would prefer to speak with your husband," or "This is too complex to discuss with you," ten seconds into the conversation. [...] When

the Pentium first came out and a heat-sink fan was needed for it, Intel made arrangements for non-technical people to be able to bring in their computer to have it installed and technical people were able to receive the fan directly and install it themselves. When I phoned to get it sent to me, I had a horrible time getting them to accept me as being qualified to do it myself. Of all my male friends who called, none of them had their technical expertise even questioned. Upon hearing a female voice on the phone, this condescending attitude by technical support services continued until the past few years. I guess I can partly blame *Spite* for most emails being addressed to me as "Dear Sir," but I have to admit, I still find it annoying. I realize that my name "Mari" is not a typical name, but I would think in other situations that most people would assume I was a woman with that name. Even though it is my name as author, many people wrote directly to my second ex-husband for technical support with the game because they assumed he was the real programmer (he ran the online league games for players).

Soderberg also cited Roberta Williams as one of her own heroines, which seems to underline the necessity for us to draw attention to these (and other) subjects who get excluded in the hegemonic processes that produces game designer technicity as "essentially" masculine.

The discursive formation of computer game culture is dominated by a very specific set of tastes, sensibilities and subjects. The optimistic "outsider" identities of the earliest years of technoculture have been superceded as their contexts have shifted. The cultures of production associated with computer games exhibit an extraordinarily high degree of homogeneity compared to other media industries. Producers are recruited on the basis of their acculturation within a common set of biographies and, once recruited, they find themselves working alongside others like themselves, producing games for more people like themselves. Particular kinds of dominant tastes emerge through the game culture that, although by no means being typical of everyone in the industry, command a disproportionate amount of cultural capital. The tastes, desires and aspirations that characterize the cultures of computer game production have so far exercised a very powerful hegemonic influence upon the kinds of games that get made, as well as upon their circulation and reception.

Academic Technicity and Authoritative Taste Cultures

To conclude we would like to draw attention to the way in which some similar contradictions can be found at work in academic approaches to computer gaming. In the recent past academics from a variety of (primarily) humanities-derived disciplines have been enabled to "come out" as computer game players. The identity of academic gamers/gamer academics as members of a subculture with its own sense of community (essentially a defensive inward looking stance) has been gradually transformed into an identity that is proactively seeking to carve out a respectable and autonomous space within the academy for research and teaching. Within this process we can observe nostalgia for a receding subcultural identity that continues to have purchase within a still-emerging and largely illegitimate field of study.

Within the academic study of games, we can also see the operation of our dominant technicity at work. We encounter this technicity most often at the margins of academic debate as a set of internalized values that provide a common subcultural enthusiasm for games research. That is to say certain kinds of games and player practices might be privileged over others since they reflect the tastes of researchers and editors — tastes which are themselves formed in relation to the dominant technicities which operate within the game industry.

The explicit goals of the journal Game Studies appear to be inclusive:

> As game scholars, we are (or should be) dedicated to understanding all games, not just the ones that sell. To us, games are not products but communicative practice. The games people play are (or should be) more important to us than the games people buy [Aarseth 2002].

A brief study of the abstracts published for articles in this new journal confirms that this commitment is carried through in the range of titles and practices being studied. However, there exists in the ironic marginalia a preferred technicity. Aki Järvinen (2002) begins his review of *Halo* with the following: "Even though a ludologist deserves a slap in the face every time s/he compares a game to a movie, I cannot help myself." Gonzalo Frasca (2001) is even more explicit,

> I must confess something that may end my career as a videogame reviewer for good. I cannot stand Tolkien. While I never read any of his books, I hated him as soon as I installed *The Hobbit*, an adventure game from the early eighties on my Sinclair ZX Spectrum. The problem is that I do not only despise Tolkien, but the fantasy genre in general. My heresy goes even further: I do not even like *Star Wars*. [...] Now that you know my little dirty secret, you will understand why I find most fantasy-related videogames quite boring. I have always preferred stories about human affairs and social issues to magic spells and mean dragons.

Frasca's disavowal of a dominant technicity, his "dirty little secret," constructs it as an imagined "other" against which his own preferred tastes will have to be measured. As reflexive critical thinkers it is essential that we also pay attention to our own internalized technicities and tastes and to the way in which they inflect and determine the choices we make about which games to study and how to study them.

Notes

1. Bourdieu (1986: 173) notes that, "[t]aste, the propensity and capacity to appropriate (materially or symbolically) a given class of classified, classifying objects or practices, is the generative formula of life style, a set of distinctive preferences which express the same expressive intention in the specific logic of each of the symbolic sub spaces, furniture, clothing...."

2. See http://www.womengamers.com/interviews/roberta.html

References

Aarseth, Espen. 2002. "The Dungeon and the Ivory Tower: Vive La Difference ou Liaison Dangereuse?" *Game Studies* 2(1) Retrieved February 13, 2006 (http://www.game studies.org/0102/).

Asakura, Reiji. 2000. *Revolutionaries at Sony: The Making of Sony Playstation and the Visionaries Who Conquered the World*. New York: McGraw Hill.

Bourdieu, Pierre. 1986. Distinction: A Social Critique of the Judgment of Taste. London: Routledge.

Butler, Judith. 1992. "Contingent Foundations." In *Feminists Theorize the Political*, edited by Judith Butler and Joan Scott. London: Routledge.

Castells, Manuel. 2000. *The Rise of the Network Society*. Oxford: Blackwell.

Coyle, Karen. 1996. "How Hard Can It Be?" In *Wired Women: Gender and New Realities in Cyberspace*, edited by Lyn Cherny and Elizabeth Reba Weise. Washington: Seal Press.

Escobar, Arturo. 2001. "Welcome to Cyberia: Notes on the Anthropology of Cyberspace." Pp. 56–76 in *The Cybercultures Reader*, edited by David Bell and Barbara M. Kennedy. London: Routledge.

Featherstone, Mike, and Roger Burrows (eds.) 1995. *Cyberspace/Cyberbodies/Cyberpunk: Cultures of Technological Embodiment*. London: Sage

Frasca, Gonzalo. 2001. "Grandmothers Are Cooler Than Trolls." *Games Studies* 1(1). Retrieved February 13, 2006 (http://www.gamestudies.org/0101/).

Gel214th. N.d. "Interview with Gary Gygax: RPG Legend." Retrieved October 04, 2004 (http://www.womengamers.com/interviews/garygygax.php).

Haraway, Donna. 1989. *Primate Visions: Gender, Race and Nature in the World of Modern Science*. London: Verso.

_____. 1991a. *Simians, Cyborgs, and Women: The Reinvention of Women*. New York: Routledge.

_____. 1991b. "The Actors Are Cyborg, Nature Is Coyote, and the Geography Is Elsewhere: Postscript to 'Cyborgs at Large.'" Pp. 21–6 in *Technoculture*, edited by Constance Penley and Andrew Ross. Minneapolis: University of Minnesota Press.

_____. 1997. *Modest Witness@Second Millenium. FemaleMan Meets OncoMouse: Feminism and Technoscience*. London: Routledge.

Hayles, N. K. 1999. *How We Became Posthuman. Virtual Bodies in Cybernetics, Literature and Informatics*. Chicago: University of Chicago Press.

Järvinen, Aki. 2002. "*Halo* and the Anatomy of the FPS." *Games Studies* 2(1). Retrieved February 13, 2005 (http://www.gamestudies.org/0102/).

King, Brad, and John Borland. 2003. *Dungeons and Dreamers: The Rise of Computer Game Culture from Geek to Chic*. San Francisco: McGraw Hill.

Kushner, David. 2003. *Masters of Doom: How Two Guys Created an Empire and Transformed Pop Culture*. London: Piatkus.

Lee, Raina. 2001. *1-Up: Adventures in Video Game Culture Metazine*, vol. 1 Winter.

Levy, S. 1984. *Hackers: Heroes of the Computer Revolution*. London: Penguin.

Lie, M. 1995. "Technology and Masculinity: The Case of the Computer." *The European Journal of Women's Studies* 2(3): 379–94

Lister, Martin (ed.). 2003. *New Media: A Critical Introduction.* London: Routledge.

Marvin, Carolyn. 1988. *When Old Technologies Were New: Thinking about Electric Communications in the Late Nineteenth Century.* Oxford: Oxford University Press.

McRae, Shannon. 1996. "Coming Apart at the Seams: Sex, Text and the Virtual Body." Pp. 242–263 in *Wired Women*, edited by Lynn Cherny and Elizabeth Reba Weise. Seattle, WA: Seal Press.

Nakamura, Lisa. 2002. *Cybertypes: Race, Ethnicity, and Identity on the Internet.* New York: Routledge.

Pemberton, Duane. 1999. "Interview with Roberta Williams." Retrieved December 20, 2005 (http://www.gdhardware.com/interviews/roberta_williams/001.htm).

Sobchack, Vivian. 2001. "New Age Mutant Ninja Hackers." Pp. 138–148 in *The Cybercultures Reader*, edited by David Bell and Barbara M. Kennedy. London: Routledge.

Springer, Claudia. 1991. "The Pleasure of the Interface." *Screen* 32(3).

Stone, Rosanne Allucquere. 1995. *The War of Desire and Technology at the Close of the Mechanical Age.* Cambridge, MA: MIT Press.

Storey, John. 2002. *Inventing Popular Culture.* London: Blackwell.

Takahashi, Dean. 2002. *Opening the Box.* Roseville, CA: Prima Publishing.

Tomas, David. 2001. "The Technophilic Body: On Technicity in William Gibson's Cyborg Culture." Pp. 175–189 in *The Cybercultures Reader*, edited by David Bell and Barbara M. Kennedy. London: Routledge.

Wakeford, Nina. 2000. "Networking Women and Grrrls with Information/Communication Technology: Surfing Tales of the World Wide Web." Pp. 350–359 in *The Cybercultures Reader*, edited by David Bell and Barbara M. Kennedy. London: Routledge.

Williams, J. Patrick, Sean Q. Hendricks, and W. Keith Winkler (eds.). 2006. *Gaming as Culture: Essays in Reality, Identity and Experience in Fantasy Games.* Jefferson, NC: McFarland.

8. Ghost Recon: Island Thunder: *Cuba in the Virtual Battlescape*

RAFAEL MIGUEL MONTES

As a Cuban-born but American-raised man who has spent a vast majority of his life in Miami, the capital of the Cuban exile enclave, much of my intellectual curiosity and professional activity has revolved around studying multiple representations of the island a scant ninety miles away from my home. Politically unable to visit my birthplace due to the circumstances of my family's migration, much of my knowledge of the island has come from the stories — both nostalgically embellished and emotionally distorted — of my parents as well as other Cubans in Miami that I have interviewed. It is through these narratives that I have been able to understand the exigencies of exile as well as the conflicted emotions that arise from the desire to return to a country, many decades after departure, that can no longer be the original country which was left behind. For many who have left the island, the perils of homecoming, an impossible act of reconciliation between the actual Cuba and the imagined Cuba, are not necessarily or even easily negotiated. Transport is always tumultuous.

My desire to investigate how Cuba is represented outside of the Cuban-American narrative framework led me to Red Storm Entertainment's 2002 release, *Tom Clancy's Ghost Recon: Island Thunder* (UbiSoft 2003). In this chapter I will show how this particular game disrupts claims that transport to elaborate virtual worlds is always enjoyable by focusing on what occurs when a Cuban-American is transformed into an American soldier engaging in squad-based jungle warfare in a mythical future Cuba. What happens when the Cuban exile community's longed for commencement of a post–Castro Cuba is instantaneously rendered for immediate consumption? And, furthermore, what happens when the player identifies more with the enemy than with the avatar?

A Note on Related Work

The desire to comprehend potentially tumultuous political and economic practices brought about by late capitalism, such as unchecked global expansionism and mass population migrations, led sociologist and postmodern cultural critic Anthony Giddens to develop his theory of structuration. According to Giddens (1986), individuals can no longer be viewed as entities wholly defined or determined by greater social structures — economic, political, national — that potentially encompass and direct their daily lives. Citizens are not classified solely by their willingness to accept or even adapt to these macro-environments nor by their resistance to them. Instead, individuals act in conjunction with those broader social structures, thus creating a relational matrix that underscores the agency potential for both.

Although there is a certain social structure in place, marked by communal adherences to traditions, institutions, and moral codes, this structure is neither static nor impassive. At the individual level (the micro-level) these structures undergo continual contouring as they are altered, rectified, reinterpreted, or in some cases abandoned altogether. Social life emanates from this interaction between individual agency and institutional power. Additionally, social transformations occur at the collective level when individual acts multiply into collective acts, usually on a national level, and deny power to the established structures set in place.

Miroslaw Filiciak (2003) employs Giddens' theory of social structuration to develop his concept of hyperidentities within the realm of the video game. Filiciak's work, concentrated mostly on the phenomenon of massively multi-player online role-playing games (MMORPGs), focuses on the interaction between player and avatar and how this particular synthesis of individual and technology helps produce what he considers a "networked self" (p. 89). This technologically developed and enhanced self, in conjunction with other networked selves, assists in creating fictive environments girded by openly displayed human desires. Relating his own experiences about his initiation into *Everquest* and the panoply of possible choices for creating an avatar, he acknowledges that "the MMORPG user situation is an idealized image of the situation of the postmodern human creature, in which a user

can freely shape his own self" (p. 90). A concomitant element of this rearticulation of self, this shaping, is the opportunity to create a series of alterations
that can substitute an ideal form vastly superior to the realistic form of the player
him/herself. Constructing an avatar becomes a moment of instantaneous gratification as well as a drastic improvement because the selected proxy becomes
a "manifestation of the self beyond the realms of the physical, existing in a
space where identity is self-defined rather than pre-ordained" (Reid 1996).

This emphasis on auto-definition stems from the fragmentary nature of
the postmodern condition: "...the pressures influencing identity are augmented
by mass media along with the lifestyle promoted by consumerism, multiply-
ing our 'self' as an effect not only of complex social relations ... but also —
and maybe even mainly — of shaping ourselves through consumption and
constructing our own image" (p. 95).[1] Given this penchant for transformation via the acquisition and consumption of products — an activity arguably
exacerbated by the consumer-oriented nature of the internet — the traditional
accoutrements of self-making such as national allegiance, family history, and
community participation have become less attractive options. Purchasing an
identity, an economic enterprise central to the initiation of any partaking in
an MMORPG and mostly ignored by both Filiciak and Reid, underscores the
liquidity of the millennial subject. As one becomes "less likely to identify
with dominant institutions, background and residence are less and less important" as markers of selfhood (Filiciak 2003: 95).

The relative unimportance given to geography and cultural heritage in
Filiciak's elaboration of the relationship between player and avatar is a cause
for some concern.[2] The concentration on the reformulation of self in a rapidly evolving world, especially defined by the consumption of technology,
reinforces the fact that power and agency remain in the hands of those capable of affording the technologies necessary to reshape themselves. Failure to
mention issues of class and access assumes that gaming is a purely democratic
enterprise instead of a marker of privilege. The conservative sum of $500 a
year spent on video game titles alone by the average consumer of this technology, as well as the monthly fee for a number of online gaming sites, (see,
e.g., Berger 2002), establishes the economic considerations necessary for participation. These considerations are reinforced in Steve Jones's 2003 study of
gaming habits of U.S. college students for the PEW *Internet and American
Life* project. Similarly, Steve Jones's (2003) study of gaming habits among U.S.
college students for the *PEW Internet and American Life* project mentions the
"$6.5 billion spent on gaming" and the additional "$2.9 billion spent on
online gaming" the year before the study. Yet little emphasis is put on the fact
that the study's sample consists of a particularly privileged demographic:
American college and university students.

Filiciak's lack of acknowledgement of the role that identity politics plays in the reformulation of self via avatar suggests an uncomplicated relationship between the user and the game itself.[3] To immerse oneself as a "social actor in the medium" (McMahan 2003: 78) is a precarious transaction that entails a complicated series of submersions. Race, class, gender, sexual orientation, physical disabilities, and even religious affiliations are, at times, constrained or even outright denied by the diegetic (i.e., narrative) content of the video game. Questioning Janet Murray's (1997: 99) assumption that "the experience of being transported to an elaborately simulated place is pleasurable in itself, regardless of the fantasy content," in the remainder of this chapter I will examine the relative value of pleasure brought about by simulation.

Ghost Recon: Island Thunder

One of the most intriguing elements of this particular entry into the Clancy-inspired video game arsenal is its interpretation of post–Castro Cuba.[4] The accompanying game booklet for the Xbox title proclaims the plot parameters for the game to be played: "The year is 2010, and great changes are afoot in Cuba. Fidel Castro's heirs have been unable to keep the fire of his revolution burning, and a popular uprising has toppled the Communist regime. In its wake, a fragile hope for democracy emerges." It is amidst this political instability that the title begins to create the diegesis of gameplay. The "fragile hope" of Cuba's nascent democracy, after nearly five decades of Castro's revolution, rests, however, not in the hands of the citizenry. The fictitious history of the island, as presented by Red Storm, has been populated by sinister external forces. The booklet stresses that there are "those in Cuba who do not want to see a democratic regime, and they will do anything it takes — subversion, violence, or open revolution — to make certain that Cuba's future is the one they create for it."

The subversive element attempting to visit his own anti-democratic despotism upon this fictive Cuba is Priego, a politician/mercenary of indeterminate national origin who has been able to fund his coercive takeover through the seemingly endless resources of a Colombian drug lord whose name is never revealed. Priego, who must remain alive in order to successfully complete the overall mission, has managed to create his own assault weapon and grenade-toting army consisting of sympathetic Cuban rebels and, again, nationally unspecific soldiers of fortune.[5] Members of his enforcement team have been situated in a number of strategic locations throughout the imagined Cuba in order to ensure the election of someone who can conceivably become Cuba's next dictator.

Post-Castro Imaginings

The premise of the game — a concentrated exercise of fictional narrative based on possible political and social scenarios upon Castro's death — is not conceptually innovative. Stories of post–Castro Cuba have been quite plentiful in a variety of genres. The work of espionage and techno-thriller authors, such as Jim DeFelice (1997), Martin Cruz-Smith (2001), and Stephen Coonts (2000), take Castro's demise and potential futures after that event as the staging ground for the action in their texts. In the world of Cuban-American memoir, especially Carlos Eire's (2004) *Waiting for Snow in Havana* and Gustavo Pérez-Firmat's (1995) *Next Year in Cuba: A Cuban's Coming of Age in America*, both imagine — sometimes covertly and sometimes quite visibly — the role of the dictatorship in the shaping of multiple generations of Cubans and Cuban-Americans. These texts ponder what will emotionally ensue once Cuba is "free" from the present regime. Writing within what can best be considered a persistent emotional-nostalgic matrix, Pérez-Firmat (1995) acknowledges the passage of time and the trauma central to those perishing in exile because of Cuba's current political conditions: "For exile families, the impact of change is not only personal but cultural, for the passing away of a generation spells the extinction of a culture.... With every first-generation exile who passes away, we in the younger generation lose words, turns of phrase, habits of thought, gestures that are distinctively Cuban" (p. 163).[6] Although some may argue that Pérez-Firmat's generational extinction theory is an obvious outcome of temporal movement and not an innate condition of exile, the deterritorialization inherent in the exile condition causes an acute cultural divide. Subsequent generations of Cuban-Americans, due to the regime and embargo and travel restrictions as well as familial strictures, become alienated from the most viable source of cultural and social replenishment. The difficulty of maintaining contact, both with those who have perished in exile and those who remained on the island, exacerbates the waiting for the commencement of a Cuba without Castro.

Outside of the world of fiction and autobiography, the imagined future has also become the ongoing project of academics, economists, entrepreneurs, and politicians. These social actors have pondered the future of Cuba and the ramifications that Castro's demise will eventually and undoubtedly bring, envisioning the Pearl of the Antilles as the next land of economic opportunity. Even a cursory glance at Edward Gonzalez and Kevin F. McCarthy's (2004) RAND Corporation report reveals the multivalent considerations necessary for an intelligent discussion in the topic. Assessing years of economic disintegration, socio-political disenfranchisement, and Castro's suspect international reputation, especially in the arena of human rights, the report argues that the future of Cuba after Castro will be a precarious one. Gonzalez and McCarthy explain that the potential for political fallout after Castro will be even greater because the state will "surely possess less legitimacy and political power than its predecessor, while also lacking the economic resources to attack these structural problems" (p. 53). They go on to urge that the problems of what they designate a "failed state" (p. 51) will be an obvious result of decades of political and cultural totalitarianism: "The weakness of the state in the post–Castro era could compound Cuba's future difficulties, leaving the island mired in a deepening demographic, social, racial, and economic crisis that could lead to the unraveling of the new Cuban state" (p. 58).

Phantasmagoric Interventions

It is within this constellation of crises that the game situates Priego. Red Storm Entertainment's fictitious future is designed exactly as the political situation of contemporary Cuba: an eerie repetition of the past. Priego and his mercenaries are not alone, however. According to the game booklet, "From the midst of the chaos, the call goes out for the Ghosts. Their mission: to ensure the integrity of the Cuban elections by thwarting any attempts made to subvert them." Prima's official strategy guide for the Xbox version of the game (Searle 2003) minimally enhances the Ghosts' back-story by representing them as "unseen soldiers who move through the night, deadly, and silent as the grave" (p. 3). Searle's narrative collapses the border between player and plot by reinforcing the player's implicit cooperation with the explicit patriotic endeavor at hand: "You are America's elite Special Forces team, U.S. Army Green Berets sent to the world's political hotspots to keep the peace at any cost. Against impossible odds you rescue hostages, eliminate hostile military factions, and recover classified documents that could change the face of a nation" (p. 3).[7] Elite, deadly, and silent, Searle's imagined player is propelled into an American military scenario that assumes, unlike Fernandez and McCarthy, the U.S. Army's principal role in the liberation of Cuba from years of authoritarianism. One could argue that the main portion of the gameplay relies primarily on the ability to "rifle through the dozen remaining enemies for the prize of a good night's sleep" (Searle 2003: 58). The game's dominant narrative finds the value in killing as narrative inertia; forward movement in a fictive world depends upon a kill that "signifies moral progress, a means to an end, not an end in itself" (Gibson 1994: 102). In fact, movement through the multiple missions entails the systematic and strategic killing of those Cubans unwilling to openly embrace an American-prescribed and militarily-installed democratic process. Coded as Priego's men, Cubans in the game, far from being the populace to be liberated, are transformed into the enemies who impede the potential advancement from mission to mission as Searle's manual implicitly attests.

Very few "everyday" Cubans appear during gameplay, either as citizens or even voters; this continues the simplistic military/political foundations of the title as a war-game in which the elite forces and the easily overtaken despotic resistance are pitted against one another. It is striking how game designers represent Cuba as a barren geography bereft of any actual population. Even when the mission moves towards the center of the city of Cienfuegos during the "Liberty Storm" campaign (a province whose population numbers well into the six digits), the streets are absolutely empty. An abandoned bus, empty buildings with intact facades, and a red 1950s-era convertible, amidst a scattering of palm trees, serve as icons of geography in some sort of tropical shorthand. A military jeep driving down the main thoroughfare and a couple of armed soldiers are the only signs of life. These significant images reify the hero-enemy dichotomy central to the game's dominant narrative. Apparently too afraid to actually populate the territory or act on their own behalf for the sake of political liberation, Cubans outside of Priego's circle of influence have been obviously made inconsequential to the game and thus have been summarily deleted from the design.

The Minutiae of War

Of the two parties present in the game — Priego's forces and the American Ghosts — the designers have also deleted the option of choosing between the two. The player must command the leadership of the elite force's Alpha team. He/she becomes the creator of not only that team but also the designer of the Bravo team, an often used partner that aids in surveillance, ambush, rescue and recovery. Due to these design parameters, the only available missions involve defeating the pre-programmed Cuban insurgency. The player's primary responsibility is to construct a team of eight soldiers, divided into two companies, who have been allocated statistical points based on weapon skill, stealth, leadership ability, and endurance potential.

Searle devotes several pages of his guide to these seemingly valuable criteria given that apt team building and success at the coalition phase will eventually translate into success in accomplishing all the missions. This focus on the minutiae of military ability, on the part of Searle, helps "facilitate the player's engagement with the fictional gameworld" (Crogan 2003: 295). The concentration necessary (even before actual gameplay commences) to create the proper elite unit that will ensure victory places the player deeply within even the most minimal employment of the game's imaginary political framework. New soldiers arrive as rewards for successful individual mission completion, making the act of coalition formation an ongoing process that further minimizes the discussion about the fictive historical moment presented by the designers. Arguably, if the focus is maneuvered almost exclusively toward the right military combination of avatars for overcoming the enemies found along the "many potential routes through the simulated event space" (Crogan 2003: 289), then the event space in question is only tangentially the island of Cuba. Cuba just happens to be the "political hotspot" selected for this particular series of campaigns. For the designers at Red Storm Entertainment, the value of the gaming experience resides exclusively in American military prowess and strategic ability.

Although Patrick Crogan (2003) chooses to "deemphasize the ethical positioning of the user/audience in favor of the demands of training for control" (p. 296) in his overview of video game titles within the military entertainment complex, I would like to suggest the necessity of evaluating these positions in order to explore how particular members of the gaming audience are either excluded outright or, in worst case scenarios, demonized by certain portrayals generated by designers. The ability of the Ghosts is generally hampered by the placement of Priego's men. It is weaponry, stealth, leadership, and endurance that maneuvers them to optimal engagement sites where the enemy can be eliminated. The "insertion zone" for Alpha and Bravo companies allows enough cover for both teams to strategically move, initially undetected, towards the fulfillment of the preconceived objectives. The avatar's slow movement and patience brings about the action for which he/she has been deployed. Agency lies in the hands of a player explicitly coded as white, male and American. The game's first-person perspective, although potentially liberating on the identity front, may fail to allow total immersion due to the emphasis on the game's nationalist agenda.

Conversely, the enemies throughout the game are solely reactive. Priego's men either become bodies cut down by American artillery or interrupters of missions — signs of strategic failure. The non-player (Cuban) characters are unable to kill as adeptly as the elite forces or reposition themselves to counter the player's plan of attack, at least no more than what has been preconceived by the designers; they operate in "the playful staging of symbolic death" (Crogan 2003: 279). They have neither the stealth nor the endurance, so central to the incoming troops, to protect themselves. According to Searle (2003), even the weaponry allotted to Priego's men fails to protect them: "When you get into some shooting, *Island Thunder* upgrades the demo expert to a Z-84 assault weapon" (p. 16). Arguably this upgrade is a vital component for victory given his remark that "the enemy uses assault weapons, but they don't get as high-tech as the demo expert's Z-84" (p. 16). As the Ghosts' cache of weapons increase, improve, and morph throughout the missions, the enemy's arsenal remains both static and rudimentary. The game's concentration on the use-value of military technology as a central component of success arguably acts as a form of tacit approval for military intervention.[8]

Digital Terraforming

Furthering the derealization established by the designers of the game, the island never quite becomes a territory capable of generating active interrogations of exilic or national subjectivities. Instead, it is used as a random site for the game's exposition of jungle warfare. *Island Thunder* is one of many titles emanating from a trend that Gray (1994: 316) refers to as "speculative military futurology" in which technological fantasies and American military culture and policy are intimately related. It seems that with every scientific breakthrough, especially in the 20th century, technology has either been created or appropriated for military use. A major consequence of this intersection between military policy and technological progress has been the creation of contested, imaginary nation spaces — battlescapes — where potential wars can be acted out, practiced, rehearsed, and (given the advent of gaming technology) started over for the sake of understanding the consequences of military intervention. Given the endless scenarios and outcomes possible, the theory behind Gray's wargames concept could conceivably lead to the end of war through the bloodless and therefore antiseptic nature of modern technoscience, an optimal scenario suggested by Richard's (1999) conceptualization of abstract conflicts without material consequences. Discussing the recent release of the U.S. Army and Department of Defense's first-person shooter, *America's Army: Operations* (U.S. Army 2002), Crogan views the game as an illustration of the military and technology collusion: "The two-way traffic between computer gaming and military simulation in the military entertainment complex signposts a significant moment in the pure war tendency" (p. 280). This merger of technology and imagination will potentially serve as the cornerstone of what Possony (1970) has labeled America's 21st century manifest destiny (cited in Gray 1994). Unlike previous conceptualizations and incarnations of national and geographic progress, Possony's vision takes place in realms and territories that are wholly uncharted and only figuratively populated. By creating virtual wars in fictional spaces, whether in books or in video games, populations are not truly displaced, resources are not truly exhausted, and casualties are not truly experienced. It is warfare, ideally made absolutely clean.

One of the essential ingredients missing from the fusion of technology and warfare is the population of the battlescapes in which these mergers occur. The concentration on artillery intervention, brought about by technological progress, elides how these tactics are, by definition, implemented against the geographies inhabited by other populations. It is in the realm of international relations where technological success is ultimately measured. Undoubtedly, native populations suffer the consequences of the type of armed maneuvers, even if solely in the arena of virtual war, that Gray (1994) discusses. The erasure of national agency, with the marked exception of American national agency, becomes the first step in the disintegration of a national identity that can potentially be defined by the citizens themselves. As a Cuban-American player of *Ghost Recon: Island Thunder*, I am asked by the dominant narrative of the game to inhibit my own multiculturality and national allegiances and to embark on a military and political crusade against those with whom I share, at least partially, a common heritage. The momentary submersion of my own roots becomes a necessary act in order to accomplish the programmed missions as they have been designed. American military agency, as well as the liberatory agenda implied by that agency, discounts a variety of other potential relationships that may arise among those present in the battlescape.

Mignolo (2000) stresses that the practice just described, which he labels local historiography, unifies and permits access to cultural and social power. It is in the adoption, adaptation, transformation and rearticulation of local histories that nations begin to participate within a global conversation. Power is therefore derived from the nation's ability to possess and, by extension, control its own biography. According to Mignolo, "[l]ocal histories are mediated by the structure of power — more specifically by the coloniality of power that articulates the colonial differences between local histories projected and exporting global designs and local histories importing and transforming them" (2000: 278). Arguably, the mediation central to this formulation must be read against the technological power that participants entering the contact zone bring to the engagement. The globalizing impulse inherent in the deployment of armed forces maximizes the distance and the difference between the participants and, via this "new civilizing design" (Mignolo 2000: 279), interrupts local history as it actively commences to transform the invaded terrain.

As I have argued, the problematic redefinition of Cuba as a site in need of Ghost reconnaissance (i.e., in need of surveillance) and, in due time, in need of applied democratization suggests the creation of a fictive landscape completely bereft of a local history and national history so vital to the exposition of a country's identity. Along with the absolute negation of a viable Cuban population (aside from a small ensemble of similar looking hostages in need of rescue) the video game designers construct the island's geography to validate the narrative content of the game. What seem particularly vilified in game are the territory where the future-war scenario takes place and the shadow population that seemingly allow it to occur. Red Storm Entertainment has created a 3-D ensemble shooter environment that paramilitarizes the territory of Cuba while maintaining its tropical ambience. Although bustling metropolitan areas do exist in the actual island, for the programmers this virtual world is one of underground bunkers, abandoned radio towers, outposts and strongholds.

As the missions unfold, the Cuban landscape seems constructed solely for the reinforcement of the message that the Ghosts need to be present and must be ultimately victorious. With every engagement there are not only Priego's armed men but also a series of military installations that mandate the intervention of the Alpha and Bravo team. A rough count of these defense structures number in the teens. Ghosts are asked to destroy ammunition dumps, take command of fortresses, purge terrorist camps, and dismantle a fully operational SAM site with an antitank missile. These otherwise-barren militaristic landscapes are dotted by small shacks and a few collapsing plantation buildings set amid sierras or swamps or isolated stretches of beach. These structures, programmed outside of the necessary architecture for the armed intervention inherent to gameplay, offer a simulacrum of Cuba and reinforce the perceived assumption of the island as a Caribbean wasteland at its most decayed. Cuba's future — on the brink of collapse, abjectly poor, and militarily defenseless except for Priego's input — can only be guaranteed via America's military assistance. Cuba is not an island as much as it is a piece of land where ghosts deploy firepower while a ghost population awaits rescue. Cuba is reduced to a campaign rather than a country. The game touts the triumph of American virtue and reinforces the myth that military achievement and technological expertise will eventually transmit freedom to populations unable to access that freedom on their own.

Even the natural terrain of the island, structures that can only suffer tangential transformation in order to maintain some level of authenticity, stop functioning as landscape or as ready supplies of natural resources. In the game, this geography becomes cover for troop advancement or tactical positions that ensure successful sniper fire. The elite forces traverse the island just as the island lends itself to triumphant traversing. The step-by-step strategy for winning the game reinforces the way in which the geography assists the player's forward movement through the missions: "Take this small gap through the rocks to arrive at location point #3. Advance south and follow the rocky plateau base southeast. You'll wind through small gaps in the mountain and a cave.... The last gap brings you out into the midst of your enemies. Tread with care" (Searle 2003: 71). The exit from the mountain leads the player, if the two guards have been eliminated, to a central tower that "offers a wonderful view of the map" and allows the shooter to "scan around with your sniper until you find an enemy target" (p. 74). Landscape and the pleasure of flora, the game's "wonderful view" is only truly wonderful insofar as it certifies some level of strategic value. Outside of its military usability, the Cuba presented is wholly irrelevant. Some would argue that this usability is, in regards to gameplay, the primary and perhaps only value of the game.

Warriors Without Borders

Fast becoming one of Amazon's Top 100 console games, the expansion pack has so far merited a number of very satisfactory reviews on the web. Interestingly though, most of the praise and/or criticism is basic gamer analysis. According to one reviewer on amazon.com, "the graphics are clearly improved upon from those in the PC version — soldiers look cleaner, and even explosions detonate much more realistically." Another satisfied customer of the Xbox live multiplayer version of the title mentions how "booming firepower from fellow gunners in all-natural environment filled with bustling leaves and thunderous falling rain completes the great soundtrack." A significant feature of this particular review is the attention to arsenals and weapons prowess. Although the discussion of the soldiers themselves is minimal aside from some positive remarks of the polygon count, these player reviews suggest that the value of the title stems from the ability to simulate the stealth and patience necessary to render oneself invisible to the enemy. This is not the combat frenzy fought from within the fog of war as players find themselves bombarded by multiple arsenals. This is covert operations built around the emotionally-driven preservation of a miniscule number of select, and therefore invaluable, operatives. The focus on firepower and military activity in these reviews also shows how untroubled these players are with the political ramifications implied by the game. Unlike my own apprehensions of participating in the elimination of Cubans for the sake of their own liberation, these players, through what appears to me to be a different ideological frame, seem to have bought into the validity of using covert operatives whenever and wherever necessary if the end result is freedom and democracy.

To this end, *Island Thunder*'s focus primarily relies on camaraderie above geography. What ideally appeals to the player is the opportunity to bond via the explosiveness of warfare with other similarly-minded individuals without the accompanying burden of actual military service or physical peril. The success of the title, especially with the multiplayer functions, is the ability to simultaneously hyperlink several players together in order to mimic the sensation of unified reconnaissance without necessarily having the other players within the room. This chance to embody the fictive ghost soldier with others in pursuit of the same gamer ideals accentuates the central danger of the contemporary virtualization of the technothriller genre. With its devout faith in one's salvation through technology (which I ideologically link to a country's salvation through the technology and weaponry of other presumed superior nations), games of this nature assume the significance of rituals of male bonding, military unity, and patriarchal bloodsport while only tangentially paying attention to the territories where these pursuits take place.

The allure of the techno-thriller for its primarily male readership lies in its prevalent message of "transforming boys into men" by merging them to their machines, first, and with each other, second (Gibson 1994: 85). Future-wars scenarios, with their evil enemies and geographic spaces/populations in dire need of taming, glorify armed combat by tapping into the symbolic implications of conflict. Speaking of fictive war experiences, Gibson describes how "they affirm male power in ways that are accessible to middle-class men. Paramilitary brothers live lives far outside the system and depend upon their own bodies and personal weapons for power" (Gray 1994: 322). For those who live within the system, fantasies of technological prowess and comfortable male camaraderie create a source of control in an increasingly alienating and chaotic world. Taming the island is a clear objective whereas taming the workplace, academia, their children, or their own bodies may be unaccomplishable. And despite its focus on current political events, potential geopolitical speculations, or outright fantastic future-war scenarios, Gibson notes that these virtual paramilitary fantasies are "all about giving birth, either to new weapons, or to new warriors" (1994: 322).

At every stage of the game, one of the player's primary responsibilities is to perform a certain task that will help him/her unlock a new specialist and a new weapon that may then be inserted into the original formulation of the Alpha and Bravo teams. Constant supervision over personnel, reinforcements, and weaponry becomes a necessary component of success as the complexity of the missions increase. In fact, certain scenarios cannot be mastered unless there has been a marked progress in firepower. Once again, individual strategic prowess becomes essential only insofar as it acts to ensure access to improved technologies. The acquisition of this technology remains the core value of the wargame experience: "[t]he more weapons the warrior owns, the more power he can appropriate from their histories, and the more fantasy adventure he can pursue" (Gibson 1994: 87). Gibson goes on to stress, however, that this acquisitive urge is never wholly divorced from the virtuous and moral ideal that necessitates the warehousing of such a variety of potentially devastating implements. "Since paramilitary culture projects a world in which the male warrior is left alone to defend himself and his loved ones — or to avenge their deaths — the boundaries of the society he has to protect become synonymous with the farthest distance he can secure against a potential enemy" (p. 87). In the case of *Island Thunder*, the real world is shorn away and privilege is granted to the world that appears before the warrior's eyes, an utterly destructive point of view regardless of the patriotic, moral or civil value with which those two intersecting lines have been imbued.

Final Reflections on a Hybridized Self

It is from such a vantage point and through such an environment (i.e., one beset by white American masculinity) that I am asked to travel. My mission successes require more comrades, more weapons, and more individual power, regardless of my own cultural heritage or political beliefs. *Island Thunder* demands my American patriotism via self-selected and highly specialized avatars embarking upon a ready-made, directed moral quest. Ensuring freedom and liberty to an island on the brink of another five decades of totalitarianism, my Ghost comes with stealth, strategy and the machineries of liberation necessary for the task. The implied attraction to the heroic task at hand, in the words of Don Pendleton, an editor of numerous men's action-adventure novels, stems from the belief that "they feel like some piece of their turf is being threatened" (quoted in Gibson 1994: 111). It is vital, however, to note that working through this threat seems always to take place on "turf" that belongs to someone else.

Notes

1. One could argue that the ultimate example of this fusion between consumption, gameplay, and identity formation is found in the recently released *The Urbz: Sims in the City* by Maxis Games. Throughout the game, one's clothing acts as the catalyst for either positive or negative communication interactions in the number of social environments developed by game designers. The philosophy behind this title is that the garments behave as surrogates for the identity of the avatars and are therefore more important than the actual personalities of the avatars themselves.

2. Filiciak envisions the virtual realm as a natural extension of the human desire to render ourselves visible outside of our corporeal selves. Acting for other members of the audience, whether through the fantasy-scapes of MMORPG or through the multiple venues for online play, we become members in a community where "everybody can star" (p. 100).

3. In fact, Filiciak (2003: 101) acknowledges that "games are the medium that most perfectly describe our existence and express the way the human 'self' functions in the contemporary world." Via his elaboration of hyperidentities, he views gameplay as an elaborate series of active communications that permit people to view each other's identities without the obstacles that could conceivably preclude these interactions.

    4. To date, given all the available platforms for video game play, there are seventy available titles under the Tom Clancy banner of military-inspired video games. Although some titles are multiple entries, due to simultaneous release for PC, PS2, XBOX, Gamecube, and PSP, the Clancy name above the title has become almost shorthand for sales success.

    5. The sympathetic Cubans who make up the vast majority of Priego's personnel are all duplicates of each other. Dressed similarly — linen pants and the traditional short sleeved guayabera — and shaded similarly-light brown skin and black hair — the varieties inherent to the general Cuban population are erased in order to represent an iconic Cuban male that will serve as targets for the Ghosts.

    6. Due to the demise of the first generation of exiles and the cultural embargo on Cuban artistic products emanating from the island, the relative isolation of Cuba, especially in regards to Cuban and American interactions, makes it possible to construct a one-dimensional history on the part of Island Thunder's designers. The presence of Fidel Castro and communism a mere ninety miles away from the United States, especially given its five decades of existence, has allowed the island to be a persistent theme within the techno-thriller and espionage genres.

    7. According to Eugene Provenzo (1991: 64–5), "video games allow the viewer[s] to engage actively in the scenarios presented.... They experience a sense of personal involvement in the action when they work the controls, and they perceive the video games as not only a source of companionship, but possibly a substitute for it."

    8. Gray (1994) concludes that one of the integral components of military environments is the construction of "rigid images" of potentially dangerous others that help perpetuate the environments in the first place: "[t]o justify itself the war establishment requires a ferociously evil and very powerful adversary" (p. 324). One reason, perhaps, for the shadowy histories of Priego and those who have installed him into power is the need to maximize the ominousness that is conspiratorial and potentially multinational or even global in nature.

References

Berger, Arthur Asa. 2002. *Video Games: A Popular Culture Phenomenon*. New Brunswick, NJ: Transaction Publishers.

Coonts, Stephen. 2000. *Cuba*. NY: St. Martin's.

Crogan, Patrick. 2003. "Gametime: History, Narrative, and Temporality in *Combat Flight Simulator 2*." Pp. 275–302 in *The Video Game Theory Reader*, edited by Mark J.P. Wolf and Bernard Perron. NY: Routledge.

Cruz-Smith, Martin. 2001. *Havana Bay*. NY: Ballantine.

DeFelice, Jim. 1997. *Havana Strike*. Wayne, PA: Leisure Books.

Eire, Carlos. 2004. *Waiting for Snow in Havana: Confessions of a Cuban Boy*. NY: Free Press.

Filiciak, Miroslaw. 2003. "Hyperidentities: Postmodern Identity Patterns in Massively Multiplayer Online Role-Playing Games." Pp. 87–102 in *The Video Game Theory Reader*, edited by Mark J.P. Wolf and Bernard Perron. NY: Routledge.

Gibson, James William. 1994. *Warrior Dreams: Violence and Manhood in Post-Vietnam America*. NY: Hill and Wang.

Giddens, Anthony. 1986. *The Constitution of Society: Outline of the Theory of Structuration*. Berkeley, CA: University of California Press.

Gonzalez, Edward, and Kevin F. McCarthy. 2004. *Cuba After Castro: Legacies, Challenges, and Impediments*. Santa Monica, CA: RAND Corporation.

Gray, Chris Hables. 1994. " 'There Will Be War!': Future War Fantasies and Militaristic Science Fiction in the 1980s." *Science Fiction Studies* 64 (21): 315–336.

Jones, Steve. 2003. "Let the Games Begin: Gaming Technology and Entertainment among College Students." Washington, DC: PEW Internet and American Life Project. Retrieved June 1, 2005. (http://www.pewinternet.org/pdfs/PIP_College_Gaming_Reporta.pdf)

McMahan, Alison. 2003. "Immersion, Engagement, and Presence: A Method for Analyzing 3-D Video Games." Pp. 67–86 in *The Video Game Theory Reader*, edited by Mark J.P. Wolf and Bernard Perron. NY: Routledge.

Mignolo, Walter D. 2000. *Local Histories/Global Designs*. Princeton, NJ: Princeton University Press.

Murray, Janet. 1997. *Hamlet on the Holodeck: The Future of Narrative in Cyberspace*. Cambridge, MA: MIT Press.

Pérez-Firmat, Gustavo. 1995. *Next Year in Cuba: A Cubano's Coming of Age in America*. NY: Anchor Books.

Possony, Stefan Thomas. 1970. *The Strategy of Technology: Winning the Decisive War*. Cambridge, MA: University Press of Cambridge.

Provenzo, Eugene. 1991. *Video Kids: Making Sense of Nintendo*. Cambridge, MA: Harvard Press.

Reid, Elizabeth. 1996. "Text-Based Virtual Realities: Identity and the Cyborg Body." In *High Noon on the Electronic Frontier: Conceptual Issues in Cyberspace*, edited by Peter Ludlow. Cambridge, MA: MIT Press.

Richard, Birgit. 1999. "Norn Attacks and Marine Doom." Pp. 339–340 in *Ars Electronica: Facing the Future: A Survey of Two Decades* edited by Timothy Druckrey. Cambridge, MA: MIT Press.

Searle, Mike. 2003. *Prima's Official Strategy Guide: Tom Clancy's Ghost Recon: Island Thunder*. Roseville, CA: Prima Games.

UbiSoft. 2003. *Tom Clancy's Ghost Recon: Island Thunder*. Platform: Xbox. Red Storm Entertainment.

U.S. Army. 2002. *America's Army: Operations*. Platform: console. U.S. Army and Secret Level.

Section 3: Experience and Identity

9. *The Player's Journey*

Mirjam Eladhari

This paper discusses in-game characterization with a special focus on the conditions for character and identity development in massively multi-player online role-playing games (MMORPGs). Characterization is one of the tools that students in any narrative art form learn about at the very start. Narrative characterization is about describing other characters to an audience, viewer, player or reader. In virtual game worlds (VGWs) things are different because players characterize themselves. While much has been written about development of identity in virtual game worlds, (e.g., Bruckman 1992; Turkle 1995) there is so far not much material approaching the development of own fictional identities — player characters — from a poetic-aesthetic perspective. It is necessary to recognize not only that virtual game world creation is an art, but also that playing is an art in itself, providing performances both for the individual player and for the virtual society of the specific game world.

Can one talk about characterization at all if it is not a performed identity, or role, but instead a real identity expressed within a fictional setting? Can one talk about "true character" when the character in question is a real person, set in a fictional world, expressing an identity which may or may not be fictional, who may or may not be role-playing while performing it? In the following I draw upon thoughts from Bartle (2003) about the concept of persona, from McKee (1997) about the notion of true character, from Campbell's (1949) concept of the hero's journey, from Fine's (1983) thoughts on role-playing versus gaming, and from other sources to see if it is possible to take a few first glimpse under the veil. In particular, I am looking for possible ways to use characterization to create more meaningful dramatic experiences and to deepen the possible immersion into the game world via closer identification with one's own player character. Methods for game mastering may be one way, while evolved rule sets and autonomous functions for player characters may be others.

MMORPGs and the Importance of the Player's Representation

MMORPGs have a set of more or less general features that control what type of game activities are available (Eladhari 2003), yet there are a few striking aspects of VGWs which make them unique and different from other forms of art. One of these aspects is how the openness of the narrative structures makes it possible for players to add their own goals to game worlds, which in turn results in added narrative potential in the world (Eladhari and Lindley 2004). This chapter, however, focuses more closely upon characterization — the core of good storytelling. In the VGW setting avatars are characterized by different persons who play. This may be compared with how literary authors try to simulate characters when their characters "come to life" with themselves driving the story. Here we have a similar situation, but it is a performance rather than a simulation.

Avatars are not only vehicles for movement or self-characterization, they are the functional cores of each individual playing experience. They are both the focus and the focalization point, i.e. the point from which to focus. As a player you see the world through the eyes of your avatar — your focalization point. When other players look at you they see your representation, your avatar — you are a focus. Furthermore, the state of your avatar controls what you can or cannot do in any given moment. From a design and engineering point of view, the avatar represents all effort to build the whole system, all of its functionality boiled down to be used by one super or base class that is the one that the player will use — to execute the whole piece; to set the world into moving, living, changing; to add to its society, its dramas, its norms, its webs of social networks, its layout and architecture and to the world soul that is the synthesis of all pieces functioning, moving and rubbing together. If a minimal design change is made in player character (PC) functionality, the whole system must be changed. One could say that the player is a concentrated mirror of the whole world — in that size, too: a small mirror that reflects the whole world. The mirror is the player's peeping hole into the VGW. It is not only an interface; the whole setup of the character is dialectically related to the world. How PCs are engineered (i.e., what possible states, abilities and properties they can have) is wholly dependent on the world mechanics itself and vice versa.

Characterization and True Character

Characters and characterization are obviously central in VGWs. But what is characterization in this context? McKee (1997: 100) makes the distinction between characterization and true character, defining characterization as such as what is merely observable:

> Characterization is the sum of all observable qualities of a human being, everything knowable through careful scrutiny: age and IQ; sex and sexuality; style of speech and gesture; choices of home, car, and dress; education and occupation; personality and nervosity; values and attitudes — all aspects of humanity we could know by taking notes on someone day in and day out.

All these things applied in a game would be what we could see and note about another PC or about a non-player character (NPC) fairly easily by having a few conversations and maybe teaming up once or twice for common causes, like hunting or questing. True character, on the other hand, would not be seen so easily. According to McKee (1997: 101), "*true character* is revealed in the choices a human being makes under pressure — the greater the pressure, the deeper the revelation, the truer the choice is to the character's essential nature."

In order to see this in another player character, a deeper, long-term relationship is needed. In most cases these are friendships, but can also be love relations, curious obsessive enmities, or any other relationship that is more than an acquaintance. In relation to us as humans it is not uncommon to ask ourselves what we would do in a critical situation. Would you deceive your friends under pressure of losing your own life? If you were in an immediate life-threatening situation, would you panic or act with rational urgency? People who have been in critical situations often reflect upon their behavior afterwards and feel that they found out more about themselves when they reflected on how they reacted. This is true in the accounts of disaster survivors such as the sinking of the *Titanic* or the destruction of the twin towers in New York City, just as it is of players in VGWs.

Role-Play, Game-Play and Persona

One question that arises in massively multiplayer online game (MMOG) contexts is whether the true character shown in the VGW is the true character of the PC or the true character of the player. We assume that in most cases what is shown is the true character of the player, this being due to two main factors. First, most players of MMOGs do not role-play a fictive character but instead play themselves in another world. Second, the assumption may be tied to one's level of immersion in the game world and thus in the identity via which the world is experienced. Bartle (2003) has described the representation of the PC in terms of levels of immersion, going from avatar to character to persona — the highest level of immersion. The persona refers to a state where the player does not differentiate between her/himself and the character. In Bartle's taxonomy, the player has an avatar if s/he only uses it as a puppet to control as her/his representative in the world. A player who regards the object that s/he controls as her/his representation in the world would have a character. The character is an extension of a player's self, a whole personality for the player when s/he is in-game. Most players play at the level of representation and often have several characters. In the most extreme state of immersion, the object that a player controls is not seen as a representation. Rather, the player has the experience of being the object:

> A persona is a player, in a virtual world. That's in it. Any separate distinction of character is gone — the player is the character. You're not role-playing a being, you are a being; you're not assuming an identity, you are that identity; you're not projecting a self, you are that self. If you're killed in a fight, you don't feel that your character has died, you feel that you have died. There's no level of indirection, no filtering, no question: You are there [Bartle 2003: 155].

A player who feels that the game character is a persona rather than an avatar has not only achieved statistical proofs of achievement, but also a sense of synthesis, of really being there, in the game world. Therefore, players can be divided into three different groups:

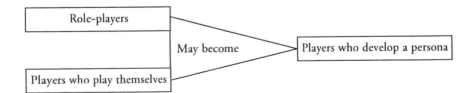

These distinctions are by no means clear-cut. A role-player may develop a persona, a player who plays her/himself can sometimes experience having a persona or role-playing, and so on. However, what all these modes of playing have in common is that the *player* is the one who carries out both the characterization of and the expression of the true character of her or his avatar/player character/persona in the current VGW.

In VGWs the characterization of the PC is done by the player within the gameplay framework provided by the developer. This means that we can divide up characterization into a number of dimensions.

1. The design of the gameplay framework, specifically the design and implementation of types of PCs (character classes).
2. The player's configuration of a PC before entering the VGW and possibly also formulation of a fictional background story for the PC.
3. The player's performance and development of the PC in the VGW.

Let us now explore these dimensions, each in turn.

Creating a Character

How a character is created depends of the details of the specific gameplay framework, but most VGWs let the player choose from among a range of different character types, such as race, class and profession. Some game designs allow players to also choose a gender (often there is a neutral gender as one of the options for certain classes) and to customize the appearance (skin, eye, or hair color, height, build, and so on). Often, different classes are better for certain professions, but usually the choice is free.[1] The main skills chosen determine what the PC is especially good at. In game this gives the player a certain role in groups that are formed to do something specific, like quests or hunting sessions. Groups usually need to be put together so that they, as a whole, have the necessary skills and properties to succeed at a certain task.

In most games player can also change the properties of the character. The properties are the game-specific properties that define how strong, fast (and so on) the character is, which is often combined with skill levels that determine how efficient a certain action is. For example, if a player creates a character that is going to use a dagger as a weapon in *Asheron's Call*, s/he will probably choose a high value for the property Quickness. If the player intends to create a character that will use magic in some form he or she will probably place higher values on all properties that are related to the mind. These specific examples of using magic and daggers apply to MMOGs having a fantasy mythos (e.g. *Asheron's Call, Asheron's Call 2, EverQuest, Final Fantasy XI*), but similar setups are found in worlds with other genre-types, such as sci-fi (e.g., *Anarchy Online, Star Wars Galaxies*). A paradox for character creation is that players need to decide on important personal properties before they have entered the game world, so at the moment of creation they may not know what will be important to them.

Player Characterization in the Game World

Once a player has entered a game, there are two dimensions to characterization. The first is how the PC can be perceived by other players, while the second is how the player perceives her or his own PC. Players can usually not see all of the properties of another player's PC.

CHARACTERISTICS AT A GLANCE

Suppose a PC approaches another PC in-game. Things that are visible and audible in close spatial proximity are the characters' class, gender, specific physical appearance, motions and possible sounds associated with the PC. In most VGWs it is also possible to target the character and ask for more information. In some games the targeted PC gets a text message that another PC is accessing their information. In some games the amount of information that can be retrieved is dependent on skills in getting information (as in *Asheron's Call*). The information usually consists of information about the character's main skill type, level of advancement and the currently-wielded weapon. In many cases (as in *Final Fantasy Online*) it is also possible to see whether the PC is interested in joining a group. So what do we make of this? Depending on our current needs, goals or preferred type of activity, we can see if it is worth starting a conversation with the other player/PC or not.

TRIAL CONVERSATION

Suppose that we start a conversation with the other PC. First of all, as in all media, dialog is a powerful tool for characterization. Cherny (1994: 11) shows an early example from the text-based VGW, *LambdaMOO*, of how players program personal and characteristic behaviors into their avatars that can be triggered by keywords typed by other players.

Besides pure dialog, in conversation it is also possible to use emotes, to add gestures and other type of information into the conversation. How much of this can be animated differs from game to game. Emotes are available in text-based MUD forms, and in many cases this gives a large degree of freedom to the player if it is combined with the freedom to program behaviors. This is usually referred to as "scripting" and is something that has become more sophisticated also in recent graphical VGWs, most notably in *Second Life* and *Star Wars Galaxies*. Scripting is often used to put together chains of highly individualized emote sequences. In *Star Wars Galaxies* it is possible to set a mood for the character. The dialog system then adds comments in addition to the typed dialog. For example, if a character has the mood set to "wounded" and types "oh" the output in the form of text is the following: ""oh" Immigrain says, dismay in her eyes." Also the facial expression is set to correspond with the mood (although not all moods have a corresponding facial expression). Another expressive feature is that certain words that the player types when talking freely in the area (i.e. not in a specific chat channel) triggers a PC animation sequence. For example, if the player types "yes," an animation shows the PC nodding.

GETTING TO KNOW

Suppose that we decide to do something together with another PC. Let us also suppose that we both have just joined the game world and that we therefore decide to do a "delivery quest" together. A quest of this type has the objective of delivering an item from one NPC to another, a type of quest given to low level characters in many MMOGs. Such quests are simple and give players opportunities to see more of the game world while becoming accustomed to the interface. Through the interactions associated with doing the quest together with another PC, we "get to know" the other character. That is, we get an idea about how this player character behaves and who s/he *is*.

"SELF–CHARACTERIZATION"?

All of this raises the question: How is characterization in VGWs different from how we get to know people in everyday, face-to-face life? One obvious difference is that it is not everyday life. Instead of being constrained by the properties we were born to, such as gender, appearance, health and conditioning by social class, by culture, by environment and by family, we are constrained by the mechanics of the game world rules and of its norm systems. If we compare this to moving to another country we could argue that both are situations where you change a lot of old constraints for new ones.

Can we still talk about characterization? In *Life on the Screen*, Sherry Turkle (1995) describes how she (as an English-speaker) felt when she lived in France. She became the "French-speaking Sherry" who "was not unrecognizable, but she was her own person. In particular, while the English-speaking Sherry had little confidence in being able to take care of herself, the French-speaking Sherry had to and got on with it" (p. 209) These things also happen in virtual worlds — but in real life we don't perceive ourselves as performing any kind of "self-characterization." We may in Goffman's (1959) sense consciously create certain appearances to make a certain impression, but we don't talk about characterization. Characterization is a concept strongly tied to pre-authored fiction. Methods for characterization are taught in contexts of learning to characterize characters in movies, novels, and, when it comes to games, NPCs. We could argue that VGWs are fictional and therefore all types of expression of information about a certain player character must be seen as characterization. But many players see the time that they spend in a VGW — and especially their lived relations with the other players — as a parallel reality, possible to compare to a vacation or to any kind of social situation that has other types of conditions than the "everyday" has. This is also comparable to Oldenburg's (1989) notion of different kinds of social places, where the home is number one, work is number two and the local pub is the third place. You go to the third place to socialize with other people, who in turn have many good effects for the individual and the community, but your primary reason for going there is that it is fun. For many players the VGW is such a third place.

In his sociological study of role-playing *Shared Fantasy*, Fine (1983) makes a distinction between game players and role players. The gamer plays the game as himself, while the player who wishes to lose himself in the fantasy is the true role-player — s/he plays the character. According to Fine, the gamer uses gaming as an extension of self, motivated by the question "Would I survive under these circumstances?" The gamer's play tends to be more oriented toward succeeding in the game scenario than in the role-playing. For role-players, on the other hand, the emphasis on the role is much greater, to the point of the player claiming to be "another person" or "schizoid" (Fine, 1983: 211).[2]

For the sake of argument, suppose that characterization is something that only the role-player does because a role-player makes a conscious effort to characterize the character s/he is performing, in a similar way that an actor would, except that there is no audience on which to make an impression apart from fellow role-players. The distinguishing factor would be the conscious act of characterization. But in fact (from a systemic point of view) the role-player and the game-player use the same tools for expression and they do make impressions that are characterizing them as players and game characters. We still make impressions, and we are still (at least most of us) conscious of how others perceive us. Considering that MMOG players on average play around 20 hours per week (Yee 2002) it is probable that gameplay styles vary over time — maybe the role-players do not role-play all the time and vice versa.

To use the term persona as described by Bartle (2003), it takes time to become a persona in a game and that time is needed for development. The intention to evolve the PC over time into a persona is probably not tied to whether the player is game-playing or role-playing. A role-player actually becomes the character s/he plays, while the game-player develops a second identity, or second self, that s/he becomes when s/he is in the game world. Is the role-player still making a conscious effort to characterize the PC? If not, we loose our distinguishing criterion. Fine's (1983: 211) assertion that the role player aspires to "loose himself to the fantasy" goes along the lines of Bartle's conception of the player becoming a persona, where "there's no level of indirection, no filtering, no question: you are there" (Bartle 2003: 155). In Bartle's view, which I share, the "celebration of identity is the fundamental, critical, absolutely core point of virtual worlds" (p. 159). To develop a second self, or a persona, is "the final level of immersion" and "virtual worlds enable you to find out who you are by letting you be who you want to be" (pp. 161, 160).

The Development of Identity

Now we seem to be entering a realm where we have gone from characterization to talk about the development of identity. Sherry Turkle (1994: 158) wrote that in MUDs, "there is an unparalleled opportunity to play with one's identity and to 'try out' new ones. MUDs are a new environment for the construction and reconstruction of self." Taking identity as a concept, it often refers to "one," just as we only each have one physical body. However, in contemporary theories the concept very often refers to having several identities depending on context; this is something that we all recognize in today's differentiated society where we use different (context-dependent) roles. Our embodiment, however, follows us into virtual spaces, despite Barlow's (1996) words in his Declaration of the Independence of Cyberspace that "our identities have no bodies." In VGWs, we are not restricted to having only one virtual body.

DEVELOPMENT OF IDENTITY THROUGH SEQUENCES OF EVENTS

The development of identity, where part of the process is to change and mature, comes with challenges. We learn about ourselves all the time, but especially in situations that are comparable to those in which fictional characters show their "true character"— under pressure, in conflict situations, and in situations that involve difficult choices. Is there a "player's journey" just as there is a "hero's journey" (Campbell 1949; Vogler 1992) in which a true character is revealed? And if yes, is this the true character of the player's character, or of the player's in-game persona?

In the hero's journey, just as in Propp's (1968) *Morphology of the Folktale*, we find a strict chronological sequence of events and a concentration around the main character: the hero. The hero is said to have a character arc, which is the path of growth that a character undergoes, and the character's choices in difficult situations reveal his or her true character. The other characters in the narrative also have character arcs, but their main functions are to function for the hero, not for themselves. They inhabit other character archetypes and include, in addition to the Hero: Mentor, Higher Self, Allies, Shape Shifter, Threshold Guardian, Trickster, Shadow and Herald.

SINGLE-HERO CENTERED STRUCTURES IN MULTIPLAYER GAMES?

In multiplayer games it is not possible to have meaningful game play for all participants if they all have the role of the hero at all times, nor if they are all merely functions for a single hero. This is an obvious fact in live-action role playing contexts, and very clearly expressed in Section 3 of the Dogma 99 manifesto (Fatland and Wingård 2003: 20): "No character shall only be a supporting part." The challenge is that of how to accomplish heroship for all PCs, while also allowing PCs to play other functional roles for other PCs in their functions as heroes.

The concept of heroism in this sense builds upon a couple of central concepts. One concept is that of singularity, to "be the one" (who saves the world), i.e. to be chosen. Another central concept is that the individual does something admirable and good according to a specific norm system. A third central concept is that heroes are the ones who songs and stories are written about. For the hero's sake, this is not anything that happens while the adventure goes on; the hero becomes a hero only once the story is told. There is no heroism if there is no scribe, or writer of ballads, and an audience to whom the story is later told. The songs are sung in contexts where the hero is seldom present. There is a part of this happening in virtual worlds — we can see it on player pages and guild pages on the Internet, but it is in most cases secondary to the play. What is most important to the player is the journey, not the tale about the journey.

THE JOURNEY AS A ROUTE TO SELF-KNOWLEDGE

Richard Bartle (2003) compares the online player's journey with the hero's journey, step-by-step along the route Campbell (1949) described. Bartle interprets the hero's adventurous journey as the player's journey towards mastering two worlds, where the player's goal in the journey within a virtual world is that the virtual self and true self become the same. In this case the player's journey begins in real life, with getting hold of an account that lets the player log into a virtual world. This represents the "departure." The "initiation" stage takes place wholly within the virtual world, while in the "return" the player is separated from the virtual world but has learned a lot about her/himself along the journey.

Exactly what players learn about their true selves varies. Amy Bruckman (1992) explores one consequence of the player's journey with a PC named Tao. Tao tells her that he learned a lot about himself through spending time in the virtual world. For example, he learned how to organize people, give orders, and went through the difficult experience of serving as a defense council for a friend. Bartle's conjecture is that "playing virtual worlds is a kind of hill climbing activity through identity space" (2003: 440). Tao's conclusion that, "these experiences have helped me to know my self better" (p. 35) is partially in line with the challenges any hero faces and is experienced by other role-players in virtual worlds (see Turkle 1995). Significantly, his conclusion is also somewhat different from the task we are used to heroes completing: successfully fighting evil.

A More Interesting Journey?

How would it be possible to make this journey more interesting? We have already seen that there are a lot of tools that provide players with the means to characterize their PCs, but what about the expression of true character? Suppose that we get along well with the PC that we went on a delivery quest with, that we start doing more things together, and eventually end up joining the same guild, a permanent grouping of players, and thus develop a social network together within the VGW. How do we see the "true" aspects of the other player's character, and how is our own true character expressed?

What I am getting at is this: How can we create situations that involve challenges, conflicts and choices that would express the true character of a player — or a PC? We could make it easier for ourselves and say that we don't care about that distinction and ask how the true character of a persona would be expressed. But in doing so, we would ignore the long phase of playing that takes place before a persona is developed. We could probably also presume that the expression of true character would help the player to develop a persona — and thereby get a deeper and more meaningful experience of playing and inhabiting a virtual game world.

For the sake of this argument we would also need to state that we see the development of a persona as a good thing — we want to find further means to support the development of a persona. An important step in this process is the first identification with the PC. The fact the PC creation is done by the player her/himself creates a sense of ownership from the beginning, comparable with an initiation ritual. But then there is a matter of deepening the bond and the sense of identification of the player with her or his PC. If the player feels that the discrepancy between the perceived real self and the PC's identity is too great, or feels uncomfortable for some reason, the player might quit the game entirely, start playing another game, or create a new character.[3]

Character classes are usually varied, and there are several tools for the players to express themselves — as themselves playing in another world, or as fictional roles they perform. The classes may be considered as more or less stereotypical, mostly depending on design heritages from the *Advanced Dungeons and Dragons* system, the different code bases that to a large extent form the game play paradigms in VGWs and on content based heritages from fantasy and science fiction mythos. Nevertheless players are provided with a large range of tools for characterization in the sense of what can be seen, including more static properties as well as behavior and styles of play and expression. And players do use this in very innovative ways. When it comes to expression of characterization and true character, players' imagination and creativity take them a long way. Nothing in the current system supports the expression of individual true characterization of the player characters or the personas. How can the game design provide more support in this? Basically there are two main ways of doing this — by game mastering and by implementing means for it in the game play framework.

Supporting Expression of True Character via Game Mastering

A controversial example of game mastering is the (now infamous) event involving the trader Malaki in the VGW *A Tale in the Desert*. Trader Malaki was said to trade valuable goods, yet he "would not trade with women, and made references to trading /for/ some of them as slaves. This did not go over well at all, and he was eventually hounded out of Sinai, by a small revolt led by Logicritus, after peddling one or two of his wares for some expensive items. He later turned up in Karnak to do the same, with the same result."[4] This stirred up a lot of emotions and discussions in online forums. What it meant game-wise was challenging and called for reactions. Some players with male PCs did trade with Malaki, while others refused. The PC Logicritus even started a small revolt. Andrew Tepper (2004), creator and owner of *A Tale in the Desert*, commented on the event:

> Along comes a foreign trader, with shiny new goods, and an attitude that's totally offensive, totally out of line with the culture that has developed in our Ancient Egypt. Would you trade with him? Would you put aside your morals, if it meant you'd get an advantage that many people don't have? In real-life, would you patronize a store that had a "No Jews allowed" policy? What if they had *really* good prices? Would you do it and hope nobody saw? Maybe feel guilty? The best books, movies, television — can provoke a range of emotions. I like books that make me feel happy, enraged, triumphant, guilty, enlightened, sad. I want to have all of those emotions available in an MMO, and emotions occur in players, not characters.

A side note: in this particular instance the riot and the negative reaction came from the *players*. Had it been only NPCs having a norm system as in ancient Egypt, or players strictly role-playing within the norms of the fictional historic society, there would have been nothing strange or notable with the trader's behavior because such behavior was not necessarily discriminatory within that normative system.

This event is important because it represents a test of the player's true character. In a role-playing situation this might instead have been reflected upon afterwards, in an out-of-game setting. But if a player plays her/himself suddenly transported to ancient Egypt, the strong emotions are more understandable. It may be argued that the player's were indeed role-playing, considering that the norm system that evolved in this particular fictional version of old Egypt does not tolerate discrimination of women and supposes that the (whole) player base shares this perspective. If so, this becomes an example of how game mastering can bring out expressions of true character not only by players, but also PCs. The danger with this is to push it too far and thereby alienate players from the game world.

Even though the world is virtual and the setting is a game, it is ill-advised to trivialize the emotional impact of events involving the player's own character — Dibbell's (1993) story about the rape committed by MrBungle in the text based virtual world LamdaMOO clearly showed that our virtual personas are vulnerable. An even earlier example is van Gelder's (1985) "The Strange Case of the Electronic Lover," which takes up issues of mind-to-mind encounters, gender swapping, deceit and construction of alternative personas. Whether the players in the virtual worlds play as themselves or adopt roles to play game mastering is a powerful tool for creating dramatic and challenging situations that can support the expression of true character.

Supporting Expression of True Character via the Framework of Game Rules

Besides game mastering, another way of supporting the expression of true character and the development of persona would be to extend the functionalities of the object the player controls to better reflect an actual personality. The personality would consist of the distinctive and characteristic patterns of thought, emotion, and behavior that define an individual's style and influence his or her interactions within the VGW. As an example, let us say that a character has a phobia for a certain type of object in the world. How shall a player deal with that if an object creates an involuntary reaction of fear for the character? Let us also suppose that this phobia is either chosen by the player her/himself, or that it was caused by a prior traumatic event within the game world. The reaction to this would also be dependent on the PC's personality and different PCs might react differently to a situation involving specific emotions. There is an obvious danger in implementing systems that make a PC behave or be inclined to behave in a certain way — too large an amount of control over the PC would be taken away from the player, thus alienating her/him, which is directly opposite of our intentions. But, for the sake of argument, we can suppose that it is possible to tweak the system in a way that does not take control away from the player, but that it instead poses a challenge.

There are innumerable ways of implementing personality-specific behavior outputs depending on the type of personality models used and the type of game play framework. There are a number of models derived from research in social sciences, and of course it is possible to define game-specific personality models from scratch. Some models are under development (Moffat 1997; Egges, et al. 2003; Eladhari and Lindley 2003), where the personality models are mainly inspired from the NEOAC model of personality traits. Considering the vast field of theories around personality, affect and temperament, this is a field that leaves room for numerous different ways of experimenting with what mind, identity and personality would mean in the context of VGWs. The prevalent gameplay paradigms derived from previous games are by no means mandatory, even though they have formed both players' and developers' expectations of what a MMOG should be like. Games having different gameplay paradigms, such as *A Tale in the Desert*, which is a non-combat game featuring political violence (metaphoric backstabbing) rather than physical violence (actual stabbing), has still been able to find a stable player base.

A system incorporating the personality modeled and developed by the player into the PC may well be a support for both creating and experiencing situations more dramatic and individualized than most VGWs currently provide. Together with game mastering this might be a tool that both expresses the true character of the PC or the persona and leads to experiencing more immersion in the game via closer identification with the object that the player controls. It may also be a basis for the creation of individual, dramatic story arcs. However, it is crucial to bear in mind that even though the creation of VGWs can be an art, playing in them and inhabiting them can also be a performative art form in itself. VGWs may in the future provide systems that support the emergence of true individual story arcs, game mastering that can bring out the true character, and more sophisticated support for the development of personas, but it is the player's task to inhabit them, play them, and maybe develop within them. That is the player's journey.

Conclusion

Most virtual game worlds today have elaborated tools for characterization of player characters, but less for bringing out their "true character." The expression of true character in game worlds could lead to deeper and more meaningful dramatic experiences as well as supporting a higher degree of immersion into the game world via closer identification with the avatar, which in turn could support the development of a persona. One hypothesis is that this may be achieved partly by game mastering and partly by developing more sophisticated architectures for the player's representations in the worlds. To author individual dramatic story arcs for each player is not possible for a designer of massively multiplayer game worlds. It is instead the player's individual journey that creates the story, along with living, creating, and developing within the world.

Notes

1. This freedom sometimes has a less efficient result for achievement or "success" within the game system if a sub-optimal race is chosen for a particular functional class. In those cases players refer to "gimped" characters.

2. It ought to be pointed out that Fine's study concerned multiplayer games, not massively multiplayer games.

3. An exhibition by Robbie Cooper, entitled Alter Ego, in Proud Galleries in London, England on October 8–26 2004 (http://www.proud.co.uk/exhibitions/exhib_ego/) consists of photographs of players of virtual worlds, alongside screen shots of their avatars. Richard Bartle reflected upon the exhibition on the TerraNova website, giving an example of the player April who left EverQuest since she felt that her representation in the game did not match her real life self. Bartle's post on Terra Nova October 16, 2004 reads: "Some of the person/avatar pairs said more than others. The one I found most interesting was a young woman called April who played as Jaynex. She claimed to have lacked confidence before she got into virtual worlds, and to have gained confidence as a result. She'd begun on [EverQuest], but had gradually become frustrated with it and had moved on to [Star Wars Galaxies]. There, she'd created an avatar that she'd made look exactly like her. Some points about this: 1) The avatar does not look exactly like her. It may look like how she sees herself, but there are some striking differences, most notably hair and eye color. 2) She had to leave [EverQuest] because her [EverQuest] self no longer matched her. In other words, the avatar wasn't a good fit any more. How many other people stop developing because they're locked into their avatar, rather than starting a new avatar (or changing the way their avatar looks)? 3) She may have the same look (in her mind) as her RL self, but she doesn't have the same name. She still doesn't feel that's her." (http://terranova.blogs.com/terra_nova/2004/10/reflections_to_.html#comments)

4. For details, go to: http://wiki.atitd.net/tale2/TheTraderMalaki

References

Barlow, John Perry. 1996. "A Declaration of the Independence of Cyberspace." Switzerland: Barlow Home Page, Retrieved July 27, 2005 (http://www.eff.org/~barlow/Declaration-Final.html).

Bartle, Richard A. 2003. *Designing Virtual Worlds.* Indianapolis, IN: New Riders.

Bartle, Richard A., and Roy Trubshaw. 1978. *MUD: Multi User Dungeon.* Platform: PC.

Bruckman, Amy. 1992 "Identity Workshop: Emergent Social and Psychological phenomena in Text-Based Virtual Reality." Technical report, Cambridge, MA: MIT Media Laboratory.

Campbell, Joseph. 1949 *The Hero with a Thousand Faces.* Princeton, NJ: Princeton University Press.

Cherny, Lynn. 1994. "'Objectifying' the Body in the Discourse of an Object-Oriented MUD." Ghostweather Papers, Retrieved January 23, 2006 (http://www.ghostweather.com/papers/objectifying%20the%20body.htm).

Curtis, Pavel. 1990. *LambdaMOO.* Platform: PC. http://www.lambdamoo.info/

Dibbell, Julian.1993. "Rape in Cyberspace." *The Village Voice,* December 21, pp 36–42.

Egenesis. 2003. *A Tale in the Desert.* Platform: PC. http://www.atitd.com.

Egges, Aarjan, Sumeda Kshirsagar and Nadia Magnenat-Thalmann. 2003. "A Model for Personality and Emotion Simulation." *Knowledge-Based Intelligent Information & Engineering Systems* KES2003.

Eladhari, Mirjam. 2003 "Trends in MMOG Development." *Game Research,* Retrieved January 23, 2006 (http://www.game-research.com/art_trends_in_mmog.asp).

_____, and Craig A. Lindley. 2003. "Player Character Design Facilitating Emotional Depth in MMORPGs." *Digital Games Research Conference 2003,* 4–6 November, Utrecht, The Netherlands: University of Utrecht.

_____, and _____. 2004. "Story Construction and Expressive Agents in Virtual Game Worlds." *Other Players: Conference on Multi Player Phenomena* December 6–8, Copenhagen, Denmark: IT University of Copenhagen.

Fatland, Erik, and Lars Wingård. 2003. "The Vow of Chastity" and "The Dogma 99 Manifesto." Pp. 20–28 in *As LARP Grows Up: Theory and Method in Larp,* edited by M. Gade, L. Thorup and M. Sander. Fredriksberg, Denmark: Projektgruppen KP03.

Fine, Gar, A. 1983. *Shared Fantasy: Role Playing Games as Social Worlds.* Chicago, IL: The University of Chicago Press.

Goffman, Erving. 1959. *The Presentation of Self in Everyday Life.* New York, NY: Doubleday.

Linden Lab. 2003. *Second Life.* Platform: PC. Linden Research. http://secondlife.com/

McKee, Robert. 1997. *Story: Substance, Structure, Style, and the Principles of Screenwriting.* New York, NY: Harper Publishers.

Moffat, Dave. 1997. "Personality Parameters and Programs." Pp 120–165 in *Creating Personalities for Synthetic Actors, Towards Autonomous Personality Agents,* edited by Trappl R. and Petta P. London, UK: Springer-Verlag.

Near Death Studios. 1996, 2001–2004. *Meridian 59.* Platform: PC. http://www.meridian 59.com.

Oldenburg, Ray. 1989. *The Great Good Place.* New York, NY: Marlowe & Company.

Propp, Vladimir. 1968. *Morphology of the Folktale* (English Translation). 2nd Edition, Austin, TX: University of Texas Press.

Sony Computer Entertainment America Inc. 1999. *EverQuest* Platform: PC. http://eqlive.station.sony.com/

Sony Online Entertainment. 2003. *Star Wars Galaxies: An Empire Divided.* Platform: PC. LucasArts http://starwarsgalaxies.station.sony.com/

Tepper, Andrew. 2004. "Event Motivation." *Slashdot,* October 22. Retrieved July 28, 2005 (http://slashdot.org/comments.pl?sid=126745&cid=10604460)

Turbine Entertainment Software. 1999. *Asheron's Call: Dark Majesty.* Platform: PC. Microsoft Corporation. http://www.microsoft.com/games/zone/asheronscall/

_____. 2002. *Asheron's Call 2: Fallen Kings.* Platform: PC. Microsoft Game Studios, Microsoft Corporation.

Turkle, Sherry. 1994. "Constructions and Reconstructions of Self in Virtual Reality: Playing in the MUDs." *Mind, Culture and Activity* 1(3): 158–167.

_____. 1995. *Life on the Screen.* New York, NY: Touchstone.

van Gelder, Lindsy. 1991. "The Strange Case of the Electronic Lover." Pp 364–375. In *Computerization and Controversy: Value Conflicts and Social Choices,* edited by C. Dunlop & R. Kling. San Diego, CA: Academic Press 1991. Originally published in *Ms. Magazine,* October 1985.

Vogler, Christopher. 1992. *The Writers Journey.* Studio City, CA: Michael Weise Productions.

Yee, Nicholas. 2002. "Codename Blue: An Ongoing Study of MMORPG Players." Retrieved January 23, 2006 (http://www.nickyee.com/codeblue/home.html).

10. *Mutual Fantasy Online: Playing with People*

TORILL ELVIRA MORTENSEN

In current computer game research, the pleasure of playing tends to be reduced to mechanic structures, where rewards follow achievements and pleasure equals mastery. A focus on narrative, structure and simple interaction models masks the complexity of human pleasure and how varied the sources of fun can be in a game played by and with other human beings. Online multi-user computer games are mainly driven by the interconnectedness and activities of the players. For many players of these games, pleasure is derived less from fancy graphics and more from a gaming environment that permits personal influence, social interaction and development in relation to other players, not just in relation to the game.

My study of text-based online multi-user games — MUDs (Multi User Dungeons) — has revealed some of the basic pleasures of gaming (Mortensen 2003). The simple, low-bandwidth text form combined with the many opportunities for in-game communication between players open games for a wide variety of gaming delights as well as social activities. These "old fashioned" games contain the basic features of online game-play and offer very quick, user-controlled interaction between users as well as with the game platform. Such games can therefore still be a significant source for understanding the delights of participation in more elaborately developed computer games.

Games are deeply connected to the newer youth culture and flavored by the multicultural, boundary-defying visions of science fiction and fantasy — exploring and expressing delight in a world where there are no limits to what is possible and where there is still room for an everyday person to become a hero. In this chapter I will look at how MUD players experience and express the pleasures they associate with playing online with other human beings. I will organize their delight in four categories, which emerged from my analysis of their discussions with me: (1) Gaming as it is represented in other media, mainly literature; (2) Identification with a certain cultural segment through fan activities and participation; (3) The expression of a personal, subjective identity; and (4) The experience of flow, which I will contrast with the more chaotic concept of seduction.

Games, Fantasy and Science Fiction

The MUDs I have been studying are adventure- and role-playing games, which coexist with table-top games, live action role-playing games (LARPs), and more graphically sophisticated computer and video games. Adventure and role-playing games are closely related to and mutually dependent on a genre of literature dubbed "science fiction and fantasy" in bookstores. Of course, the culture of fantastic fiction stretches widely beyond bookshelves and computers. The fantasies in writing link into the fantasy acted out in table-top games, LARPs and also less game-oriented and more re-enactment oriented activities, and have penetrated mainstream popular culture through, for instance, movies that reach a mass audience, television series and an expanding variety in graphic novels (see Mackay 2001).

Computer games tend to be associated with virtual reality — a reality that is thought to be better than real, more seductive, and which disrupts the player's understanding of self. Those who are concerned with the power of computer games see this as a destructive factor, a subversion of the mind into patterns of death, destruction and despair. Those who are curious about or positive toward computer games tend to defend them by pointing out how they build character, particularly in the way they give players an option to safely explore their personality and establish their own identity (see Williams, Hendricks, and Winkler 2006). Piers Anthony wrote from this latter point of view in his notes from 1981, the notes that later became *Killobyte* (Anthony 1993), a fantasy/sci-fi flick happening inside a virtual reality multiplayer game. In *Killobyte* Anthony has the main character question the interplay between mind and body by asking what comprises the nature of his character in a world where he can experience free movement and play independent of the position and abilities of his physical body:

> So what was his nature? Before it had become irrelevant in life as well as in the game, because of the accident? Walter considered, and realized that for the first

time since the accident he just might be able to look at it halfway objectively. Because this *was* a game, not reality [Anthony 1993: 62].

Anthony's ontological perspective is very similar to that used by Sherry Turkle (1995), which assumes that lack of physical reality liberates the conscious mind from the restrictions of the physical reality, opening up for the real playfulness of the uninhibited personality. "A MUD can become a context for discovering who one is and wishes to be. In this way, the games are laboratories for the construction of identity" (Turkle 1995: 184). Anthony does however turn around and point out something that reveals knowledge of players' distinction between what belongs out of character (OOC) and what is in character (IC), making a clear distinction between the identity of the player and the identity of the character:

"It's only a game. One fake man is as good as another. Here I have a body to madden men's minds. I want to use it while I can. I wouldn't do this in real life, but this isn't real life. For the purpose of the game, you can tell the others that I screamed and fought. Okay?" She stepped out of her bra and panties, and stood naked before him. She was glorious [Anthony 1993: 107].

The main characters in *Killobyte* display multiplayer role-playing behavior as they attempt to figure out where the lines go between their roles and their personal identities. This awareness is frequently lacking in other descriptions of virtual worlds, as they are more aimed at the fantasy of a virtual reality so real that manipulations in cyberspace are as real as fleshspace. This is true of the world William Gibson (1984) portrays in *Neuromancer*. Here, Case, our perhaps-hero, is inside cyberspace:

They floated in the center of a perfectly square room, walls and ceiling paneled in rectangular sections of dark wood. The floor was covered by a single square of brilliant carpet patterned after a microchip, circuits traced in blue and scarlet wool. In the exact center of the room, aligned precisely with the carpet pattern, stood a square pedestal of frosted glass [Gibson 1984: 172].

In this description the physical detail and the meaning of the representation (necessary in order to resolve real world tasks) is more important than the knowledge that this is not a physical world. Such knowledge is only important when it impacts the body, while the mind stays active, as when Case "flatlines"—when he appears to be brain-dead—but is negotiating with a cyberspace construct.

There is not too much to be gained by comparing the widely different styles of authors like Anthony and Gibson, yet the way they treat the same topic—virtual reality—*is* worth looking at. While Gibson has coined some of the most popular phrases for understanding the world which may be possible beyond the limitations of the physical body, Anthony has described the experience of the gamers. Anthony's description goes into the nitty-gritty detail of equipment, the dangers to the physical body and the importance of a meta-understanding of where and what a character represents in a game. While both descriptions carry with them a strong sense of science fiction, Anthony's work remains fixed in the realism of IC and OOC, game-victory versus flesh-world worries, and loyalty beyond the game through human interaction and human friendship. This awareness of the distinction between IC and OOC was well known and very strong among the players I interviewed in 1999, interviews which I refer to and quote here and elsewhere (Mortensen 2003). For the gamers, knowing the difference was essential to good role play because confusing them would pollute the play and pull game concerns into the real world, and vice versa. An example of such pollution might be a player claiming it needed to win because it had such a crappy day at school and losing a confrontation in the game would make it worse. The rule is that what happens in the game is only valid in the game — IC — and if you learn something outside of the game — OOC — that might be valid for the game, your character does not know this until it has been told in-game.

The connection between literary popular culture and gaming culture is closer than the representations of games in literature show, as we can see for instance from the use of settings from literary worlds in gaming. There is a long list of such games, both for computers and for the table-top; some commercial and some created by amateur enthusiasts. *Dragon Realms*, the computer game created by the trio who used the names Topaz, Elwyn and Scarabae, was an original creation but was, according to the creators in an interview in Melbourne in May 2003, still heavily influenced by a series by Glenn Cook, featuring the mercenary Black Company (Cook 1984). This is visible not so much in the story or setting as in the dystopic nature of the game, the endless loss-loss situations and the delight with betrayal, double-crossing and betrayal within the double-cross. Yet another connection can be made, though one not quite that visible. This is the connection between amateur gaming culture and the creation of literature. At least two of the players I interviewed used their role-playing as a way to practice the creation of fiction, and there are strong ties between the fan culture of fiction and general creativity and the gaming community.

The players were all at some level or another aware of the self-expressive part of gaming, and the connection to expressions through other media. Elisabeth Sierro saw the connection to painting:

> ES: Definitely. I mean — I think it's — In some ways the interaction is simplified, but in terms of forms of expression it's actually much more complicated I think to try to express something on a MUD than to express something on a painting. (...) I think it requires a lot more attention to express something on the MUD if

only because of the complexity, the layeredness of it, the fact that if you act something onto it, it acts back.

Other players used the game as a way to test out their fictional characters, and flesh in the character concept by testing it on others. In cases like this realism was not important; it was much more important that the character appeared believable. Matthew Taylor described one of his characters in an interview, explaining how he used the MUD *The Infinite Point* to test out his characters and think about them:

> TORILL: If he's a shapechanger, why not?
>
> MT: He isn't though, he has been changed. Shapechangers are one of these powerful characters that have been overused, because they can change into a mouse and to a dragon and this and that. And I actually have rules in my own head to guide myself to avoid doing something stupid like that. He was changed and he can't go back, which is his dilemma. He wants to go back but if he did go back he'd be hunted down and killed. It's complicated anyway... Hopefully I'll come out with a book and send you a free copy.

Several of the interviewees displayed a high level of analytical and critical thinking about the games, questioning the technical and narrative choices made by designers. Below, Tom Kentley elaborates on the invention of the joystick, the challenge of learning something new and his admiration of the designer's creativity:

> TK: I mean, the successors of some really successful games, I mean *Final Fantasy* has been through 8 editions, and the 8th version of the game and the first version of the game is essentially the same game (...) it's a game people feel is worth purchasing because they know what they are paying for. (...) In fiction I like long stories, I like being in book two and know there's a long series ahead, but in terms of books I like the ones that made strong choices and took the risks. In games this means you could convince yourself that yes, if you actually wanted to learn how to deal with this new interface, thing would get better. As an example: the Nintendo 64 when it first came out had an analogue control stick, rather than a control-pad on it, but everybody was using a control pad, which is essentially a button which you push with your thumb. Then Nintendo 64 came out with a little stick, which was essentially a little joystick, a wiggling stick, and the advantage with the analogue stick it wasn't on or off, it was however gradient of 90 degrees the stick was moving in any direction. So that one stick could let the tip-toe dude slow walk, jog, run, sprint depending on how far you shifted the stick off of 90 degrees, and to me that was great, that was like WOW I have never seen this before and nobody have ever done anything like it.

Tom Kentley talked about how he read science fiction for the "strong choices," the original ideas that make a certain piece of literature stand out. He compared this directly to technical innovations and viewed the physical object and the new interface as equally part of the experience of expressive culture, i.e., the computer game. Related to how a book's binding, paper quality and visual design influence the book-reading experience, the physical manifestation of the technology plays a much larger role in the experience of computer-mediated texts. The gadget value of technology holds a cultural significance similar to reading the "right" books, seeing the "right" movies, listening to the "right" music. Thus, understanding the subtle differences of digital gadgets becomes part of the requirements for distinction, a way to measure the skill and sophistication of the critic (Bourdieu 1986).

Pop Culture and Games

Players of online multi-player games are not isolated from the popular literary culture. They move back and forth between modes of playing and different types of media consumption, rather than staying locked to their monitors. Their rich experiences and self-expression are recorded in interviews with some very active players and game-administrators from three online games. They are also recorded in the logs of gaming sessions, where mutual and individual fantasy creation, competition and OOC interactions were logged through a year of playing.

The participants in my study of MUD players back in 1999 were not average computer games players. In fact, what I discovered was that it is very unlikely that there is such a thing as an average player. Player bases may be possible to position in different demographics, but even within rather homogenous groups the motivation for each single player is unique and individual. Most of them had one thing in common though. They were deeply involved with the wide range of the cultural expressions of science fiction and fantasy.

Members of the group were conversant with literature that is still pushed into the back shelves of bookstores, or the cheap section along with harlequin romances. Their literary choice was not mainstream literature. Some authors, particularly of science fiction, have become accepted into the mainstream of literature and have left their impression on both academic and popular culture; the previously mentioned William Gibson being one of these. But the mass production of fantastic literature is — and in some cases with good reason — considered trash literature. This "trash" has however proved to be extremely fertile ground. From series such as Anne McCaffrey's *Pern* novels, movies such as *Star Wars* and television series such as *Star Trek*, fan culture participants have facilitated the development of a fluency in using language, telling stories and enacting them through directing these stories at each other. Simple, straight-forward stories have branched into a conglomerate of amateur and commercial games.

A quick search at Mudconnect.com, the main base for finding MUDs and mudders, revealed four existing MUDs set within Anne McCaffrey's *Pern* fiction. There were also six *Buffy* MUDs and MUSHes, while more than 50 were listed for the query *Star Wars* and 26 were listed as *Star Trek* based. There were a few pay-to-play MUDs listed, but they numbered 23 out of 1740 and were therefore an insignificant part of the MUD universe. It is quite clear from my research and participation in these communities that MUDs are games run by amateurs — people who make games for a wide range of reasons, none of which include immediate economic reward. This is typical fan-culture behavior, as Henry Jenkins describes:

> Fan writing builds upon the interpretive practices of the fan community, taking the collective meta-text as the base from which to generate a wide range of media-related stories. Fans, as one long-time Trekker explained "treat the program like silly putty," stretching its boundaries to incorporate their concerns, remolding its characters to better suit their desires [Jenkins 1992: 156].

All MUDs are multi-player games, although some of them feel like single-player spaces — silent, haunted places with a potential for activity — which makes them feel as empty as a large school when all the students are gone. Single-player games such as *Dragon Riders: Chronicles of Pern* (Ubi Studios UK 2001) still exist within a social sphere though, and older games such as *Dragon Riders of Pern* (Everlasting Software N.d.) are available free at Old-Ware or AbandonWare online. The worldwide web opens up for game-related interaction outside of the game. *Dragon Riders: Chronicles of Pern* has a quite simple website online,[1] but through commentaries and discussion sites players share information about the game, for example when players commented on Gestalt's (2001) review from the *EuroGamer* website.

These traces of games, which are not heavily marketed or pushed for consumption, are not just traces of abandoned objects but of human interaction and a culture of gaming that extends beyond both the limited multi-player space as well as the marketing scope of companies. In much the same way as book-rings, players talk about, swap and analyze games. Dawn Marks described the experience of being thrown into a local area network to play *Starcraft* (Blizzard Entertainment 1998) with friends and compared it with playing it online:

> DM: I have played Starcraft across the net, but that has been with people I knew already. I only did it a couple of times and it was more for... It was fun, I'd probably do it again. It's one of the things we do around here, except it's not online, we set up like six computers in a network and play against each other, with Starcraft. We do it down at Reed. That's how I learned to play Starcraft, they threw me in and said everyone against everyone. I was Beyne's ally, and he

even wiped me out once. It was like "you're too slow — Sssshhht." When I played across the net with Lyle ... I was so slow, and he was quicker than I so he tried to help me, so the computer just wiped us out. I made a bad decision but I definitely learned that playing against other people and playing by yourself is two different experiences.

The practice of playing is not something asocial, detached from the lives of the gamers. It is very much a part of their cultural practice, and they learn from each other, develop skills necessary to participate in the activities of their subculture, and are able to describe and analyze these processes in their own words.

Identity and Cultural Background — Legends and Social Structures

Personal development, mastery, social development, friendships and explorations of identity and social roles are vital aspects of playing with people, and players' delights are embedded in the social rewards of multi-user games. They underline the importance of a well-developed and internationally dispersed culture, where Asian, Norse, Celtic and American Indian mingle effortlessly with new fictitious myths and hybrid legends for modern dreamers. This is a mesh that tends to lack the ironic distance of bricolage, taking on instead a sincerity that resonates with other areas of life, making the players pull their reality into their games (and the other way around). Playing is not a postmodern activity, but rather expresses a new sincerity attached to the use of media. The players are no longer seen as just an active audience, but as *active* participants in their mediated experiences.

One player used the game as a testing-ground for her sociology thesis. This is nothing new, as some of the most well-known articles in the field of game studies are based on using theory developed for flesh-world interaction. An early example is Edward Castronova's (2001) article on the economy of Norrath, the world in *EverQuest* (Sony Online Entertainment 1999). This foundational article has since seeded academia with studies of in-game and out-of-game economies, and the mingling thereof. It is a playful article in which Castronova — with both insight and skill, but also a certain amount of tongue-in-cheek — analyzes the economy of a virtual nation as if it was a geographically based nation state. This is a hyperreal approach, and it slips easily in with a post-modern sensibility:

These new objects are the poles of simulation around which is elaborated, in contrast to old train stations, factories, or traditional transportation networks, something other than a "modernity": a hyperreality, a simultaneity of all the functions without a past, without a future, an operationality on every level. And doubtless also crises, or even new catastrophes [Baudrillard 1994: 78].

Castronova treats Norrath as if it were a "real" state with a history resulting from accumulated years and human migrations, not a few years of fiction written while coding went on in the next room.

Mariah, who wrote her sociology thesis about gender roles in the game we both played, did not treat *Dragon Realms* as a geographical, "real" place. To her the non-reality of the game was the important aspect which let her do her experiments with her own potential in the many characters she donned:

> MPK: I'm a social science major, so I am very interested in people and how they interact with things, and how the communities form and break up, and how people are choosing to portray a specific character. Hopefully you are not playing yourself all the time, but you have a character in your mind. If you think "my character is shy," then you have to use the stereotype of shy and portray this character as shy, and I am very interested in what people think shy is, and what people think angry is and what people think cold is ... icy, and angry, and I'm very interested in how people are choosing to portray a specific person, and I think that the really good people are the ones who are willing to sacrifice their own personal way of doing things in order to do something in the way of the character in a stuck situation.

Mariah's online experiments depended on the fictional quality of the games. She would not play around with the different representations of what she considered parts of herself if she did not feel confident about her own and her fellow gamers' understanding of the difference between IC and OOC. This distinction is what makes her treatment of the game different from many of the scholars who do in-game research (such as Castronova), but it echoes the game understanding described in users of *The Dreamscape* (Taylor 2002: 40). As one of Taylor's interviewees, Meg, says, "[i]n effect, I suppose I was unknowingly using my second reality as a social experiment and it has become very much a learning experience for me." Taylor's research is not from a strictly role-play intensive environment and so perhaps this is why its users lack the vocabulary of the more dedicated role-players when it comes to expressing the difference between the perceived self and the played character. Whereas Meg unknowingly used her second reality as a social experiment, Mariah did this deliberately, and the social experiment goes beyond her own feelings about it. Mariah wanted to see their effect on others, not just feel them for herself.

What Mariah did is a kind of bricolage, the way Claude Levi-Strauss describes it in *A Savage Mind* (1966). Derrida (1978) further discusses this bricolage:

> The *bricoleur*, says Levi-Strauss, is someone who uses the "means at hand," that is, the instruments he finds at his disposition around him, those which are

already there, which had not been especially conceived with an eye to the operation for which they are to be used and to which one tries by trial and error to adapt them, not hesitating to change them when it appears necessary, or to try several of them at once, even if their form and their origins are heterogenous — and so forth.

Mariah used the means at hand — the MUD — for her own purposes and thus may be seen as a bricoleur, as are most of the other players of the game. They use the game for fun, but the game has a wide set of secondary uses as well: Dawn got free long-distance; Tom Kentley shaped his own theories of a society where games could be used for political consciousness-raising; Doris Olson used it to meet a boy she liked to hang out with and that boy, Matthew Taylor, used it to test out his virtual characters.

Derrida recontextualizes Levi-Strauss' ethnological concept of bricolage and connects the activity to play through his critique of the finite nature of empiric data. In his deconstruction of bricolage he points out that the field in question (which he claims is language) "excludes totalization," thereby suggesting that the field may just as well be one of play, a field of endless repositioning. It is interesting to see how smoothly these things fit together and how Derrida's critique ceases to be critique, becoming a confirmation of Levi-Strauss' work. This is especially significant when we apply the methodology not to a "real" world of measurable truths, but to a world where intent and experience are the only tools by which a "truth" can be measured, a virtual world. All empirical facts that relate to the player's experience of the game depend on the interpretation of the individual. This does not make it less important or less true. Games and virtual worlds are human constructions, and natural laws or scientific or social facts hold only contextual interest.

Flow and Seduction — Subversive Pleasures and Constructive Achievement

If the players who use games for purposes other than playing are bricoleurs, then I suggest that the bricoleurs of gaming are the players who achieve pleasure. This is, however, not "true" enjoyment through the autotelic experience in Csikszentmihalyi's (2002) terms. According to Csikszentmihalyi, the autotelic experience is one of achievement, of constantly bettering yourself at the game, while pleasure comes from secondary effects such as social connections created and maintained in the field. Elsewhere I have discussed how Csikszentmihalyi's *flow* concept relates to Baudrillard's *seduction* in relation to play (Mortensen 2004). The conclusion from this discussion was that the concept of flow is one of production and mastery that relates to the self-made person — he or she who creates his or her own happiness. This is very different from the pleasure of seduction: delight through letting go, through losing control.

The concept of flow — the productive, goal-oriented idea of pleasure through mastery — is one which fits smoothly into much of the research done on games and pleasure. Several researchers studying people's attraction to games, such as Turkle (1995), Bruckman (1987) and Taylor (2002; 2003) consider the reason for playing games to be something outside of the game itself, something the game can be used for. This is an act of bricolage by the player: how the player takes the tool at hand (the game) and uses it to understand him or herself, to create an identity or achieve a sense of achievement and connectedness to others. The more problematic concept of seduction has however not been researched much, perhaps because it defies language, or defies our understanding of the answers. In an interview, David Inthiadaka talked about it like this:

TORILL: Why do you play computer games?

DI: I hate to say this, but — the answer that comes into my mind is — they are fun.

With this reply, which was otherwise comprised of insightful and precise statements about his online gaming experience, David revealed the subversive pleasure of playing — it is just plain fun.

This is a difficult aspect of play to study and so far most researchers of games and game culture have focused on the parts of gaming which can be expressed, described or observed. The gaming experience itself is elusive, and as the interviews show, almost impossible to express. When asked why they like games, players tended to search for the kind of productive answers that fit with a more ludic understanding rather than one grounded in the simple (and complex) idea of "fun." Fun needs to be dissected and the activities leading to fun described in order for the researcher to analyze it. So far, studies of games have tended to find that games are productive and useful and stated that this is what makes them entertaining.

Still, David's reply indicates that this traditional research activity is not sufficient to describe gaming. So what do I suggest? There are some methodologies which describe fragile research processes, where the researcher influences the research as much as he or she studies it. One direction of research which follows this line is called action research. Action research (or participatory research) goes beyond traditional ethnographic strategies and delves further into an area where subject and object blur. It is based in the 1970's movement toward empowerment of those who might otherwise have no voice with which to define and categorize themselves; it is built upon participation between researcher and object.

While I am not really worried about the democratic rights of computer gamers in the way one might worry about the rights of illiterates in Tanzania (Hall 2001), the virtual community invites more immersive research that action research describes. There is not yet a properly developed language of the experiences players have in computer-mediated universes. Even the fairly simple MUD universes are hard to express and explain in words, *and those are made of words.* How much harder is it to describe and analyze the multi-mediated experiences of more complex game worlds? To break through and understand the experiences of playing and the essence of fun in computer-mediated games (or in any games), the researcher must immerse herself in the experience and risk contaminating or being contaminated in the way the action researcher opens up and submits to the power to structure the process for the people who are also the object of the research. This process makes the subjects and herself the same: objects to be studied and criticized.

Conclusion

Games link closely to popular culture, but mainly to that of fantasy and science fiction. There is a neat parallel between the science fiction-like nature of computer technology, where fantastic inventions have become commonplace, and the dreams of limitless magic and technological innovation found in the literature. Living with new gadgets can permit a life so far only described through film tricks. Further, the cool new designs apply to functions which have today gone far beyond automatization of common, manual tasks and into creating tasks we never knew we needed a gadget to perform. The need for a field to analyze computer games sounds in a way like science fiction, and the fact that I can write this chapter here in Norway and then send it to the other side of the planet in a moment is nothing short of magic — or at least magical to a woman who was past thirty before sending off the first email.

Behavior and social rules are normally transferred from parents to children. In this case — when the medium (both the hardware and the software) upon which gamers rely for communication is new — the parent generation knows how to behave even less than the children. This means that the project of learning how to play and how to behave on the playing field is at best a joint project, but mostly a task for young people to struggle at alone. A very useful tool for this is role-play, as the open access and low bandwidth of computer-mediated communication invites heavy editing of the personality.

It becomes very hard to convey everything that is normally communicated through a short face-to-face meeting through the information exchanged in a computer game. This means that in order to communicate well there needs to be an understanding of the distinction between the character which is being played and the person who is playing. In role-play-intensive contexts this means distinguishing between IC and OOC. In the environments where role-play is less obvious and more understated, more along the lines of Erving Goffman's (1959) ideas of role-play in everyday life, the lines may blur and create a frustration with what is real and what is the edited self. As Taylor's (2002; 2003) research shows, there is a certain awareness of how the online self is a more edited version of the self. This is an issue among the players.

In the study of games there is a tendency to focus on what seems reasonable and acceptable and the strategies and pleasures of playing are understood as productive, disciplined and controlled. To recognize, describe and then research that which is liminal and subversive is not yet easily within the grasp of game scholars. Critical theory has sharp limits and we tend to end up in new dichotomies of player experiences. While play is experienced as immersion and sensation, it needs to be described through scholarship. Hence we turn playing into the same kind of intellectual exercise as when we do analysis: the more complex, the more we enjoy mastering it. The experience of flow is near and dear to many highly-trained scholars. But in this manner we forget the other pleasure of gaming — play as a deeply subjective pleasure, where we have fun "just because" or "despite." In the words of Baudrillard (1990: 133): "In games there is nothing to redeem, no accounts to settle with the past. For this reason, games appear unaware of the dialectic of the possible and the impossible, there being no accounts to settle with the future." Games are so attractive because they release us from the boundaries of our achievements in other arenas and set us free to measure ourselves by different standards, not just because they reduce the world to factors that can be learned, controlled and mastered.

The practice of playing computer games is here now, whether it is the simple games of *Tetris* or *Solitaire* or large, complex social games. It is irrevocably a part of our culture and a product of it. At some point we will learn to speak its language of delight and touch its interface of pleasure without reducing it to production. Or we will just accept the mystery. But what player does not want to penetrate beyond the explored boundaries to see whether the limits can be pushed just a little further into the unknown? Activate the auto mapping and let's go seek the meaning of fun!

Notes

1. http://dragonriders.ubi.com/news.html

Bibliography

Anthony, Piers. 1993. *Killobyte.* New York: Ace/Putnam.

Baudrillard, Jean. 1990. *Seduction.* New York: St Martin's Press.

_____. 1994. *Simulacra and Simulation.* Ann Arbor: University of Michigan Press.

Blizzard Entertainment. 1998. *Starcraft.* Platform: PC. Blizzard Entertainment.

Bourdieu, Pierre.1986. *Distinction: A Social Critique of the Judgement of Taste.* London: Routledge and Kegan Paul.

Bruckman, Amy Susan. 1987. *Moose Crossing: Construction, Community and Learning in Networked Virtual World for Kids.* Boston: MIT University Press.

Castronova, Edward. 2001. "Virtual Worlds: A First-Hand Account of Market and Society on the Cyberian Frontier." Retrieved February 01, 2006 (http://papers.ssrn.com/sol3/papers.cfm?abstract_id=294828) published by CESifo, Center for Economic Studies, University of Münich, and the Ifo Institute for Economic Research (http://www.cesifo.de/home).

Cook, Glenn. 1984. *Black Company.* New York: Tor Books.

Csikzentmihalyi, Mihaly. 2002. *Flow: The Classic Work on How to Achieve Happiness.* London: Rider.

Derrida, Jaques. 1978. *Writing and Difference.* Chicago: the University of Chicago Press.

Everlasting Software. N.d. *DragonRiders of Pern.* Platform: PC. Everlasting Software, download at Game Downloads, Retrieved January 01, 2006. (http://free-game-downloads.mosw.com/abandonware/pc/strategy_games/games_d/dragonriders_of_pern.html)

Gestalt. 2001. Review of "Dragon Riders: Chronicles of Pern" in *EuroGamer.* Retrieved February 01, 2006 (http://www.eurogamer.net/article.php?article_id=1405)

Gibson, William. 1984. *Neuromancer.* New York: Ace books.

Goffman, Erving. 1959. *The Presentation of Self in Everyday Life.* New York: Doubleday.

Hall, Butt L. 2001. "I Wish This Were a Poem of Practices of Participatory Research." Pp. 171–178 in *Handbook of Action Research*, edited by Reason, Peter and Hillary Bradbury. London: Sage.

Jenkins, Henry. 1992. *Textual Poachers: Television Fans and Participatory Culture.* New York: Routledge.

Levi-Strauss, Claude. 1966. *The Savage Mind.* Chicago: University of Chicago Press.

Mackay, Daniel. 2001. *The Fantasy Role-Playing Game: A New Performing Art.* Jefferson, NC: McFarland.

Mortensen, Torill Elvira. 2003. *Pleasures of the Player: Flow and Control in Online Games.* Unpublished dissertation. University of Bergen, Volda University College.

_____. 2004. "Flow, Seduction and Mutual Pleasure." In *Other Players* conference proceedings (http://www.itu.dk/op/), edited by Miguel Sicart and Jonas Heide Smith. Center for Computer Game Research, IT University of Copenhagen, Denmark, 6–8 December 2004. Retrieved February 01, 2006 (http://www.itu.dk/op/papers/mortensen.pdf).

Sony Online Entertainment. 1999. *EverQuest.* Platform: Windows. Verant Interactive.

Taylor, T. L. 2002. "Living Digitally: Embodiment in Virtual Worlds." Pp. 40–62 in *The Social Life of Avatars: Presence and Interaction in Shared Virtual Environments*, edited by R. Schroeder. London: Springer-Verlag.

_____. 2003. "Multiple Pleasures: Women and Online Gaming." *Convergence* 9(1): 21–46.

Turkle, Sherry. 1995. *Life on the Screen: Identity in the Age of the Internet.* New York: Simon and Schuster.

Ubi Studios UK. 2001. *Dragon Riders: Chronicles of Pern.* Platform: PC. Ubi Soft Entertainment.
Williams, J. Patrick, Sean Q. Hendricks, and W. Keith Winkler. 2006. "Fantasy Games,
Gaming Cultures and Social Life." Pp. 1–18 in J. Patrick Williams, Sean Q. Hendricks,
and W. Keith Winkler (eds.) *Gaming as Culture: Essays in Reality, Identity and Experience in Fantasy Games.* Jefferson, NC: McFarland.

11. From Dollhouse to Metaverse: What Happened When The Sims *Went Online*[1]

Mia Consalvo

After a long day at work, Addie and Lola go out to dinner together downtown and spend way too much money on the meal. After doing a little shopping, they take a cab home, wash up and go to bed, in their safe (burglar-alarmed) suburban neighborhood.
— The Sims

Spent time looking around. Found a place called Perkz that was good for building skills. Talked with the property leader, Tina, for a while... She's a founder, and a few of her roommates haven't been online in a while. I said if she got rid of any to let me know. She asked how old I was and how often I was online. I responded "33, online 3–4 times a week, 3–4 hours at a time." She said to stop by the next day. Did a bit more wandering, built some skills and made a little bit of money.
— The Sims Online[2]

When I first started playing *The Sims,* I quickly became addicted to bossing my miniature households around, and was intrigued as to how I could direct my Sims but never entirely control them. I started collecting the expansion packs, and wrote about the game and its representations of sexuality (Consalvo, 2003a). I was aware of the coming launch of *The Sims Online,* and watched curiously as the game gained attention from media outlets not normally known for their positive coverage (if any at all) of the game world. And I too was sucked in to the promise of a Metaverse.

When the online version came out I bought it and eagerly logged online. But after the initial newness of the experience wore off, I found myself confronted with a dilemma. That dilemma is characterized by the above two quotations (and others that follow throughout this chapter), the first from my experiences playing *The Sims* (*TS*) and the second from my fieldnotes in *The Sims Online* (*TSO*). While I had no trouble creating interesting situations and telling the occasional good story with my controllable multitudes, my experiences in *The Sims Online* seemed to fall flat, lacking nuance, interest or intrigue. Why did I enjoy making my virtual Sims clean the bathroom, but disdain watching Kazumi (my first *TSO* avatar) build her twentieth gnome in a row? Where were the interesting people to talk to? Why were roommate interviews tied to how frequently I would be online? Why did skill building take so long?

I had to confront the truth — I was a solitary game player. I enjoyed games as an escape from reality ... and sociality. I did not play to be more social, but to be more asocial.[3] *TSO* had tricked me — what had happened? When initial sales goals for the game fell much lower than expected, I wondered if my experience was a common one. The thing to do was to study the games, their individual components, and unique elements of gameplay. Only then could I approach an answer as to why, when *TS* went online, the millions playing on their own failed to follow, and whether there was anything special or different about the people that did. To do this, I investigated both games in the context of their common content, the "everyday," and through the element of control, which is central to (but different in) the gameplay experience of each game.

How pervasive had the original *TS* become? Released in 2000 with expansion packs coming at a rate of about two per year, the franchise has sold over 50 million copies (Coleman 2005) and most impressively now boasts a player base that is 52% female (Lewis 2003). A game of electronic dollhouse, the game has expanded to include more objects (*Livin' Large*), party gear (*House Party*), vacations for over-worked Sims (*Vacation*), a downtown area for hooking up (*Hot Date*), gardens and pets (*Unleashed*), a chance for your Sim to become famous (*Superstar*), and the ability for Sims to do magic (*Makin' Magic*). The game has also migrated to the console and handheld world, and been translated into seventeen languages (Coleman 2005). More recently the game engine has been overhauled and the platform has moved to 3D with *The Sims 2*, which sold more than 4 million units in its first five months of release and again received critical acclaim (Coleman 2005). It seems that naming something "*The Sims*" is a license to print money, but there is always an exception to the rule. At the end of 2002 Electronic Arts/Maxis released *The Sims Online* to great fanfare, both in the gaming and mainstream press. The Massively Multiplayer Online Game (MMOG) was supposed to be *the* breakthrough online game that would finally crack the mass market. Over the past decade the most successful online games have remained fantasy and sci-fi RPGs, which currently command 85% of the MMOG market (Woodcock 2005). Leaders in the past have included *Everquest* (which had at its peak approximately 450,000 users), and *Lineage* (with over two million users) (Woodcock 2005). More recently, games such as *World of Warcraft* (*WoW*) have gained dominance (with over two million paid subscribers) over *Everquest* and the older *Ultima Online*, but again, *WoW* is a fantasy themed RPG. Such games are more specifically Massively Multiplayer Online *Role-Playing* Games (MMORPGs) featuring opportunities for players to fashion avatars as elves and halflings, battle monsters (or "mobs") alone and with guilds, and amass wealth and prestige through dedicated gameplay.

TSO was meant to bring online gaming to a wider networked public not interested in killing monsters, but who might be drawn to virtual socializing and friendly competition. With production costs for games rising and publishers becoming more risk averse, the model of one game being played for months or years, with a monthly subscription fee over and above the purchase price of the game, is quite attractive. And tapping into the lucrative "casual" gaming market would be necessary to achieve that. The hardcore market for MMORPGs was already divided between several games, mentioned above, with similar offerings constantly in development. How many people who wanted to be an elf didn't already have an opportunity to play one? *TSO* was a place for the casual gamer to make the move to online gaming through a careful alteration of *TS* into an online, persistent world.

Because of the phenomenal success of *TS* as a game franchise, the launching of *TSO* was no small event to be relegated solely to the gaming press. Although specialist magazines such as *PC Gamer* ran regular updates on the evolving game and gave it a cover in September 2001 (a full 14 months prior to its release), the mainstream press waited until closer to the launch, but then covered the event like the premiere of a major movie. Newspapers from the *San Francisco Chronicle* to *The Atlanta Journal-Constitution* reviewed the game, and three major U.S. weekly newsmagazines ran stories either given over to *TSO* or featuring the game prominently (Croal 2002; Emling 2002; Grossman and Song 2002; Hartlaub 2002; Pethokoukis 2002). *Newsweek* went so far as to put *TSO* on the cover of its special report issue (The Next Frontiers), titled "The New World of Internet Games: The Sims Online" (Croal 2002).

Lowered Expectations

TSO did not meet the industry's high expectations. Released in December 2002, *TSO* was supposed to dominate the all important fourth quarter sales and Christmas shopping period. Yet when the dust had cleared in early January 2003, sales were far lower than expected. After an initial peak of slightly more than 100,000 subscribers in 2003, user interest steadily fell with subscriptions in mid–2005 numbering 30,000–40,000 (Woodcock 2005). Shortly after the commercial release of the game, ex-players (mostly beta-testers) of *TSO* loudly panned the game in places like Amazon's reviews, calling the game an "expensive chat room" where nothing of consequence happened. Players also complained about differences from the original *TS* game and the lack of activities in *TSO*.

In this chapter I consider what happened through a comparison of the design of the original *TS* and *TSO*. I explore the history and gameplay of each game and how their gameplay diverges in important ways. Through that examination I question how the content of "everydayness" at first brought a successful gameplay experience to *TS*, but then inhibited pleasurable control of the gaming situation in *TSO*. In that move, a key element was lost — not the consumer desires so often thought of in relation to TS, but *control desires*. So while on the surface the two games looked similar, the different rule sets resulted in greatly different play experiences, and a loss of a critical element, control, that players of *TS* had initially found pleasurable. The implications of the particular content of *TS*, the importance of genre, and the pleasures of control are all brought together at the end to further theorize gameplay and its central components.

I played more than 350 game "days" in *TS* and had a user account on *TSO* for more than a year with three Sim avatars. My Sims in *TS* and *TSO* built houses, held down jobs, advanced through careers, built up skills, were roommates, visited other neighborhoods and houses, and chatted with the "natives." Although I cannot claim to have done all there is to do in either game — and my activities in *TSO* have been more limited than my explorations of *TS* — I offer my own interpretations and analyses of the differences between the games and how their modes of gameplay differ, as well as the implications that arise from those differences. I also draw on industry interviews and popular and business accounts of both games in helping to understand the business decisions and constraints that affected each game in its development and ultimate reception. I do not believe that I can reveal any "true" reason that *TS* succeeded wildly while *TSO* did not, or that these particular gameplay differences are the only ones in the games that are significant. However, my analysis can lead to a better understanding of the two games, how they differ, and how changing the rules for gameplay can radically alter player experience.

Game Studies Levels Up

Just as the gaming magazines constantly divulge information about new and upcoming game releases, the academic field of game studies is now comprised of new and exciting work examining the industry, games themselves, and how players make sense of gaming and particular games. Studies from fields as diverse as education (Gee 2003), economics (Castronova 2004–2005), psychology (Schott and Horrell 2000), and media studies (Stald 2004; Taylor 2003) have appeared, and a dedicated approach to studying games, ludology, is being developed (Aarseth 1997; Frasca 2003; Juul 2005).

For this project I draw on some of the tenets of ludology in exploring the gameplay variations in *TS* and *TSO*, including the idea that games should be studied as spaces for play and/or exploration, rather than simply as "texts" that tell a story. Likewise, I build off T. L. Taylor's (2003) work on women who play *Everquest* and their reasons for doing so in an attempt to explore different ideas about what constitutes good gameplay for various sorts of players. Additionally, I integrate findings from Royse, Baasanjav, Hopson, and Consalvo (forthcoming), which explore the importance of control as a facilitator of pleasure in gameplay for women in particular.

In order to best talk about both games, I will focus on four areas of interest, loosely based on a method still in development for analyzing games (Consalvo 2003b). This method helped me study *The Sims* and how it structured sexuality (Consalvo 2003a) and through continued modification works as a starting point for the textual analysis of games. It acknowledges that games have both static and dynamic elements, that games are rule-based systems that players must interact with to experience, and that game design has ideological underpinnings which players may or may not recognize, accept, or challenge. The method includes examining four elements of a game (and its cultural context): the objects, the interface, interactions within the game, and gameplay. The first two categories are relatively static, with an object inventory serving to explore the world of objects in a particular game, their variety and uses, and how they are part of the gameworld and gameplay. Interfaces are the key area for players to connect (or not) with a game, and so it is crucial to study how interfaces offer as well as withhold certain options for players. Mapping the interaction in a game serves to explore a more dynamic aspect of gameplay: How characters (and NPCs) communicate with one another, and how open or closed this system can be. Exploring these interactions can help a researcher determine if a game really is branching and how "free" the players are to choose their own path. Finally, scrutinizing the gameplay tackles the gameworld, allowing the researcher to study such things as intertextual references in a game, the coherence of the gameworld, genre considerations, and other broader concerns. These four areas, taken together, can allow a researcher to study any number of conceptual or substantive issues, from sexuality (Consalvo 2003a) to between-game comparisons.

Level One: Interface Design/ Interfacing with the Games

> Given the sales of The Sims and its expansion packs, it's pretty reasonable to expect The Sims Online to have huge appeal. Will it be the first truly mainstream massively multiplayer game? We'd say it's "Sim"-ply inevitable. [Morris 2001: 17]

Just as a player depends upon the interface of a game to interact with the software, so too the interested reader seeks out information about a game through the interface of reviews, previews, and general game news. Over the years those interfaces have become standardized, and have likely shaped players' expectations for how to "read" or anticipate a game. Reports often rely on a combination of reporting and critique of the game, with a standard complement of screenshots. The prominence of screenshots has grown over time, as game graphics have developed in sophistication. As a result, the game screenshot has become an established benchmark for previewing and reviewing a game, a way for potential game players to better determine if they will enjoy (or at least be intrigued by) the gameplay offered within.

Pre-release publicity for *TSO* followed a typical path for new games, with numerous screenshots of the game and its controls prominently featured in most stories. One of the most striking (or maybe unremarkable) things about these screenshots was how closely they resembled screenshots from the original *Sims* games. For example, on the opening pages of the *Newsweek* article "Sims family values," there was a page-and-a-half image of the game, presumably an enlarged screenshot, featuring various Sims engaged in different activities, including fighting, cheering, playing musical instruments, and chatting with each other. The avatars and objects were almost identical to the original Sims' universe, with a few new objects present, presumably to pique the interest of current players of *TS*.

Much of the text related to promoting the new game also drew on that sense of familiarity and success. For example, a *Wired* magazine article stated that "the basic playability [of *TS* and *TSO*] was the same — each Sim pursues primary needs such as food, sleep, a social life, and the shortest path to the bathroom. But the online version dispenses with AI" (Levine 2002: 176). Likewise, a *Newsweek* article linked the success of TSO to its predecessor: "since The Sims, which was released in 2000, is already the best-selling PC game ever, many are predicting that The Sims Online will shoot to the top of the online-gaming charts as well" (Croal 2002: 48).

Although such articles were quick to point out the new features of *TSO*, including the addition of online multi-play, that alteration was presented as either an improvement or a new feature, not something that would radically alter players' current gameplay style. Some initial problems with the gameplay were raised, such as one author recounting that he was "voted out of the house" for not spending enough time online, and other players' discontent with the lack of options available, but for the most part the online space of *TSO* was touted as the realization of the "Metaverse" envisioned by cyberpunk author Neal Stephenson in his influential novel *Snow Crash* (Croal 2002; Levine 2002).

Yet when examining the game itself, the interface of *TSO* has some important differences from *TS*. The addition of chat and communication apparatuses was new and suggested that the gameplay would be quite distinct from the single-player version. *TSO* players could not only move their Sims around, queue up actions, and advance them through their lives and their days, but also chat with other players in real time, with the communication appearing as a text bubble above their Sim puppet. They could send email messages and make "phone calls" to other players, and chat privately (whisper) with others while in crowded rooms. These interfaces were easy to use and their familiar terms made them accessible to individuals new to online game playing, the targeted demographic of *TSO*. Yet the presence of these interfaces was not really remarked on in pre-release publicity and other changes to the style and nature of gameplay were largely overlooked. The combination of familiar scenes and little discussion of new features perhaps combined to create a false sense of familiarity with the game, which might have led to some of the early dissatisfaction with *TSO*, as *TS* players discovered its very different style of gameplay.

Although in the original *TS* the avatars communicated with each other, that communication was largely symbolic, depending on the player to extrapolate (or ignore) meanings arising from the Sim gibberish and pictorial cues that are a hallmark of the game. For example a player could direct a Sim to "talk about the weather," resulting in an interface and text balloons which were iconic and had to be "decoded" by the player in order to furnish the semantic sense of simulated conversations. With *TSO*, icons reverted to real text. The player could not just press a button to "chat about Hollywood" but had to come up with actual conversation, either "real life" or role-played in some way. That demand became a persistent one as players were encouraged to interact with other players as a central part of gameplay. Because of that, each player depended on her own role-playing or conversational skills, which might or might not be equal to the challenge.

For example, players need money to finance their various activities, including building larger houses and furnishing them, acquiring pets or hiring service NPCs, and buying new clothes. Yet until the recent addition of job objects, there were few ways for players to earn money that didn't entail interactions with other players. A player could work at a canning station making jam alone in her house, but payouts were higher if more players worked simultaneously on similar job objects. That coding choice by the developers led (perhaps unintentionally) to large houses devoted to skilling and money making, generally focusing on one or two ways to make money, such as pizza palaces, gnome factories, and the like.

Job houses brought together many *Sims* players who, once settled into building gnomes, for example, had little to do but stare at the screen, or socialize with other players. Sometimes it could be entertaining, and sometimes it was akin to watching paint dry. While researchers such as Taylor (2003) have remarked on the sociality found in *Everquest*, that game's social factor is often based around goals that can only be achieved through group action and interest, as well as friendships that form from shared interests. In *TSO*, it is difficult to get to a point of common interest because so many houses are, on the surface, the same, filled with semi-anonymous Sim avatars all doing the same things. There is also no real need for any one particular Sim to be present, and no player skill involved in making sure the activities continue. In short, group interdependence is not required, nor does it offer any real advantage in the game, other than as roommates. Without a further need to depend on others or build skills to advance the group in addition to yourself, there appeared to be little to tie Sim players together in much of a meaningful way, beyond socialization for its own sake.

In opening the game space of *TSO* to allow for socialization (seen here through the expanded interface options given over to communicating in various ways), not enough thought was given to the goals of that socialization, or the needs driving it. While players "needed" roommates to build bigger houses, and "needed" visitors to make money or advance through popularity listings, that need was largely one of corralling Sim bodies, rather than Sim minds. So, to make money with my house in Alphaville, I could try to draw Sims in to visit, but it made little difference who these Sims were, or how good or bad they were at canning jam, provided they stayed as long as possible (and thus made me more money). As Mark LeBlanc argues in *Re:Play,* "even when 'socialization' is your primary form of entertainment, the goal of the game still has a purpose; it adds structure to the socialization. Goals are the difference between a game and a chat room" (Scholder and Zimmerman 2003: 56). Without offering Sim players real needs for interdependence facilitated by socialization, the game often felt like a chat room, with little in the way of recognizable goals.

In summary, although the interface options changed dramatically from *TS* to *TSO*, those changes were not remarked on much in popular news accounts of the new game. The move from symbolic to mediated/real communication led to a new style of gameplay that players of *TS* perhaps were less comfortable with, and the addition of socialization, although superficially mentioned in pre-release publicity, was not tied to game goals in a way that overcame the radical alterations in gameplay that it engendered.

Level Two: Interaction Map

> *Malcolm gives Lola a friendly hug when she arrives at his house. They dance slowly to music, but she refuses to let him kiss her passionately, as their relationship isn't of the romantic sort.*—The Sims

> *Kazumi enters Standard Telemarketing and receives the standard "hi Kazumi!" from the host. After finding an open phone she gets to work, and largely ignores the rest of her "coworkers."*—The Sims Online

Drawing on the previous discussion of the change in interface from *TS* to *TSO*, another key difference between the two games is the interaction options available to players. Practically, although the look and feel of the two games did not dramatically differ, the choices for how players could control their Sims, and the feedback that they would receive in doing so, altered the resulting *genre* of the game. That change led to a shift in how players conceptualized and strategized the game, because embedded game rules altered the type of gameplay that players could expect.

Here again, although the games are based on a loose concept of "everydayness" or home life, different rules pushed the player in very different directions. What changed was a key element: control. While other game scholars have investigated how rules are integrated into gameplay and structure games (Salen and Zimmerman 2005), little research has explored the component of control. Drawing from Foucault (1975) and his relations of power, we see how the player can exercise power in games through control in many different ways. For example, an individual can exercise control through specific acts: playing/not playing games at all, choosing a specific game, choosing when to play and for how long, choosing which avatars to play, which directions to take, and how to direct character actions along the way. All of those choices are dependent on what the developer offers to the player. However, the opportunities for control (often conceptualized as choice) and the taking of control constitute for many gamers a pleasurable element of the play experience (Royse et al. forthcoming). Therefore, we need to take the concept of control into account and explore how such elements as interactions within games, and genres of games, can offer or withdraw control and its various expressions for different sorts of players.

The Sims, although defying easy categorization in a game genre, could be loosely grouped with or between the genres "simulation" and "god game." The game claims to be, and does a great job of, modeling real life with its banal elements. Players build simulated houses; they create simulated people, send them off to simulated jobs, and make Simoleons, or simulated money. But *TS* is also partially a god game in that it offers players an all-seeing view of the action and the opportunity to control a dynamic environment in many different ways.[4] It allows for a variety of actions and options in game play and then creates feedback and allows the player to succeed or fail based on their own particular choices. The game is also a god game because the player controls many Sims, can zoom between houses and neighborhoods, and more practically, controls every aspect of their Sim lives. Players can be kind or vengeful gods, making their Sims happy and well-adjusted, or miserable and impoverished.

Although there is no "end" to *TS*, players can create objectives based on the elements of the game (successful careers, many friends, great houses, numerous zombies, etc) provided, and determine whether they measure up or not. Additionally, players can direct interactions but never completely control them, due to the various in-built elements of the game (personalities; moods; time of day; type and level of relationship; and the presence, if allowed, of "free will" in Sims).

Players of *TS* can expect a particular type of interaction in the game. Specifically, that means interactions modeled after "real life," such as talking, hugging, joking, and interacting with familiar objects from the home ("flush" the toilet, "clean up" the mess on the floor). It also means learning how interactions between Sims can and do change over time, and how players can help to encourage or discourage certain interactions, but can never be completely sure of reactions to potential interactions. Players are also expected to control the interactions of numerous Sims in multiple houses, neighborhoods, and "outside' establishments. They grow to expect different interaction options for romantic and jealous Sims, and learn how personalities shape interaction options (and reactions) despite their best intentions.

As ludology theorists might argue, some of the greatest pleasures of *TS* are the evolving, dynamic level of interactions within the game (rather than any story or narrative), as Sims grow more familiar with one another, and how the interplay of various Sim relationships (jealous lovers, zombies) can affect those interactions in interesting ways. Additionally, because the player is in control of most Sims with the computer puppeteering the rest, players are allowed a level of experimentation with the game not allowed in real life. So, Jane can yell at Jill and even slap her if she becomes upset enough. Jill could then choose to either beg forgiveness, or perhaps move to another house. These aspects of the interactions create a space for players to create multiple scenarios based on interest as well as whim, and see how each interaction will affect the ultimate status of a household.

Rather than being a fulfillment of consumer desire, *TS* embodies a fantasy of control that players may not have in their daily lives (how many of us can control our families to the degree we can in *TS*?). The marriage of household content and the interest many players have for control as a central pleasure in gameplay led to a design expectation that was altered with *TSO*. Simply speaking, the pleasure of control was largely stripped away. Although in *TSO* the creation of avatars is very important, players may only create three, which must reside in separate cities, with only one available to control at a time. Because of those restrictions, players are encouraged to invest more time and energy in a specific avatar, becoming attached to one particular Simulated person, rather than having the more impersonal job of managing legions. Avatars can be personalized to a great degree, and can model many non-verbal communications such as "shrug," "cheer," "act bored," and the like. Players can also initiate an interaction with another Sim avatar, such as "dance" but here the interaction must be accepted or declined by the other Sim, here controlled by another player and not the computer AI. In *TSO* all Sim avatars are puppeteered by individuals, and so are not the raw material with which one player creates her desired interaction types. Even if Kazumi likes DJ2Cute, she cannot make the two Sims dance together — the person puppeteering DJ must agree to the interaction request. And although in *TS* an AI-controlled Sim can refuse to comply, those actions are based on an internal logic of previous choices, rather than the whims of a (perhaps unknown) live person.

The style of interaction described for *TSO* is clearly out of the range of simulations and god games — here we have moved into the realm of the virtual community, or MUDS and MOOs, without the possibility of running into non-service oriented NPCs along the way. Interaction becomes communication-based, as players are now regularly dealing with other players, rather than playing a single-player game. Other game theorists have chronicled the history of MUDs and in particular how more social versions have come to dominate the form (LamdaMoo and MediaMoo being the most famous). In such spaces, players can either role-play a character or interact as "themselves" (Turkle 1995).

In *TSO* there have been efforts to form Role-Playing houses and neighborhoods (designated in their house name with the "-rp" modifier) to support such a style of interaction. Yet, those efforts have not been very successful, at least as far as I have seen. Perhaps one problem is that the player of *TSO* is creating a character from a more mundane world than other online game realms. Although there are opportunities for players to create dramatic situations, those seem to be the exception rather than the rule. As a cursory example, more player names seem to resemble chat room and IM names than those of serious role-players.[5]

Such elements combine to create a gameworld where interaction options begin as limitless in terms of communication and language, but can end up being superficial and repetitive. Without a common experience or goal to drive them (beyond practicing logic skills, for example), players often default to the lowest common denominator of conversational topics — sex, work, the weather, or chores to be done in the house.

The addition of some elements to gameplay (i.e., communication between players, the addition of multiple players present simultaneously online) and the deletion of others (symbolic communication is mostly gone; the ability to puppet multiple Sims) resulted in a genre-shift from *TS* to *TSO* that had radical effects on what players could and could not do in the game space. Likewise, the banal world of everyday life that worked very well in the single-player version created more of a challenge when the god-game turned virtual community. These changes indicate the importance of game design choices, and how certain choices can attract or repel particular players expecting a certain type of gameplay.

Likewise, such shifts demonstrate how control plays out in a gameplay environment. Although *TSO* gave players new ways to control their activities through various communications channels and through new interaction options, it also changed other elements, which made the experiences of *TSO* and *TS* quite different. While games need rules (upon which control is based) and endless options for control would likely be uninteresting, it appears that control is a defining factor. Combining control with the original "everyday" content of *TS* led to player expectations for similar modes of experience in *TSO*. New types of control failed to compensate for the control that had been stripped away. Returning to Foucault and notions of power, the player experienced in *TSO* a reduction in power through the loss of control. New elements that offered potential power as compensation were not equivalent and therefore failed. We can summarize, then: power is not simply about limitless control, or many different sorts of control, but about keeping control consistent, and/or believable within a particular gameplay universe.

Level Three: Object Inventory

Objects play a central role in *TS*, giving Sims comfort, providing them with fun, and allowing them to be social in particular ways. Objects fall into various categories, from the functional (toilet; smoke alarm; bed) to the entertaining (pinball machine; dollhouse) to the entirely frivolous (statuary; artificial plants). Each new expansion pack touts additional new objects for decorating houses, as well as creating new and better downtowns, old towns, and vacation spots. While *TS* has been criticized for an over-reliance on objects (see Flanagan [2003] for more on this topic), many of these objects are multi-use, meaning that they can help Sims in their socializing as well as pursuit of friendships and romance. Items such as couches for snuggling, pools for swimming, and campfires for singing 'round, can all help players keep their Sims happy and social, and add a tone of whimsy to the game with the comical definitions and satires on brand names that the game offers (such as a Soma Plasma TV).

From a functional standpoint, *TS* players can build and furnish houses with as many objects as they wish, provided they have the available funds to do so. More expensive items are more efficient, in that they replenish a Sims' needs faster than do cheaper items, encouraging players to earn more money through Sim job advancements as well as strategic marriages among households. The wide variety of building objects and decorating options allows players freedom to create themed houses and neighborhoods, as well as loudly overdone, garish accommodations. The widely known money cheat ("rosebud") further allows players that might not be interested in careers or friends to build monoliths and decorate to their hearts' content. All of these elements of *TS* objects allow the player great freedom in building houses and interacting with these objects.

In *TSO*, most of the same building materials and objects appear amidst many other new options and the promise of continual additions and upgrades. Yet there are important differences in how these objects can function in the online version of the game. For example, players are allowed a limited number of objects per avatar, although this number increases every 7–14 days (Lewis 2004). That number does not include building components such as wall segments or doors, but instead applies to functional, decorative and fun objects, including things like refrigerators, beds, and stereo systems. The stated reason for this limit is to encourage sociality: As players build bigger houses and wish to furnish them with more stuff, they bump against the limit and so need roommates to help with acquisitions. A house can hold a maximum of eight people, allowing for many more potential items. But, the limit serves to encourage players to not go it alone, especially if they have dreams of a pleasure palace on the beach.[6]

Objects also continue a function in *TSO* that was started in *TS*: as mood regulators. Your Sims still need to visit the bathroom and sleep in a bed from time to time, whether you are in *TS* or *TSO*. However, the objects in *TSO* are designed differently in relation to zoning laws so that needs can arise more quickly (or more slowly) in certain places, but not others. Likewise, game time flows differently, with critical implications for objects and Sim needs. In *TS*, if Sims need to sleep, the player can put the Sim in bed and throw the clock to high speed to get past the down time of energy replenishment. In *TSO* however there is no control over the game speed. Players must put their Sim avatars through their paces and wait while the process completes. The process has been speeded up (Sim time is faster than "real time") but still remains a functional necessity. However, because the style of gameplay has changed, interactions with objects have also changed. Interactions which once could be sped up or slowed down depending on player desire, now mainly serve to interrupt the flow of the "real" gameplay for the player, as potentially interesting social interactions may have to be interrupted to "green up" an ailing avatar.

Overall, objects still play an important role, but have become secondary (and troublesome) in certain situations due to the new controls in *TSO*. While objects may play into consumer fantasies in *TS*, they do allow for rich and varied gameplay options, and players can choose among multiple ways for Sims to have fun and socialize as well as relax and replenish themselves. The stock of objects in *TS* is unlimited (particularly with a cheat code), thus allowing players to pursue design and building interests if they so desire. With *TSO* however, objects play a more circumscribed role. There are more items to choose from, yet choices must be made because of the restrictions in number. One particularly open area of gameplay has been reduced through a simple change in rules regarding ownership of objects and the (loss of) control over time. Gameplay has moved from the player controlling object interaction speeds, to object interaction speeds controlling the player.

Level Four: Gameplay Log

*To be social, Stewart called his former housemate (and lover) Michael,
to ask if he wanted to come over. Michael accepted, and brought
along some flowers for Stewart as well as his current wife, Esme.*

Surprisingly, the evening went well and everyone got along famously, watching TV and eating pizza. —The Sims

Monday, January 20, 2003
Had $92 visitor bonus. Party tonight at our house. Got there about a half hour late. Darla (or someone) had put up bunches of balloons around our dancing room. Very cool. There was a female Sim dancing on the floor, but did not respond to chat. Kandy and Darla both there, but no other roomies. Who are these people!? Had a few visitors, including Siren and Ronnie. —The Sims Online

In different ways, the worlds of *TS* and *TSO* are both large and small. The single-play style of *TS* is bounded by the computer and its AI, and the extent to which the player wishes to build houses, downtowns, and other types of lots, as well as families and social circles. Here the world can be designed as cozy or spacious, depending on players' whims. It can also change dynamically — players can demolish, evict, redecorate and change things around daily. Yet the play is always constrained by the motives of the player and the interaction of the AI.

Likewise, *TSO* is big and small, but in different ways. The player has a singular puppet to command, rather than legions. The number of houses or lots for the player to control are also fewer. Yet, the universe of other Sims and other lots is vastly expanded: New houses, entertainment and gaming places open (and close) daily, parties occur and job lots come and go. A player can spend weeks just exploring the vast terrain, limited only by the constraints of the city size. The player need not rely on her own creativity to have fun, but can shop around for the right place to do so. And with changing moods and needs, the player can easily move to suit those as well, all the while interacting with other players. Except for pets and service–NPCs, everyone your Sim meets in a city is a "real" person, whatever that might mean. A player poses as one Sim among many other masqueraders, rather than commanding artificial multitudes.

That change is significant. Just as other human players can anticipate my needs and wants perhaps better than a computer (and offer far more opportunities for pleasure and diversion), so too comes an accompanying responsibility. When I play against (or with) a computer/AI, there is no reciprocity expected. I don't say to the computer, "no, you go first, I insist." I don't thank the game for directing another Sim to accept my Sim's marriage proposal. Nor do I expect the AI to be upset at me for goading my Sim into fighting with a neighbor over something trivial. But my expectations are altered with a real person, even if that person is a stranger.

In *TS*, players are encouraged to play virtual dollhouse and direct the lives of the inhabitants. Directing lives can mean making unpleasant choices, either out of necessity or fun. Given an artificial situation, players can experiment, allowing them to see what happens when a Sim nags another Sim for too long. There are no "real" consequences involved.[7] Yet when the other Sim is a real person, even if it's a person I do not know, my feelings change. I can nag a computer easily; another person is more difficult. And likewise, even if I really wanted to have my Sim slap that other Sim (or just peck her on the cheek), the other Sim now has the opportunity to refuse. Not that the computer AI couldn't, but it was somehow different.

Previous researchers investigating text-based online virtual worlds have found that players do develop norms for behavior in those spaces (Dibbell 1999). It is possible that because *TSO* is so similar to real life, I and other players have transferred our behavioral norms. Just as I wouldn't expect to be able to slap a stranger on the street IRL, neither can I do so in *TSO*. That norm is not so pronounced in other types of online games, where situations are more fantastical, and different behavioral norms already more established. The underlying point is that players either bring along, or invent, expectations for interactions, when other people are involved. Those norms have consequences for how they behave. It also suggests that the look and feel of a virtual world can inspire in players certain behavioral norms, and as we see the rise of more non–sci-fi and fantastical MMOGs, behavioral norms will likely change, as both the environment and player base change as well.

What implication does that have for understanding electronic forms of play? How does gameplay both structure and respond to player activity? While early play theorists wrote about the magic circle (Huizinga 1955) as a place apart, it seems that contemporary electronic games are now more like overlapping spaces to daily life than separate spheres. They are not removed from the politics and bad behaviors of various players, nor are they separated physically from our other activities. As we see games like *TS* and *TSO* that incorporate the mundane into gameplay and make it fun, we see the magic circle continue to warp. As different sorts of players encounter a variety of different games, magic circles will multiply and not be held apart from the everyday. Given that, we can better see how even the everyday can become central to a gaming experience, and how it can expand our horizons for experimenting with affordances of power and control; key elements of gaming pleasure. Exploring those variables can help us better understand games and their role in our lives, and how their structures can enable and/or restrict certain joys and certain forms of choice.

Boss Fight: Implications and Conclusions

Electronic Arts has (as of mid–2005) responded to many TSO player concerns, adding more experiences similar to *TS*, including pets, service NPCs, and more structured jobs. Now you can go with your Sim to work, instead of waving goodbye as the carpool pulls away. Such actions indicate their awareness of problems with early gameplay — the need to give players more to do now that time is not manipulable, and more ways to have fun since players are not creating the lavish, original scenarios previously envisioned (Lewis 2003). Yet the marketing of the game has also changed. EA now seeks adult women who can use a credit card (rather than its original target market of teen girls), who claim to be at least somewhat social, and who are players of *TS*. In doing so, they have acknowledged how different the initial *TSO* was from *TS* and can target their audience and content accordingly. This suggests for game studies some important things. First, with more online games we can expect more games that actively evolve, both from the developer and player standpoint. Although not all voices are equal, player demand and interest must ultimately drive development for a game to succeed.

Second, even seemingly small changes in style of gameplay can drastically alter the game that is created. This study demonstrates how close study of digital games, and the identification of key elements that either differ or parallel one another in those games, can yield important insights into how certain games form an engaging base for some types of players and not others. The importance of control and its multiple forms of expression in games, for example, has been demonstrated by comparing the different types of control offered (and withdrawn) in *TS* and *TSO*. Such central elements of gaming pleasure must be carefully studied to see how they shape the play experience. Likewise, content variations in online (or any multiplayer) games can help to generate and limit behavioral expectations from players, with resulting benefits and drawbacks. As we move away from the complete dominance of fantasy and sci-fi oriented online games, further empirical investigations into player behaviors will be necessary.

Third, more detailed and varied methodologies for studying games and those who play them need to be developed. Clearly there is no one-size-fits-all approach, but game studies scholars must work to make this process more transparent. In addition to playing the games (itself a large advance over previous generations of game scholars), elucidation of the method for studying these games should be an important item on the agenda for contemporary digital game studies. This study, for example, could have also been conducted by engaging in play sessions with different players of both games, or through focus group interviews with them. Different disciplinary literatures could have been added, such as anthropology, to bring additional insights and perspectives into the analysis. Finally, to arrive at better understandings of how games function and how individuals take them up and play with them, we need to keep refining our activities and scholarship, to see how players and games are mutually implicated in the activity of playing games.

Notes

1. An earlier version of this paper was published in Italian in Bittanti's *Videogames, Aesthetics, Politics and (V)ideologies* (see Consalvo 2005).

2. The above excerpts, and similar ones following in this text, are taken from two sources. Material from *The Sims Online* is excerpted from my field notes of the virtual ethnography I conducted in the game during 2003. All identifying names have been changed to protect the privacy of players. The pieces from *The Sims* are narratives I constructed for this chapter that illustrate some of the situations and events that happened while I played the game during 2002 and 2003. The events are taken from the various characters and households I created, including those that I consciously directed and those that happened out of my direct control. I will examine the implications and differences between these two types of excerpts throughout this piece.

3. Here the plot thickens — it turns out I'm not a completely solitary gamer after all — I was just looking in the wrong space. In summer of 2004 I gave online games another try and started playing the MMORPG *Final Fantasy XI*, which I now greatly enjoy and play regularly, despite a dialup connection in my home. Perhaps it was related to my prior interest in the *Final Fantasy* series (although my interest in *The Sims* couldn't keep me going in *The Sims Online*) or the style of gameplay in *FFXI* was closer to my ideal, but now I have to say that I am not entirely a solitary gamer, and can understand the draw of Massively Multiplayer Online Games, at least in certain contexts. However, I do still understand the position of the solitary gamer, and feel that the belief that "everyone" will want to play online games (currently espoused by some developers and publishers) is misguided.

4. This view of the action differs from simulators like Microsoft's *Flight Simulator* series, or racing sims such as *Gran Turismo 3*, which put the player in a 3D space with a more constrained perspective.

5. In this chapter I don't delve into the activities of the Sim Mafia or the attention given to The Alphaville Herald. These came after my observation period ended, and although I have followed the activities with interest, I have no direct experience with them. This also raises the very pertinent question of researcher scope in analysis, especially with persistent online worlds. When can observation end? What conclusions can be drawn from playing on one server or living in one city? Should breadth be "sacrificed" for depth? These are all fascinating questions that must be separately addressed.

6. House lots also come in varying sizes, and players must have an appropriate number of roommates to create a larger house and lot. There is a way around this stricture: players can pay an additional fee to upgrade the lot while continuing to live alone, but the fee is steep, and would take players a fair amount of time to achieve.

7. Even this is somewhat misleading. When playing *The Sims* I have killed off various Sims that were either annoying me, or as an experiment. In all of these situations I felt guilt about the deed, and in one case even reverted back to a pre-saved version, to undo a drowning.

References

Aarseth, Espen J. 1997.*Cybertext: Perspectives on Ergodic Literature.* Baltimore, MD: The Johns Hopkins University Press.

Castronova, Edward. 2004–2005. "The Right to Play." *New York Law School Law Review* 49(1): 185–210.

Coleman, Stephen. 2005. "The Sims Franchise Celebrates its Fifth Anniversary." Retrieved October 1, 2005 (http://wire.ign.com/articles/585/585856p1.html).

Consalvo, Mia. 2003a. "It's a Queer World After All: Studying *The Sims* and Sexuality. Gay and Lesbian Alliance Against Defamation, Retrieved January 15, 2005 (http://www.glaad.org/publications/).

_____. 2003b. "Game Analysis: Developing a Methodological Toolkit for the Qualitative Analysis of Games." Paper presented at the New Research for New Media: Innovative Research Methods Symposium, Minneapolis, Minnesota, September, 2003.

_____. 2005. "Da Casa Delle Bambole a 'Metaverso': Il Trasloco Sofferto di 'The Sims Online.'" Pp. 62–82 in *Gli Strumenti del Videogiocare: Logique, Estetiche e (V)ideologie,* edited by Matteo Bittanti. Milano: Costa & Nolan.

Croal, N'Gai. 2002. "Sims Family Values." *Newsweek,* November 25, pp. 46–54.

Dibbell, Julian. 1999. *My Tiny Life: Crime and Passion in a Virtual World.* New York, NY: Owl Books.

Emling, Shelley. 2002. "World of Sims debuts on Web." *The Atlanta Journal-Constitution,* December 17, p. 2c.

Flanagan, Mary. 2003. "SIMple & Personal: Domestic Space & *The Sims.*" Paper presented at the Melbourne DAC 2003 conference.

Foucault, Michel. 1975. *Discipline and Punish: The Birth of the Prison.* New York, NY: Basic Books.

Frasca, Gonzalo. 2003. "Simulation Versus Narrative: Introduction to Ludology." Pp. 221–235 in *The Video Game Theory Reader,* edited by M. Wolf & B. Perron. New York, NY: Routledge.

Gee, James. 2003. *What Videogames Have to Teach Us About Learning and Literacy.* New York, NY: Palgrave.

Grossman, Lev & Sora Song. 2002. "Sim Nation." *Time,* November 25, p. 22.

Hartlaub, Peter. 2002. "The Game of Life." *San Francisco Chronicle,* December 17, p. D1.

Huizinga, Johann. 1955. *Homo Ludens: A Study of the Play Element in Culture.* Boston, MA: Boston Beacon Press.

Juul, Jesper. 2005. "Games Telling Stories?" Pp. 219–226 in *Handbook of Computer Game Studies,* edited by J. Raessens & J. Goldstein. Cambridge, MA: The MIT Press.

Levine, Robert. 2002. "The Mayor of SimCity Conquers the World." *Wired,* October, pp. 176–179.

Lewis, Jessica. 2003. "*The Sims Online:* A Case Study." *Gamasutra.com.* Retrieved January 15, 2005 (http://www.gamasutra.com/resource_guide/20030916/lewis_pfv.htm).

_____. 2004. Personal communication, March 8.

Morris, Dan. 2001. "The Sims Online." *PC Gamer,* September, pp. 10–17.

Pethokoukis, James. 2002. "Screen Wars." *U.S. News & World Report,* December 16, p. 38.

Royse, Pamela, J. Lee, U. Baasanjav, M. Hopson & M. Consalvo. Forthcoming. "Women and Games: Technologies of the Gendered Self." *New Media & Society.*

Salen, Katie, and Eric Zimmerman. 2005. "Game Design and Meaningful Play." Pp. 59–79 in *Handbook of Computer Game Studies,* edited by J. Raessens & J. Goldstein. Cambridge, MA: The MIT Press.

Scholder, Amy, and Eric Zimmerman, Eds. 2003. *Re:Play: Game Design + Game Culture.* New York, NY: Peter Lang.

Schott, Gareth, and K. Horrell. 2000. "Girl Gamers and Their Relationship With Gaming Culture. *Convergence 6* (4): 36–53.

Stald, Gitte. 2004. "Global Reach, Local Roots: Young Danes and the Internet." Pp. 129–140 in *Internet Research Annual: Selected Papers from the Association of Internet Researchers Conferences,* edited by M. Consalvo, N. Baym, J. Hunsinger, K. B. Jensen, J. Logie, M. Murero, & L. R. Shade. New York, NY: Peter Lang.

Taylor, T.L. 2003. "Multiple Pleasures: Women and Online Gaming." *Convergence, 9* (1): 21–46.

Turkle, Sherry. 1995. *Life on the Screen: Identity in the Age of the Internet.* New York, NY: Touchstone.

Woodcock, Bruce. 2005. "An Analysis of MMOG Subscription Growth — Version 18.0." Retrieved March 15, 2005 (http://www.mmogchart.com).

12. Platform Dependent:
Console and Computer Cultures
Laurie N. Taylor

As game studies emerges from new media as a new interdisciplinary field, its scholars focus on many new media-related issues like interactivity and immersion. In order to do so, they often truncate games into one unified field rather than examining them as related, yet disparate, fields of computer and console games. Computer and console games differ in use and in the cultures that they create because of differences in game-play, game usage, and game type. Academic study has traditionally focused on computer games because of their ease of access, with most academics having better access to computers than consoles; their ease of use, due to easy cheating methods for computer games; and because of their generally older gaming populations. Console games, on the other hand, have been studied far less because they require additional materials, are more difficult to play and to cheat at playing, and because their gaming communities are generally younger. Further, most academic game studies have examined only the cultures present in multiplayer games, rather than including the large gaming communities that are formed around single-player games as these cultures begin and develop in online discussion, bulletin boards, forums, magazines, and other venues.

The differences between console and computer gaming communities are formed through the game interfaces, the spaces of game play, and through player perceptions that often mislabel consoles as boys' territory and computers as systems for girls or older players. These different gaming communities are then fostered through online and face-to-face discussion, magazines targeted at particular platform players, and through player perceptions on the types of games that belong on a certain platform. Academia has situated itself more closely with computer gaming communities despite the importance of console gaming communities for console game studies and for game studies as a whole. As Gee (2003) rightly notes:

> A good number of people play both platform games and computer games, of course. Nonetheless, somewhat different affinity groups, with different attitudes and values, have arisen around each domain, with lots of overlap in between. There are people who play in both domains but have strong opinions about what sorts of games are best played on platforms and what sorts are best played on computers [p. 35].

This chapter traces the reasons for the divisions between console and computer gaming cultures so that the different cultures may be noted for historical accuracy, for studies of gaming cultures and of gaming genres as they relate to platform, and for future game studies (particularly mobile gaming studies). For game studies, the gaming platform relates directly to game play and to game genre because of the manner in which gaming interfaces and gaming key configurations are used as tropes for particular game types and particular gaming cultures. These connections based on platform are necessary to note for the differences in game types, game narratives, and gaming cultures that emerge in relation to the platform.

Distinguishing between console and computer gaming cultures aids in differentiating studies of audiences as much research divides audiences by age, gender, skills, education, and so on. Gaming communities and cultures have been examined primarily for the manner in which they surround multiplayer play. However, gaming cultures also emerge from single-player play and are structured around specific video game titles, in much the same manner as other subcultures operate (e.g., *Star Trek*, *Xena*, and *Buffy the Vampire Slayer* fan communities). Gaming cultures often divide themselves based not only on game titles (e.g., *Star Wars*) or game narrative types (e.g., horror games), but also based on gaming platforms (e.g., Xbox). Academic research that accounts for platform differences will become increasingly useful as the XBox 360 and Nintendo Revolution promise to act as virtual consoles, allowing for legal emulation, but emulation that alters the nostalgia that often fosters console gaming communities. Further, as consoles increasingly support online gaming culture, the differences between online gaming cultures and offline gaming cultures (through magazines, websites, and shared physical play spaces) will need to be nuanced in relation to the gaming platform.

Studies of gaming cultures also need to take into account the importance of platform as the portable gaming market expands. With the release of the Nintendo DS and Sony PSP, along with other portable gaming systems embedded in cell phones and PDAs, the portable gaming market is growing at a rapid pace. The portable gaming market directly relates to the gaming platform because the manner of game-play and the games themselves are specialized, especially as game developers create games for a so-called casual, quick-play market. Notions of platform and its relationship to game studies aid in bridging portable game studies with studies of other portable devices like the wealth of scholarship on the Sony Walkman.

Academics and Computer vs. Console Games

Many of the academics first analyzing video games studied video games as a new media art form akin to film or hypertext. These scholars tended to focus on computer games, and on computer games in relation to new media, as with Aarseth's (1997) *Cybertext*, Douglas' (2000) *The End of Books—or Books Without End?*, and Manovich's (2001) *The Language of New Media*. They also tended to focus on computer games like *Myst* and *Riven* and did not include console games like those played on Nintendo and Atari systems. Their work has proven useful when applied to video games in general, yet the differences between console and computer games still need to be noted because of their significance for gaming and for gaming cultures.

Video games, a single field existing as multiple, heterogeneous genres, contain critical differences that originate in the platform type and that are more pervasive and significant than simplified issues of interface (which are found with all electronic media). Indeed, while some scholars have specifically studied gaming cultures, their studies generally focus on multiplayer computer gaming cultures (e.g., Turkle 1984, 1995; Morris 2002). Wolf (2001) argues that computer games are a subset of video games, stating: "Computer games, then are most usefully seen as a subset of video games, due to the shared technologies such as the microprocessor and the cathode-ray tube. Furthermore, many games are now released across multiple platforms at once" (p. 17). All video games are played on computer systems; however, for video games — on computers or consoles — distinctions among them can only be reduced with caution. Classifying video games as one field with the platform as a subcategory risks simplifying game studies and obscuring significant aspects of game-play. For example, such an approach may overlook particular games being released only on particular platforms and the cultures that accompany those platforms, effectively closing investigation of those relationships. In short, categorizing computer games as a subset of video games effectively hides issues of platform, culture, and gaming interface.

The ever-advancing technology in console systems, with their hard drives and network adapters, continues to blur the divisions between consoles and computers. The distinctions between console and computer games may soon become technically insignificant, yet the gaming cultures that these differences create ought not to be forgotten. Despite this slow merging and blurring, games have traditionally been, and indeed still are, wedded to their platforms in manners that are significant enough to warrant recognition. Currently, there seems to be a move toward "games [that] are ... 'ported' (rewritten into different computer languages or systems) from one platform to another, broadening their markets and appearing in multiple modes of exhibition" (2001: 27). Focusing on porting, however, neglects the fact that these ports are generally not as successful on the secondary systems (Klepek 2004). One of the most popular of the *Resident Evil* series, *Resident Evil— Code: Veronica—* (2000) has still not been ported as a computer game, despite winning "game of the year" awards from several gaming publications. The games that have been transferred have received consistently lower ratings for their computer editions,[1] further indicating significant differences that exist both for the gaming platform and for the culture around it.

Game interfaces, as they relate to specific platforms, also require greater attention because of the ways in which they shape the gaming experience. Lahti (2003) argues that force feedback controllers aid in blurring the boundaries between user and interface, providing "a tactile feedback from the computer to the body that literalizes the implied bodily sensations conveyed through visual and sonic effects used in earlier games" (p. 162). Lahti also argues that games peripherals (e.g., joysticks, pedals, steering systems) make players cyborgs through their relationship to the games and to the game interfaces by foregrounding "haptic interaction and simultaneously encapsulate players in a game world complete with bodily sensation" (p. 169). There needs to be increased attention to console controllers, computer peripherals, and how these correlate to players' experiences with specific platforms.

Internal Divisions: Console Wars

In addition to the separate gaming cultures formed by the division of console and computer games, we find that each platform type is heterogeneous. Individual gaming systems like the Game Boy, GameCube, PlayStation, and XBox serve to create unique gaming cultures. This is due in part to the availability of a game on a particular system and to the fact that many gamers have access to only one or a few systems. Gaming cultures are influenced by the gamers' only having access to that or those systems and games and have spawned forums and magazines devoted to particular console systems like *Nintendo Power, XBox Nation* and *PlayStation Monthly.* Gaming cultures are also supplemented by internet discussions and by production from the gaming culture itself. Consalvo (2003) describes in her study of video game fans:

> Game players excited about specific games such as *The Legend of Zelda: Majora's Mask* can jump on the internet, where they engage in chat, read newsgroups, hang out on Internet Relay Chat, and create and surf web sites devoted to their creators, there are also numerous sites devoted to games that are created by players of the game who have become fans of the individual game or various game series [p. 327].

As Poole (2000: 4) posits regarding the 1980s and 1990s: "Already by this stage a great number of teenagers were more interested in videogames than in pop music. And Nintendo and Sega inspired fanatical loyalty." That loyalty served to harness many players and to keep them tied to a particular console type (or to consoles generally). In delimiting the different gaming cultures, many single games embody the divisions between the different player communities and cultures, and these divisions often cause controversies.

Controversies include the "console wars," in which the different console types struggle against each other to secure portions of the console gaming market with their specific games and interfaces (Leitch 2002). For instance, Nintendo's GameCube won the right to exclusively release the latest *Resident Evil* game, *Resident Evil 0* (2002), as well as several remakes. Nintendo fought for the exclusive rights because the console gaming industry recognized that the *Resident Evil* series featured prominently in console gaming culture and so players would purchase the GameCube specifically to play these games. Lake (2001) argues that Nintendo also recognized that exclusive rights to this Mature-Rated series would make the GameCube appear as a more mature system so it could appeal to a larger gaming culture with older gamers.

Controversies also include arguments among players over where certain game titles or types "belong," for example with the arguments around the sequel to *StarCraft* (1998) being released on consoles, instead of on a computer system. *StarCraft* began solely on computers as a real-time strategy game (generally a computer gaming genre). Players often argue that a particular game such as *StarCraft* belongs on a computer or a console and that the game cannot operate properly on the other platform (Malcivar 2004). Such arguments are voiced from a distinctive fan culture which has emerged because many games do remain wedded to a particular platform despite potential economic rewards for releasing on multiple systems. These cultures are formed in part by the technological differences in the game systems and can be differentiated by several factors that also relate to those technical differences like game-play conventions, the gaming interface, and game genres. Each of these technical differences relates heavily to console or computer gaming and, thus, to their respective gaming cultures.

Game Interface

Despite the blurring of divisions by academia, the technical apparatus for console and computer play differs greatly and these differences are perhaps one of the most visible divisions between console and computer gaming cultures. Many video games can now be played on either consoles or computers because of emulation programs and multi-platform games. Furthermore, many console games can now be played through additional peripherals like keyboards and computer games can be played through additional peripherals like controller pads. However, the typical manner of play remains largely tied to the traditional interface for a given platform.

The typical console interface features a controller pad with several buttons and directional-sticks or pads for movement. This configuration is present on the controllers that are included with the majority of console game systems including the Game Boy, Game Boy Advance, all of the Nintendo Home Systems, the two PlayStation Systems, the Sega Systems, and the Xbox. The typical computer interface consists of a keyboard and mouse. While the difference in keystrokes and button configurations may seem insignificant, Crampton Smith and Tabor (1996: 43) contend that interface design affects users: "There is a commonly held assumption that content is somehow separate from form. [...] We think that this assumption is mistaken. Content cannot be perceived without form, and the form of a message affects the content." Winograd (1996: xviii) also argues for the importance of the interface to the actual work: "Design cannot neatly be divided into compartments for software and for devices. The possibilities for software are both created and constrained by the physical interfaces." Software must be designed with a platform in mind. As such, the platform affects the manner of software design, which in turn affects the software user. Because of this, the interfaces for consoles and computers affect the games on each, and the types of games that are available on each. They also affect both how the players play the games on each platform and whether the players play on multiple platforms. This affects players' participation in computer and console gaming cultures.

From the field of human-computer interaction, Donald Norman (1988: 22) notes that for interface design, "controls with more than one function are indeed harder to remember and use." Computer game interfaces are generally more programmable than console interfaces because computer games can assign a single function to a single keyboard "hot" key and because most computer games allow players to assign each skill to a key. Console games, on the other hand, generally allow between one and three preset button configurations. These configurations cannot be changed, so players must learn the configurations in order to play. However, for skilled console players, the preset configurations are normally related to the popular key sets for other console games. The reuse of similar configurations makes console games easier to play for those familiar with them, and makes them more difficult for those unfamiliar with consoles. The difficulty levels for console or computer gaming interfaces are exacerbated when moving between the two forms, which in turn reinforces the boundaries between console and computer gaming cultures.

The *Resident Evil* game series' implementation of extremely limited game controls illustrates the importance of control configurations. The *Resident Evil* games use a character-relative control configuration, which simply means that pressing a direction on the directional pad will always make the character move in that direction relative to the character's viewpoint on the screen. However, these games combine the character-relative controls within changing screens that are sharply divided into small segments so that pressing up over one screen can quickly result in the player moving in the opposite direction in a new screen because of the game design. For instance, a player could be pressing up to have the character run down a hallway. As the character moves down the hallway, the screen may shift, and the character's view could be reversed and the character could subsequently be running up the hallway. Character-relative controls are more often embraced by hardcore gamers. They are most often found in console horror games, which suggests a connection between control schemes and platform as well as control schemes and game genre.

As Zovni (2002) mentions in his review of *Silent Hill 2* (2001), a game that offers both camera and character-relative controls: "Thankfully, those of us with reflex-problems can now switch between camera-relative and character-relative controls that finally allow you to handle your character in a more natural way when placed under the game's kickass but often awkward camera positions" (para. 6). Character-relative controls are difficult for players who have not learned them, and they require a longer than average learning curve. However, *Resident Evil* was first released in 1996 on the PlayStation, with many subsequent games on various systems, and so many console players learned the controls, especially with console players being more familiar with the overall use of a controller. Computer players did see the release of *Resident Evil* a year later, as well as later releases of several other *Resident Evil* games; however, the gaming controls are still seen as relatively obtuse for many computer games.

While interfaces differ from console to console system, the primary differences are between console and computer games. Gee remarks (when referring to console games as platforms as they are generally referred to in gaming magazines) that "[m]any platform-game players think keyboards are a bad way to play video games, while some computer-game players think they are a good way. In turn, these matters are connected to their identities as game players" (2003: 34). While the differences between console and computer interfaces can be mitigated through the use of peripherals, console and computer gamers (and thus their gaming cultures) generally view the differences not simply as aspects of the interface, but as intrinsic to the game type and therefore as extremely significant to game-play.

Consoles Are for Kids

Interface differences are also the basis for gaming community biases as console and computer gaming communities are further separated by the representation of the console community as less skilled, more childish, or in some way less mature than the computer community. This depiction continues in academic studies. Crawford (2003) divides milestone games into "videogames" and "computer games" and states that in their early development computer games and video games were easily separated: "videogames played on consoles didn't have much computer power and tended to appeal to younger kids, while computer games were played on more expensive personal computers and so tended to appeal to older boys" (p. 20).

The perception of consoles as children's systems and computers as gaming systems for adults continued through both gaming cultures and through much of the older within-game studies. Norman (1988: 138–9) stated that the Nintendo is "meant to be used by children" and even describes the system as "The Nintendo Children's Toy." While the arguments over platforms and age appropriateness have evolved since that time, Norman (2004) later argues that consoles are for young people, specifically young males. Like Norman, Ray (2004) confines her analysis of games to age and gender in relation to platform. Both Norman and Ray's divisions of console and computer games implicitly construct a gaming culture based on a particular platform; in this case, they define consoles as more for boys or dedicated gamers and computers as more available for girls, older players, or atypical players in general. While problematic, these divisions do carry some validity and do underlie some of the divisions in gaming cultures because young boys are more likely to have console systems available for them while girls and older players are more likely to have access only to computers (Ray 2004). These divisions are also due in part to the fact that computer games require a higher initial cost for the computer. The perception of consoles as for children and computer gaming as for older players also relates directly to the spaces in which the games are played.

Places and Ways of Play: Living Rooms, Online Hints, and Game Play Conventions

In addition to the technical aspects of consoles and computers the physical placement of the systems differs. Early gaming culture derived from arcade games where one or two players played while others watched. Players who excelled were able to record their names or initials on the screen. The social space around arcade games, combined with acknowledgement for high scores, led to the establishment of small location-based communities. These individual gaming cultures were united by the types of games they played, the places where they played, and the manner of game-play. Like arcade games, computer and console gaming cultures were and are structured largely within the spaces in which they are played.

> Arcade games, home video games, and desktop computer games each operate within their own social space[....] Home video games must be played where the television is located, which is often a large and public room. Although one or two people can actively participate, everyone who sits in or walks through the room shares the experience of the game[....] Desktop computer games, played where the computer is located in an office or perhaps a bedroom, are comparatively antisocial, for they are often designed for a single player. On the other hand, desktop games may use networking to expand their social space [Bolter and Grusin 1999: 102].

The physical space of game-play thus leads to different gaming cultures because the television space required of console games places console games in a localized communal space. In this communal space, several people often participate in the playing of a single game.

Computer games, however, are often played in an office or in a bedroom and require that the player be closer to the screen. The physical design of computers as single-user units, combined with increasing broad-band internet access, has led to games being played without others participating in the same physical location. Computer games are more easily connected to networks for virtual community play. Because of the differences in play spaces, computer gaming cultures became more immediately tied to online culture, and console gaming cultures remained more concretely based in small groups of players and more reliant on magazines for larger gaming culture discussions. Now, the XBox and PS2 allow for multiplayer online play, but this has only recently become the case.

Because of the more localized spaces of play for console games, and because those spaces most often reside in communal areas, console games have founded communities based around single-player games like the *Resident Evil* series, the many games in the Mario world (of which several can be played as multiplayer games), and games like *Devil May Cry* (2001). These communities, based around single-player games, either originate through the small, localized play groups that play and watch the games being played, or through external discussion of the games in magazines and forums. While many scholars have investigated the gaming communities present in online multiplayer games, much less attention has been paid to the gaming communities present with single-player games. These cultures are much more difficult to study because they exist asynchronously from game-play, yet they are significant because they affect the gaming culture as a whole.

Before the internet revolution — with forums, bulletin boards, and chat sessions focusing on aspects of video game culture — there was *Nintendo Power*. *Nintendo Power*, the largest-circulation magazine for kids in America by 1989 (Sheff 1993: 179), was first released in the spring of 1988 and featured high score lists, gaming contests, letters to the editor, fan art, and other media that fostered the creation of a Nintendo gaming culture based on the primarily single-player games for the original Nintendo Entertainment System. Game journalism initially split between the console magazines like *Nintendo Power* and *Electronic Gaming Monthly* (*EGM*) and the magazines dedicated to computer games like *Computer Gaming World*. However, their split is now being minimized as console and computer games continue to overlap and as magazines share articles and websites like 1UP.com, which supplements console magazines like *EGM* and *XBox Nation* as well as computer magazines like *Computer Gaming World*.

Acknowledging the differences in computer gaming audiences and games, Klepek claims that the differences are often invisible even within the industry. "Having found success on consoles, however, many publishers may be coming into the PC world without much of an idea of how the audiences and markets differ" (2004: 33). Magazines and their websites, as well as fan sites, offer walkthroughs, maps, and hint guides. These exist as external texts to the games and game cultures, yet they still operate for the creation and continuance of gaming cultures (Gee 2003). Because the game walkthroughs, maps, and tips all refer to specific games — even with ported games, these texts often differ based on the game system — these texts all serve to engender a gaming culture specifically tied to the game system. The hints and walkthroughs connect to the overall gaming culture, which is tied by issues of interface and gaming convention and which then fosters the culture through the repeated use of those conventions, including cheating.

Gaming conventions differ for consoles and computer games, making game-play and game design for each format differ based on the gaming platform. Some of the more significant differences include saving and cheating. Computer games normally allow players to save at any point in game-play. Console games, on the other hand, often limit the number and frequency of game saves as determined by their limited memory space. Gee suggests that console gamers are more accustomed to extended replay: "in my experience, many platform users do not see playing large parts of a game over and over again as repetition in the way in which I do" (2003: 34). This extended replay is necessary for console games because of the limited save allowances, yet limited saves are often counted against computer games when games are reviewed.

One of the most extreme examples of limited saves can be found in the *Resident Evil* series. "The method by which you save games will infuriate PC purists, as it is not only sporadic, but requires an item of which there are a limited number" (Dulin 1999: para. 7). Originally, the game saves were limited due to technological constraints for memory space. However, this has become a cultural convention for the series and many players cannot win because the game severely limits ammunition and saves so that the player is easily killed and replay becomes more difficult. This forced replay and limited save system is part of the reason for the failure of *Resident Evil* on computer systems; the conventions for computer games and the *Resident Evil* games are at odds.

Cheating is easier to perform on a computer system because cheat codes and hacks are readily available through codes that increase weapons, defense and in-game knowledge (such as map hacks) and often make avatars unkillable. For console games, cheat codes can usually only be administered through additional peripheral materials that must be purchased and then configured. Because cheating was generally more difficult on consoles, easy cheating methods became part of the console gaming culture. One example of this is the *Metroid* (1985) "JUSTIN BAILEY" cheat code that gave the player almost all of the game powers, the *Contra* (1988) and *Life Force* (1987) code for additional lives, which was done using the controller keys "Up, Up, Down, Down, Left, Right, Left, Right, Select, Start." In fact, the popularity of these codes as part of the culture now feeds t-shirt sales with businesses like Game Skins.com, as mentioned earlier, selling shirts with these codes on them.[2] One important distinction here is the source of cheats. In computer gaming culture, cheats and hacks tend to be third-party, unauthorized creations, while in console gaming culture, cheats are coded into the software by company programmers.

Like cheating, game modifications prove simpler on computers because computer games are meant to be modifiable for corrections. Computer players are familiar and accustomed to being given incomplete games and downloading patches to update their games. Because of the need for patches, computer players are also readily familiar with the need to alter their existing games, through both the games' sponsored patches and through player-made modifications or "mods." These mods have even fostered mod communities where groups of players work together to create personalized mods of games, like specific-themed *Quake* (1996) mods and *Sims* (2001) character mods (Morris 2002).

Console gamers, on the other hand, have not had the possibility for mods until recently. In prior (and many of the contemporary) gaming consoles, mods are not possible because the game's coding is sealed in the game cartridge or disc. While the PlayStation2 and XBox now have hard drives for their systems, enabling console players to use game or player created mods, game mods were almost entirely unavailable until now. In fact, the culture of console gamers has come to expect games to be fully developed; as Rider notes:

> PC gamers are often tech junkies. They like to fiddle with their boxes, take great pride in pumping up their video resolution until their graphics card screams and begs for mercy, and they like to share and show off their knowledge[....] Console gamers just don't want to be that bothered with the technology — they don't want to install patches, tweak settings, or work to play the game. Consoles are made to be powered up and played with little to no hassle [2002: para. 5–6].

Computer gamers often developed communities around game modifications and patches, but because console players had to rely on the game cartridge or disc, their communities often developed because of the cultural commonalities in dealing with cartridge and disc errors. One of these commonalities is the method of cleaning dust from the original NES cartridges. Many players used cotton-tipped swabs with rubbing alcohol to clean the dust from the cartridges, despite the fact that Nintendo specifically advised against it. Other players developed special methods of blowing into the cartridges to clean out the dust. In addition to legal mods, there are illicit mods and methods of copying games which have fostered subcultures for both computer and console gamers. Because computer games are available on full computers, the games are more easily copied even with copy protection.

Conclusion: Platforms for Academics

In some ways, the significance of platform type for consoles and computers is diminishing with technological improvements. However, the differences for portable gaming systems like cell phones and PDAs are rapidly developing. Aside from mobile gaming platform differences, console and computer game interfaces still differ and those differences still factor largely for gaming culture in general, as well as for gaming genres and the act of gameplay. Game studies needs to further recognize the impact of the platform and interface for purposes of historical accuracy and for the significance of platform given the changes in platforms with the Nintendo DS radicalizing the handheld market, and with the rise of other gaming platforms. Attempts to study games without regard to their platform and to their gaming culture would serve to further instantiate an academic gaming culture that has already begun in its preference for computer games. The differences in gaming platform, as these differences inform all gaming aspects, must be further investigated.

The academic gaming culture is driven in part by the desire to have replicable gaming experiences through the multiple saves offered by computer games, and the desire to archive the games for later use. Console game emulators make older games available for play on computers; however the method of play is still drastically changed, often in fundamental ways that alter gameplay and game reception. Once the differences between computer and console games are recognized, then the academic desire to protect data may come to include console games and pieces of console gaming culture through the archiving of console gaming systems instead of just their code through the archiving of emulators. Whether or not this archiving can be successful, the recognition of the differences between console and computer games would still serve to inform investigations of gaming systems, mobile gaming, and gaming cultures.

Notes

1. See for instance Gamespot.com's overall rankings of the *Resident Evil* games. The first received an 8.2 for the Playstation release and a 7.2 for the computer release; the second received an 8.9 on the PlayStation and a 7.0 on the computer.

2. Even the gaming clothing divides computer and console gamers with the clothes on GameSkins.com most often depicting console gaming icons and the clothes on sites like ThinkGeek.com most often depicting geek culture with computer coding and computer gaming icons.

References

Aarseth, Espen. 1997. *Cybertext: Perspectives on Ergodic Literature*. Baltimore, MD: Johns Hopkins UP.

Blizzard. 1998. *StarCraft*. Platform: PC. Publisher: Blizzard.

Bolter, Jay David, and Richard Grusin. 1999. *Remediation: Understanding New Media*. Cambridge, MA: MIT Press.

Capcom. 1996. *Resident Evil.* Platform: Playstation. Publisher: Capcom.

_____. 1997. *Resident Evil 2.* Platform: Playstation. Publisher: Capcom.

_____. 1999. *Resident Evil 3: Nemesis.* Platform: Playstation. Publisher: Capcom.

_____. 2000. *Resident Evil, Code: Veronica.* Platform: Dreamcast. Publisher: Capcom.

_____. 2001. *Devil May Cry.* Platform: PS2. Publisher: Capcom.

_____. 2002. *Resident Evil 0.* Platform: GameCube. Publisher: Capcom.

Consalvo, Mia. 2003. "Zelda 64 and Video Game Fans." *Television and New Media* 4: 3 August: 321–334.

Crampton Smith, Gillian, and Philip Tabor. 1996. "The Role of the Artist-Designer." Pp. 37–57 in *Bringing Design to Software,* edited by Terry Winograd. New York: ACM Press.

Crawford, Chris. 2003. *Chris Crawford on Game Design.* Indianapolis, IN: New Riders.

Douglas, J. Yellowlees. 2000. *The End of Books — Or Books Without End?: Reading Interactive Narratives.* Ann Arbor, MI: University of Michigan Press.

Dulin, Ron. 1999. "Review of *Resident Evil 2.*" *Gamespot,* March 26. Retrieved Aug. 10, 2004. (http://www.gamespot.com/pc/action/residentevil2/review.html).

Gee, James Paul. 2003. *What Video Games Have to Teach Us About Learning and Literacy.* New York: Palgrave, 2003.

id Software. 1996. *Quake.* Platform: PC. Publisher: Activision.

KCET. 2001. *Silent Hill 2: Restless Dreams.* Platform: PS2. Publisher: Konami.

Klepek, Patrick. 2004. "Console Publishers Get PC." *Computer Gaming World.* 245, December, pp. 32–3.

Konami. 1987. *Life Force.* Platform: NES. Publisher: Konami.

_____. 1988. *Contra.* Platform: NES. Publisher: Konami.

Lahti, Martti. 2003. "As We Become Machines: Corporealized Pleasures in Video Games." Pp. 157–170 *The Video Game Theory Reader,* edited by Mark J.P. Wolf and Bernard Perron. New York: Routledge.

Lake, Max. 2001. "*Resident Evil* Series: GameCube Exclusive." *Planet GameCube,* Sept. 31. Retrieved Oct. 1, 2004. (http://www.planetgamecube.com/news.cfm?action=item& id=2071).

Leitch, Sam. 2002. "Console Wars." *Videogames NZ,* May 12. Retrieved Oct. 1, 2004 (http://www.videogames.co.nz/showfeature.php?id=2).

Malcivar. 2004. "User Comments, Starcraft: Ghost Demo at E3." *Geek.com,* May 13. Retrieved Oct. 1, 2004. (http://www.geek.com/news/geeknews/2004May/bga2004051 3025123.htm).

Manovich, Lev. 2001. *The Language of New Media.* Cambridge, MA: MIT Press.

Maxis. 2001. *The Sims.* Platform: PC. Publisher: Maxis.

Morris, Sue. 2002. "First-Person Shooters — A Game Apparatus." Pp. 81–97 in *Screenplay: Cinema/Videogames/Interfaces,* edited by Geoff King and Tanya Krzywinska. London: Wallflower Press.

Nintendo. 1985. *Metroid.* Platform: NES. Publisher: Nintendo of America.

Norman, Donald A. 1988. *The Design of Everyday Things.* New York: Basic Books.

_____. 2004. *Emotional Design: Why We Love or Hate Everyday Things.* New York: Basic Books.

Poole, Steven. 2000. *Trigger Happy: Video Games and the Entertainment Revolution.* New York: Arcade Publishing.

Ray, Sheri Graner. 2004. *Gender Inclusive Game Design: Expanding the Market.* Hingham, MA: Charles River Media.

Rider, Shawn. 2002. "Back to the Front: The Console Wars Go Online." *Games First,* May 29. Retrieved Oct. 1, 2004. (http://www.gamesfirst.com/articles/shawn/console_ war_online/consoles_online.htm).

Sheff, David. 1993. Game Over: How Nintendo Zapped an American Industry, Captured Your Dollars, and Enslaved Your Children. New York: Random House.

Turkle, Sherry. 1984. *The Second Self: Computers and the Human Spirit.* New York: Simon and Schuster.

_____. 1995. Life on the Screen: Identity in the Age of the Internet. New York: Simon and Schuster.

Winograd, Terry. 1996. "Introduction." Pp. xiii–xxv in *Bringing Design to Software,* edited by Terry Winograd. New York: ACM Press.

Wolf, Mark J. P. 2001. "The Video Game as a Medium." Pp. 13–33 in *The Medium of the Video Game,* edited by Mark J. P. Wolf. Austin, TX: University of Texas Press.

Zovni. 2002. "Review of *Silent Hill 2.*" *Moby Games,* Dec. 5. Retrieved Sept. 1, 2004. (http://www.mobygames.com/game/view_review/reviewerId,3250/gameId,5069/platformId,3/).

Section 4: Consumption and Community

13. Mapping Independent Game Design

Jason Wilson

"I don't think you'll ever really get rid of the bedroom coders. At least not without some kind of very powerful pesticide..."
Indie Game designer Graham Goring,
interviewed in *Retrogamer* [Carroll, 2004]

Critical concerns about a narrowing of scope in game design — an increase in genre-based videogame production — are not only premised upon a misunderstanding of the nature of commercial development and the dynamics of popular media, but also contrive to ignore the long, ongoing history of innovative, independent design that expresses new possibilities for the production, aesthetics and meaning of videogames.

Recently, videogames industry news service gamesindustry.biz offered a short feature on developer Planet Moon's decision to shy away from making games for any future flagship consoles. The design house had announced its intention to concentrate their efforts on producing games for Sony's looming PSP handheld platform. It was argued by gamesindustry.biz's writer, Tom Bramwell, that the time and resources needed to create blockbuster games to meet market expectations in a brutally competitive console development industry represent too great an entrepreneurial risk for small companies. The conclusion of the piece, that Planet Moon's decision to deliberately scale down these costs and expectations might signal a new model for commercial game production, led Bramwell to risk a cross-media comparison:

In a sense, it's a lot like an independent film studio... [I]t's unusual for studios under a certain size to commission the kind of effects-heavy, high-risk block-busters that dominate the silver screen all year round, precisely because they know they can't afford to choke down on a big, multi-million-pound loss in the same way a company like Universal perhaps could... [I]t may just be that the PSP (and to a similar extent the Nintendo DS) gives small developers a more realistic set of goals, allowing them to express themselves comfortably and cre-atively without having to worry about betting the entire stable on one horse every time they put fingers to keyboard on a new project [Bramwell 2004].

It is implied here that the withdrawal to low-cost development brings aesthetic and commercial constraints *and* opportunities; the analogy with film carries a hint of the prospect of "art-house" values and modes of production. Planet Moon's move, if successful, could see such a stance become increas-ingly important — already other smaller developers such as New Zealand/ Aoeteroa's Sidhe are, apparently, going down the same path (Sidhe Interac-tive 2004).

Gamesindustry tends, like much of the rest of the games media (as well as many games and new media scholars) to focus on the increasingly concen-trated industrial nexus of what we might call "big gaming": the linked com-plex of big developers, big publishers and big retailers supplying users of the major platforms with bleeding-edge digital play. Because of this, Bramwell can be forgiven for the hints of amnesia and myopia in his otherwise provoca-tive piece. His implication that top-down refocusing among established devel-opers might lead to a greater prevalence of low-cost indie development runs the risk of ignoring independent game design as it already operates. The fact is that independent game design has a long and ongoing history (arguably it has a *longer* history than that of gaming as a commercial reality). If we use "independent game design" as a term to describe generally what happens out-side the circuits of "big gaming," we will find that it embodies a range of games, made from a range of motivations, with a range of relationships to mainstream production, distribution and consumption.

This chapter provides a necessarily selective survey of the sprawling diver-sity of indie game development, not as a means of developing a category of "art" that is opposed to the industry, nor by way of describing a field that might "redeem" the alleged cultural bankruptcy of gaming conceived as "new media's other" (Lister et al. 2003), but rather as an exploration of a diverse group of sites and practitioners who alternatively use the freedom that inde-pendence from the games industry gives and struggle against the limitations of their externality for a range of purposes. Briefly, I will describe the char-acteristics of the current global, mainstream gaming market by using an overview of Electronic Arts — perhaps its biggest player — to map its economic and cultural scale and importance. The main focus, though, is the alternatives to this version of gaming that arise in the worlds of indie design, around and beyond the margins and scope of consolidating global games production and distribution. I will explore how indie practitioners are variously start-up entrepreneurs, producers of politically-engaged inflections of current game genres, hackers and modifiers of existing game software and hardware, vintage gameplay revivalists, and explorers of the possibilities of the physical interface. In offering these examples, I will maintain mostly, though not exclusively, an Australian focus and will show how indie design continues to be at once a crucial driver of innovation in game design, a parallel sphere of artisanal digital craft, and a site of critique.

"Big Gaming": An Overview

Contemporary "big gaming" is characterized by a mode of development involving large, salaried, highly skilled and specialized teams of designers and artists, working for firms with major investments in high-end technological infrastructures, who are often carrying out licensed and/or franchise-based development for one of the major proprietary consoles (PlayStation 2; Nintendo GameCube; XBox) or for PCs. The results are spectacular 3D worlds that usually require the advanced consumer technologies of current-generation game consoles or high-end PCs to play in. If they are not the in-house productions of major international publishers, developments are often tied to distribution deals with these now-enormous and highly profitable entities. In the absence of any articulation with the considerable marketing and distribution networks of the big publishers, smaller developers may not recover their production costs. Australian developers for example, like Auran or Beam, have had their recent international hits only by dint of their distribution deals with, or takeovers by, major publishers like Activision or Atari. Inevitably, this means that publishers often have considerable and often quite direct influence over creative decisions during the development process. Another powerful element in this system are the retail chains to and through which games are largely sold to end-users, and whose brand values and retailing priorities can themselves feed back into development decisions, constraining developers' creative control. Lastly, developments are publicized in a large and growing on- and offline games publishing industry.

The organization that epitomizes such structural arrangements is, perhaps, US development and publishing giant Electronic Arts Inc. (EA). Since their incorporation in 1982, EA has combined licensed in-house development, publishing and distribution of games for major platforms — forty-two to date. I personally have seen the EA logo on games I have played over the course of twenty years on the Commodore 64, Commodore Amiga, Sega Master System and Sega Megadrive, PC, PlayStation and PS 2 and Xbox. Their earliest games — *Doctor J and Larry Bird Go One-On-One* (1983), *M.U.L.E.* (1983), *Skyfox* (1984) *World Tour Golf* (1985), and *Mail-Order Monsters* (1985) — show exactly how early their concentration on reliable mass-market genres like sports simulations, strategy games, flight simulators and arcade-action conversions began. Since their beginnings EA have extended their cultural and economic importance as a licensed third-party developer, paying fees to manufacturers for the right to publish games on their consoles but never engaging in hardware production themselves, thus remaining flexible across a history of changing hardware platforms and increasing concentration of software production. EA gradually entrenched its position and then enormously expanded its business by designing and releasing blockbuster titles in proven genres, and cementing the dominance of its own big-name franchises.

By the end of fiscal year 2003, EA was operating in two business segments with three major brands: EA Games (publishers of *Harry Potter and the Chamber of Secrets* [2002], *The Sims* [2000] and *Command and Conquer: Generals* [2001]); EA Sports (*FIFA Soccer 2003* [2002], *Rugby 2004* [2003], *Madden NFL 2003* [2002]); and an edgier EA Sports Big label (*Def Jam: Vendetta* [2003], *NBA Street* [2001]). It had in-house development and production studios in six international locations, and numerous agreements with other third-party developers whose games EA publishes, markets and distributes, e.g., *Battlefield 1942* (2002), which they published on behalf of developers Digital Illusions. The company's products are distributed to over 80,000 global retail locations. They have developed close relationships with giant North American and international retail chains like Wal-Mart, and specialists like the globally franchised games retailer Electronics Boutique. The company makes large-scale, ongoing professional advertising and PR efforts pitched both at mainstream and gaming media, and includes sports sponsorships and endorsements and cross-media tie-ins with major film franchises like *Lord of the Rings* and *Harry Potter*. As a result, in 2003 twenty-two of their games sold over a million copies, and 42% of the firm's net revenue was generated outside the US. If market capitalization is used as a measure, while selling nothing but games, they are now the fifth largest software corporation listed on the New York Stock Exchange (Yahoo! Finance 2004). Their ownership is almost exclusively large institutional investors whose noted risk-aversion is clearly not triggered by the entirely debt-free EA's prospects. Recent rumors and boardroom appointments have suggested Viacom's strong interest in acquiring the company, but they are apparently unwilling or unable to come up with the US $20 billion that would be required to acquire the company and deliver shareholders a reasonable premium (Fahey 2004b).

Independent game production, with its long history and great diversity and depth, can be defined as that which occurs outside the kind of nexus EA exemplifies. Indie design, however, is not a unitary field. It now overlaps variously with new media art, political activism, new economy start-up entrepreneurship and even new age movements. Sometimes it defines itself against mainstream game production and sometimes it hovers on its margins of the industry, seeking an entry. Indie game designers vary in the positions they take on games themselves and their history. Some seek to critique games as they are, or to force gaming in new directions; some seek to lovingly recreate or modify past styles of gameplay as an aesthetic or ideological comment, or from pure fandom; others maintain a happy distance from game cultures, servicing a particular constituency with styles of gameplay that have fallen from favor in mainstream design. What indie designers share are the costs of production outside the games industry's growing and concentrating capital flows, and the benefits conferred by widespread technological literacy, the falling costs (in the West) of powerful information and communication technologies (for both designers and their constituencies), new channels of on- and offline distribution and networking, and, whether or not they are self-conscious in this, the ethic of DIY and cultural appropriation that have recently characterized new media cultures and new artistic movements.

One versus Many: *Learning the Interface*

The Australian artist Richard Allen's *One versus Many* is an ingenious hardware modification that extends digital conglomerate Konami's design insights — in games like *Dance Dance Revolution* (Konami 1999) — while bearing down hard on the characteristics and the potential of embodied play's physical interface. Like so many contemporary practitioners, Allen's own biography shows him criss-crossing the boundaries of commercial game and software design and new media art in a way that makes him and his practice hard to define. *One versus Many*, though a gallery-sited work, shows how deeply his sensibility has been marked by the visual aesthetic and attentive regimes of gaming.

Using an Atari 2600 console and a familiar 1970s title — *Combat* (Atari 1978) — Allen's work intervenes at the point of the game controller. Instead of the iconic Atari joystick, the user must control her tank in the two-player game by means of a series of pressure sensors embedded in footpads made of recycled hubcaps, and lit up by flashing LEDs. These are arranged non-intuitively before a large projection of the gameplay screen. Instead of cradling the joystick in her hand, the player must leap around from footpad to footpad, and sometimes needs to attempt to stand on two of the trickily spaced pads in combination in order to get her tank to move in the right direction.

The screen projection blows up Atari's blocky raster vehicles to an epic size, filling the player's field of view. The actions the player needs to take viscerally increase the tension of the game and illuminate the physical demands that gameplay always makes. Together, projection and player's actions create an unusual spectacle in gallery space, and by using obsolescent forms of CGI Allen draws attention to the effects of size and the possibilities of engendering performance through the science and art of the interface. *One versus Many* has the effect of satirizing critical discourses that, on the basis of their visual component, make an unreflexive connection between games' derealized spectacles of combat, forms of derealization in broadcast news, and ideologies and institutions of the military-industrial or military-entertainment state (Nichols 1988; Virilio 2002). The juxtaposition of such spectacle and giggling gallery visitors trying to make sense of the relationship between their actions, the interface and the screen disrupts the easy connections made on the basis of visual resemblance and insists on games as specific forms of image (co-)production.

The relationship with *Dance Dance Revolution* is clear, and Allen can be seen to play with the ideas (and ideologies) of technological progress that characterize parts of the popular reception of gaming. *One versus Many* is a work that creates novel effects by bringing together forms of play from opposite ends of gaming history in a jumble of recycled materials, ironic futurism and home-baked electronics. The principal difference between *Dance Dance Revolution* and *One versus Many* is that one characteristically offers the enthralling rhythms of subcultural and cyborg performance, and one visualizes and extends the chaotic and exhilarating moment of *learning an interface*.

Escape from Woomera: *Playful Protest*

Though *Escape from Woomera* is one of the most discussed examples of contemporary, Australian indie games production, it has only recently been available in a playable form. Like *Counter-Strike* (Sierra On-Line 2000), the game is a modification of *Half-Life* (Sierra On-Line 1998), which turns the game engine to uses that differ from those of the commercial release. In an appropriation of a familiar game industry marketing technique, the projected game was first available only as an unplayable teaser, and in May 2004 a playable prototype became available from the developers' website. This, though, is part of what the project seeks to draw attention to, namely the difficulty of producing certain kinds of games within the prevailing organization of games development.

As the name suggests, *Escape from Woomera*'s central gameplay imperative is absconding from one of Australia's largest immigration detention centers in Central Australia. The game utilizes the hegemonic aesthetic of the First-Person Shooter established in games like *Wolfenstein 3D* (id Software 1992) and *Doom* (id Software 1994) and perpetuated in series like *Quake* (id Software 1996) and *Unreal* (GT Interactive 1998) to at once critique the politics of such gameplay (as in the *Quake*-based works of Chinese artist Feng Mengbo) and the Australian government's policy of incarcerating refugee claimants. Instead of the dark underground mazes that characterize the commercial genre, the player will have a first-person perspective of the huts, dry earth and bright, cloudless sky of the central Australian detention center. The player, unarmed, will be required to avoid camp security and find a way out to freedom.

The capacity for overt, spectacular violence that is usually present in FPS games is absent here, but this only succeeds in drawing attention to the submerged or routine institutional violence embedded in long-term detention. The institutional spaces of incarceration become, like the levels of *Quake*, an architecture of intensity and fear, with the player ever-alert for potential sources of danger around every corner in the form of camp guards. The unarmed helplessness of the player not only draws attention to the structure of power in such conditions of imprisonment, but also chimes with the "stealthy" gameplay options in titles such as *Thief* (Eidos Interactive 1998). The marking of banal landscapes with profound, violent conflict mirrors the charge of games like those of the *Grand Theft Auto* series (DMA/Rockstar 1997–), but with significantly different player-positioning, and different implications, too.

It is worth noting that some of those working on the project are themselves temporary or intermittent "refugees" from the games industry. Working and speaking to their work under aliases, and only fitfully being able to advance the project, they draw attention to the sometimes–Draconian labor arrangements in the games industry. It is not only that many in the industry work under contracts that grant their employer ownership of all and any intellectual property they produce, but that many PR–sensitive design companies would almost certainly dismiss employees engaged in such forms of political expression. From their largely unprotesting acceptance of a tough classification regime in the early 1990s, to their restriction of IP rights and politically-engaged outside work, the Australian games industry has a poor record when it comes to ensuring their employees' cultural and political freedoms.

Needless to say, the games industry is profoundly uninterested in funding the significant development costs of a first-person shooter of this nature. Alternative sources of funding have also been difficult to access, since the development fell between the cracks in not meeting the institutional criteria of either new media art *or* a viable new economy start-up — two powerful legitimating discourses of digital creativity. As long as the game remains unfunded and unfinished, it represents a provocative problem for any would-be architect of new media policy, or for anyone who criticizes games on the basis of their allegedly limited subject matter: how can we get this made, distributed, and played?

In all of this — its difficulties in securing financial backing, its necessarily partly-covert production, its ingenious play with a prevalent aesthetic, and its use of same as a tool of protest — *Escape from Woomera* manages to raise some crucial questions around the politics of gameplay and the politics of detention. The game makes a connection with contemporary guerrilla and indie media movements, and with the entire modern history of politically-engaged visual-cultural production, from Goya to Gaetano. But what kind of connection is it, and what are the political effects of bringing gameplay into contact with political protest? It also raises questions about the relationship of new forms of protest and new protest movements with more established organizations and forms of activism. Given that the game drew criticism both from the federal government (by way of the then–Minister for Immigration, Multicultural and Indigenous Affairs, Philip Ruddock) *and* the Human Rights and Equal Opportunity Commission, who oppose the policy of detention (and claimed it exploited the position of refugees), it brings us to ask how the acceptable parameters of protest ought to be determined, and by whom (Swalwell 2003). Presumably a film or TV documentary about the issue would not have drawn such a reaction from either side, or at least not from *both*. This raises the issue of the cultural status of games, which, as Lister et al. (2003) point out, are still conceived of in many quarters as "new media's other." Perhaps it exposes generational tensions within human rights activism *and* within styles of media consumption. Lastly, it brings us to consider the often invidious working conditions in the "creative industries," where not only is creativity itself seriously constrained at work, but where many companies contrive to own *all* of their workers' creative output. It should be noted that, although the teaser and the preview have had all these effects and posed these questions, the design team are frank in saying that until *Escape from Woomera* is a playable game, they consider it unfinished.

La Molleindustria: Designs on Power

Italian collective La Molleindustria also makes politically engaged games, though in genres different than *Escape from Woomera*—and with different critical targets. Its games run in Macromedia Flash, by now a long-established family of software applications for producing and replaying web animations, games and pop-ups. Molleindustria makes games that resemble the flash and shockwave games that crowd the servers of shockwave.com or are used to advertise commodities, from energy drinks to political candidates like Howard Dean. The resemblance is made manifest in their visuals, the basic gameplay discipline (mouse-pointer), and in their emergence in discrete browser windows. The difference is that these are games that seek, for example, to make trenchant criticisms of ever-more "flexible" labor markets and to visualize and make playable the claims of queer theory about the mutability of sexual identity, pleasure and desire.

Molleindustria explicitly positions its work in opposition to the mainstream industry, which it sees as having been invaded by global entertainment giants. It simultaneously positions its work alongside broader indie media movements:

> We believe that the explosive slogan that spread quickly after the Anti-WTO demonstrations in Seattle, "Don't hate the media, become the media," applies to this medium. We can free videogames from the "dictatorship of entertainment," using them instead to describe pressing social needs, and to express our feelings or ideas just as we do in other forms of art. But if we want to express an alternative to dominant forms of gameplay we must rethink game genres, styles and languages. The ideology of a game resides in its rules, in its invisible mechanics, and not only in its narrative parts. That's why a global renewal of this medium will be anything but easy [Molleindustria 2004].

Molleindustria's website shows its explicit connections with organizations like Euro Mayday, which stages a yearly event that is a rallying point for new social movements. Molleindustria explains, too, its decision to distribute its games freely online:

> We chose to start with online gaming in order to sidestep mainstream distribution channels and to overcome our lack of means. Using simple but sharp games we hope to give a starting point for a new generation of critical game developers and, above all, to experiment with practices that can be easily emulated and virally diffused [Molleindustria 2004].

With such serious critical aims, it may be a surprise for their site's visitors to discover how much fun their games are. One game, *Tuboflex*, is introduced as being set in the near future:

Year 2010. The need of mobility has grown to excess since the first years of the millennium. That's why Tuboflex Inc., the world's leading Human Resources Services organization, created a complex tube system that make it possible to dislocate employees in real time, depending on demand. Playing the part of a Tuboflex workhand, you will have to survive in this dynamic labor market [Molleindustria 2004].

In *Tuboflex* the player, armed with her mouse, must negotiate different tasks set for her (cute) avatar in different virtual workplaces, from a fast-food drive-through counter, to a factory floor, to a clerical cubicle, to a Christmastime shopping-center wherein she must play Santa to demanding children. The avatar is sucked from one job to another without warning. And while the tasks become progressively harder, in between there are periods of unemployment where the clock ticks as the player's avatar sits idly in an armchair.

In *Tuboflex*, La Molleindustria's ideological sympathy with new kinds and forms of political protest such as Euro Mayday and its Netparade is clear. Of Netparade, which is an online, participatory manifestation of the annual Euro Mayday parades in Milan and Barcelona, and which online visitors are invited to add an avatar to, the organizers say:

> The marching avatars are digital simulacra of today's exploited masses of neoliberalism: précaires, precari@s, precari, cognitarie, contingent knowledge and service workers. We are a mixed bunch, a heterogeneous multitude of precarious jobs and lives. Yet we have not spawn out of Fordist assembly chains, but out of dystopian retail chains and office spaces [euromayday.org 2004].

Tuboflex speaks to and simulates the conditions of the same constituency: postmodern, post–Fordist, largely young and Western service and information workers.

Queerpower: Welcome to Queerland is another of La Molleindustria's Flash games, this time focused on the politics of sexuality and identity. The game's intro sets the scene: "Queerland inhabitants don't have fixed sexual orientations and roles. They fornicate following their highly changeable desires" (Molleindustria 2004). Players (1–2) must choose a preference before play begins ("dick lover," "pussy lover," or "other or confused" [Molleindustria 2004]). When play begins, the instruction "Fuck!" appears as players' avatars face each other. A number of actions are available: the player may approach or retreat from the opposing avatar, change shape between masculine and feminine forms, and between a number of sexual poses, and instruct their avatar to engage with their opposite number, from which pleasure is (unevenly) distributed. Progression in the game is measured by the two on-screen bars for each player that measure how much desire one's avatar feels for the gender-posture combination of the other avatar at any given time. This, along with the shapes assumed at intimate moments, forms the matrix of the queers' "dynamics of desire;" one that measures "the satisfaction level of your queer" (Molleindustria 2004). The game ends when one avatar or another's satisfaction level maxes out at orgasm.

There is a clear inversion here of the imperatives of 2D beat-em-ups from *Street Fighter* (Capcom 1987) or *Mortal Kombat* (Midway Games 1992) forward, though it resembles them in taking the logic of *Pong* (Atari 1972) to a certain conclusion. Like *Tekken* (Namco 1994) or *Soul Calibur* (Namco 1999), *Queerpower: Welcome to Queerland* makes a number of abilities, postures and special moves available to the player in their tangle with their opposite number. Beat-em-ups use (ever-diminishing) health bars to indicate how much damage a player has sustained (and the equation of such damage with pain is underlined and extended to the player's body in hardware mods/artworks like C level's *Tekken Torture* [2002]). *Queer Power*, in contrast, invites the player to accumulate and grant pleasure.

There are a range of interfaces between the game and influential strands of queer theory. Indeed, it could be said that the game visualizes and makes playable some of its key claims or problems relating gender and sexuality. The polymorphy of players' avatars and the blur of shifting preferences and identifications illustrate claims about the constructedness, or even the arbitrariness, of inviolable categories of homo-, hetero-, masculine and feminine. Identities such as these are here equated with something as mutable and evanescent as the "skins" that players choose for their avatars in mass-market games like *The Sims* (Maxis 2000). It is open for players to make it their object either to compete to reach orgasm first, to reverse this and be the first to fill up the other player's satisfaction bar, or to try to reach this point together. Either way, the game plays up the power inscribed in such encounters and raises a number of questions about power, pleasure, domination and submission.

Mulawa: Digital Craft, Virtual Tourism

Not so strongly articulating any oppositional politics, and located in a sphere of what we might call digital craft, parallel to the games industry, are small, artisanal enterprises such as Townsville-based Mulawa. Mulawa's games are the work of a single practitioner, Peter Hewitt, and so far there are two that are commercially available, *Xiama* (2000) and *Magnetic* (2003), which Mulawa self-publishes and sells both online and at a stall in Townsville's Cotter's Markets. The games are thoroughly rooted in the lost tradition, so beloved of earlier games scholarship, of *Myst* (Cyan/Red Orb Entertainment 1994) its sequel *Riven* (Cyan/Red Orb Entertainment 1997) or *Jewels of the Oracle* (Eloi

Productions 1995): essentially gameplay is a passage through a series of static, panoramic scenes, where progress is dependent upon puzzle-solving and clue-collection.

There are important differences, though, between Mulawa's games and the adventure-puzzles of a decade ago. Where the earlier games took advantage of the increasing graphical sophistication of mid–1990s mass-market PCs, and set their games in finely-textured CGI fantasy worlds, Mulawa's games ask the player to make her way through a world composed of digitally-photographed scenes from the natural environment surrounding Townsville. While *Xiama* is composed of scenes from Bowling Green Bay National Park, *Magnetic* contains images of Magnetic Island, located just off Townsville. To progress through these picturesque tableaux (which are photographed by Hewitt himself) the player must, for example, solve geometrical puzzles and collect scraps of paper from the environment which add up to a message or a poem. Mulawa's web presence offers players an open and direct dialogue with Hewitt, a diary that details the development of the game and Hewitt's own motivations in its creation. This highly personalized and artisanal form of games authorship, where close links between a game's author and its public are forged, is distinct from the studio- or publisher-branded products of the games industry — even from those instances where developers attempt to exploit relationships with a fan community to feed back into the development process, or where the product of fan labor remains the property of publishers.

Aesthetically, though visually modest by comparison to contemporary games like *Final Fantasy X2* (SquareSoft 2004), Mulawa's games still manage to raise some important questions for game studies. However fetching they may be, without the connecting puzzles, Hewitt's photographs would simply be a slide show. With them, though they are often quite simple in their character, the game takes on a narrative dimension, or perhaps becomes what Henry Jenkins calls "narrative architecture" as the photographs become spectacular rewards in a highly engaging ludic practice. What, we may ask from here, are gameplay's minimal conditions? The aestheticized images of rainforest not only answer those who would argue that there are no games with Australian content, but they give rise to a kind of virtual tourism, where the embodied spectator must carry out forms of cultural labor in order to traverse imagined spaces. What are the consequences of at once making such images available to a geographically dispersed audience, locating games in local spaces, commodifying these spaces in a commercial product, and incorporating them in gameplay's ludic economy? Do these games depend on the pleasures of spectacular possession, or are they an attempt to connect gaming with an environmental and local consciousness?

Playing with Toys: Eness and Virsual

Eness is an industrial and software design team from Melbourne that straddles the line between art and commerce, and whose "virtual rocking horse," *Virsual*, provokes questions about the borders of categories like artwork, product, technology and toy. *Virsual* is composed of an elaborately manufactured, futuristically styled rocking horse facing a large-screen digital projection of a first-person perspective on a very bright and friendly virtual environment. By rocking and leaning in various ways, the user (atop the horse) can influence the speed and direction of movement on-screen. The imperatives of this navigation mesh neatly with its deliberately unthreatening, child-friendly character: the player collects golden rings, at her own pace, from a range of magical characters in enchanting on-screen environments.

Like Konami's recent hardware-software innovations in standalone arcade games and its home console ports, or indeed like Richard Allen's work, *Virsual* seeks to effect new incorporations of the playing body in new forms of gameplay. The soothing motion of rocking and the rocking-horse's connotation of childhood fantasy harmonize with the on-screen environment and with the history of this particular kind of toy in children's culture, yet they introduce something quite novel to embodied gameplay.

Work such as Eness's may put us in mind of new media art theorist Oliver Grau's figure of the media artist, who

> Represent[s] a new type of artist, who not only sounds out the aesthetic potential of advanced methods of creating images and formulates new options of perception and artistic positions in this media revolution, but also specifically research[es] innovative forms of interaction and interface design, thus contributing to the development of the medium in key areas, both as artist and as scientist. Art and science are once more allied in the service of today's most complex methods of producing images [Grau 2003: 3–4].

The construction of a new and charming interface taps the history of children's culture, i.e., that of commercial gameplay[1] and extends the range of embodied virtual play, is enabled by the highly technologized solution to a series of technical problems. Some of these solutions are ingenious. For example, controlling *Virsual* by means of rocking is made possible by the adaptation and incorporation of wireless mouse technology. *Virsual*'s biomorphic-futurist shape is the result of digitally-controlled, laser-tooled manufacturing processes. A high level of efficiency in project coordination is necessary where the completed toy requires a seamless fit between physical manufacturing, electronic circuit design, coding sophisticated on-screen worlds and operating within a start-up budget gleaned from institutional grants and corporate sponsorships.

Thus far, Eness representatives have exhibited *Virsual* in gallery spaces and spoken to the project at arts festivals and Indie Game Developer conferences. Yet, they are unabashed in their wish for *Virsual* to become a mass-market toy, though they acknowledge that it would be an expensive proposition for manufacturers and consumers alike. The development of *Virsual* shows local indie firms refusing to be constrained by institutional discourses of art and commerce, or clichés about artisanal, altruistic artworks and cultural-industrial commodities.

Playing with History: Vintage Remakes

While Eness looks to a future where the potentialities of embodied interaction are expanded, the retro remakes scene is a largely online culture of (usually) unpaid hobbyist practitioners remaking vintage games from classic platforms for contemporary PC and Mac users. This needs to be distinguished from emulation cultures. Programmers making emulators like MAME seek to preserve arcade games in a playable state by emulating the hardware functionality of original, stand-alone machines. The practices highlighted in online clearing-houses and community forums such as www.remakes.org or http:// retrospec.sgn.net, however, add up to something different than emulation, where programmers often make use of the play in the notion of the "remake" by creating games that reprise something of originals like *Breakout* (Atari 1976), *Tetris* (Pazhnitov 1985), or *Manic Miner* (Smith 1983) but with changed graphical styles, additional features or the incorporation of other kinds of gameplay. This can be compared with film remakes, where the audiences have an expectation that filmmakers will make changes and add something of themselves to the original to reflect their own preoccupations or broader cultural changes.

Indeed, the hobbyist culture of remakes is one of the spaces in game culture where games are most heavily marked as authored. On www.remakes.org, a section entitled "Heroes" includes fan-style interviews with prominent remakers like Andy Noble, who is responsible for highly-esteemed new versions of *Manic Miner* and *Jet Set Willy* (Smith 1984). Popular publishing titles such as *Retrogamer* not only provide subcultural visibility for all kinds of practices associated with the games of the past, they also give prominence to remake auteurs, for example when *Retrogamer* recently featuring an interview with Graham Goring from Retrospec and Stu Collier from Ovine by Design.

Designers like Noble, Goring and Collier make no money from their remakes, but they are near the top of a hierarchy of auteurs who receive kudos from a thriving on- and offline culture. There is another reason that only social and cultural capital can flow in the remakes economy: these designers often sail close to the wind of copyright infringement and are also working outside their occupations as commercial game designers, with all the constraints that befall those so employed. As Goring explained to *Retrogamer,*

> I work on commercial games for a living so I couldn't make money out of this even if I wanted to — it'd be a contractual no-no. But personally I'd avoid making remakes for money just because of all the legal problems that would arise out of a money-making venture. The copyrights on a lot of these old games indirectly belong to big companies... [When contacted for copyright permission] some of the companies have taken a "don't ask, don't tell" policy ... [but] there are certain companies whose games you don't bother trying to remake because their stance is well known [Carroll 2004: 28].

The increasing importance of corporate remakes of vintage games in extending gameplay to, and driving sales of new media technologies such as JAVA–enabled mobile phones may see the squeeze on hobbyist developers tighten. (In the European Leisure Software Developers' Association's first mobile phone game download chart, *Tetris* (IFone 2004) was number 1 (here reprising the market-busting role it had in the GameBoy's success); the next month it was *Pac-Man* (Namco 2004) (Fahey 2004a). For now, though, some companies at least allow retro remaking to continue, knowing that remakes are the drivers of fan communities convened around the deeps of the digital back-catalog and that remaking is an important venue for present and future developers to hone their skills. Meanwhile, remakes and their publics raise important questions about the nature of the nostalgia here expressed and entrenched (What, precisely, is its object? What are its uses?) and the history of the reception of gameplay.

Conclusion

From this survey, we struggle to find a universal aesthetics or ethics of independent game design, and the activities and motivations of these designers suggest a range of relationships among the different sites of indie production and the mainstream games industry. Necessarily, all of these producers have an ambivalent relationship with the technologies, aesthetics, institutions, and the past and present of big mainstream gaming. Variously, indie production looks like a crucial driver of innovation and expansion in game design, a proving ground for games industry professionals, a harsh critic of the values of big-budget games, an appropriator of the forms of commercial gameplay for the purposes of nostalgia or political activism, a parallel set of digital craft practices, and a marker of the limits of commercial design wherein games without commercial viability are made from other motivations. If part of what gamesindustry.biz says is true, and modes resembling current independent game design are set to become more prevalent, scholars of gameplay and new media alike will do well to continue to attend to indie's past, present and future.

Note

1. The task of collecting rings refers us to late 1980s and early 1990s games such as *Sonic the Hedgehog* (Sega 1991).

References

Baer, R. 2003. "Video Game History." Ralph Baer Associates. Retrieved May 5 2004. (http://www.ralphbaer.com)

Bramwell, T. 2004. "Developer Planet Moon Refocuses Exclusively on PlayStation Portable." Retrieved 1st June 2004 (http://www.gamesindustry.biz/content_page.php?section_name=dev&aid=3536,).

Burnham, V. 2001. *Supercade: A Visual History of the Videogame Age, 1971–1984.* Cambridge, MA: MIT Press.

Carroll, M. 2004. "Retro Remakes." *Retrogamer* 2: 27–31.

Cubitt, S. 2001. "prestondigitation." Sean Cubitt. Retrieved June 5 2004. (http://130.217.159.224/~seanc/seanwriting/prestonframeset.html).

Euromayday.org. 2004. "Mayday Net Parade." Retrieved June 14 2004. (http://www.euromayday.org/netparade/).

Fahey, R. 2004a. "Pac-Man Tops UK Mobile Games Chart in April." Gamesindustry.biz. Retrieved: June 18 2004 (http://www.gamesindustry.biz/content_page.php?section_name=new&aid=3639).

_____. 2004b. "Viacom baulks at $20 billion EA price tag." Gamesindustry.biz. Retrieved: June 23 2004 (http://www.gamesindustry.biz/content_page.php?section_name=pub&aid=3564).

Grau, O. 2003. *Virtual Art.* Cambridge, MA: MIT Press.

Herman, L. 1997. *Phoenix: The Fall and Rise of Home Videogames.* Union, N.J: Rolenta Press.

Lister, M., J. Dovey, S. Giddings, I. Grant, and K. Kelly. 2003. *New Media: A Critical Introduction.* London: Routledge.

Molleindustria. 2004. "La Molleindustria." www.molleindustria.it. Retrieved 14 June (http://www.molleindustria.it/home-eng.php#queerpower).

Nichols, B. 1988. "The Work of Culture in the Age of Cybernetic Systems." *Screen* 29(1): 22–47.

Sidhe Interactive. 2004. "Sidhe Receives Funding For PlayStation(tm) Portable Game Research." Retrieved June 22 2004. (http://www.sidhe.co.nz).

Swalwell, M. 2003. "The Meme Game: Escape From Woomera." *RealTimeArts.*

Virilio, P. 2002. *Desert Screen: War at the Speed of Light.* London: Continuum.

Winter, D. 1999. "Pong-story." Retrieved March 24 2002. (http://www.pong-story.com).

Yahoo! Finance. 2004. "Yahoo! Finance: Electronic Arts Inc. (ERTS): Quotes and Info." Retrieved 6 July 2004. (http://finance.yahoo.com/q/pr?s=ERTS).

14. Desire for Commodities and Fantastic Consumption in Digital Games

MIKE MOLESWORTH AND JANICE DENEGRI-KNOTT

One question posed by digital games is about their relationship to, or impact on, the ordinary lives of players. Is digital play liberating, separate from and a substitute for "real" life experience, or inevitably connected to, influenced by and in turn able to influence "real" life? In this chapter we consider possible connections between the experiences individuals have while playing popular digital games and their experiences in a consumer society. Specifically, we evaluate the connection between virtual goods and consumer culture by examining the possibilities for relationships of stimulation and/or substitution between digital games and "real" consumption. We argue that desire for consumer goods easily finds its way into digital games, that some experiences in games may ask players to re-examine their consumer lifestyles, and that some games open up the potential for consumption experiences based on fantasies beyond what is available in the material world.

It is only recently possible to view digital games as places where consumption occurs. Developments in digital game hardware now allow for very detailed graphics capable of depicting realistic branded goods (Poole 2000). This has resulted in many games — mainly sports simulations and driving games — carrying representations of real brands (cars, advertising, sponsorship) as a way to enhance realism. Game developers often pay a license to

brand owners for use of brand names, but as advertisers have started to recognize potential benefits from brand placement in games, we are seeing more
brand placement deals (Edwards 2003). Recent examples include Dole
Bananas who paid Sega to include their brand in *Super Monkey Ball*, Pizza
Hut and KFC who both appear in *Crazi Taxi* and Motorola who appear in
the game *Die Hard* (Emery 2002). It is now possible to buy simulations of
consumer goods for real money. Consumers can savor driving a "real" car in
video games, build a virtual dream home, or enhance their digital lives with
rare and expensive magic artifacts. Marketers are also producing their own,
branded console games and online "advergames" out of a desire to reach
difficult audiences (Edwards 2003). It seems that opportunities for virtual consumption are set to increase.

The development of opportunities to engage with virtual brands and
products in video games presents a challenge for most theories informing our
understanding of consumer behavior. Much literature on consumption deals
with material commodities that are needed, wanted, used conspicuously and
owned in a physical sense. But deprived of material substance, the popularity of virtual commodities is indicative of a type of consumption that defies
the premises of utility-based explanations, for example a virtual car cannot
take you to work. Consequently, making sense of consumption in digital
games requires an appreciation of consumer behavior that considers the more
salient imaginary and symbolic qualities of goods as well as the potential interface between the consumption of intangible, digital commodities and the
desire for and acquisition of material goods. Consumption of digital commodities may also be studied in light of the many criticisms of exacerbated
materialism. These include the systematic alienation of consumers into one-
dimensional beings (Marcuse 1964); the inability of goods to lead to a satis-
fying state of being (Fromm 1976), and depletion of natural resources with
few psychological benefits (Csikszentmihalyi 2000).

In order to unpack these relationships we discuss the types of pleasures
a consumer may derive from simulated goods (whether they are sensory-based
or imaginary); the role of "real" brands in generating pleasure during digital
game play; and the interplay between experiences of playing with simulations of brands and the desire for material consumption experiences. We first
attempt to account for the emergence of virtualized consumption, arguing that consumers are increasingly familiar with hyperreal and even virtual
consumption environments for the acquisition of goods. We then explore
the role of digital games as resources for consumer dreams and fantasies,
assessing how they may be treated as objects of desire themselves. Finally, we
explore how digital games may or may not stimulate desire for "real" commodities. Conceptually, we draw on theories of consumption and desire, illus-

trating them with three popular digital games; *Gran Turismo*, *The Sims* and *Everquest*.

Gran Turismo is one of the best selling console games of all time with world-wide sales of up to 30 million units (Gamezone 2003). Although perhaps often thought of as a driving simulation, the game is of interest here because it also simulates aspects of consumption (buying new automobiles) and provides evidence of the potential of brand placement in games. The cars featured in the game are representations of real cars available in the marketplace. The Sims series of games is considered to be the best-selling PC game of all time (e.g., Howson 2003). It has also been described as "virtualized consumerism" (Kline, Dyer-Withford, and DePeuter 2003). In *The Sims*, players are free to create a wide range of characters and family units. They are then able/required to build a virtual home based on a multitude of designs and to fill that home with all the usual household goods. In the recent online version of *The Sims* players interact with other Sims, controlled by other players. They also get to interact (for the first time in this game) with "real" brands. Sims may visit a McDonald's, for example and increase their happiness and health by consuming a burger. A Sim may also "buy" a PC, complete with Intel processor (Reuters 2002). In Western countries, *Everquest* was until recently the most popular massively multi-player online game (MMOG). At its peak 500,000 players signed up to the game (Thompson 2003) each paying £100 a year subscription.[1] In *Everquest* players quest for magic spells, enchanted armor, powerful swords and other such fantasy objects, which they can also buy and sell in a virtual marketplace. They may also choose the race, gender, skills and strength of their characters from a range of options, as a consumer may choose a new outfit.

The Emergence of Virtualized Consumption

Several factors may help to explain the increased occurrence of consumption-like activities in videogames. There are growing concerns amongst marketers about the decline in effectiveness of "traditional" communication techniques. Marketing (2003) cites Henley Centre research which indicates that consumers are "all spent out" and increasingly disappointed with over-peddled promises of materialism as a bridge to achieve well-being. Marketers' endless attempts to find ways of re-invigorating jaded markets have resulted in marketing being accused of being both "parasitic," borrowing from popular cultural forms (MacAllister 1995) and "geographically imperialistic," seeking out new places to present persuasive messages (Leiss, Kline and Jhaily

1990). The popularity of video games makes them a potential new domain for innovative marketing communications.

The increasingly imaginary, symbolic and playful dimensions of consumption may also have aided the colonization of digital games by marketing forces. Not only is the symbolic value of goods now said to be of more importance than their utility value (see Gabriel and Lang [1993] for a detailed discussion), but consumption in itself can be constructed as a game. If the pleasures of consumption derive from the symbolic value of goods, then digital games come to represent intelligible spaces to see, desire and even purchase commodities. This emerging supremacy of the sign value of goods over use value has been captured in literature addressing contemporary consumer culture. For example, Baudrillard (1994) sees consumers as "trapped" in an endless, playful, consumption-orientated, media-produced simulation, where symbolic meanings are all that is important. Others have noted that playful leisure activities are themselves incomplete without opportunities to consume (Urry 1995) and that shopping malls and superstores are no longer organized for efficient shopping, but are themed entertainment centers where consumers play (Gottdiener 2000). Featherstone (1991) argues that the spectacle of shopping malls in some way replaces the previous playful regression of the carnival or fair. More recently, online shops have begun reproducing these environments as virtual simulations (Ryan 2001) and online auction sites such as Ebay are also turning buying and selling into an elaborate game (Levy 2002).

Technologies simultaneously reflect and (re)present the society in which they are developed (Woolgar 1996) and digital products (including games) are products of the consumer society that we have just described (Darley 2000; Kline et al. 2003). Game designers', programmers' and producers' experiences as consumers may thus influence their input into games, regardless of any brand placement deal. Kline et al. (2003) make this very clear, warning against the tendency for technological determinism which ignores the fact that technology is used and modified by members of society whose actions determine the subsequent use for the technology. The implication is that, although consumption in games may reflect a consumer society this reflection is imperfect. In allowing a new space for consumption digital games may also modify behavior producing new consumer culture and attitudes towards commodities.

Digital Games as Resources for Consumer Dreams and Fantasies

A number of authors explore in detail how consumption may be driven by internal, imaginative idealizations of objects of consumption. This departure from accepted hierarchical models that schematize the workings of a rational economic consumer is well established by more experiential and hedonic explanations of consumption (Addis and Holbrook 2001; Caru and Cova 2003; Havlena and Holbrook, 1986; Hirschman and Holbrook 1982; Holbrook 1997). For example, Holbrook and Hirschman (1982) have produced a rich catalog of research exploring hedonic and experiential aspects, where fantasies, feelings and fun are central in the consumption experience. Recently, Belk and his colleagues, in a series of articles (Belk 1998; Belk, Guliz and Askegaard 1996; 2000; 2003) have attempted to shift the focus from a needs-satisfaction discourse for understanding consumer behavior to that of consumer desire. Desires are defined by Belk et al. (2003: 99) as "specific wishes inflamed by imagination, fantasy and longing for transcendent pleasure." Desire, they postulate, would enable an understanding of the processes leading to consumption, unlike needs that, as Campbell (1987) points out, are usually assumed to pre-exist. Consideration of desire allows for an understanding of how consumers develop an affinity towards the embodied, sensuous pleasures of consumption experiences (Holbrook and Hirschman 1982; O'Shaughnessy and O'Shaughnessy 2002) as well as the anticipatory pleasures of the imagination (Campbell 1987; McCracken 1985).

McCracken's (1988) work on displaced meanings explores, from a cultural stance, why certain objects become coveted by consumers and why a cycle of yearning for new goods is inexhaustible. He argues that the attraction of goods lies in their ability to act as bridges between consumers and coveted displaced meanings — meanings that come to signify an idealized state of being and have been deliberately removed from an everyday context to avoid the possibility of their destruction through exposure to reality. The evasive nature of displaced meanings, as desirable states that are never to be fully obtained, fuels desire. Since the emphasis is on "if only I had, then..." the role played by consumers' imaginations is pivotal in fuelling desire towards objects.

Similarly, Campbell (1987: 77) defines consumers as dream-artists who "employ their creative, imaginative powers to construct mental images, which they consume for the intrinsic pleasure they provide." Campbell's autonomous hedonist consumer is one who is a product of a Romantic ethic that celebrates the powers of the imagination and emotional sensibilities. His thesis harbors a playful, emotional element that resonates with characteristics of play. For example, Huizinga (1938: 9) defines play as "freedom," "unreality," and "outside the immediate satisfaction of wants and appetites" and Sutton-Smith (1997) highlights a whole rhetoric of play based on the same Romantic foundations as Campbell's thesis. For Campbell the locus of pleasure is sustained upon emotional experiences rather than sensory (physical) ones, hence stimulation energized by intense feelings exceeds that provided by real experiences.

Campbell's treatise on imaginary consumption is the story of the development of the modern, romantic hedonist. He contrasts this with a more traditional hedonist, for whom sensual pleasure is a result of thrilling, physical experiences. From a psychological perspective, perhaps relevant to digital game play, Poole (2001) suggests something similar: individuals seek flow. Flow is a desirable state of being, an optimal experience which individuals desire to attain and re-attain (Csikszentmihalyi 1975), but which is experienced in the present and therefore suppresses the speculative imagination. A desire to return to pleasurable consumption experiences is also identified by Belk et al. (2003). Although digital games undoubtedly produce pleasurable flow through play (in a traditionally hedonistic way), they may also constitute a resource to build more enduring daydreams.

The imaginary in consumption is encapsulated in what Campbell defines as modern hedonism. Modern hedonism is not only a disembodied-mentalist experience, as Boden and Williams (2003) suggest in their critique of Campbell's work, but one where daydreaming may result in a behavioral response in the form of consumption. Like McCracken's displaced meaning, Campbell's hedonist consumer attempts to perpetuate day-dreams by choosing to attach them to objects of desire, unhooking them only once these objects are attained and experienced. It is this unhooking and hooking of anticipatory illusions about forthcoming events or desired goods through which autonomy is exercised. Consumers, as autonomous self-illusory dream-artists, "employ their creative, imaginative powers to construct mental images, which they consume for the intrinsic pleasure they provide" (Campbell 1987: 77). They are free to pick from various sources available in everyday consumer culture to craft personalized daydreams which they then consume in their imagination.

The experiences of playing digital games may be useful resources for these daydreams. *Gran Turismo* is promoted by publisher Sony in this way: "Featuring over 160 real-life cars from authentic manufacturers, 11 tracks, and the ability to realistically upgrade your cars, Gran Turismo is a world streamlined for the car enthusiast." In encouraging daydreams of ownership, *Gran Turismo* potentially provides an ideal model for marketers wishing to stimulate consumer desires through digital play. All the pleasures of the "perfect" experiences of the game may be imagined in the real ownership experience. Lienert (2004) cites players of *Gran Turismo* who claim "You really know the product. You can pick a car, accessorize it, tune it and drive it in the game under realistic conditions. It's better than any brochure." These same players (students) even claim a desire to buy specific cars featured in the game when they start work. Such was the desire of players of *Gran Turismo* for the Mitsubishi Lancer featured in the game, but not available from real US dealerships, that their requests to buy the real thing led Mitsubishi to change its US import strategy (Gamasutra 2002).

At the start of the game a player is awarded money and invited to visit the virtual showrooms of leading car manufacturers, complete with accurate ranges and color schemes. The player starts out with sufficient money only to buy the cheapest cars, although they may browse all of them. Immediately the player sees that some cars (by virtue of their higher price and higher performance) are more desirable than the ones that they can currently afford. This simulated shopping experience is important for the game. Although the most obvious objective of the game is to win races, this is also the only way that a player gains "money" in order to buy a more desirable car. An end purpose of the game seems to be to acquire a garage full of the most desirable cars. The races are just an exciting way to delay their acquisition, thus actually making them more desirable. If daydreaming strengthens desire (Campbell 1987), then a playful simulation of desired objects, like the cars represented in *Gran Turismo*, could expand the dream-artist's ability to conjure desired images of a consumer good. The game in itself encourages this by inviting players to desire ever more expensive cars, imagining through their efforts what it would be like to buy the real thing. They can even watch and re-watch themselves driving these cars using a "record" and "playback" function. These recordings may act like "advertisements" featuring the player driving her dream car in "ideal" conditions (which, incidentally, would not be acceptable in a "real" advertisement due to concerns about incitement of dangerous driving). Recalled experiences of the game may come to represent aids for the imagination and in doing so could increase the anticipatory pleasures of consumption.

Yet, can experiences in animated digital games really be considered legitimate platforms to conjure up images for the purpose of desire for the "real" thing? Miller and Miller (1996) considered the effects of direct and indirect (vicarious or mediated) experience on attitudes and on predicted behavior. Overall, direct experience tended to result in stronger attitudes which were a better predictor of future behavior. These ideas have been applied to interactive media and marketing communication experiments, the results of which suggest that virtual environments that produce more presence (mediated experiences imagined as real) produce stronger attitudes (Coyle and Thorson 2001; Kim, cited in Lombard and Ditton 1997). Other human-computer interaction researchers have highlighted that individuals may have problems in distinguishing between real and simulated experiences, especially when they are recalled from memory (Shapiro and Lang 1991) and especially when the mediated experience was from virtual reality simulations (Shapiro and McDonald 1992). Presence (or telepresence) may be determined by the vividness and interactivity of the medium (Steuer 1995).[2] Steuer highlights that currently only video games score highly on both dimensions and they therefore seem most likely to readily produce telepresence. He goes on to advise that as these new technologies develop so too do the possibilities for using them to "manipulate and control beliefs and opinions" (Steuer 1995: 53). There is therefore an element of realness to the actions that take place on the video game screen. Consequently a more vivid and elaborate daydream built in and through a playful virtual environment is likely to strengthen the desire for the "real" more effectively than print, or even TV advertising.

"Owning" cars in *Gran Turismo* is perhaps an enjoyable experience, but there are limits to the consumption simulation. You cannot park the car outside your own home. You cannot actually sit in it or drive it to work and you cannot choose not to buy new, more expensive cars and still progress through the game. The experience of ownership of a particular car is therefore incomplete. Players can eventually achieve this limited virtual ownership of all the cars they desire and complete all the races.[3] An end to the game constitutes an end to the ongoing imagining of owning virtual representations of cars, and the enjoyment ascribed to this activity by Campbell, unless desire can be redirected somewhere else. *Gran Turismo* therefore includes the opportunity for desire to be directed outside the game towards the "real" commodities in order to continue crafting pleasurable daydreams. A player may still enjoy the game by seeking lower lap times but the dream of owning cars may seek other outlets. This may explain the earlier comments of Lienert's students and the requests made to Mitsubishi.

The Sims simulates consumer lifestyles in a more comprehensive manner, therefore offering a wider range of resources for the construction of consumer day-dreams. Sims are almost infinitely customizable and players can also visit numerous, "unofficial" web sites to download a wide range of clothes and other commodities. Many of these sites are themselves displayed like shopping malls, highlighting the game's focus on consumption (Nutt and Railton 2003). The Sims' popularity can be attributed to the ease with which players may play out dreams related to everyday consumption activities, as this quote posted from a player on the official Sims bulletin board illustrates: "I think that playing *The Sims* is like a fantasy world. You can be rich and live in a house like Shaq or living in a shack. I think this game is great for interior design and construction of houses." Players' daydreams and desires within the game are often consistent with their desires in real life. They want a family and friends, they want a comfortable home, filled with commodities — and perhaps like real life, in *The Sims*, work takes place only as a means to achieve the wealth required to sustain a consumer lifestyle. Game play ignores the work environment and instead focuses on leisure (Nutt and Railton 2003).

Gran Turismo and *The Sims* represent the actualization of consumer daydreams. Yet, Campbell (1987) stresses a difference between daydream and fantasy. Fantasy represents an unrestricted usage of the imagination in crafting unrealistic scenarios, whereas the daydream is bolted onto a real object, making the daydream instrumental in anticipating the consummation of desire. Although fantasy feeds from an unlimited use of the imagination, and therefore has the potential for more pleasurable imagined experiences, the trade-off is that the absence of reality reduces its ability to create the sense of longing required by desire. As a result fantasy can be fleeting and short-lived and therefore lead to less overall pleasure. Belk et al. (2003) suggest that desire requires there to be hope that the object of desire can be obtained. Likewise, McCracken identifies the need to believe that desired states of being are achievable, even if they are never actually reached. Fantasies, therefore, do not produce desire because there is no hope of their fulfillment — I may desire a new car or home, but I do not desire to be a powerful wizard, even though I may fantasize about being one.

An interesting aspect of digital games, however, is their ability to simulate both "realistic" experiences and fantastic ones. Desire in fantastical digital spaces encourages unlimited use of the imagination. This is reflected by *Everquest*'s official website, which promotes the game by suggesting: "Meet new friends from around the world to face epic challenges. Make yourself a noble human knight, a vicious dark elf thief, a greedy dwarven merchant, or whatever suits your desire." The objects of desire in *Everquest* are not the mundane commodities of *The Sims* or *Gran Turismo*. The official site claims that players have "[t]housands of items to discover and collect, both magical and mundane, including artifacts of great power." In *Everquest* players aim for rare prestigious clothing, magic swords, staffs, and other such fantasy. One key attraction of the game is a medieval style marketplace where players may come to buy and sell or simply to browse for bargains. A key activity for players is searching for goods in the hope of finding a rare item, either at a bargain price in the market or through questing. *Everquest* may not therefore support brand placement easily, but has considerable potential to stimulate desire for virtual commodities themselves.

Digital Games and Consumer Culture

Unlike *Gran Turismo*, *The Sims* and *Everquest* offer potentially endless play.[4] There is no obvious conclusion to either game and in fact the publishers constantly update with new content. So what are the implications for the cycle of desire for commodities when a player is never confronted with an end to the simulated experience, but rather invited to endlessly seek new experiences, including new commodities or artifacts within the simulation?

For Campbell (1987: 86) the "desiring mode constitutes a state of enjoyable discomfort, and that wanting rather than having is the main focus of pleasure-seeking." Hence any postponement in the consummation of desire is accepted, or actually desirable. His thesis suggests that modern consumer culture has its roots in Puritanism which encouraged the suppression of an overt gratification of desires and therefore encouraged the development of a romantic consumer ethic. In postponing consumption, the individual can extract more pleasure from the experience by indulging in the "discomforts of desire." Campbell explains this discomfort as a prolonging of the pleasures associated with the crafting of daydreams. He frames this through a construction of real, lived experiences as inherently deficient in their ability to generate such heightened states of pleasure. McCracken (1988) also suggests that when a commodity is acquired, desire for that which was previously hoped for fades and consumers soon find new objects to desire, because desire is what is aimed for. For this reason objects of desire are often deliberately difficult to obtain.

Revisiting Campbell (1987), the emphasis has been on the disenchanting nature of real objects as a source of renewed desire (see also Belk et al. 2003; Gabriel and Lang 1995; Shankar and Fitchett 2002). However it is actually the loss of the daydream, rather than a disappointing object that stimulates desire for another commodity. Campbell views commodities as little more than transient carriers of a dream that a person is likely to attach to other objects in order to re-experience the illusory pleasures of daydreaming. This autotelic vision of desire is also evident in Belk et al.'s (2003) inquiry into passionate consumption which stresses that it is the desire to desire rather than disappointment that infuses the cycle of desire. The experience of renewed desire is not therefore dependent on an unsatisfactory encounter with physical commodities. The virtual representation could easily become "real enough" to endlessly resuscitate the cycle within the game by allowing an endless supply of new items to long for. Castronova (2003) suggests that game players revel in the difficulty of achieving goals. In play, individuals deliberately and self-consciously agree to rules that make the achievement of arbitrary objectives more difficult (Sutton-Smith 1997). So perhaps modern digital games have the potential to help the individual achieve endless desire in addition to encouraging desire to seek the "real" (as with other marketing communication forms). For the player of open ended games like *The Sims* and *Everquest* there may be a separation between their mundane, everyday consumer lives and their ability to create, fulfill and recreate daydreams within the game. This separation or distance from everyday consumption activities may allow for a reflection on or moderation of consumer culture.

One logic behind placing brands in games is to stimulate consumer desire for "real" commodities in order to increase profits. However, not all the daydreams generated by games may be wanted by companies whose brands are placed in the game. Walsh (2002), for example, incites players of *The Sims Online* to demonstrate outside the virtual McDonald's as an easy substitute for "real" demonstrations against McDonald's. Likewise, Turkle (1995) maintains that simulation games may have the ability to allow players to come to see something about real-life systems. As a result of this (and possibly more than other media), games may encourage individuals to transform aspects of their real lives. Gee (2003) also suggests that games can produce powerful learning experiences as a result of the reflection they encourage in players. One player revealed as much in a post to *The Sims* bulletin board:

> I started looking at my life differently, in terms of what needs do I have? I actually think of talking as social building, and sleeping as greening my energy bar. It helps me break my life down into the basic "needs" of my life and helps me decide which need is the lowest... It really has helped me lead a more solid life, since I don't go to bed without filling all my needs for that day. Hmmm, maybe I DO play The Sims too much.

Molesworth (2003) cites another *The Sims* player who came to understand that, just like in real life, a Sim cannot be made permanently happy by buying things — they must always be bought things. Nutt and Railton (2003) also highlight the ability that the game gives players to acquire a better understanding of the way that society works. Players are free within the game to ask "what if" questions about behavior including relationships, but also consumption. Kline, et al. (2003: 276) suggest that in *The Sims*, "[t]he lesson that is taught, or at least reinforced, is that one must negotiate the daily events and crises occasioned by a life in which commodity consumption is the raison d'etre." Klimmt (2003) also describes this characteristic of some digital games in terms of psychologists' understanding of play — as something that helps individuals make sense of real life, including the relationship between actions and emotion.

While the nature of consumer desires is made transparent by *The Sims*, the open-ended nature of games like *The Sims* or *Everquest* may suggest that players do not necessarily direct desire to objects outside the game. Rather, the rules built into the game can be used by players to experiment with their attitudes to various activities. Because *The Sims* places so much focus on consumption, it is likely that players will be able to use the game to explore what consumption means for them, they may see the circle of desire at work. Frasca

(2003) suggests that the ability to act out different scenarios (to ask "what if" and get different answers) is a key distinction between the rhetoric of games and the rhetoric of other media. Campbell (2004) has suggested that shopping may even have an ontological function. By allowing consumers endless opportunity to test their reactions to goods and experiences available in the market and thereby experience "who they are" digital games obviously vastly extend the range of experiences available.

Rather than asking players to question consumer lifestyles, digital games like *Everquest* provide the potential for consumers to desire artifacts unavailable in their "real" lives. With *Everquest*, fantasy becomes palpable through the vividness of hypermedia and the hierarchical structure based on skill that sustains the game. This, coupled to the desire created by objects within the game and the challenges it presents to its players, allows for a continual rekindling of desire. For many the result is a compelling experience. The regeneration of desire within the confinements of such a fantastical environment could explain why the game has acquired an "addictive" quality (McCandless 2003). Even players themselves refer to the game as "Evercrack," or "heroinware" because of players' tendency to let the game take over their lives (Becker 2002). Seemingly for some players the power of these games is to render all other activity meaningless. A player whose fantasies and desires are satisfied (and re-kindled) by these games may look less for desire in mundane consumption. Castronova (2003) considers the economics of MMOGs, suggesting that the "satisfaction"/cost differences between "real" life and games will determine the level of substitution of games over "real" life. Where games offer more satisfaction — in this case the experience of desire — individuals may be drawn to spend more time playing them, rather than other "real-life" consumption games. Potentially the longing for an elusive "Duck Staff" in *Everquest* may offer more pleasure than the desire for a new pair of jeans or even an automobile. This may be even truer at a time when the acquisition of consumer goods has become easier through higher disposable income and access to immediate credit and therefore the opportunities for pleasure through anticipation is reduced. The acquisition of commodities in games generally remains pleasurably difficult.

The Social and Commercial Construction of What Is Desirable

We have already suggested a link between what people come to desire and the efforts of marketers. The desirability of consumer brands is carefully constructed through the efforts of brand managers and advertisers (e.g., see

Kapferer 1997). To be desirable there generally needs to be awareness among others of the value of a brand and this is a key role for marketing communications. But how do commodities in games, which are not always simulations of existing "real" brands, therefore become desirable? We know that, far from the picture of game players as isolated and unsociable, players frequently play with others and discuss games during social interactions and in numerous online forums (Poole 2000; Sherry, Lucas, Rechsteiner, Brooks and Wilson 2001). If the social influence exerted by present or imagined "others" in digital games is felt by players, then they can be considered relevant forces dictating what is to be desired.

Campbell's (1987) thesis could be read as antagonistic to the importance of the social in understanding the cycle of desire. For example, Campbell rejects Veblen's (1899/1992) emphasis on consumers' need to outdo others and communicate status as short in explaining how wants are generated and updated. In Campbell's thesis, the social life of desire is subdued by the autonomy of the consumer since it is the pleasure found in controlling stimuli through the imagination that explains how a want is generated. Yet, "attitudes of others exert an influence over which new products becomes the focus of desire" (Campbell 1987: 91). While producers do not manipulate consumers, they can attach symbolic meaning to products. Belk et al. (2003) establish and develop clear linkages between desire and the socio-cultural context. Desire is not attached to an object because of its intrinsic qualities, "but [depends] on the consumers' own hopes for an altered state of being, involving an altered set of social relationships" (p. 348). The imagination that produces desire is therefore not entirely individual, but social. Society generates an accepted view of what is desirable. Campbell also recognizes the potential for novels, films and TV to provide individuals with the raw material for daydreams. Individuals may desire what they see others desiring through the media, especially marketing communication, which dominates and structures media consumption. We might now want to add digital games to Campbell's list of media.

Arguably players of *Gran Turismo* must make decisions about which cars they want based on some pre-existing knowledge of cars. They must already have desire for cars to be interested in the game. Although the pre-existing, socially constructed hierarchy of car brands creates the motivation to play, the Mitsubishi example also demonstrates that a previously unfamiliar car can be effectively positioned in the market by its inclusion in the game and its status within the game relative to other, more familiar vehicles. The game may allow the exploration of a wider range of cars than would otherwise be the case for a consumer restricted to what is available locally and what they can afford to purchase. The game may encourage desire for the more expensive cars and therefore a rejection of lesser models that are no longer the stuff of daydreams. However, unlike mass media advertising, *Gran Turismo* offers players a chance to evaluate different cars "first hand" alongside each other. Molesworth (2003) cites players who claim a dislike for specific models of car, based only on their experiences with them in the game. If pre-existing attitudes to car brands attract players to the game, it may also be that playing the game influences "common knowledge" of what constitutes a desirable car. The game may allow opportunities to reflect on the types of cars that are favored as a result of the simulated ownership experience.

In *The Sims Online* and *Everquest* a player may directly observe the choices made by other players and use these to form opinions about what they might hope for their avatar. Like *Gran Turismo*, the Sims player is aided by accepted "rules" of the marketplace. It may be easy for them to make assumptions about what constitutes desirable homes and commodities, without the aid of immediately recognizable brand names. But in *Everquest* the connection to the social is not the "ordinary" lives of players but a common understanding about fantasy and myth that forms the basis for how players make sense of artifacts. So does this connection to myth and fantasy also limit their appeal as the raw material for desire? Individuals may vary in their imaginative capabilities, finding it harder to "get into role" in *Everquest* than in the "everyday life" of *The Sims*. Of course many digital games are now based on popular films, so it may be that consumption of the film constitutes the necessary context in order for players to "believe" in the fantasy world of a game. Molesworth (2003) cites a player who expresses pleasure derived from reenacting moments from his favorite film (*Star Wars*) in digital games, for example. The world of *Everquest* is not dissimilar to Tolkien's *Lord of the Rings*, a perennially favorite book and the subject of the most popular films of recent years (Bellaby, 2001). The choice between playing *Everquest* and playing *The Sims* is therefore a choice between the familiarity of being a consumer and the excitement of acting out fantasies developed from other media consumption.

Players attracted to games like *Everquest* are unlikely to develop fantasies related to mundane consumption as a result of play, but as with the real marketplace, items do become valuable as a result of their scarcity and association only with experienced, "wealthy" players. The desire for powerful characters in the game has even produced a grey market. For example, on eBay consumers will pay real money for the assets and characters that exist only in the game (Birch 2003; Dibbell 2004). This may be further evidence that individuals do desire simulations of commodities as they might real commodities, even though it may reduce the pleasure experienced in achieving this success. Players of *Everquest* can see what other players desire, what they have bought and what they value, and may use this to form their own judgments about what is worth having. In this way desire may still be influenced by social interaction. And if anything these objects may prove even more desirable because of their (artificial) scarcity and the effort taken to obtain them. Intangibility does not reduce digital games' ability to stimulate desire or mean they have no value. Strong feelings of ownership have been documented in several cases where players, seeking compensation for the loss of a valued virtual commodity, have taken legal action in the "real" world (Lyman 2003).

Games like *Everquest* may not promote the consumption of real commodities but they may be seen as an elaborate and potentially effective way for the market, in this case the electronic entertainment market, to make money from consumers' desires. Campbell rejected fantasy as a source of pleasurable desire, but digital games now provide a way for the market to fulfill even our most imaginative fantasy. *Everquest* players may be less interested in consuming other goods, but as long as they continue to pay for online games the circle of capitalism continues. In fact, Kline et al. (2003) suggest that digital games may be the ideal goods of a postmodern society. Games do not just reflect existing markets; they produce new trajectories for consumption ranging from the introduction of new brands as "cool," the instigation and reassessments of consumption practices, and even the establishment of new consumer worlds.

Conclusions

In this chapter we have explored digital games as spaces for consumer daydreams and fantasies. We have argued that this phenomenon requires theoretical consideration and we have suggested that an understanding of consumption, imagination and desire provides useful insights. We have used this approach to consider three popular games. Through these examples we have speculated several relationships between play and consumer desires and therefore argued for the potential impact of digital games on consumer culture. Table 14.1 summarizes key considerations stemming from this evaluation.

Digital games may obviously allow for a traditional hedonism based on sensory experience and physical pleasure — the optimal experience of flow. But they may also be useful artifacts for the experience of "modern" hedonism based on the imagination. Games are spaces where individuals can experiment with daydreams and fantasies including relating to consumption. In experimenting, daydreams and fantasies may be developed, reinvented or rejected in favor of new imaginings and experiences that can generate pleasure.

Game	Type of Game-play	Focus	Relationship with desire and consumption
Gran Turismo	Restricted	Daydreams	The game may be stimulative of desire for real commodities. Desire is initially directed internally but ultimately directed externally towards the ownership of expensive "real world" commodities.
The Sims	Open	Daydreams	The game may be both stimulative and substitutive of desire for real commodities. Desire is mainly directed internally, allowing a player to see over time the process of consumer desire at play.
Everquest	Open	Fantasies	The game may be substitutive of desire for real commodities. Desire is directed internally, allowing a player the pleasure of almost endlessly desiring the most fantastic objects and achievements.

Table 14.1: Types of games and their relationship to desire and consumption

Games like *Gran Turismo* are restricted simulations of consumption. They may allow consumers to imagine what it would be like to own and drive luxury sports cars and therefore become a stimulus for enjoyable daydreams about car ownership. But they are limited in the simulation of that ownership and in duration of game play. As a result they may readily cause the redirection of desire towards the actual ownership of cars.

Games like *The Sims* are attractive to players because they allow more acting-out of consumer daydreams. But the game is open-ended. Whatever desires are created and acted-out within the game, they may constantly be redirected to other aspects of the game. Perhaps games like this can therefore also create new places for displaced meaning, new places where consumers' idealizations of life are safe from the harsh realities of the real world, and therefore compensate for failings or disappointments as a real consumer. Virtual goods may also act as satisfactory bridges for displaced meaning. This would seem consistent with Sutton-Smith's (1997: 231) explanation of play "as a lifelong simulation of the key neonatal characteristics of unrealistic optimism, egocentricity, and reactivity, all of which are guarantors of persistence in the face of adversity." *The Sims* allows for a more complete experience of consumption than *Gran Turismo* and therefore may also allow players to evaluate their experiences as a consumer, providing a critique of the role of consumption in their real lives. Games like *Everquest* may go even further. In *Everquest* individual fantasy can be imagined, played out and re-imagined in new forms. If a reflective *Sims* player questions the value of a consumer lifestyle, the dedicated *Everquest* player dismisses it completely, rendering it irrelevant as a source of pleasure.

According to consumer researchers, one virtue of consumption is that it is a mechanism through which mundane existence is transformed into a resource for individuals' daydreams, allowing them to experience the pleasures of desire. Within digital games, commodities — especially branded ones, rich in symbolic meanings — allow players to act-out their daydreams, fulfilling, but also renewing them. Games also allow players to act out a wider range of fantasies. Game design deliberately prevents the easy acquisition of the most desired objects, thereby further encouraging daydreams and fantasies. This could be contrasted with "real" life where the acquisition of goods is made ever easier by improved distribution of goods and readily available credit that reduce the potential for the pleasures of anticipation. In this environment it is perhaps not surprising to see the growth of digital games like *The Sims* and *Everquest*. As consumers reject the material pleasures of consumption and seek instead "experiential" consumption, digital games provide opportunities for new, engaging and exciting play.

Those concerned with the insidious nature of commercial messages and the promotion of materialistic dreams will no doubt view our observations about *Gran Turismo* as further evidence of the market's imperialism as it invades and conquers yet another area of life. Currently, marketers may seek involvement in restricted games like *Gran Turismo* that direct desire towards actual consumption. It is players' everyday desire for commodities that makes consumption-games fun. The potential for consumption experiences to be playful also makes commodities attractive as source material for games. Games developers can use them to make engaging and meaningful in-game experiences, such as the showroom in *Gran Turismo*, the marketplace in *Everquest* and the whole of *The Sims*. But open, social games may also allow players to renegotiate the symbolic meaning of things within the game, reducing the importance of pre-existing commodities as objects of desire — a potential problem for marketers of desirable consumer goods. Marketers may prefer games more like *Gran Turismo* and less like *The Sims* or *Everquest*, yet the preferred approaches of marketers are still subject to the strategies of games producers, themselves skillful marketers. If fantasies unrelated to "real" world consumption, and/or open-ended, multi-player simulations are popular — if they sell — then games producers may make more of them so that more consumers will play them. Games like *Everquest* and *The Sims* constitute new forms of consumer culture, as yet little studied, despite the many millions of consumers already indulging. Consumption presents a multitude of opportunities for play. But our desire to play new games is also a driving force in new consumption experiences. This is another way of expressing the now widely acknowledged idea among consumer researchers that the relationship between individuals and consumption is not based on the development and satisfaction of ever more sophisticated needs, but rather on desire, stimulated by perpetual novelty. In other words, consumption in digital games is better understood as a contemporary aspect of emotional and playful consumer culture rather than a rational and utilitarian one.

Notes

1. The more recent game *World of WarCraft* now has more than seven million subscribers.

2. Vividness refers to the range of senses addressed and the quality of reproduction of inputs. Interactivity refers to the speed of inputs a user can make, the number of possible inputs and the degree to which inputs "map" natural behavior (e.g., using a steering wheel input device to control a simulated car in a video game).

3. The importance of exploring a range of cars is emphasized on the official *Gran Turismo* website, where it is stated that "Gran Turismo 4 will feature over 650 cars vs. 150 in GT3."

4. Although, there is a trend to market game sequels and expansion packs, including downloadable extra content. *Gran Turismo* is now on its fourth installment, suggesting that even this game may be endlessly extended.

References

Addis, Michaela, and Morris Holbrook. 2001. "On the Conceptual Link Between Mass Customization and Experiential Consumption: An Explosion of Subjectivity." *Journal of Consumer Behaviour* 1: 55–66.

Baudrillard, Jean. 1994. *Simulacra and Simulation*. Ann Arbor: University of Michigan Press.

Becker, D. 2002. "When games stop being fun." *C/net News.com*. April 12. Retrieved June 4, 2003 (http//news.com.com/2102–1040_3–881673.html?tag+st_util_print)

Bellaby, Mara D. 2001. "Hobbits Still Charming Readers." *The One Ring*. March 9. Retrieved September 4 (http://www.theonering.net/perl/newsview/8/999550306)

Belk, Russell W. 1998. "In the Arms of the overcoat, on luxury, romanticism and consumer desire." Pp.41–55 in *Romancing the Market*, edited by S. Brown, A.M. Doherty, A.M., and B. Clarke. London: Routledge.

Belk, Russell W., Guliz Ger, and Soren Askegaard. "Metaphors of Consumer Desire." *Advances of Consumer Research* 23: 368–373.

_____, _____, and _____. 2000. "The missing streetcar named desire." Pp. 98–119 in *The Why of Consumption: Contemporary Perspectives on Consumer Motives, Goals and Desires*, edited by S. Ratneshwar, D. Glen Mick, and C. Huffman. London: Routledge.

_____, _____, and _____. 2003. "The Fire of Desire: A Multisided Inquiry into Consumer Passion." *Journal of Consumer Research* 30: 326–351.

Birch, Dave. 2003. "Second sight." *The Guardian*, July 17. Retrieved July 17, 2003 (http://www.guardian.co.uk/online/story/0,,999226,00.html)

Boden, Sharon, and Simon J. Williams. 2003. "Consumption and Emotion: the Romantic Ethic Revisited." *Sociology* 36: 493–512.

Campbell, Colin. 1987. The Romantic Ethic and the Spirit of Modern Consumerism. UK: Blackwell–IDEAS.

_____. 2004. "I Shop Therefore I Know That I Am." Pp. 27–44 in *Elusive Consumption*, edited by K.M. Ekstrom and H. Brembeck. Oxford: Berg.

Caru, Antonella, and Bernard Cova. 2003. "Revisiting Consumption Experience: A More Humble But Complete View of the Concept." *Marketing Theory* 3: 267–286.

Castronova, Edward. 2003. "On Virtual Economies." *Game Studies* 3(2). Retrieved May 26, 2004 (http://www.gamestudies.org/0302/castronova/)

Coyle, James R., and Esther Thorson. 2001. "The Effects of Progressive Levels of Interactivity and Vividness in Web Marketing Sites." *Journal of Advertising* 30: 65–77.

Csikszentmihalyi, Mihaly. 1975. "Play and Intrinsic Reward." *Journal of Humanistic Psychology* 15: 41–63.

_____. 2000. "The Costs and Benefits of Consuming." *Journal of Consumer Research* 27: 267–272.

Darley, Andrew. 2000. Visual Digital Culture: Surface Play and Spectacle in New Media Genres. Routledge: London.

Dibbell, Julian. 2004. "Real Profits from Play Money." *The Guardian*, April 15. Retrieved April 20, 2004 (http://www.guardian.co.uk/online/story/0,,1191678,00.html)

Edwards, Ellen. 2003. "Plug (the Product) and Play." *Washington Post*, January 26, 2003, A01.

Emery, Gene. 2002. "What's In a Name: Product Placement in Games." *Game Zone*, January 30. Retrieved May 2002 (http://www.usatoday.com/techn/techreviews/games/2002/1/30/spotlight.htm)

Featherstone, Mike. 1991. *Consumer Culture and Postmodernism*. London: Sage.

Frasca, Gonzalo. 2003. "Simulation versus Narrative: Introduction to Ludology." Pp 221–236 in *The Video Game Theory Reader,* edited by Mark J. P. Wolf, and Bernard Perron. London: Routledge.

Fromm, Erich. 1976. *To Have or to Be?* London: Abacus.

Gabriel, Yiannis, and Tim Lang. 1995. The Unmanageable Consumer: Contemporary Consumption and its Fragmentation. London: Sage.

Gamasutra. 2002. "Gran Turismo Moulds Decisions of Car Manufacturers." *Gamasutra*, December, 13. Retrieved January 6, 2003) http://gamasutra.com/php-bin/industry_news_display?story=1525)

Gamezone. 2003. "Critically-acclaimed blockbuster racing franchise pushes Playstation2 technology to new heights by capturing the automotive lifestyle in *Gran Turismo*4." *Gamezone*, May 14. Retrieved June 3, 2004 (http://ps2.gamezone.com/news/05_14_03_02_00pm.htm)

Gee, James P. 2003 What Video Games Have to Teach Us about Learning and Literacy. New York: Palgrave Macmillan.

Gottdiener, Mark. 2000. "The Consumption of Space and the Spaces of Consumption." Pp.265–286 in *New Forms of Consumption*, edited by M. Gottdiener, Boston: Rowman and Littelfield.

Havlena, William, and Morris Holbrook. 1986. "The Varieties of Consumption Experience: Comparing Two Typologies of Emotion in Consumer Behaviour." *Journal of Consumer Research* 13: 394–404.

Hirschman, Elizabeth. 1991. "Secular Morality and the Dark Side of Consumer Behavior: Or How Semiotics Saved My Life." *Advances in Consumer Research* 18: 1–4.

Hirschman, Elizabeth, and Morris Holbrook. 1982. "Hedonic Consumption: Emerging Concepts, Methods and Propositions." *Journal of Marketing* 46: 93–101.

Holbrook, Morris. 1997. "Romanticism, Introspection and the Roots of Experiential Consumption." *Consumer, Markets and Culture* 1: 97–164.

Howson, Greg. 2003. "Games Watch: The Sims." *The Guardian*, February 6. Retrieved March 30, 2004 (http://www.guardian.co.uk/online/story/0,,889307,00.html)

Huizinga, Johan. 1938. *Homo Ludens*. Boston: The Beacon Press.

Kapferer, Jean-Noel. 1997. *Strategic Brand Management*. London: Kogan Page.

Klimmt, Cristoph. 2003. "Dimensions and Determinants of the Enjoyment of Playing

Digital Games." In *Level up: Digital Games Research Conference Proceedings,* edited by M. Copier and J. Raessens. Utrecht, Netherlands.

Kline, Stephen, Nick Dyer-Witheford, and Greig de Peuter. 2003. *Digital Play: The Interaction of Technology, Culture, and Marketing.* Canada: McGill-Queen's University Press.

Laramee, Francois. 1999. "The Game Industry and the Economics of Failure." *Game Dev.net,* November 23. Retrieved April 3, 2002 (http://www.gamedev.net/reference/articles/article867.asp)

Levy, Steven. 2002. "How to Play the eBay Game." *Newsweek,* June 17. p. 58.

Lienert, Anita. 2004. "Video Games Open New Path to Market Cars." *The Detroit News Business,* February 15. Retrieved June 12, 2004 (http://www.detnews.com/2004/business/0402/16/b01–64356.htm)

Lombard, Mathew, and Theresa Ditton. 1997. "At the Heart of It All: The Concept of Presence." *Journal of Computer-Mediated Communication* 3. Retrieved July 6, 2003 (http://jcmc.indiana.edu/vol3/issue2/Lombard.html)

Lyman, Jay. 2003. "Gamer Wins Lawsuit in Chinese Court over Stolen Virtual Winnings." *Technewsworld,* December 19. Retrieved December 28 2003 (http://technewsworld.com/story/32441.html)

Marcuse, Herbert. 1964. *One-Dimensional Man.* London: Routledge.

McCandless, David. 2003. "Just One More Go..." *The Guardian,* April 3. Retrieved May 30 2004 (http://www.guardian.co.uk/online/story/0,,928102,00.html)

McCracken, Grant. 1988. *Culture and Consumption*: New Approaches to the Symbolic Character of Consumer Goods and Activities. Bloomington: Indiana University Press.

Millar, M.G., and K. U. Millar. 1996. "The Effects of Direct and Indirect Experience on Affective and Cognitive Responses and the Attitude-Behavior Relation." *Journal of Experimental Social Psychology* 32: 561–579.

Molesworth, Michael. 2003. "Encounters with Consumption During Computer-Mediated Play: The Development of Digital Games as Marketing Communication Media." In *Level Up: Digital Games Research Conference Proceedings,* edited by M. Copier and J. Raessens. Utrecht, Netherlands.

Nutt, Diane, and Diane Railton. 2003. "*The Sims*: Real Life as Genre." *Information, Communication and Society* 6: 577–592.

O'Shaugnessy, John, and Nicholas O'Shaugnessy. 2002. Marketing, the Consumer Society and Hedonism. *European Journal of Marketing* 35: 524–547.

Poole, Stephen. 2000. *Trigger Happy. The Inner Life of Video Games.* London: Fourth Estate.

Reuters. 2002. "Intel, McDonalds enter *Sims*' World." *Reuters,* September 16.

Ryan, Christopher. 2001. "Virtual Reality in Marketing." *Direct Marketing* 63: 57–62.

Shankar, Avi, and James Fitchett. 2002. "Having, Being and Consumption.*" Journal of Marketing Management* 18: 501–516.

Shapiro, Mike A., and Annie Lang. 1991. "Making Television Reality: Unconscious Processes in the Construction of Social Reality." *Communication Research* 18: 685–705.

Shapiro Mike A., and D. G. McDonald. 1992. "I'm Not a Real Doctor, but I Play One in Virtual Reality: Implications of Virtual Reality for Judgments About Reality." *Journal of Communication* 42(4): 94–114.

Sherry, John, Kristen Lucas, Stephany Rechtsteiner, Christi Brooks, and Brian Wilson. 2001. "Video Game Uses and Gratifications as Predictors of Use and Game Preference." Mass Communication Division, International Communication Association Annual Convention, San Diego, CA.

Simms, Jean. 2003. "Intangible Desires." *Marketing,* November 7. p. 28.

Steuer, Jonathan. 1995. "Defining Virtual Reality: Dimensions Determining Telepresence, Reality" in *Communication in the Age of Virtual Reality,* edited by F. Biocca and M. Levy. Hillsdale, NJ: Erlbaum.

Sutton-Smith, Brian. 1997. *The Ambiguity of Play*. Cambridge, MA: Harvard University Press.

Thompson, B. 2003. "Are You Game?" *BBC Webwise*. March 10. Retrieved September 4, 2003 (http://www.bbc.co.uk/webwise/column/column100303.shtml).

Turkle, Sherry. 1995. *Life on the Screen*. New York: Simon and Schuster.

Urry, John. 1995. *Consuming Places*. London: Routledge.

Veblen, Thorstein. 1899/1992. *The Theory of the Leisure Class*. New Brunswick, NJ: Transaction.

Walsh, T. 2002. "Big Mac Attacked." *Shift.com*, November 7. Retrieved March 3, 2003 (http://www.shift.com/print/web/425/1.html).

Woodcock, B. S. 2005. "An Analysis of MMOG Subscription Growth — Version 18.0." May 4. Retrieved May 20, 2004 (http://mmogchart.com/).

Woolgar, Steven. 1996. "Technologies as Cultural Artifacts." Pp.87–103 in *Information and Communication Technologies: Visions and Realities*, edited by W. Dutton. Oxford: Oxford University Press.

15. Reading and Playing: What Makes Interactive Fiction Unique

Daniel Keller

Zork. Hitchhiker's Guide to the Galaxy. Planetfall. These are three of the most well-known, successful computer games of all time, yet they seem utterly out of place in computer gaming history to those whose exposure is limited to the beloved games of recent years — *The Sims, EverQuest, Halo, Half-Life.* Players of *Myst* and *The Longest Journey* might find some familiarities in play structure, with the heavy emphasis on gathering objects and solving puzzles. However, one big difference would stand out rather clearly: the complete lack of graphics in the former titles. *Zork, Hitchhiker's Guide, Planetfall* and others like them are the text-based games of Interactive Fiction (IF), a genre which has received an increasing amount of attention from scholars in recent years. Part of this increase has to do with IF's connection with other digital texts that have garnered more interest: hypertext fiction, MUDs, and MOOs. Evidence for this connection can be seen in recent works by Janet Murray (1997), Espen Aarseth (1997), and J. Yellowlees Douglas (2000), all of which mention IF tangentially while discussing hypertext fiction. Other recent scholars have focused more attention to IF: Sarah Sloane (2000) devotes entire chapters to the subject; Lara Baker Whelan (2002) questions the interactive nature of the genre, and Nick Montfort (2003) is the first author to devote an entire book to IF. Douglas Jerz and Emily Short's (N.d.) manuscript, *IF Theory*, will undoubtedly increase interest in the subject.

I mention the growing interest in the subject because it relates to some of the points I explore in this chapter. As an avid player of IF during its formative years in the 1980s, I watched the genre quietly die as the decade came to a close and text-based games were replaced by games with ever-more-impressive graphics and sound. As an avid reader of both print and digital texts, I made a reluctant transition to playing the flashy new games that filled store shelves. Now, as a scholar in a discipline wedded to alphabetic literacy, I am curious about the revival of IF: first as a form of entertainment, and second as a subject of scholarship. When I look at the writers of recent and upcoming scholarship on the subject, I realize I am not alone. The scholars mentioned above — Montfort, Whelan, Jerz, and Short — are also players[1] of IF, and Montfort and Short have created award-winning IF. The other part of this growing scholarly interest in IF seems due to the socio-historical contexts that not only produced IF and its audience during the 1980s (when digital texts were becoming available to a certain part of the public), but that also maintained that audience until some of its members became scholars at a time when research on the intersections of print and digital media became more prevalent.

Certainly the scholarship was happening all along, but the intersections of print and digital media seemed to become clearer in recent years after writers stopped ordering funerals for print, revised the well-written obituaries (all-text, no picture — of course), and generally realized that Gutenberg could rest easy. With the rising interest in recent video games, it only makes sense to look back at IF as a major genre of print and digital media gaming, with due consideration given to the authors and players that comprise it. Arguably, the primary reason IF is still around is because of the communities that formed on Internet Usenet groups. Without these communities — without the authors and audiences who create and maintain the contemporary version of this genre — the scholarship would either not exist or would be limited to classic games from the 1980s. While the previously mentioned scholars have made valuable contributions to the subject, they do not provide room for the voices of players. Including the voices of those participating in the genre is crucial, especially when statements are made about how readers interact with IF. As IF scholarship develops further, both in its examination of theory and of practice, readers need to be included as an active part of the genre.

Since I am primarily interested in why IF still exists and what it does for its players, I consulted them.[2] My main interest in doing so was not only to give IF readers a voice, but to explore several substantive questions through their words. What exactly is IF? Who reads IF? Do readers believe IF is truly interactive? What does IF provide readers vis-à-vis other game genres?

What Is IF?

IF generally refers to text-based computer games. An author uses a software program to create a potential narrative, programming moments that permit the player to type in directions that allow her to advance the narrative and explore the setting. The player commonly types in such directions as "go west" or "in" to explore. Other typed directions can be as simple as "look" or "pick up key" or as complicated as "Take the iron key from the table and unlock the wooden door."

While the player is free to type whatever she wants, her level of interaction is limited by the author's design; i.e., a player can only perform a possible range of actions that have been anticipated by the game's author. If the author does not want the player to be able to complete a certain action (e.g., "kill king with axe"), he/she will create a response that blocks such an action (e.g., "You decide not to when you see the ten hulking guards in the room"). If the author has not anticipated such a move and has not created a response, the player receives a generic — and ultimately — frustrating response (often something like "I don't understand").

Some scholars would have a problem with my designating these games as Interactive Fiction, particularly because such games do not seem interactive to them (e.g., Aarseth 1997; Joyce 1995; Whelan 2002). I have no interest in debating the genre title in this space except to say that IF could also describe other digital and print media: hypertext, graphic-based computer games, and books such as Julio Cortazar's *Hopscotch* (1975). I see no harm in genre distinctions being flexible. For this chapter, however, IF refers principally to text-based computer games.

Who Reads IF?

To answer this question, I devised a survey for people participating within IF communities. To find respondents, I posted a request for survey participants on two Internet Usenet groups.[3] I received thirty responses from willing participants, to whom I e-mailed surveys. Twenty surveys, which were comprised of several open-ended questions, were returned. Even though the sample was small, the demographic results were interesting in how they resemble the IF audience of the 1980s. Readers of IF during the 1980s were most likely to be well-educated men (presumably Caucasian). Out of the twenty participants in this survey, seventeen are male. Twelve of the twenty describe themselves as Caucasians[4] and seven reported having "some college experience." Three respondents were college graduates, nine were in graduate school, with six describing themselves as PhD students. One respondent reported having received a PhD. Overall, the sample was biased toward highly-educated Caucasian males.

Since few studies have been done on the fans of IF, it is hard to tell whether this small sample is representative. A survey by Eileen Mullin (1995), who maintains the IF webzine *XYZZYNews*, provides some support for my findings. In her survey, 168 of 186 respondents were male and almost half of all respondents described themselves as "academic/student." The median age was 24 for men and 29 for women. Since her survey primarily involved opinions on the Infocom games of the 1980s, it could be safely assumed that many of these respondents had discovered IF during its formative years.

It seems that those participating in the contemporary era of IF also participated in the classic era of IF. Only one participant reported discovering IF in recent years. The rest first experienced IF years ago, from as early as 1976 to as late as 1988. Respondents supplied a variety of details about their earliest experiences with IF and the two following accounts are fairly representative. The first is from Vivienne Dunstan,[5] a 31-year-old history PhD student:

> I've been playing IF for about 22 years or so, dating back to early experiences with the Infocom games. Usually, I'd be playing IF on the Commodore 64 and IF was a very long-drawn out experience then, typically waiting ages for the game to load, quite a pause between turns, and disk-loading of new sections.

The second is from Rachel Henry, a 29-year-old graduate from MIT:

> I played the "old" games back when they came out, including one called *Crystal Caverns* that I would dearly like to get my hands on. I also played *Zyll* and of course the old Infocom games. When graphics became available I moved on. I would class *Myst* and the old *King's Quest* games as being "in the spirit" of Interactive Fiction.

When the era died in the early 1990s, several of these readers lost track of IF until the past few years. The possibility that many of the current IF readers were also readers during the genre's formative years raises two questions: How do players first get involved with the genre? How is their interest held over time?

Determining the relationship between authors and audiences is no easy task. In recent years, scholars have observed the need to examine the socio-historical situations that influence authors and audiences (Brodhead 1993; Radway 1991). Social situations, literary history, and the material production of texts all interact with each other recursively, creating texts and contexts, authors and audiences. Writing is never just the sole creation of the author, mining the genius of her mind, free from social influence and literary history.

Rather, the production of writing "is bound up with a distinct social audience: *in* its production each addresses and helps call together some particular social grouping, a portion of the whole potential public identified by its readerly interests but by other unifying social interests as well" (Brodhead, 1993: 5). By examining the means of production of classic IF and the social situations of its audiences, we can get a clearer understanding of how this genre formed, peaked, and plummeted within a decade, but still managed to maintain much of the same audience today.

History of IF

Interactive Fiction has its origin in the role-playing game *Dungeons & Dragons* (*D&D*), which was published in 1974. Before *D&D* swept through college campuses in the mid–1970s, text games had been short and unsophisticated (King and Borland 2003). Programmers saw similarities not only in *D&D*'s random number generator (the dice), but also in the game's "*if-then*" structure: "*if* the character slays the orcs, *then* he is allowed to open the door and find the treasure" (p. 27). The imaginative depth of *D&D* inspired the creation of a number of text games, predominantly by male high school and college students in the late 1970s (p. 27). The most influential and popular game was *Zork*, created and released by a group of ten male MIT students in 1979 under their company Infocom (Doherty 1995).

The sources of inspiration for Infocom and IF were then found in male-dominated contexts: *D&D* and computing. As Cassell and Jenkins (1998) note, computers have been and continue to be used more by males than females, regardless of age. Throughout the short history of computers, men — whether in school, at home, or in computer-related jobs — have been given more access to computers and have received more encouragement to use them (p. 12–14). Another crucial factor in the formation of the IF audience was money. Because a computer cost a few thousand dollars at that time, it was an item owned primarily by well-educated, middle-upper class families (Briceno 2000b). In the classic era, then, IF was available to well-educated families on a medium primarily used by men. The audience seems to have reflected the composition of Infocom itself: most of the game designers were men, having been educated at MIT; only two authors were women (Scheyen 1999).

With the current proliferation of computers and the popularity of computer games, it is hard to imagine anything computer-related being a tough sale. To put Infocom's situation into context, imagine trying to persuade people to fork over a few thousand dollars for electronic equipment that looked like something they already owned (a TV) to use for games that utilized not graphics, but the printed word (something you could pull off the shelf). In its marketing strategies, Infocom attempted to accomplish two primary goals: attract readers of print texts to these new electronic stories; and knock the poor graphics offered by other computer games. Graphic technology was rudimentary at the time and only allowed for simple line drawings and a limited color palette. Infocom could play up its ability to create a world out of words. An early ad featured a graphic image of a blocky red character that resembled a demon while the Infocom tagline asks: "Would you shell out $1000 to match wits with this?" (Briceno 2000). Through such strategies, Infocom attempted to pull in potential readers by offering them something different from other game companies: "Instead of putting funny little creatures on your screen, we put you inside our stories" (see Figure 15.1).

Another ad, this one for the underground adventure *Zork* (Infocom 1980), featured an open book. On one side of the book's page is text; on the other page, a trapdoor opens down into a mysterious green light (see Figure 15.2). With this ad, it seems Infocom was suggesting that readers could get even deeper into a story with *Zork* than they could with a regular book (note that the mysterious green light shining from the trapdoor is reminiscent of the typical screen color of computer monitors of the time). As the interviews with players will show, the offer to put "you inside our stories" seems to have been the lasting appeal of IF.

Infocom's other attempts to draw in consumers also show a desire to pull in readers of print texts. One of the more untraditional marketing moves by Infocom was to sell its games not only in computer stores, but in bookstores as well (Briceno 2000a). Selling their games in bookstores went hand-in-hand with making references to a game's literary antecedents. The box description of *A Mind Forever Voyaging* (Infocom 1985) likened the sci-fi game to Huxley's *Brave New World* and Orwell's *1984*. The horror game *The Lurking Horror* was described as part Lovecraft and part Stephen King. And, one of the best-selling Infocom games, *The Hitchhiker's Guide to the Galaxy* (Infocom 1984) was co-written by the novel's author Douglas Adams.

Infocom also set itself apart in how it packaged its games. Most computer game companies usually included two items in computer game packages: the disk and a slim instruction manual. You still find this today; pick up almost any game box, shake it, and you'll hear a manual and CDs rustling against the cardboard interior. Consumers of Infocom games, however, received much more. Infocom provided "browsies" (often short magazines related to the game's story [see Figure 15.3]) and "feelies" (objects readers would find while playing the game [see Figure 15.4]) with each package. Sure, these "browsies" and "feelies" were used to prevent software piracy, but they

WOULD YOU SHELL OUT $1000 TO MATCH WITS WITH THIS?

MEET YOUR MATCH. MEET INFOCOM GAMES-PERHAPS THE BEST REASON IN SOFTWARE FOR OWNING A PERSONAL COMPUTER.

In fact, people have been known to purchase computers and disk drives solely for the purpose of playing our games. And they haven't been disappointed. Because Infocom's prose stimulates your imagination to a degree nothing else in software approaches. Instead of putting funny little creatures on your screen, we put you inside our stories. And we confront you with startlingly realistic environments alive with situations, personalities, and logical puzzles the like of which you won't find elsewhere. The secret? We've found the way to plug our prose right into your imagination, and catapult you into a whole new dimension.

If you think such an extraordinary experience is worth having, you're not alone. Everything we've ever written—ZORK® I, II, and III, DEADLINE, STARCROSS, and SUSPENDED—has become an instant best-seller. For the simple reason that Infocom offers you something as rare and valuable as anything in software—real entertainment.

At last, you can fritter away your evenings playing a computer game without feeling like you're frittering away your computer investment.

Step up to Infocom. All words. No pictures. The secret reaches of your mind are beckoning. A whole new dimension is in there waiting for you.

INFOCOM™
The next dimension.

Infocom, Inc., 55 Wheeler St., Cambridge, MA 02138

For your: Apple II, Atari, Commodore 64, CP/M 8", DEC Rainbow, DEC RT-11, IBM, NEC APC, NEC PC 8000, Osborne 1, TI Professional, TRS-80 Model I, TRS-60 Model III

Figure 15.1: Infocom pokes fun at the shoddy graphics of other games *(copyright © Activision; used with permission).*

Figure 15.2: In this ad, Infocom states: "For the first time, you can be more than the passive reader" *(copyright © Activision; used with permission)*.

had a larger purpose — readers were given tangible objects that could be enjoyed separately from the game.

For a while, the boxes even mimicked books. Before 1984, Infocom games were packaged in "folios" that related to the theme of the game; for instance, the detective mystery *Deadline* (Infocom 1982) was packaged in a police file (Infocom 2003). Between 1984 and 1989, games were released in boxes that opened like books to reveal the game's contents (see Figure 15.5). Infocom's attention to detail regarding the items included inside game boxes earned the company rave reviews at the time from such magazines as *Rolling Stone* and *Discover* (Infocom 2003). While Infocom might have had the simple intentions of trying out different packaging strategies, another possibility is more likely — if readers could be given objects and magazines they could touch and read, perhaps readers would feel more comfortable trading a story they could hold in their hands for a story that existed only on a computer screen.

During its run, Infocom released more than thirty text-based games encompassing a wide range of genres: fantasy, mystery, sci-fi, comedy, romance, adventure, and horror (Infocom 2004). While these games cannot be pinned down to any single narrative type (e.g., knight rescues damsel in

A Mind Forever Voyaging

Perry Simm was four years old when he became lost in the largest department store in the city.

He let go of Mother's hand to pick up the video cube. He rotated it with wonderment, touching the control knobs and squealing with delight as the images shifted . . .

Figur 15.3: This is one page of a short story "browsie" included with *A Mind Forever Voyaging* (copyright © Activision; used with permission).

distress), their basic structure required readers to solve puzzles and collect items to work towards what was usually one successful ending. Contemporary IF also embraces a wide range of genres, but makes no promises on puzzles or items or any one "true" ending. Some current IF does employ the gather-and-solve structure of classic IF, but most of the acclaimed IF of recent

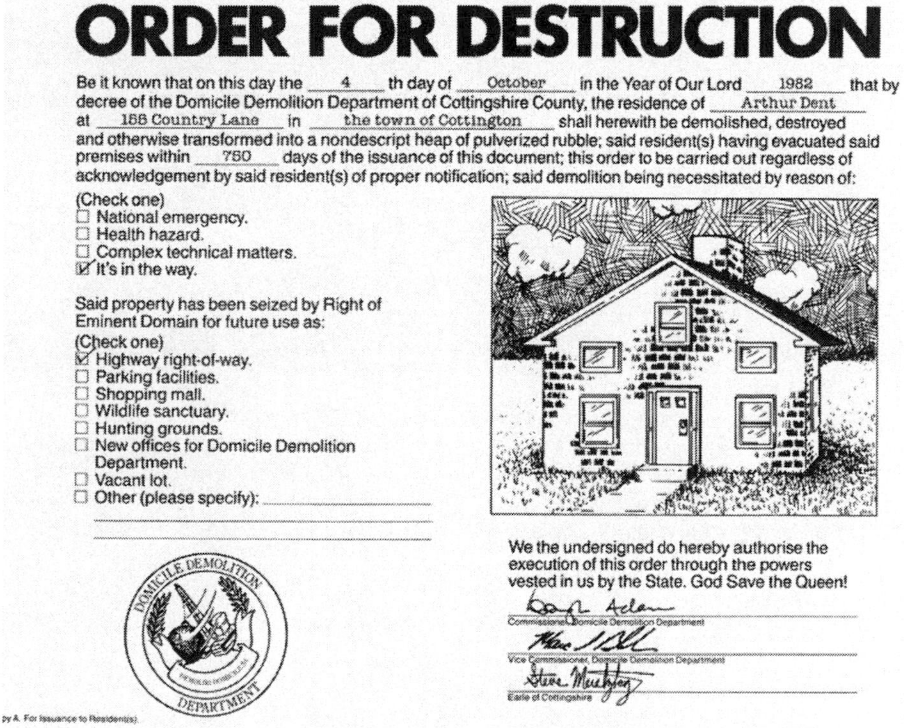

ORDER FOR DESTRUCTION

Be it known that on this day the ___4___ th day of ___October___ in the Year of Our Lord ___1982___ that by decree of the Domicile Demolition Department of Cottingshire County, the residence of ___Arthur Dent___ at ___155 Country Lane___ in ___the town of Cottington___ shall herewith be demolished, destroyed and otherwise transformed into a nondescript heap of pulverized rubble; said resident(s) having evacuated said premises within ___750___ days of the issuance of this document; this order to be carried out regardless of acknowledgement by said resident(s) of proper notification; said demolition being necessitated by reason of:

(Check one)
☐ National emergency.
☐ Health hazard.
☐ Complex technical matters.
☑ It's in the way.

Said property has been seized by Right of Eminent Domain for future use as:

(Check one)
☑ Highway right-of-way.
☐ Parking facilities.
☐ Shopping mall.
☐ Wildlife sanctuary.
☐ Hunting grounds.
☐ New offices for Domicile Demolition Department.
☐ Vacant lot.
☐ Other (please specify): _____

We the undersigned do hereby authorise the execution of this order through the powers vested in us by the State. God Save the Queen!

[signature]
Commissioner, Domicile Demolition Department

[signature]
Vice Commissioner, Domicile Demolition Department

[signature]
Earle of Cottingshire

Figure 15.4: This is a "feelie" included with *Hitchhiker's Guide to the Galaxy*. Picked up by the player during the game, it is a notice ordering the destruction of the player character's house *(copyright © Activision; used with permission).*

years reads like smart, experimental fiction that depends upon the medium for its effectiveness.

What unites classic IF and contemporary IF is a love of text and the possibility of immersion in the story. Classic IF showed this love in many games. *A Mind Forever Voyaging*, which puts the player in the role of a sentient computer that monitors simulations of the future, feels more like exploring a sci-fi novel than playing a game because it is incredibly rich in detail and has nearly all of its (incredibly tough) puzzles near the game's end. Part of the pleasure in playing *Hitchhiker's Guide to the Galaxy* is exploring the scenes from the novel as Arthur, Ford, and Trillian. Another pleasure is delighting in the wordplay, with players gathering items such as "tea" and "no tea" and having to argue with the game at one point. And while not to everyone's taste, *Nord and Bert Couldn't Make Head or Tail of It* (Infocom 1989) is nothing but wordplay, with puzzles being solved through knowledge of puns and clichés.

Figure 15.5: The object on the far right is the game box to *Zork*. The front cover opens to the left, revealing the "browsie" inside: "The Great Underground Empire: A History." Lifting the "browsie" reveals the other items displayed here: the map, the gold coin (both "feelies"), and the game disk *(copyright © Activision; used with permission)*.

Unfortunately for Infocom, words in the late 1980s were about to take a long siesta in published gaming. As computers became more advanced and allowed for more sophisticated graphics, the gaming market changed and text games became uncompetitive.[6] Infocom eventually made four games that combined text and graphics, but fans of the text games were resistant to this change (Infocom 2004). As Infocom folded, other companies tried to fill the gap left in the genre. In the late 1980s and early 1990s, Legend Entertainment and Magnetic Scrolls were two companies that released text-heavy games offering graphics as an option — players could turn off the graphics at any point and play solely through text. While many of these games were critically acclaimed and continued the gather-and-solve structure of Infocom's games, they could not sustain the genre and IF games dropped out of professional publication by 1993. A text parser remained in numerous graphic-based games, most notably those published by Sierra (famous at the time for the *King's Quest* and *Space Quest* series). It wasn't too long, though, before the text parser vanished, replaced with a point-and-click interface. When it came to gaming interface, text was dead.

However, text-based interactive fiction is thriving in online communities. Pinpointing when these communities formed is difficult, but they show no sign of dissipating. *XYZZYnews*, a popular IF webzine, appeared in 1995 and has sponsored an annual IF contest since 1996 (Mullin 2004b). Many current IF authors are as well-known as classic IF authors. Emily Short, Andrew Plotkin, Graham Nelson, and Adam Cadre are among the most acclaimed contemporary authors — they are the subjects of interviews in various webzines and were mentioned by nearly all of my respondents. Plotkin's status is such that he became the subject of *Being Andrew Plotkin*, a clever IF game that demands knowledge not only of Plotkin's other games but also knowledge of Plotkin from interviews and IF award ceremonies. Such a game could only succeed in a tightly-knit community.

Current game designers have expanded the genre well beyond its beginnings in terms of creativity and depth. While quite a few works of modern IF still involve solving puzzles and collecting items, many also experiment with the form. This experimentation is what distinguishes contemporary IF from classic IF. For example, Adam Cadre's (1998) puzzle-free *Photopia* features a dizzying, fragmented narrative in which the player experiences dislocations in time and perspective as she inhabits multiple roles. Such games keep Infocom's promise to "put you inside our stories." Since winning and losing are not options, and solving puzzles isn't part of the challenge, the point is to see the story through and become a part of it.

Another puzzle-free game, *Rematch* (Pontious 2000) is a one-move game that allows the player to enter only one command, concluding the game. One-move games are not terribly popular, but they're more intriguing than they sound. Knowing only one move is available, but guessing that many possible moves exist, the player gets to re-explore the same moment with different outcomes. Such experimentation in contemporary IF is in part spurred on by the fact that current authors do not have to sell their games. Infocom authors had to make sure that readers were getting their money's worth by providing a long gaming experience filled with puzzles. Yet as one of my respondents observed, "The fact that modern IF is done for the love of it (not much money to be made) means that the authors really care about their work. Of course, this won't turn a bad author into a good one, but it does mean that most works are a labor of love."

Modern IF wouldn't be possible without distribution through the Worldwide Web. With the spread of high-speed Internet availability and the ubiquity of server space, authors are now able to make their games available for free download if they choose. Because IF authors cannot reasonably earn money through their games (the games could be pirated easily), they gain a sense of achievement by being able to have others experience their creations. Paul Ardis, a 20-year-old computer science major, explained that he enjoys writing IF for the "thrill of creating something which will then go on to entertain someone later. When I'm done, I'll have something that I'll be proud of which I hope others will enjoy." Not every author expressed a similar reason for writing IF, but this sense of having players enjoy their creations, as well as possibly receiving a community's acknowledgement through the annual IF award ceremonies factors into the reason IF communities persist.

Another important factor in IF's survival is nostalgia. Some current authors have even gone so far as to recreate the pleasure given by the "feelies" and "browsies" included with early Infocom games. Acclaimed author of modern IF, Emily Short is involved with feelies.org, which creates tangible items players can find in contemporary games despite the fact that she and others make little or no money from the project.

What Does IF Offer?

When asked why he writes IF, Adam Cadre (quoted in Montfort 2003: 230) responded, "to impress Jodie Foster." Nick Montfort observes that the "absurdity of the question" is met well with Cadre's clever response. Yet the question itself is not as ridiculous as the idea of there being an ultimate answer. However, some tentative explanations can be offered for why participants continue to work within this particular genre today. These explanations are embedded in the idea that IF offers readers things that books, hypertext, and graphic video games do not.

Perhaps the most obvious reason why readers remain engaged with this genre is the interactivity it offers. This position has been criticized. Whelan (2002) questions the notion of interactivity in IF, arguing that IF is no more interactive than traditional books. Drawing on Tzvetan Todorov, Whelan states that narratives, even postmodern narratives with branching possibilities, such as those found in IF, "gain their momentum from a series of disruptions to an initially stable situation" (p. 80). The pattern of disruption and restoration gives readers a sense of fulfillment and drives them to the end of the narrative. These moments of disruption and restoration occur in IF with the puzzles that readers must solve to advance the narrative (pp. 80–81). Since both readers of IF and readers of traditional texts want to advance the narrative, IF is therefore not any more interactive than a traditional text. Citing an example of this, Whelan shows negative responses to an IF Competition game, David Ledyard's "What_IF," in which readers complained about the game because they "felt it was too difficult to resolve a particular problem or crisis, which resulted in an utter lack of narrative movement — i.e., the reader got 'stuck' in a situation and couldn't move beyond it" (p. 81).

Yet, her assertion seems to run counter to Infocom's claim to "put you inside our stories." While Whelan's attempt at bringing in readers' voices should be applauded, she examines only specific reader complaints about several IF works. Given such specificity, she does not study how these readers view broader IF concepts such as interactivity, narrative, and reader fulfillment, all of which she defines for her argument. In essence, the complaints give her some insight into the readers' problems with particular IF games, but they do not illuminate the readers' views of IF as a genre.

How does Whelan's definition of *interactive* compare to the definition given by readers of IF? For Whelan, a requirement of interactivity is that "the reader give something to the narrative (other than choosing a pre-determined path or screen) as much as the narrative gives something to the reader" (p. 78). It seems then, that, for IF to be truly interactive (to Whelan), readers would have to be able to alter the narrative in a way that was not planned by the author, a condition which is practically impossible given the current state of artificial intelligence.

When asked to define "interactive," most of my participants acknowledged that they were choosing a "pre-determined path" set up by the author. They did not seem to believe that they were creating a new narrative with their actions and they realized that they were limited to the author's design. However, many participants expressed the belief that they were telling the story *with* the author in some fashion. No participant spoke of being a "co-author," but many participants used words such as "discovering" and "guiding" to describe their involvement in the story. Vivienne Dunstan saw the author and player working together to create a story, but gave the author more control:

> For me it's a mix of the game designer and the game player. I suppose I view the designer as providing a story template which the player then uses to create their own story experience. How much this happens depends on how the game has been designed and how much freedom the designer has given the player in terms of what can happen.

Even though players admitted that their control over the narrative itself was limited by the author's programmed possible actions and events, they did not feel the experience to be any less interactive. Several respondents observed the importance of being fooled by the "illusory" nature of the interaction. As 42-year-old writer Johan Herrenberg stated, "IF *simulates* interactivity through a very clever manipulation of narrative elements. 'Interactive' is: when you have the illusion your freedom is not compromised by any necessity directing your ways." Adam Thornton, a 32-year-old Internet consultant and IF author, states that the author's job is to maintain this illusion: "...if it's done well, the fact that it's all smoke and mirrors is not evident at all."

The purpose of illusion is to give players the sense that they are in control. By recognizing the illusory nature of their control over the story's narrative, players realize that they are not creating anything new. They do not begrudge the illusion that they are in control; rather, they appreciate the illusion. Giving the player this sense of control is important for Vivienne Dunstan as she writes IF; for her, the player has to be able to influence the narrative in some way for the experience to be interactive:

In IF — for me anyway — the player is intrinsic to the storytelling. Not realizing that sufficiently well would lead to a poor interactive experience and the impression that the author is just telling a story, a preset story, and the player is just playing it straight back, with little opportunity to influence it, or to discover it in new ways.

To give the illusion of control, the player should be allowed to "influence" the story and "discover it in new ways." If the author anticipates the actions a player might take and programs a large number of actions and a large number of results, the player might think of one action over another, thus sending the story in a different path and discovering the story in a different way. Dunstan describes a "poor interactive experience" as one in which a player is engaged with a "preset story" and is merely "playing it straight back." In this sense, the player has even less control. Some games are more or less interactive, depending upon the author.

For players of IF, then, interactivity is measured in degrees, not determined by an either/or state, as defined by Whelan. Brett Witty, a 23-year-old PhD student, states that a player's ability to add something new to the narrative — Whelan's definition of *interactive*— would make IF "perfectly interactive":

> IF is fiction that you can direct. You don't mould the work of fiction, but the player definitely directs it. IF is certainly interactive so long as it isn't a slideshow. Even if you can just mess with the game world in a way that doesn't alter the plot of the game, I'd still call that interactive. A perfectly interactive IF game would allow you to interact with the game world and shape the plot. Of course, you can still be IF without this.

While many participants expressed hope for the improved game design and advanced artificial intelligence that would be required for "perfectly interactive" IF, they seem content with the illusion of control and the ability to discover the story in different ways, even if it involves "mess[ing] with the game world in a way that doesn't alter the plot of the game." Many participants noted the value of being able to "mess with the game world," a concept that has become important in game studies as scholars have recognized that computer games are not just literature and do not just offer puzzles and obstacles — they simulate social worlds.

Do endings have the importance stated by Whelan? Stressing the importance of endings in IF is understandable since one of the apparent draws of the genre today is the possibility of multiple narratives, multiple actions, and multiple endings. Yet, Whelan does not quote any readers on how much endings mean to them. In many places she speaks for IF readers: "part of the reader's enjoyment of IF is the discovery of a variety of end points" (p. 82). In other words, readers of IF enjoy trying different actions to find different possible endings, even if those endings are unsuccessful and result in death. Even when readers reach the end of the IF narrative, that ending "is constructed by the author, not by the readers themselves" (p. 83). In this way, too, Whelan finds IF similar to traditional books. Whelan's focus on the end points of IF is based on the assumption that IF readers are focused on the end of the narrative, much in the way that readers are focused on the end of regular books.

Many IF readers do not seem particularly concerned about the end, however. When asked about the emotions they experience while playing or about their fondest memories of playing IF, participants mentioned endings, but did not elevate them above other experiences. In describing his fondest memories of playing IF, Adam Thornton mentioned finishing a game, but the ending was included with other memories of solving puzzles and reaching emotionally significant moments in other games:

> I felt intensely clever when I figured out Nalian [a puzzle]. I felt like I'd been punched in the gut when Mitch dragged my wife away in *A Mind Forever Voyaging*. I felt like crying when I sang Floyd "The Ballad of the Starcrossed Minor." I got a Lovecraftian frisson of ickiness upon reading the book in the church in *Anchorhead*. I gasped in wonder when I got the bounded-in-a-nutshell ending in *Metamorphoses*.

Of course, readers of novels and viewers of films would probably give similar responses about their emotional experiences and favorite memories. Endings are not unimportant to readers of IF, but they do not seem to be the motivating factor in advancing the narrative that Whelan perceives them to be. For Whelan, readers solve the game's puzzles to bring stability back to the narrative, advancing it toward some end (p. 80–81). My readers, however, seemed to view the logical puzzles in IF as offering certain opportunities not allowed by regular prose fiction or even hypertext.

Readers approach puzzles as opportunities for frustration and pleasure. Brett Witty observed how "[s]everal puzzles have been great to solve. After much head-scratching and annoyance the solution finally dawns and you get through it. It's very rewarding." Not all players love puzzles, and some find them interminably frustrating. Johan Herrenberg admitted that "some games had puzzles which had taxed my logic to breaking-point. I'm no good at cryptograms, my mind simply doesn't work that way." However, he also stated that the pleasure of solving a puzzle can only be gained from IF:

> There is nothing quite like the sight of prose coursing down your screen after you did something essential. A recent example: in *Slouching towards Bedlam* there is a hall full of flies, but you can't get them. There is a spider-like machine that retrieves them for you. When I made it work, I was delighted and surprised by the wonderful description that ensued. These experiences, unavailable to other art-forms, are the things I play IF for.

When writing IF, Vivienne Dunstan worries about puzzles overshadowing the story: "Sometimes in IF there can be too much player awareness of completing each act of the story and moving to the next one. This can make the meta-level of narrative too apparent to that player and potentially distract from the story that they are experiencing."

Several players observed that one has to "earn the story" in IF, whereas a traditional book can simply keep turning the pages. Explaining the difference between IF and traditional print prose, Brett Witty stated: "Traditional literature cannot allow for the piece to evolve in completely different ways upon rereading — choices are made and cannot be undone, nor can you take an alternative route. You can in IF." This balance of puzzle and story is important to players and crucial to IF.

Even though they disagree on which element matters more, readers of IF regularly talk about wanting both story and puzzles. The combination of puzzle and story is one major element that separates IF from regular prose fiction and hypertext fiction. As Adam Thornton noted, "Hypertext is easier [than IF]: it basically is 'text with Boolean switches,' or at best a Choose-Your-Own Adventure story. The branching structure is usually trivially evident to the reader." Comparing IF to hypertext, Johan Herrenberg stated: "It's very easy to go on to the next page with hypertext, but that kind of clickable answer will rarely suffice with IF — to see the next page you have to earn it." In "earning it," people engaged in IF, then, are both readers and players. They read an engaging story and play with challenging puzzles along the way. Explaining the appeal of IF, Paul Ardis wrote, "It's amusing to play and engaging to read ... interactive fiction provides the opportunity to simultaneously do both." Rachel Henry concurred: "I love puzzles and games and books. The combination is deadly."

The importance of puzzles is somewhat complicated by the fact that puzzle-free IF is a popular contemporary form of the genre. This complication is cleared up when we do not treat reading and playing as separate activities in the IF game. When a person reads a paragraph of descriptive text in IF, she is also playing at the same time. All participants flip between *playing* and *reading* to describe their engagement in IF. Herrenberg linked the two as he explained how the sense of play made his reading more active: "[What IF offers is t]he illusion of being and acting inside the fictional space. The sense that reading is acting." This "being and acting inside the fictional space" is not only what allows the reader to play with puzzles, but also to play roles, to become protagonists, to become further engaged in the story, which gives readers a sense of play in all IF, even the puzzle-free kind. Reading and playing is about becoming involved in — "messing with" — a gameworld. IF, as Infocom promised, still puts players inside the story.

Immersion in the fictional space is another major element that separates IF from regular prose fiction. IF allows readers to become protagonists, thus they find a sense of engagement in IF that is unavailable in most novels. As Vivienne Dunstan stated, "the closest that short stories and novels can come to this is if they are written in the first person, but what that person sees and experiences is predefined by the author and cannot be changed. IF offers the chance both to be the protagonist and interact with their world." IF readers are not only able to see a world through another's eyes, they are also able to *play* with that world as that person. As Adam Thornton noted, "I adored playing the female servant in *Metamorphoses*, and I understood how being female and of the lower classes critically informed her perspective on her job and her life, which showed up, very subtly, as I dug through the game."

Graphic-based computer games also allow players to become protagonists who can "interact with their world." In fact, nearly half of the respondents reported playing and enjoying graphic-based computer games. However, they did not report enjoying graphical games as much, partly because of nostalgia and partly because of the depth of imagination offered by text. Vivienne Dunstan stated that part of the appeal of IF is the ability to "visualize the game world that is described purely through text." She admitted that she likes the "text-only environment, possibly partly for nostalgia reasons (that's what computers were like when I started using them) but also because of its rich potential to describe a scene." Several respondents also noted that the text-only environment made the game experience more personal.

Many respondents shared feelings of nostalgia for text and the imaginative possibilities offered by it. Since nearly all of the respondents had experienced IF in its early years, such nostalgia is understandable, even predictable. Yet, readers of IF seem to be engaged with it for reasons beyond mere nostalgia. They are drawn to a combination of factors that are only made available through IF: the potential to feel in control of a narrative; the ability to play and read at the same time; the opportunity to become the story's protagonist; and the chance to use one's imagination to make the reading experience more personal.

Conclusion

While a good deal of attention in both popular and academic circles has been given to graphic-heavy games such as *Myst* and *Grand Theft Auto*, text games have not been forgotten. Perhaps IF's current popularity could be reduced to the same nostalgic reasons why old Atari and Nintendo games are still in circulation through gaming stores and online emulators. However, the creation of new games seems to suggest more than mere nostalgia. IF players are still fond of tracking down and playing classic Infocom games, but they also seem intent on exploring the possibilities of many more non-graphical games — the possibilities that emerge at that intersection of the book and the game, of the print and the digital. Such explorations are entertaining (evident in the proliferation of games) and intellectually stimulating, which can be seen in the scholarship about IF.

The scholarship by IF players shows a certain investment on the part of the IF community, though IF scholarship is not limited to print texts by the academics who also happen to play IF. Some authors' websites and games offer explorations of the genre that also tie its concerns to issues of narrative and identity. In particular, Adam Thornton's *Stiffy Makane: The Undiscovered Country* (2001) not only parodies "Adult IF," but offers a response to Aarseth's (1997) writings on ergodic literature and the premise behind Crawford's (2004) Erasmatron storytelling engine. Player Johan Herrenberg is fascinated by "how an art form/genre that isn't commercially viable anymore, that came into existence on the cusp of the print culture passing into a visual one, is now really thinking through its own premises." We now know that the death of print was exaggerated and we've been re-estimating the value of text. The study of IF is one facet of that reevaluation. After all, digital gaming is one arena in which people would expect text to receive a fatal blow. Yet, the players here get something different from graphic-based games and IF.

The experiential, textual nature of IF can help inform the growing field of game studies. When one of the major debates between narratology and ludology is the narrative aspects of gaming, IF could serve as a valuable example. Both classic and current IF are difficult to categorize, but the latter poses particular problems with its puzzle-free, experimental offerings. Indeed, much parsing has occurred over the designations of "game" or "work" to recent IF. Some might see Cadre's puzzle-free *Photopia* not as a game but as a piece of experimental fiction, but I cannot help but see it as both — as something that depends upon the medium of IF. How does Infocom's claim to "put you inside our stories" mesh with narratology and ludology, especially when modern IF authors and players believe in the immersion and interactivity offered by these games? The differing viewpoints of Whelan (2002) and my participants on the narrative qualities of IF offer a challenge to scholars: While theorists are also players, how do players' viewpoints affect our understanding of games? Certainly theory provides us with the tools to unlock and unpack complicated texts, but those tools also come to us with a history of being shaped and used in particular ways; ways that don't always fit new locks and bags and can sometimes hinder the process.

Future attention devoted to the relationship between player and player-character should include IF as another site in which to test and broaden theories and concepts. If this relationship depends upon the type of platform and perspective — side-scrolling *Sonic the Hedgehog*, first-person shooting *Halo* — and the player's involvement in the gameworld, then the textual environment of IF deserves a closer look. The players I interviewed spoke at length about the importance of the relationship between player and player-character and how IF offered them a richness scarcely available in other digital games. Messing with the gameworld through typing feels different — is different phenomenologically — from clicking with a mouse, from hypersmashing buttons on a joystick.

Since we still live in a textual culture — print magazines, books, hypertext — the graphic-based games come to us surrounded by text. We read online and print magazine reviews; we read advertisements; we read box descriptions. We know what to expect and have imagined the gameworld before the receipt has been printed and the game has been installed. And even though text has been abandoned as the primary interface in graphic-based games, it still helps create the gameworld in numerous instances, from supplying status information in action games to dialogue options in adventures. As scholars pay more attention to overlooked features of videogames — cinematic cut scenes and music, for example — they should also return to text.

The history of IF may give us an idea of what digital gaming may become. As modders become more prevalent and as game design engines become easier to use, how will games change? Many, like *Counter-Strike*, will follow the architecture of cutting-edge technology. Yet, as IF has become less like the gather-and-solve adventures of old and more like experimental fiction — exploring the possibilities of print and digital media — so too might graphic-based games become more like experimental film or artistic expression. Studying IF can give us a glimpse of what is to come in the future of digital gaming. We've come a long way since *Zork*.

Notes

1. When describing those who interact with IF, I will use *player* and *reader* interchangeably, just as my survey participants do. Recently, scholars (e.g., Montfort; Murray) have used the term *interactor* to describe the reader-player.

2. My methods were partially inspired by Radway (1991). In her book, Radway interviews readers of romance novels to give them a voice in the criticism of the genre. Following Fish's theory of interpretive communities, Radway assumes that "textual interpretations are constructed by interpretive communities using specific strategies" (p. 7). Since literary critics of romance constituted a different interpretive community from fans of the genre, Radway hoped to compare the different readings of the two groups. Like Radway, I want to compare the readings of IF critics with the readings of IF fans.

3. While many Interactive Fiction communities exist, two in particular, the news-groups rec.arts.int-fiction and rec.games.int-fiction, were approached because of their long history with this form of IF.

4. The number of Caucasian respondents may be higher, but because I left the question open-ended, I cannot be sure. One reported racial description was "mixed," while another was simply "human."

5. All participant names are real. And I would like to thank them for giving their time and generous insight for this study. This study met with IRB approval.

6. Infocom's foray into business software was also a significant blow with the commercial failure of the database system *Cornerstone*.

References

Aarseth, Espen. 1997. *Cybertext: Perspectives on Ergodic Literature.* Baltimore, MD: Johns Hopkins UP.

Briceno, Hector. 2000a. "Marketing." *Down from the Top of Its Game: The Story of Infocom.* MIT Archive, Retrieved April 10, 2004. <http://web.mit.edu/6.933/www/Fall2000/Infocom/marketing.html>

_____. 2000b. "The Z-Machine." *Down from the Top of Its Game: The Story of Infocom.* MIT Archive. Retrieved 10 Apr. 2004. <http://web.mit.edu/6.933/www/Fall2000/Infocom/z-machine.html>

Brodhead, Richard H. 1993. *Cultures of Letters: Scenes of Reading and Writing in Nineteenth-Century America.* Chicago: University of Chicago Press.

Cadre, Adam. 1998. *Photopia.* Platform: PC. Publisher: Freeware.

Cassell, Justine, and Henry Jenkins. 1998. "Chess for Girls? Feminism and Computer Games." Pp. 2–45 in *From Barbie to Mortal Kombat: Gender and Computer Games,* edited by Justine Cassell and Hentry Jenkins. Cambridge: MIT Press.

Cortazar, Julio. 1975. *Hopscotch.* New York: Avon.

Crawford, Chris. 2004. *Chris Crawford on Interactive Storytelling.* Berkeley: New Riders Press.

Cyan Worlds. 1993. *Myst.* Platform: PC. Publisher: Broderbund Software, Inc.

Doherty, Paul David. 1995. "Infocom Fact Sheet." *IF Archive.* Retrieved 13 Apr. 2004. <http://www.ifarchive.org/if-archive/Infocom/info/fact-sheet.txt>

Douglas, J. Yellowlees. 2000. *The End of Books — Or Books without End?: Reading Interactive Narratives.* Ann Arbor: University of Michigan Press.

Gee, James Paul. 2003. *What Video Games Have to Teach Us About Learning and Literacy.* New York: Palgrave MacMillan.

Infocom. 1980. *Zork: The Great Underground Empire.* Platform: PC. Publisher: Infocom.

_____. 1982. *Deadline.* Platform: PC. Publisher: Infocom.

_____. 1984. *The Hitchhiker's Guide to the Galaxy.* Platform: PC. Publisher: Infocom.

_____. 1985. *A Mind Forever Voyaging.* Platform: PC. Publisher: Infocom.

_____. 1989. *Nord and Bert Couldn't Make Head or Tail of It.* Platform: PC. Publisher: Infocom.

_____. 2003. "Infocom Gallery." Retrieved 10 Apr. 2004. <http://Infocom.elsewhere.org/gallery/>

_____. 2004. "Infocom: Company History" Retrieved 3 Mar. 2004. <http://www.-Infocom-if.org/company/company.html.>

Jerz, Douglas, and Emily Short. N.d. *IF Theory.* Unpublished manuscript.

Joyce, Michael. 1995. *Of Two Minds: Hypertext Pedagogy and Poetics.* Ann Arbor: University of Michigan Press.

King, Brad, and John Borland. 2003. *Dungeons and Dreamers: The Rise of Computer Game Culture from Geek to Chic.* New York: McGraw-Hill.

Montfort, Nick. 2003. *Twisty Little Passages: An Approach to Interactive Fiction.* Cambridge: MIT Press.

Mullin, Eileen. 2004. "Reader Survey." Retrieved April 3, 2004. <http://www.xyzzynews. com/xyzzy.5f.html>

_____. "XYZZYnews FAQ." Retrieved March 10, 2004. <http://www.xyzzynews.com/ xyzzyfaq.html>

Murray, Janet H. 1997. *Hamlet on the Holodeck: The Future of Narrative in Cyberspace.* New York: Free Press.

Pontious, Andrew. 2000. *Rematch.* Platform: PC. Publisher: Freeware.

Radway, Janice. 1991. *Reading the Romance: Women, Patriarchy, and Popular Culture.* Chapel Hill: University of North Carolina Press.

Scheyen, Peter. "Infocom Imps." *Infocom WebPages.* Retrieved 8 Apr. 2004. <http://www. csd.uwo.ca/~pete>

Sloane, Sarah. 2000. *Digital Fictions: Storytelling in a Material World.* Stamford, CT: Ablex Publishing.

Thornton, Adam. 2001. *Stiffy Makane: The Undiscovered Country.* Platform: PC. Freeware.

Wheeler, J. Robinson. 2000. *Being Andrew Plotkin.* Platform: PC. Publisher: Freeware.

Whelan, Lara Baker. 2002. "Narrative and Reader Interaction: Revisiting the Question of Genre in Interactive Fiction." *TEXT Technology* 11.2: 75–95.

About the Contributors

Mia Consalvo is an associate professor in the School of Telecommunications at Ohio University. Her research interests center on new media and popular culture, with a focus on digital games. She has published work about games and culture in *New Media & Society*, *Game Studies*, and *On the Horizon*. She is the author of *Cheating: Gaining Advantage in Videogames* (forthcoming) and is currently researching the interrelations between U.S. and Japanese art, business and culture as they influence digital games. Email: consalvo@ohio.edu

Aaron Delwiche is an assistant professor in the Department of Communication at Trinity University, where he teaches courses on media literacy, new media, and game studies. His research focuses on propaganda analysis, multiplayer games, and global youth culture. Since 1994, he has maintained Propagandacritic.com, a Web site devoted to fundamental techniques of propaganda analysis. Email: aaron.delwiche@trinity.edu

Janice Denegri-Knott has a background in communications for development. She has worked in both corporate and marketing communications in not-for-profit organizations in South America. She currently lectures in consumer behavior at Bournemouth University. Her main research interests relate to understanding power struggles between consumers and producers in online environments. She has presented at the Academy of Marketing Conference in the UK and the Home-Oriented Informatics and Telematics conference in the U.S. She has also published articles in the *Journal of Computer-Mediated Communication*, the *Journal of Consumer Behaviour* and *Corporate Communications: An International Review*. Email: jdknott@bournemouth.ac.uk

Jonathan Dovey is a reader in the Department of Drama, Theatre, Film and Television. He is author of the monograph *Freakshows: First Person Media and Factual*

TV (2000) and editor of *Fractal Dreams*, a collection of essays on the politics of New Media (1995). He is co-author of *New Media — A Critical Introduction* (2002). He has been involved in media production for more than twenty years in a variety of roles, including producer and director. In 1994 he produced his first piece of multimedia, the parody game "Media Myth & Mania," for a CD ROM , *Silver to Silicon* (1996). He also produced an artists' Web site, 3Gen, based on three generations of migrant heritage.

Mirjam Eladhari is a Ph.D. candidate working on the topic of "Player Character Mind Models for Deep Characterization and Emergent Story Construction in Massively Multiplayer Game Worlds." This research is conducted within the game research group at the Department of Technology, Art and New Media at Gotland University in Sweden, and within the School of Computing at the University of Teesside, UK. Mirjam has studied computing science, literature and behavioral science and holds an M.A. in literary studies. Mirjam has worked as a game programmer at Liquid Media in Sweden where she worked on a number of game titles including *The Diamond Mystery of Rosemond Valley*, a mystery game in real time 3D, for which she was the lead game programmer. She has also worked as tech lead and researcher at the Zero-Game Studio, a part of the Interactive Institute, primarily with the open research MMOG engine *Purgatory*. Email: Mirjam.Eladhari@hgo.se

Sara M. Grimes is a doctoral student with the School of Communication at Simon Fraser University. Her research explores the legal and ethical issues surrounding children's use of new media technologies, with a special focus on digital gaming. She has recently published articles on intellectual property in multiplayer online games (*New Media & Society*), data-mining practices in children's online games (co-authored with Grace Chung, *Canadian Journal of Communication*), and game community *Neopets.com* (co-authored with Leslie Regan Shade, *International Journal of Media and Cultural Politics*). Sara is currently working on a three-year research project funded by the Social Sciences and Humanities Research Council (SSHRC) of Canada, exploring social conceptualizations of the "cyberchild." Email: smgrimes@sfu.ca

Nadezhda Kaneva is a doctoral candidate at the School of Journalism and Mass Communication, University of Colorado at Boulder, and holds a master's degree from Syracuse University. Her primary research agenda draws on critical theories of culture and communication to explore collective identities and memories in various contexts, both online and offline. In relation to online environments, she is particularly interested in examining how narrative and ritual serve as means of constructing shared realities and communities. Her research has been published in academic journals and edited volumes in the U.S and Mexico. Email: nadia.kaneva@gmail.com

Daniel Keller is a Ph.D. candidate in the University of Louisville's English Department. He received his M.A. and B.A. from Southern University Illinois Edwardsville. Publications include the instructor manuals for Donald and Christine McQuade's *Seeing & Writing 2* (2003) and *Seeing & Writing 3* (2006), and articles in the forthcoming collections *Gaming Lives in the 21st Century: Literate Connections* and *Multimodal Composition for the 21st Century: A Resource Book for Teachers*. Dan's current research project examines college students' reading practices of various media in and out of school. Email: daniel.keller@louisville.edu

Helen W. Kennedy is senior lecturer and MA Award Leader, School of Cultural Studies, University of the West of England. She has spoken at a number of academic and industry conferences on the role of women in computer games and computer games culture. She was invited speaker at the GDC Europe Academic Summit August 2003 and the Women in Games conference June 2004. She has published articles in *Game Studies*, *Edge Computer Games* magazine, and *Tekka*, and has contributions in *Feminism in Popular Culture* (2005), *Game Cultures: Computer Games as New Media* (2004), and *Understanding Digital Games* (2004). Email: hwk@blueyonder.co.uk

Lars Konzack is an assistant professor in interactive digital media at Aalborg University. Chairman of spilforskning.dk (the Danish game research organization) since 2001, he is a dedicated game researcher and an avid role-player. In 2003 he finished his Ph.D. on edutainment in computer games. He maintains a weblog, *Ludologica*, and his scholarly work is on fields such as geek culture, ludology, game analysis, experience design, and sub-creation. Email: lars@konzack.dk

Mike Molesworth has previously worked in sales and marketing and is now a lecturer in online behavior and interactive media in the Media School at Bournemouth University. His main research interest is playful consumer behaviors in computer-mediated environments. He is a regular presenter at the Academy of Marketing conference in the UK and presented at the first Digital Games Research Association conference in Utrecht in 2003. He has also published papers in the *Journal of Marketing Management*, the *Journal of Consumer Behaviour*, *Corporate Communications: An International Review* and *Innovations in Education and Teaching International*. Email: mmoleswo@bournemouth.ac.uk

Rafael Miguel Montes is an assistant professor in the Department of English, Humanities and Communication Arts at St. Thomas University. He is the author of *Making Places — Haciendo Lugares: Intergenerational Traumas in Contemporary Cuban-American Literature*. His work primarily discusses the ways in which Cuban exile culture intersects with a variety of political, cultural, territorial and digital structures. Email: wedprez@aol.com

Torill Elvira Mortensen is an associate professor working at Volda University College, Norway, Department of Media Studies, with public information and media theory. In 2003 she finished her Ph.D. on text-based multi-user games (MUDs) with the dissertation "Pleasures of the Player — Flow and Control in Online Games." She maintains a weblog, *thinking with my fingers*, and her scholarly focus is on games, blogs and user experiences in cyber-culture. Email: torill.mortensen@hivolda.no

Jonas Heide Smith has a game studies Ph.D. from the Center for Computer Games Research at the IT University of Copenhagen, Denmark. His research is centered on player interaction and the issue of cooperation and conflict in multiplayer games. He co-edits the www.game-research.com resource site and is co-author of the forthcoming textbook *Understanding Video Games*. Email: jonas@autofire.dk

Laurie N. Taylor has a Ph.D. from the University of Florida. Her research focuses on horror video games and digital media accessibility. She has published articles in *Game Studies, Media/Culture, Computers and Composition Online* and *Image-TexT*, and has forthcoming articles in several collections on video games. She also writes a newspaper gaming column, an online gaming column, and radio programs for the public radio program *Recess!* Email: laurientaylor@gmail.com

Mel White is a retired computer geek who has been an administrator and wizard on various BBSs and Internet sites and games since the early 1980s. She has a master's degree in computer medicine and is currently finishing a second master's in applied anthropology at the University of North Texas. Email: cyberwizard@spamcop.net

J. Patrick Williams is a sociologist and social psychologist who does ethnographic research on youth (sub)cultures and digital culture. His work has appeared in a variety of journals and books, including *Symbolic Interaction, Journal of Contemporary Ethnography, International Journal of Deviant Behavior, Media International Australia*, and *Youth Subcultures: Exploring Underground America*. He is also co-editor of *Gaming as Culture: Essays in Social Reality, Identity and Experience in Fantasy Games* (McFarland 2006). Email: subcultures@gmail.com

Jason Wilson has submitted a Ph.D. at Griffith University (Australia) focusing on the aesthetics and cultural history of videogames as popular digital art. He is currently researching and teaching at the University of Luton (UK). His research attempts to locate videogames in a longer and broader history of visual media, technology and art. He has published and presented papers based on his research in a range of international venues including journals, arts events and scholarly conferences. Email: jason_a_wilson@yahoo.com.au

Index